KHAKI CAPITAL

NIAS–Nordic Institute of Asian Studies
NIAS Studies in Asian Topics

NIAS Press is the autonomous publishing arm of NIAS – Nordic Institute of Asian Studies, a research institute located at the University of Copenhagen. NIAS is partially funded by the governments of Denmark, Finland, Iceland, Norway and Sweden via the Nordic Council of Ministers, and works to encourage and support Asian studies in the Nordic countries. In so doing, NIAS has been publishing books since 1969, with more than two hundred titles produced in the past few years.

UNIVERSITY OF COPENHAGEN

Nordic Council of Ministers

KHAKI CAPITAL

The Political Economy of the Military in Southeast Asia

edited by

Paul Chambers and Napisa Waitoolkiat

Khaki Capital
The Political Economy of the Military in Southeast Asia
Edited by Paul Chambers and Napisa Waitoolkiat

Nordic Institute of Asian Studies
Studies in Asian Topics, no. 61

First published in 2017 by NIAS Press
NIAS – Nordic Institute of Asian Studies
Øster Farimagsgade 5, 1353 Copenhagen K, Denmark
Tel: +45 3532 9501 • Fax: +45 3532 9549
E-mail: books@nias.ku.dk • Online: www.niaspress.dk

A CIP catalogue record for this book is available from the British Library

ISBN: 978-87-7694-224-3 (hbk)
ISBN: 978-87-7694-225-0 (pbk)

Typeset in Arno Pro 12/14.4
Typesetting by NIAS Press

Printed and bound in the United States
by Maple Press, York, PA

Dedicated to the memories of beloved "Mother" Somsri Waitoolkiat,
Dr. M. Ladd Thomas and Dr. Danny Unger

Contents

Maps and Figures

Tables

Preface

The journey of the book you are now reading began in 2013, when a group of academics interested in Southeast Asian military affairs broached the question of why some militaries as opposed to others in Southeast Asia have persisted in entrenching their power on the political stage. One answer was political economy, understood as the potential economic power that initially lured security officials to want to participate in power struggles as well as their interest in perpetuating that clout. However, no comparative studies to date have taken on the task of devising a theory of what we call "khaki capital" and then testing it across Southeast Asia. That could well be because of the difficulties in finding evidence to substantiate arguments of "khaki capital" motivations, as well as fears among academics that they might be threatened (or worse) by security officials for even considering such studies. Other feasibility issues include a dearth of time and funding to make this volume come about.

Despite these challenges, the authors conducted research about their particular country cases and eventually handed in chapter manuscripts, which were peer reviewed and subsequently modified. Some of these chapters were first presented at the 8th Asian Political and International Studies Association (APISA) Conference, under the auspices of the Faculty of Law, Chiang Mai University, in Chiang Mai, Thailand on 19–20 September 2014. Funding for our presentations came from Friedrich-Ebert-Stiftung (FES). Modified versions of almost all of these papers were later presented on 2–3 July 2015 at a smaller conference in Phnom Penh, Cambodia entitled "The Impact and Implications of Climate Change: Strategies and Security for ASEAN Member States," which was organized by the Cambodian Institute for Cooperation and Peace (CICP) and funded by Konrad-Adenauer-Stiftung (KAS).

Meanwhile, changing events in the country cases themselves caused a re-working of many of the chapters. In May 2014 a military coup in Thailand overthrew democracy, replacing it with a dictatorship that has lasted until today. Two months later, elections in Indonesia brought the civilian populist Joko Widodo to the presidency. In November 2015, Aung San Suu Kyi's National League for Democracy won a landslide general election, upsetting the Tatmadaw's longtime military control over the country. Finally, in May 2016, Rodrigo Duterte swept to electoral victory in the Philippines, though his triumph appeared to perhaps be destined to take that country back to its previous authoritarian experiences. All of these events and others caused chapter contributors to re-work some of their conclusions. In 2017, following even more revisions, this edited volume finds itself completed.

The editors and authors hope that the theory presented herein and the accompanying country case studies successfully shed light for different types of readers – social scientists, area specialists, or laypeople – on the complex connection between militaries and money in Southeast Asia. We realize that more can and should be said about "khaki capital" than our discussions provide, but we hope that our volume can offer at least a small dent or beginning to approach this issue among the countries of Southeast Asia. Perhaps our theory can even be transferred to countries beyond.

We would like to acknowledge the assistance of a great many people who were essential to this volume's research. But the far majority requested anonymity. Others were crucial in that without them, this volume might never have seen the light of day. These persons include first and foremost Gerald Jackson, editor-in-chief of NIAS Press, who patiently stood by us from the get-go. We also thank NIAS's copy editor David Stuligross, who offered valuable comments and suggestions. In addition, we want to acknowledge the aid of Friedrich-Ebert-Stiftung (thanks especially to Marc Saxer); Konrad-Adenauer-Stiftung; the Asian Political and International Studies Association (APISA); and the Cambodian Institute for Cooperation and Peace (CICP). Within CICP, we would like to specifically thank His Royal Highness Prince Norodom Sirivudh, Chairman of its Board of Directors; the Honourable Ambassador Pou Sothirak, its Executive Director; and Pou Sovachana, the Deputy Executive Director. Beyond these acknowledgements, we would like to thank Assistant Professor Dr. Piratorn Punyaratabandhu, Vice President, Naresuan University, Phitsanulok, Thailand, who encouraged this project. In addition, we are indebted to former Dean Assistant Professor Chatree Rueangdetnarong, Associate Professor Somchai Preecha-silpakul, Ajaan Kanya Hirunwattanapong, Dean Assistant Professor Dr. Pornchai Wisuttisak of Chiang Mai University Faculty of Law. That faculty boldly sponsored the 8th APISA Congress (containing our critical research) only four months after the Thai coup. Support for the research and writing of the Philippines chapter was provided by the University of the Philippines Visayas Francisco Nemenzo Professorial Chair Grant. Still other acknowledgements go to Dr. Katsuyuki Takahashi, Poowin Bunyavejchewin, Jaratporn Jantham Lipp, Mathieu Pellerin, Dr. Stephen Heder, Dr. Trond Gilberg, Kevin Nauen, Kim Sun, Martin Rathie, and Dr. Michael Vickery.

Some might wonder why we did not include chapters about Malaysia, Singapore, Timor Leste or Negara Brunei Darussalam (hereafter referred to as Brunei). Problems of feasibility are our only answer. But there is certainly room for examinations of these cases in future works. Finally, we want to point out that the political economy of the military in a volatile setting such as Southeast Asia is not static and will likely be changing in the years ahead, with some militaries becoming either more politically and economically fastened under civilian control or moving to be more increasingly unfettered as free-wheeling, predatory extractors of rent.

Paul Chambers and Napisa Waitoolkiat
July 2017

Contributors

Dr. **MARCO BÜNTE** is Associate Professor at Monash University, Malaysia Campus. At the same time, he is external research fellow at the German Institute of Global and Area Studies (GIGA) in Hamburg (Germany). He has published widely on issues of democratization and regime change. His work has appeared in peer reviewed outlets such as Armed Forces and Society, Asian Survey, Contemporary Southeast Asia and the Journal of Current Southeast Asian Affairs, amongst others. He is the co-editor of *The Crisis of Democratic Governance in Southeast Asia* (Palgrave 2011).

Dr. **PAUL CHAMBERS** serves as Professor and Researcher, College of ASEAN Community Studies, Naresuan University, Phitsanulok, Thailand. He is also concurrently a Research Fellow at the Peace Research Institute Frankfurt (Germany), and the German Institute of Global and Area Studies, Hamburg (Germany). He has written extensively on democracy and civil–military relations in Southeast Asia and has published widely as the author of books, chapters and journal articles.

Dr. **ROSALIE ARCALA HALL** is Professor of Political Science at the University of the Philippines, Visayas. Rosalie has also conducted research on post-conflict civil–military relations in the Aceh, Indonesia; Dili, East Timor; and Mindanao, Philippines. She is currently working on research projects with American and European collaborators on military mergers; asymmetric warfare and on Muslim women in the security forces.

Dr. **JUN HONNA** is Professor of Political Science, Department of International Relations, Ritsumeikan University, Japan. He is concurrently adjunct professor, Faculty of Social and Political Sciences, University of Indonesia, and Visiting Lecturer, National Graduate Institute for Policy Studies (GRIPS), Japan. He has written books and articles about Southeast Asia, particularly focusing on civil–military relations and democratization in Indonesia.

Dr. **HANS LIPP** studied at the University of Bayreuth as well as at the Natural Resources Institute, University of Manitoba, before earning a Diploma in Geography at the University of Trier in 1994. In 2017 he graduated with a Ph.D. (Dr. phil) in Geography/Regional Planning from the Faculty of Natural Sciences and Mathematics, Eberhard Karls University of Tübingen (Germany). He specializes in Southeast Asia, concentrating on Laos and Thailand, and regional, tourism development in rural areas.

Dr. **CARLYLE A. THAYER** is Emeritus Professor, The University of New South Wales at the Australian Defence Force Academy in Canberra. Thayer is a Southeast Asia regional specialist with special expertise on Vietnam. He is the author of Southeast Asia: Patterns of Security Cooperation (Canberra: Australian Strategic Policy Institute, 2012). He writes a weekly column on Southeast Asian defence and security affairs for the *The Diplomat*. He has held senior appointments at the International Institute for Strategic Studies in London; Asia-Pacific Center for Security Studies in Honolulu; School of Advanced International Studies, Johns Hopkins University; Center for International Affairs, Ohio University; Australian Command and Staff College; and the Center for Defence and Strategic Studies at the Australian Defence College. Thayer was educated at Brown, holds an M.A. in Southeast Asian Studies from Yale and a PhD in International Relations from The Australian National University.

Dr. **NAPISA WAITOOLKIAT** serves as Director, College of ASEAN Community Studies, Naresuan University, Phitsanulok, Thailand. Her work has appeared in numerous book chapters and journal articles. Her research interests focus upon emerging democracies in the areas of electoral politics, party politics, voting behaviour, political institutions, civil–military relations, political accountability, corruption, processes of democratization, and human security in Southeast Asia. Recently, she has also pursued research in the study of migration and political economy across ASEAN member states.

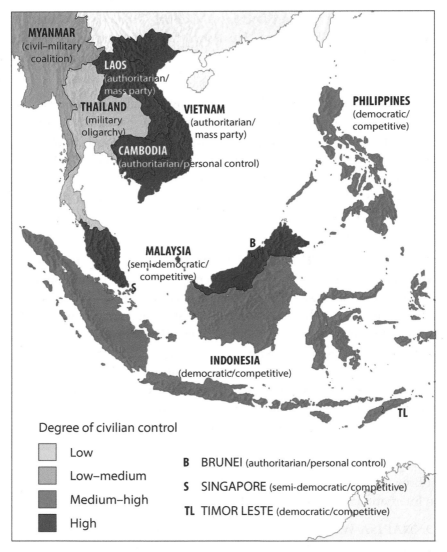

Map 0.1: Civilian control over khaki capital in Southeast Asia

CHAPTER 1

Theorizing Khaki Capital
The Political Economy of Security

Paul Chambers and Napisa Waitoolkiat

Introduction

The military is integral to the formation, expansion and durability of the state. It is a vital institution tasked with defending the state from external and internal threats alike. The definition of the military is more widely shared than that of the 'state' it is charged with defending. Under international law, states are juristic 'persons' which possess '(a) a permanent population; (b) a defined territory; (c) government; and (d) capacity to enter into relations with other states' (Article 1, Montevideo Convention, 1933). Turning to the domestic level, for Marxists the state functions as a critical actor 'to maintain and defend class domination and exploitation' (Bottomore, 1991, p. 520). The political economist John Martinussen, heavily influenced by sociologist Nicos Poulantzas, describes four dimensions of the state.

1. a product of competing interests and power struggles
2. a manifestation of structures which ... to some extent determine the behaviour of the citizens
3. an arena for interaction and conflict between contending social forces
4. an actor in its own right, which ... exerts a relatively autonomous influence on outcomes of conflicts and other processes in society (Martinussen 1997: 221–2).

From the lens of these four dimensions, the military can be analysed as an intrastate 'competing interest', one of many state 'structures', part of the 'contending social forces' and finally a principal means by which states exert 'autonomous influence.' It competes with other interest groups or social forces including civilian bureaucracies, multi-national corporations and organized labour. In fact, within the military itself, the armed forces of the army, navy and air force, if coordinated cohesively, can transcend civilian state control. The military is thus an exceptionally important actor within states. However, since the armed forces possess an enormous role in preserving national security, they also maintain control over force of arms in the state. To do so, a sufficient level of finance – from income and/or state expenditures – is required to en- sure basic sustenance. The extent to which civilians control funding of the military is of paramount importance, and given that the military is to some extent self-financing – a condition described in this book as *khaki capital* – the ability of even the best intentioned of elected civil- ian government to control its military is often even more limited than many observers imagine (Brömmelhörster and Paes 2003; Siddiqa 2007; Mani 2011). On the one hand, it is challenging to achieve civilian supremacy over militaries that completely bankroll themselves outside of or despite civilian monitoring and legislative budgets. On the other, civilian control becomes easier when civilians have their hands on the levers of khaki capital. In most countries, both hands are relevant; some militaries manage to control special financial resources directly, even as they remain generally dependent on the regular disbursement of budget- ary capital from legislative authorities. Most emerging democracies are characterized by a shifting tug-of-war between civilians and militaries across the continuum of control over labour, infrastructure and land.

The overall argument in this volume is that the greater control which militaries have over economic resources, then the more insulated they tend to be from civilian political control. The dominance of the military over its own wealth leads to greater autonomy of the military from civilian supremacy. This in turn becomes the inertia for sustaining and/or expanding the military's economic 'empire'. Once their invested economic interest becomes highly institutionalized, any reverse course of it could only be regarded by them as unacceptable. Though starting off by adhering to economic interest maximization, the military needs political power to oversee and secure its economic returns, which, rationally speaking, makes them reluctant to be under the control of civilian leaders. As a result, any civilian-led initiative or policy centring upon transparency or accountability would be naturally opposed by the armed forces. Finally, the political economy of the military takes place in the context of where wealth itself is transformed into political power. This then serves as a self-perpetuating power mechanism. This khaki capital cycle has ramifications for the ability of militaries to maintain independence vis-à-vis potential civilian control in several issue-areas, including national security, rule of law, observance of human rights standards, guaranteeing the well-being of the population and – with regard to the subject of this study – in the military's economic activities. The careful case studies of Southeast Asian countries lend confidence to this general claim.

The study thus sets out to understand the political economy of military capital or khaki capital. It does so by first offering a conceptualization of formal and informal military economic influence. Though khaki capital could be construed as having multiple potential meanings, including the potential goodwill a military organisation builds as a defender of the body politic or notions of the public interest, this study examines the term parsimoniously as the economic assets of security forces. Second, using historical institutionalism, it scrutinizes the path-dependent evolution of military finance over time amidst the quality of oversight by executive authorities. Third, it examines the resultant equilibria across various developing countries in Southeast Asia. The degree of military control over its own financing tends to affect the ability of civilians to achieve control over the armed forces. Ultimately, where historical-cultural legacies allow for a military to be autonomous from civilian supremacy, where the military is united against civilian attempts to monitor it and where structural factors favour proactive armed forces across society, then militaries are likely to maintain complete, unchecked control over their economic activities. Where militaries can completely control their own economic activities, financing for non-military activities and civilian control become imperilled.

Conceptualization

Civil–military relations in developing countries
Since the 1950s, a multitude of studies have focused attention upon civil–military relations.[1] Though traditionally, political scientists exam-

---

1. See, for example, Colton 1979; Pion-Berlin 1992: 83–102; Agüero 2001; Alagappa 2001: 29–66; Trinkunas 2000: 77–109; Croissant *et al.* 2013.

ined only soldiers and the organisations in which they serve,[2] scholarly attention has more recently expanded to what is called security sector governance: the plethora of state security organisations that includes police, paramilitary forces, courts and related entities (Forster 2002: 78; Cottey, Edmunds and Forster 2000). However, we share the opinion of Bruneau and Cristiana (2008: 914): 'security sector governance', which can be broadened to include all actors involved with the direction, enforcement and interpretation of security (state and non-state forces; executive, legislative and judicial branches), is far too encompassing to be of analytical value. As such, this study limits its scope to the political economies of *militaries*, by which we mean 'all of the permanent state organisations and their members whose primary function, authorized by law, is to apply coercive power in order to defend the territory of the state against external threats' (Croissant *et al.* 2013: 12). In other words, we are talking about the army, navy, air force and supreme command.

Civilians are non-military individuals of the executive, legislative and judicial branches of government who are either elected or appointed by elected civilians (Edmonds 1988). While retired members of the military are technically civilians, they often identify with and share the same interests as active-duty soldiers. Former soldiers often take direct leadership roles in khaki capitalist enterprises. Close connections between active-duty and retired security officials become significant when the latter are appointed to civilian posts, especially if that posting involves oversight of active-duty security personnel.

This study defines civil–military relations as those interactions that in some way relate to the power to make political decisions (Welche 1976: 2). Kohn vaguely describes civilian control as a situation where 'civilians make all the rules and can change them at any time' (Kohn 1997: 142). 'This means that civilians have exclusive authority to decide on national politics and their implementation...while the military has no decision-making power outside those areas specifically defined by civilians' (Croissant *et al.* 2013:25).

In the political security market, violence is both a public and private commodity. As a public commodity it offers state-controlled order, and as a private commodity it offers its services for the purpose of earning a profit. Militaries are generally the largest providers of the service of

2. See, for example, Huntington 1957.

violence within states, often (though not always) maintaining indirect control over police and certain paramilitary forces. In many young democracies, militaries (or certain parts of or forces serving under them) direct their oligopoly of violence toward private 'consumers', who can purchase violence or potential violence to serve their needs. Alternatively, militaries extort profits or pressure governments to give senior military officers economically lucrative positions through the potential use of force (Ngunyi and Katumanga 2014: 5-8).

Given that militaries possess this oligopoly of violence, 'they may be tempted to act in a partisan or praetorian manner in relation to domestic politics... [Alternatively,] they may be the subject of attempts by partisan factions within the civilian sector to... disrupt democratic processes. Thus, effective and democratic civilian control of the security sector is a key component of any process of democratization' (Edmunds 2003: 13). Constitutionally-entrenched civilian supremacy implies that the arrangements of civilian control over security forces must be enshrined into law. Nevertheless, military officials sometimes engage in behaviour that is informal (outside the purview or reach of the law), which helps them resist civilian control since civilians are rarely aware of it (Pion-Berlin 2010: 527–30). Moreover, on some occasions, civilians are unwilling to enforce constitutionally-embedded civilian control over the military. All in all, 'civilian control' in practice has shifted across time and space; it is never an absolute but rather 'a matter of degree' (Welche 1976: 2–3).

Militaries and economic predation

Economics and rational choice institutionalism teach us that political actors tend to acquire and deploy resources in order to maximize profits so as to achieve optimal payoffs in distributional conflicts. These actors face legal parameters provided by the institutional environment which constrains their behaviour. Ultimately, actors use strategic cost-benefit calculations to maximize their set preferences in the form of concrete policy outcomes (Hall and Taylor 1996: 936–57). Where political actors are powerful state institutions, the quest for institutional aggrandizement of resources can be an overriding reason to seek domination over other state (or even non-state) institutions. Militaries are one among sometimes many powerful state actors. In many cases, they are influential economic actors – institutionalized profit seekers engaged in an entire range of commercial activities. In militaries, the rent extracted does not remain with the leadership but is allowed to trickle down, asymmetrically, to lower rungs of the armed forces. Further, when a military organisation acquires control over substantial and productive economic resources, it will seek to remain politically indispensable in order to perpetuate its ability to create and distribute economic largesse. As a result, development of civilian control or democracy can be hindered by military organizations that refuse to reduce their political and economic roles in society.

Such predatory capitalistic practices tend to be common in many developing countries, where militaries are leading political institutions. Predatory capital exists where finance is obtained through plunder, extortion, exploitation or some form of malfeasance. Patron kings in medieval Europe offered security assistance to client princes in exchange for tribute. Similarly, contemporary mafias have offered 'protection' to merchants in exchange for remuneration to prevent damage that the racketeers themselves might otherwise deliver (Tilly 1985: 169–71). Such dues and payments have been quite surreptitious. The efficacy of protection has furthermore often depended upon the legitimacy of the managers of violence and their level of singular control over states which themselves often have differing degrees of cohesion.

The quality whereby militaries tend to be economic predators in their use of extortion and malfeasance to gain income gives rise to their accumulation of predatory capital, or more specifically khaki capital. Khaki capital itself generally denotes all financing – formal and informal – which bankrolls the military as an economic actor. Literature regarding military capital has generally focused only on the informal military economy. One 2003 study focuses upon 'military business', defined as 'economic activities falling under the influence of the armed forces, regardless of whether they are controlled by the defence ministries or the various branches of the armed forces or specific units, or individual officers.' These include military-owned corporations, welfare foundations or economic enterprises run by smaller groups or individuals within the military (Brömmelhörster and Paes, 2003: 1–4).

A second study, which examined the case of Pakistan's military political economy, also focuses upon *military business*, calling it 'MILBUS', which concentrates upon 'military capital used for the benefit of the military fraternity, especially the officer cadre, which is not recorded as part of the defence budget' (Siddiqa 2007: 5). The shadowy parameters of MILBUS contain not only the provision of security to private non-state actors, but also engagement in a wide range of 'non-security areas including farming, hotels, airlines, bank, real estate companies, etc; military holdings of state property; resources for retired armed forces personnel; the allocation of business opportunities for both active-duty and retired military officers; and finally money lost on training military personnel who retire early to start alternative careers' (ibid. 6).

The most recent analysis examines 'military entrepreneurship', defined as:

> the innovative creation of resources and means of production by commissioned military officers acting in an institutional capacity as formal owners, managers and stakeholders of enterprises that generate financial resources or goods directly benefiting the military. Their activities are generally legal and politically sanctioned, though not necessarily just or transparent... Yet what stands out is that military entrepreneurs are public actors whose loyalties are formally ascribed to the national state, while at the same time they are actively pursuing institutional interests through their economic activities. Their public loyalties and institutional interests are by no means always compatible (Mani 2010: 2–3).

While these studies offer useful definitions, they are limited as they fail to look at some important aspects of a military's political economy. These include the politics of defence budgeting, United Nations peacekeeping as a part of a military's political economy, and foreign military assistance.

The study at hand draws upon the aforementioned studies, especially that of Siddiqa. However, it goes further. It postulates that if we really want to understand military economy, we must analyse both its formal and informal sources. Thus, we propose a detailed definition of khaki capital as a form of income generation whereby the military, as the state-legitimized and dominant custodian-of-violence, establishes a mode of production that enables it (a) to influence state budgets to extract open or covert financial allocations; (b) to extract, transfer and distribute financial resources; and (c) to create financial or career opportunities that allow for the direct or indirect enhancement of its dividends at both the institutional and the individual level. Such enhancements include military business enterprises, foundations operated by and creating income for elements of (or all of) the military or defence ministry, and individual entitlements (e.g. sinecures).

Traditionally, as in Myanmar for example, military state-owned enterprises (with military managers) were corrupt, inefficient and often devoid of profit. Their advantages included the ability to use coercion and insider knowledge of state policies to obtain better terms than private corporations. Other advantages were militaries' higher degree of organisation relative to other institutions and their easy access to state funding to support their businesses. Military businesses are either managed by the military directly or sub-managed by civilian technocrats. Yet given that most military businesses are motivated by the maximization of profit, many military officials tend to seek for them the most able and professional management possible. It is for this very reason that many militaries tend to choose civilian professionals as managers of military businesses. Other militaries care less about securing profitable businesses and parasitically leech off of state support without turning profits.

Khaki capital possesses a formal and an informal dimension. *Formally*, it denotes budgetary allocations that are either directly or indirectly budgeted to the armed forces by the legislature (as approved by the executive branch). This also includes legal land-holdings by the armed forces, military pensions and retirement programmes, social welfare for soldiers killed or disabled in the line of duty (and their families) and legal military investments in private enterprises (including the holding of partially or wholly-owned businesses); Political economy on these issues comes alive when leading military officials use influence to lobby legislators or make threats to civilian governments to maximize their formalized capital preferences.

Informally, it can refer to activities that slide on a scale ranging from the semi-legal to the clearly illegal. This includes secret military budgetary slush funds, the use of soldiers for private security purposes, semi-legal or illegal military investments in private enterprises (including the holding of partially or wholly-owned businesses), military-related commercial opportunities for senior brass before or after retirement, military plunder of the state budget (corruption) and even military collusion with criminal interests. Political economy on these issues occurs where soldiers use coercion to acquire or demand a greater amount of such commercial resources.

This definition might seem overly materialistic since some might think that it under-scrutinizes the importance of military legitimacy, ideology, professionalization and links between the military and national or public interest. However, such a definition is intentionally materialistic because it aims to remain as parsimonious as possible, thus largely ignoring societal or normative factors which can influence military behaviour. Moreover, this study does emphasize the clash between military and public interests in terms of the fact that often in Southeast Asia civilians have been unable to exert control over militaries which are then able to possess massive amounts of khaki capital.

Some khaki capital is stashed legally and transparently in national budgetary or onshore accounts. Other domestic khaki capital is stashed in opaque slush funds. Military banks such as the Thai Military Bank have in the past served the role of keeping abundant amounts of capital available for military officials outside of public scrutiny. Some khaki capital is parked in non-transparent offshore accounts accessible only to the military account holders themselves. In fact, militaries tend to be distinctive as state actors both willing and able to invest proceeds from business and predatory activities offshore.

Ultimately, in many developing countries, khaki capital is predatory (manipulative and plunderous) in nature (Siddiqa 2007: 2). This is because first, aside from the more transparent defence budgets, military resources tend to be opaque. Indeed, such budgets are often not scrutinized by civilians, with the result that military expenditures are much higher than the budget allocated for particular military purposes. Moreover, parts of military budgets can be hidden in other budget categories or stashed away in secret slush funds (Brömmelhörster & Paes 2003: 13). Thus, such military economic activities are often 'off the books', or unaccountable to civilian monitoring agencies since they are monitored only by the military itself. Second, militaries, as powerful institutional actors, often demand that they should retain or obtain more of a country's economic pie. In sum, the ability of a military to achieve greater khaki capital depends upon the preponderance of power it wields vis-à-vis elected civilian actors. Such power is wielded in terms of the extent to which the military possesses political prerogatives which can keep civilian supremacy at bay. Almost by definition, the greater an equilibrium favours military power within a political system, the more financial resources the military will possess. On the other hand, where the equilibrium decidedly favours civilians, the political economy of khaki capital is weak. Where there is a rough balance between the two sides, then a tug-of-war over decision-making and resources might ensue, which can lead to military coups. Counter-intuitively perhaps, in certain cases, an equilibrium that favours the military need not be headed by the military and, since both civilian and military actors are likely to understand their place, the threat of a military coup can sometimes be relatively low.

A difficulty of this study is that there is often little accessible information available to pursue conclusive quantitative research on such an opaque subject as khaki capital. Indeed, the less pluralistic the country case in question, the less transparent khaki capital appears to be. An exception would be defence budgets. Nevertheless, parts of military budgets (or slush funds) tend to be classified for reasons of national security and publicly divulging such information can lead to imprisonment. Ultimately, because of the general opaqueness of khaki capital, many of the sources for the chapters herein have tended to be much more qualitative in nature (Siddiqa 2007: 24).

Historical institutionalism and khaki capital

Historical institutionalism is useful in explaining persistence and change in civil–military relations across time (Croissant, *et al.* 2013). Historical institutionalists stress how institutions shape not only strategies in a single historical moment, but also the evolution of preferences, goals and interests (Thelen and Steinmo 1992: 9). The historical-institutionalist development of khaki capital involves three concepts: historical-cultural legacies, path dependence and critical junctures.

The first, *historical-cultural legacies*, are prior contextual conditions of the past, which, once created, become self-reproducing and entrenching (Collier and Collier 1991; Pierson 2004). Historical legacies pave the way for military economies (as parts of powerful institutions) to sink deep roots. In this sense, 'legacies of the authoritarian past linger over the years of democratic transition and precondition the behavioural propensities and interactions of collective actors under democratic politics' (Lee 2011). Such legacies can thus lead to path dependence.

The second concept, *path dependence*, has been defined as an evolutionary trajectory whereby, once actors make certain institutional choices, 'the costs of reversal are very high. There will be other choice points, but the entrenchments of certain institutional arrangements obstruct an easy reversal of the initial choice' (Levi 1997: 28). Path dependence has two dimensions: one is structural and captures the notion of *increasing returns*, the other relates to *agency* in terms of the resources which actors can mobilize in order to initiate or guard against institutional change (Mahoney 2000; Moe 2005; Thelen 2003; Pierson 2000). Regarding khaki capital, where armed forces begin to extract rents and thus expand their economic power base, path dependence has tended to build up and entrench the military's khaki clout. This owes to the fact that the success of militaries to generate dividends tends to produce increasing returns: civilian elites often need assistance from senior military brass to sustain themselves in office. It thus becomes necessary to give financial or material perks to the armed forces to appease them.

Third, the concept of *critical junctures* reflects the importance of ascertaining a beginning point of a path across time (Capoccia and Kelemen 2007). Critical junctures are defined as 'short, time-defined periods, where antecedent conditions allow contingent choices that set a specific trajectory of institutional modification that is difficult to reverse' (Page 2006: 8). Critical junctures can influence khaki capital in the sense of major politico-economic structural phenomena that can retrench institutional configurations. Examples of critical junctures include where colonies achieve independence, revolutions overthrow regimes, or countries suffer invasion.

The approach offers explanations about how events in history either constrained or offered opportunities that affected institutional resilience or transformation.[3] Such transformations involve alterations in the distribution of power among societal actors across time as reflected in political institutions (Mahoney and Thelen 2010: 18). Beginning from the institutional point of origin, initial institutional patterns become chronologically reinforced, producing persistent impacts upon contemporary configurations (Pierson 2004). The framework emphasizes the importance of historical dynamics and contingency rather than staticity

---

3. See K. Thelen and S. Steinmo 1992; Pierson 2000: 251–67; Pierson 2004; Mahoney, Rueschmeyer, and Dietrich (eds) 2003; P. Pierson and T. Skocpol 2002.

and determinism. As such, it is practical in showing how a sequential series of events helps to reinforce configurations that have later effects. In addition, historical institutionalism emphasizes how institutions develop over time and reflect the relative bargaining power of actors that created them.

Historical institutionalism can be useful in understanding the evolution of khaki capital across time. It can demonstrate how military economic interests, goals, preferences and strategies were historically shaped, as well as how deeply militaries carved out their influence within a given economy. In addition, an historical institutionalist analysis of military political economy sheds light on the military's institutional development. Indeed, it can elucidate the extent to which historical legacies have helped to entrench an evolutionary path and whether any critical junctures worked to prolong this path dependence or shift its course. It emphasizes how chronological changes may have affected military economy at the institutional or individual level. Some of these transitions may have responded to changes in the global economy towards greater or lesser economic dependency (Mani 2010: 9–10).

Explaining the evolution of khaki capital in Southeast Asia

In the Europe of 400 BCE, Thucydides, the Athenian general, offered three basic motives for war: fear, honour and interest (Thucydides 1982: 76). While such rationales have continued to exist across time, the systems in which political units thrived have changed. Indeed, where kingdoms flourished in medieval and pre-industrial Europe, it was necessary for kings and lords to collect tribute to support themselves. Such 'taxes' from locals were paid in the form of finance, material or corvée labour. Moreover, these tribute systems involved suzerainty ties among polities with different degrees of power. Wallerstein (1974) has referred to these systems as 'world-empires'. During this time, armies were short-lived affairs, raised for temporary actions often from the peasants themselves. In this sense, a kingdom's legitimacy (or sometimes even survival) depended upon guarantees for its existence based upon the amount of tribute it provided its patron(s) or, if it was itself a patron, how long it could persevere in that role. According to Tilly (1985), the role of states in this period was four-fold: external war, keeping internal order, protecting vassals, and extracting resources for the purposes of performing the first three goals (Tilly 1985: 185). Legitimate managers of violence (militaries) only began to become clear in Europe in the 17th century, as states as well as state-sponsored armed forces achieved greater unity and degree of permanency (Tilly 1985: 173). Though armies often were forced to 'live off the land' for their subsistence, when it came to collecting tribute, as the managers of violence, they would demand higher wages. This corresponded with a new motive for war: the acquisition and agglomeration of territory. The 1648 Treaty of Westphalia to some extent ended Europe's system of feudalism and suzerainty, substituting it with a sovereign state system. Thereupon, there was a 1650–1730 recession in Europe, owing to intermittent wars, social strife and religious upheaval at the time. At this point, the European state system devolved into a mercantilist competition for power within a capitalist world economy centred upon one state at a time (Wallerstein 1974: 407). Because of mercantilism, European states became interested in acquiring colonies to produce and export goods back to the motherland. The growing power of states in Europe paralleled the centralization of bureaucracy, establishment of permanent standing armies and conversion of soldiers of fortune into wage-earners. With permanent, professional armies, European states could now fight wars over territory to build colonies and acquire profit by means of mercantilist enterprises. By the 19th century, military economies in most of Europe had become completely subsumed within the bureaucratic state. Soldiers were wage-earning civil servants. Any other income based upon coercion was deemed to be outside the military bureaucracy and thus illegal. The ability of civilian leaders to transform militaries into mere appendages of bureaucracies and make soldiers dependent upon civilians for their finance worked to harness civilian supremacy over the military (Tilly 1983: 3–4). By the 21st century, this long-time entrenchment of the military under civilian control helped to guarantee that the social construction of such civil 'servitude' would persevere.

Armies in pre-colonial Southeast Asia behaved in similar fashion to armies in Europe prior to the 1600s. As in Europe, armies were composed of peasant farmers, raised and compelled to temporarily serve the king during inter-kingdom battles in the dry season. According to some writers, rather than seeking expansion of territory, wars were primarily fought to enhance available manpower, especially given that labour was something in short supply in Southeast Asia (Reid 1988: 123; Akin 1969: 10). Labourers acquired through war enslavement were necessary for feeding kingdoms and their armies, building infrastructure and serving as temporary soldiers themselves. Depopulating enemy kingdoms was also simply another way of weakening them. Other authors dismiss the manpower theory, instead seeing the search for land as a more primary objective of kingdoms at this time (Vickery 2003: 3). Obtaining war booty was another objective, with captured kingdoms plundered and looted before the invading armies returned home. Moreover, kings would use war victories to increase their regal legitimacy, which they expected to cement their stature, esteem and respect among nobles, peasants and potential enemies. Finally, it sometimes was perceived to be necessary to wage warfare in a defensive capacity, that is, to pre-empt an expected attempt by an outside force to sack one's own kingdom. Ultimately, the motives of war for Southeast Asian kingdoms at this time included 1) plunder (to acquire manpower, land and loot), prestige and preventive security (Battye 1974: 2).

As in pre-industrial Europe, armies in Southeast Asia were briefly-composed affairs, raised temporarily to fight a war and then disbanded. Indeed, 'armies, now levied now disbanded, had a short life' (Battye 1974: 10–11). Armies did not exist during times of peace. Indeed, kings had to oblige nobles of the realm to call up their own men at their own expense to serve in wars, and these peasant-farmer soldiers thus missed working the farms that propped up the economic positions of the nobles themselves. The notables were thus generally reluctant to do without such labour for long (Reid 1988: 123). Moreover, such short-term soldiers 'traditionally had to fend for and feed themselves even when on duty...' (ibid. 71). The peasant-farmer troops had to live off the land. Sometimes this meant planting, maintaining and harvesting crops themselves; other times it meant extorting food and supplies from those unlucky enough to live where the soldiers were waging war.

In most, if not all of Southeast Asia, *historical-cultural legacies* of the pre-colonial period were generally the same: armies were ephemerally in existence; they were perceived by both soldiers and the general population to have total power; and soldiers, with the permission of their liege, could loot the vanquished as they saw fit, especially given that militaries did not receive salaries. The disappearance of pre-colonial kingdom-military relationships occurred as European colonists began to arrive to different parts of Southeast Asia: Portugal in Malacca (1511); Spain in the Philippines (1565); the Netherlands in Indonesia (1603); the British in Burma (completed in 1885) and Malaya (1824); and the French in Indochina (completed in 1893). Though Siam was never officially colonized, the Siamese kingdom generally mimicked European methods in neighbouring colonies with regard to the establishment of a permanent, professional army in 1870 (Battye 1974: 113).

Given that colonization occurred incrementally over most of Southeast Asia and at widely divergent times (1500s–1800s), it can hardly be viewed collectively as a time-dependent *critical juncture*. Rather, colonization was another collection of evolutionary moments that, together, constitute historical legacies which directly impinged upon the region. The new European colonial overlords in Southeast Asia utilized three methods to police their peripheries: 1) soldiers from the homeland; 2) security forces from other colonies; and 3) the creation of a colonial military through the recruitment of locals, based upon European bureaucratic designs. The result was a revolution in security for Southeast Asia. Soldiers drew closer to the colonizer, especially as they were now wage-earners, and all senior security officials were from the mother country. Moreover, the establishment of a national security bureaucracy across each colony helped to centralize control under colonial officials (Day 2002: 31).

For example, in Burma, the British used their own forces to quell the Burmese in three colonial wars. Thereupon, Indian soldiers from British colonial India were brought in to enforce order. After World War I, the British recruited Burmese ethnic minorities, although Burmans themselves were banned from the military until the 1930s. Meanwhile, a series of laws, such as Crosswaite's Village Act (1895), legalized the frequent use of martial law and facilitated military repression (Callahan 2002).

Turning to Indonesia, the Royal Netherlands East Indies Army (RNEIA), formed in 1830, was responsible for keeping order over the Indonesian archipelago. It was a force commanded at senior levels by Dutchmen, though most of its positions were filled by local indigenous recruits. The RNEIA regularly imposed martial law to legitimize its use of repression (Cribb and Kahin 2004: 221; Vickers 2005: 13).

Finally, in the colonial Philippines, the Spanish military directly governed many provinces and Spanish soldiers had a ubiquitous presence in everyday life. When the United States assumed colonial control in 1899, US soldiers forcibly kept order. However, Washington also established a constabulary in 1901 and the Armed Forces of the Philippines (AFP) in 1935. Both services were composed of local recruits. The Philippine Constitution (1935) and National Defence Act (1935) heightened military authority within the Commonwealth but it cemented civilian control under both US colonial tutelage and colonial Philippine democracy (Berlin 2008: 12–21)

All in all, four patterns tended to sustain colonial armies in Southeast Asia. First, their rationale for existence was strong, as they were constantly needed to fight insurgencies and maintain order. They thus played a major role within colonial administration. Second, the importance of colonial armies meant that they received continuing budgets from the mother country. Third, laws created during colonial periods gave militaries more power. Finally, as colonial governors were constantly being rotated, colonial militaries – far from the motherland – became the only powerful actors in the colonial environment.

The character of militaries in Southeast Asia today can be traced back and indeed classified according to their relationship with colonialism and time of formation. First there were non-colonial armies, such as in Thailand and Turkey. These tended to perpetuate military traditions of the more distant past. Second, as in the Philippines, Malaysia, and Singapore, there were ex-colonial armies, which were formed by colonizers but which still existed at the time of peaceful decolonization. These militaries tended to allow post-independence civilian governments to exert civilian control over them. Third, there were armies formed during national liberation, as exemplified in Vietnam and Indonesia. These armies were not constructed by the colonizer, were riven with revolutionary ideology, and had to spearhead armed struggle to expel colonizers from newly independent countries. Finally, there were armies formed during post-liberation, which had little connection to the independence struggle itself (Janowitz 1988 [1964]: 89). These armies, as exemplified in South Vietnam and post-1993 Cambodia, have tended to be the most loosely united and underdeveloped.

During World War II, militaries in Southeast Asia once again had to find their own ways to sustain themselves, eking out an existence from the land the best that they could. In fact, the post-World War II period produced either new or reorganized armies in all countries of Southeast Asia. Moreover, most modern Southeast Asian armies today derive from organisations formed as national liberation militias, begun during the early 1940s, first with imperial Japan and then against it as exemplified by Myanmar's Tatmadaw, Indonesia's TNI (Tentara Nasional Indonesia), Vietnam's Viet Minh, Laos's Lao Issara, and Cambodia's Khmer Issarak militias. After leading independence struggles to new countries in Southeast Asia, these insurrectionist forces became powerful new societal forces. By the late 1940s, most of Southeast Asia's infrastructure had been destroyed and economies were in a shambles, owing first to the ravages of World War II and second to costly struggles to achieve independence which continued on in many Southeast Asian countries (Tarling 1999: 60–79). With the exception of colonial armies, the only actors with any foundation at the time were the insurgent armies themselves. As the newly independent countries in Southeast Asia (as well as Thailand) began to rebuild their economies and embark on national development strategies, only these armies could guarantee stability; elected civilians could not. It was thus only natural that they would come to control vast tracts of land, corporations and sources of energy, as well as be granted generous annual budgets. After all, the necessities of national security justified the military's economic involvement. Either formally or informally – or both formally and informally – khaki capital increased across the board in every emerging nation of Southeast Asia after World War II. Once they gained control of economic resources, these militaries – as any actor playing bureaucratic politics – tried as best they could to keep it (Brömmelhörster and Paes 2003: 1–4). Even in retirement, military officers persisted in amassing economic largesse. Ultimately, the transition from colony to independent state (as stimulated by World War II) became the first *critical juncture* to affect militaries and khaki capital in Southeast Asia. This historic episode transformed militaries from colonial civil servant to agent of independence.

A path dependence involving historical-cultural legacies of traditionally strong militaries was difficult to break. And indeed, while military reorganisation did occur following decolonization after World War II, militaries remained powerful in all countries of Southeast Asia. As such, these militaries tried to acquire as well as maintain khaki capital at high levels relative to the national budget and indeed militaries became economic predators. Following World War II, the international dimension crucially affected the power of Southeast Asian militaries. The 1947–91 Cold War between the United States and the Soviet Union led to a growing degree of great power involvement in Southeast Asia. During this period, the Philippines, Thailand, both North and South Vietnam, Laos, Cambodia, Indonesia, Malaya (Malaysia) and Burma/Myanmar all became Cold War theatres and each used its militaries to counter and/or sponsor insurgencies. The United States, Soviet Union and post-1949 China each sent massive amounts of military and economic aid as well as advisors to bolster their allies in the region. The United States even sent combat troops and bombed Vietnam, Cambodia and Laos. These militaries increasingly took the spotlight given that they were tasked with guaranteeing national security and advancing development in rural areas. These important objectives gave the militaries a renewed impetus and justification to amass khaki capital. The bottom line was that foreign military assistance and training, primarily from the United States, the Soviet Union and China helped to subsidize regional proxy wars and the Southeast Asian armies fighting them, expanding the size and might of these militaries as well as promoting the economic-political stature of victorious militaries (Beeson and Bellamy 2008: 16).

Meanwhile, since the 1980s and especially following the end of the Cold War in 1991, external factors increasingly influenced Southeast Asia including globalization, the growing involvement of international organisations (e.g. the United Nations), multinational corporations, regional integration initiatives (such as the Asian Development Bank's 1992 Greater Mekong Subregion programme), and the post-1985 rise of Japan in the region followed by the post-2000 rapid ascent of Chinese economic clout in Asia. Foreign corporations have worked with Southeast Asian militaries in some countries such as Cambodia and Laos to evict villagers from lands and secure their holdings.

In the rapidly globalizing world, there has been a drive by Southeast Asian militaries to acquire financing through participation in United Nations Peace-keeping operations. Cambodia, Indonesia, Malaysia, the Philippines, Thailand and Vietnam have each been involved in such operations. Aside from providing outside finance from needy security forces, these projects also help keep militaries busy to reduce the risk that they might plot against governments in power.

There is furthermore an interstate dimension of military commercial activities in Southeast Asia whereby militaries work with as well as observe, interact, and learn from each other. One aspect of this relates to the historical development of militaries. The 1975 unification of Vietnam, Vietnam-supported revolution in Laos that year and Vietnam's occupation of Cambodia in 1979–89 assisted Vietnam in exerting influence over the security forces of Laos and Cambodia alike for decades to come. The militaries of the three countries have often worked with each other since. Laos and Cambodia have observed and adopted organisational methods of the Vietnamese armed forces. Vietnamese military economic influence in both countries continues to this day. A second aspect deals with regional institutional cooperation. The Association of Southeast Asian Nations (ASEAN) has provided a forum for meetings among security officials from the different ASEAN member states. Such meetings include the ASEAN Military Operations Informal Meeting, the ASEAN Military Intelligence Informal Meeting and the ASEAN Defence Ministers Meeting.

The late 1980s and early 1990s initiated a watershed event with regard to the military in Southeast Asia. Indeed, it seemed that 'a new wave of democracy' was sweeping across the world (Huntington 1991). The influx of democracy into Southeast Asia meant that elected civilian managers would achieve more monitoring abilities over the armed forces. Moreover, especially in the aftermath of the 1997 Asian Financial Crisis, military budgeting was increasingly targeted around the region and an emphasis was placed on state transparency and accountability (Beeson and Bellamy 2008: 76). Ultimately then, democratization has been a second *critical juncture* in parts of Southeast Asia, with the subsequent imposition of civilian control over the military. However, this has not meant that militaries have become overshadowed by civilian supremacy. Rather, in the Philippines (after 1986), Thailand (after 1988), Indonesia (after 1998) East Timor (after 1999) and Burma/Myanmar (after 2010), militaries have fully or partially insulated themselves from civilian control, slightly diminished their political roles, or succeeded in hiding acts of malfeasance from civilian oversight. In terms of khaki capital, democratization has meant different things for the military in different countries. In Burma/Myanmar, the military remains thoroughly insulated. In Cambodia, the military has been co-opted by the dominant political party which shields it from oversight. In Thailand, the military is really only answerable to the monarch and there is thus full insulation from elected civilian control – though since the 2014 coup, there has not been any elected civilian government at all. In Indonesia, despite civilian control since 1998, the economic role of the military has only slightly diminished. Finally, in the Philippines, where the military is expected to exist exclusively through governmental budgetary disbursements, and informal khaki capital is against the law, parts of the military have been involved in surreptitious corruption.

As for Vietnam and Lao PDR, two post-communist non-democracies in Southeast Asia, there are differences among them in terms of civil–military relations. Regarding Vietnam, though a single party dominates politics in the country, it is impossible to determine civilian versus military control (Thayer 2003). With regard to Lao PDR however, civilian control has been achieved over the military though the military remains highly influential (Evans 2002). In both countries, militaries possess enormous economic/political power within domestic society (Thayer 2003; Evans 2002).

The country cases in this book each shines light on the diversity of the armed forces' share of control over their country's economies. Table 1.1 illustrates the degree of military insulation from civilian monitoring over khaki capital. To measure this variable, we turn to the Government Defence Anti-Corruption Index.[4] This Index measures five prominent risk areas (i.e., finance, procurement, operations, politics, and personnel) where the military can assert its control over civilians especially in the economic realm. This study thus takes the index as a proxy for the degree of military control over khaki capital as well as military dominance over civilian affairs. The Index analyses corruption and insulation from civilian monitoring in the defence sectors of 82 countries. Countries were grouped in different bands, from very low risk (A) to critical risk (F). The Index placed the Philippines between bands C and

---

4. The Government Defence Anti-Corruption Index is published each year by Transparency International (TI). This chapter utilized the 2015 Index.

Table 1.1: Degree of military insulation from civilian monitoring over khaki capital

Country	Government Defence Anti-Corruption Index
Cambodia	F
Indonesia	D
Lao PDR	N/A
Myanmar	F
Philippines	C–D
Thailand	E
Vietnam	N/A

Source: Transparency International, Government Defence Anti-Corruption Index, 2015, http://government.defenceindex.org/#close.

Note: Transparency International did not produce measurements for Vietnam or Laos. We have thus transcribed these as "Not Available" (N/A) for both countries.

D; Indonesia squarely in Band D; Thailand in Band E; Cambodia in Band F and Burma/Myanmar also in Band F.

What drives khaki capital? An answer can be found based upon the analysis of agency and structure. At the individual level, khaki capitalism is driven by the greed of members of the military's senior brass (Siddiqa 2007: 10). Besides simple greed, military leaders seek to expand khaki capital in order to retain control over lower-echelon soldiers by creating personal-dependent relationships. Furthermore there is often a tendency for military leaders to make the military bureaucracy reflect their own personal interests, which sometimes results in the armed forces as an institution becoming a mere mechanism for the venal needs of the senior brass. Such military leaders identify their own interests as being in opposition to a military bureaucracy which would putatively try to control them. Thus, where top military leaders fear either external, internal or bureaucratic enemies, they will take advantage of the military institution, building up their personal wealth in the name of military itself. A final factor to note in terms of agency is the relative cohesion of militaries themselves. More united militaries are more likely either to expand khaki capital or to prevent civilian efforts to diminish it.

Meanwhile, at the structural level, historical-cultural legacies and path dependence help to account for what propels khaki capital.

Legacies of the past tell the story of militaries that traditionally had to live off the land, with peasant-farmers either forcibly recruited as soldiers or required to work in other labour capacities for the benefit of the army. Colonial experiences added to khaki capital the notion of wage labour for soldiers; the notion that soldiers needed to be under civilian (colonial) control; a permanent standing army must exist; various legal decrees needed to justify military actions; and finally that armies must follow an entire assortment of standard operating procedures. Despite colonialism, the perception remained embedded in soldiers and the general populace alike that where soldiers moved, they could take whatever materials they needed from the people – a surviving vestige from pre-colonial days (Croissant 2013). World War II witnessed the build-up of Southeast Asian rebel forces which, with regard to khaki capital, followed the example of pre-colonial armies in living off the land (except in the case of Thailand, which was never colonized). Finally, the heady days of early independence revealed that in most cases, the most powerful actors in Southeast Asia were the military. A path dependence embracing long-embedded historical-cultural legacies of militaries perceived in society as leading institutions which took care of themselves contributed to the military 'feeding itself' as in earlier times through setting up of or acquisition of interest in businesses and other elements of khaki capital.

Ultimately khaki capital has been driven by a combination of agency and structure. Human agency, when it is united as one single actor rather than multiple factions or sub-bureaucracies, initiates movements toward political outcomes. In the case at hand, such movements are made for purposes of acquiring or holding khaki capital but agents' strategies are only realized through the conditioning of structure. In this sense, the structural driving force of khaki capital has been the historical evolution of militaries, while the individual driving force has been the decisions of military commanders as agents to act.

A typology of civil–military relations and khaki capital

This study examines and compares the political economy of the military in diverse regimes across Southeast Asia. Khaki capital is obtained in different ways under different regimes. We stipulate that the extent to which the military controls its own economic resources determines the level of elected civilian supremacy over the military which in turn can sustain or even increase the military power to expand further control over its own wealth. In other words, the higher the level of military control over its own economic resources, the lower the level of civilian control over the military.

This study distinguishes between three levels of civilian control: high, medium and low (Croissant *et al.* 2013). Civilian control itself marks one swing of a pendulum while military control is on the other. Where civilian control is absolute, civilians exert absolute control over decision-making, including leadership selection, public policy, internal security, national defence and military organisation. Where civilian control is at a medium level, civilian decision-making in these aforementioned areas is limited to certain aspects. Finally, where civilian control is low, the military assumes most of the control in all five areas (Croissant *et al.* 2013: 32).

Within this tripartite differentiation of civilian control, the study in hand also offers a typology of civil–military relations (CMR) which identifies different forms of linkages between civilian and military dimensions, especially as illustrated by the different forms of CMR in Southeast Asia. This typology is also important because it accounts for the different levels of civilian versus military control over the economic capital (as well as the political capital) in different Southeast Asian countries. There have been several previous typologies, though not all of them specifically classify relative power of civilians and militaries across different regime types.[5] Finer (1962: 3) offers a four-fold classification that distinguishes

---

5. There have been a plethora of civil–military typologies. Among the most famous, Huntington (1963) distinguishes among palace coups, reform coups and revolutionary coups (Huntington, 1963: 32–3). Meanwhile, Nordlinger differentiated among militaries who act as 'moderators', 'guardians', and 'rulers' (Nordlinger, 1977: 22). Moderators tend to exert power over the government on a multitude of issues without assuming power themselves. Guardians, overthrow governments but only stay for a limited time before returning to the barracks. Rulers take direct control over the state and society (Nordlinger, 1977: 22). Moreover, Perlmutter (1980) argues that there were five types of military regimes: corporative, market-bureaucratic, socialist-oligarchic, army-party and tyrannical military (Perlmutter, 1980: 96–120). In addition, he stated that military dictatorships come in two variants: the arbitrator type and the ruler type (Perlmutter 1981: 22). Finally, Clapham and Philip classify military regimes in terms of how they utilize power. Thus, their typology is as follows: veto, moderator, factional and breakthrough.

between 1) where officers have exercised constitutional and legitimate influence a civilian government to obtain a favourable budget; 2) where officers have used threat or blackmail to achieve similar goals; 3) where officers militarily replace a civilian government with another one to prioritize military objectives; and 4) where officers simply displace a civilian government and rule by themselves. Janowitz meanwhile posits five types of civil–military relations: authoritarian-personal control, authoritarian-mass party, democratic competitive and semi-competitive systems, civil–military coalition, and military oligarchy' (Janowitz 1988 [1964]: 81). In the first three classifications, military influence is subsumed under civilian control. The authoritarian-personal variant is where a personalistic civilian dictator reigns supreme over a single polity while the military follows his/her dictates. Meanwhile, the authoritarian-mass party type describes single party regimes where the military stands as junior partner. However, in such systems, the military may be poorly developed and hence find itself competing with other security agencies. Democratic and semi-democratic systems refer to polities where militaries are either firmly under democratic control or semi-democratic control. Such firm civilian control may owe to colonial experiences where militaries became successfully subsumed under civilian leaderships. In the last two classifications, militaries are more powerful than civilians. In the civil–military coalition model, armed forces serve as a power bloc which can be instrumental in one civilian group coming to office. Alternatively, the loss of military support can spell the doom of a civilian government. Militaries may even be called upon to place a temporary government in power. Regardless, militaries in this category play the role of umpire or mediator between opposing political groups. Finally, in the last type, military oligarchy, the armed forces directly rule a country (ibid.). Though Janowitz's classification has been criticized for failing to clarify the degree of autonomy which civilian leaders can have from the military, in terms of delineating a continuum of different forms of relative power between civilians and the military, the typology has generally weathered the times well (Karabelias 1998: 11). Siddiqa (2007:33) offered a much more recent typology which, like that of Janowitz, disaggregates regimes in terms of civilian and military dimen-

---

The authors also classify military regimes in terms of the end-result of a military regime: simple hand-backs, civilian renewal, authoritarian, factional clientelism, military-party state and the case of an impasse (Clapham and Philip 1985: 8–10).

sions. These CMR types are 1) civil–military partnership; 2) authoritarian-political-bureaucratic partnership; 3) ruler military domination; 4) arbitrator military domination; 5) parent-guardian military domination; and 6) warlord domination. The first of these, civil–military partnership, is akin to Janowitz's democratic competitive or semi-competitive systems variant. Type two, authoritarian-political-bureaucratic partnership, is also very similar to Janowitz's authoritarian-mass party variant. Type three (ruler military domination), meanwhile, can be found in Janowitz's military oligarchy model. Types four and five (arbitrator military domination and parent guardian military domination) moreover are conflated into Janowitz's single variant, civil–military coalition. Siddiqa does, however, bring in a sixth new variant: the warlord type. Indeed, she calls into attention states which have suffered a complete breakdown of centralized political power. As such, different warlord armies compete for power. Nevertheless, there is no reason why this variant cannot be subsumed under Janowitz's authoritarian-personal type of control. Indeed, Janowitz does not discount the possibility that this variant might not exist under civil war conditions. For this reason, this study drops Siddiqa's warlord type, and is thus left with the five-fold taxonomy of Janowitz. Yet even Janowitz's typology needs modifications. Mention must be made of systems where actors with enormous clout exist outside of militaries or civilians. By this we mean powerful religious, monarchical, landed elite or even tribal leaders. If one of these outside groups can dominate militaries, then a new variant must be added. For this reason, as shown in Table 1.2, this study introduces a sixth variant: parallel-state semi-democracy.

Though Janowitz offered a quite useful classification of civil–military relations in 1964, more than 50 years of history as well as theoretical

Table 1.2: A modified Janowitzian typology of civil–military relations

1	authoritarian-personal control
2	authoritarian-mass party
3	democratic-competitive, semi-democratic competitive
4	Parallel-state Semi-democratic
5	Civil–military coalition
6	Military oligarchy (*Caesarism*)

Source: Based on Janowitz 1988 [1964], p. 81.

developments have led us to make some modifications. Our modified Janowitzian model offers some additions to Janowitz's original five variants but also adds a sixth type. These six variants are each explained below.

Authoritarian-personal control

In this first model, power is not politically diffused beyond a single person who controls (directly or indirectly) the political dimensions of a given polity. This person can be a monarch or non-military strongman. His/her dictatorship may include a political party or even fall in step with the trappings of democracy. However, any such party or democratic system operates as mere camouflage to the reality that this person exerts total, personalistic power. Moreover, such a form of control can exist where a country is in civil war, as with a warlord who physically controls a swathe of land and its people. Finally, rather than the military penetrating to control this person, it is the other way around, with this person exercising personal control over the military. Most finances for the military are first overseen by the personalist leader, who, in this way, keeps a check on the armed forces' power. He/she might also acquiesce to military control over certain economic holdings in return for loyalty. Examples of this model can be found in Brunei; Philippines (1972–86); and Cambodia (1955–70; 1997–present).

Authoritarian-mass party

In this system, a highly-vertical single-party structure exercises complete control over a society – including the military. Such power originates in a politburo or directorate led by senior party leaders who rotate into and out of these posts. Civilian control is high, though there is hardly any pluralism to speak of; this variant is most often seen in communist systems. The military receives a small amount of financing from party coffers, and is permitted to develop its own projects to supplement its financing. As such, there is often a lack of transparency for khaki capital in these systems. Examples of this model can be found in Vietnam (1975–present), Lao PDR (1975–present), and Singapore.

(Semi-) democratic-competition

In this model, militaries are transparent and accountable to elected civilian governments, as well as to government-appointed agencies. In those systems deemed semi-competitive, democracy is only partially embedded or consolidated (Merkel 2004). The only type of formal khaki capital, under this variant, is the transparent budget allocated by the legislature and approved by the executive. Naturally, corruption within the budget could allow for the military's acquisition of informal khaki capital. This model possesses a very high degree of civilian control, including democratically-elected civilians who are able to constantly monitor and oversee the armed forces. The military senior brass are constantly rotated in and out of their posts and indeed a bureaucratic culture has developed which politically socializes military officers and soldiers to value democratic civilian control of the military. Examples of this model include the United States and Japan. In Southeast Asia, the Philippines (1946–72; 1986–present); Indonesia (1998–present); and East Timor (1999–present) may be characterized as falling under this variant.

Parallel-state semi-democracy

Sometimes referred to as 'deep state' or 'state within a state', this variant is an aristocracy-dominant form of *khakistocracy* (military plus aristocracy). In this system, a shadowy network of elite 'players' dominates politics and the military is a mechanism that enforces their decisions; democracy itself is generally peripheral to public policy making. According to Briscoe's (2008) notion of parallel state, a powerful, informal (which can sometimes also be formal) network is organically connected to the state and can exude formal political authority, but also informally possesses its own institutional interests outside those of civilian leaders. This network can exude a high level of civilian control, though it is deficient in democratic civilian control. Such networks include constitutional monarchies (e.g. Thailand [1992–2006; 2008–14] and Jordan) or quasi-theocratic states (e.g. Iran since 1979). Elected state leadership can only solidify its position by acquiescing to the autonomy of the informal power structure. The frailty of formally elected civilian governance offers an advantage to this shadowy network, given that de facto powers can in many cases manipulate and subvert decision-making by influencing the judiciary, security forces, political parties, parliament and so on. Transactions between elected civilians and the informal structure, based upon context and institutional interest, determine the political equilibrium. Regarding khaki capital, the armed forces are really only beholden to the informal network of power and not to the state, making their financial transactions generally opaque (Briscoe 2008).

Civil–military coalition

In this model, the armed forces prefer to act as back-room dealers, acting in coalition with various elite groups to place civilian governments in power or occasionally leading military coups and then quickly returning to the barracks. Perlmutter (1981) refers to such militaries as 'arbitrator militaries', which negotiate relationships among such groups as political parties, civilian bureaucrats, (including judges), businesspeople, religious orders, ethnic groups and diverse civil society organisations. These elite groups or partners assist the military in resolving not only perceived national security problems, but perhaps also in expanding military corporate interests. In this model, militaries see themselves as the guardian of the state. They also generally despise elected civilian governments, which they perceive as corrupt, self-serving and failing to serve the interests not only of the military but also of the vast majority of the civilian population. Nonetheless, the armed forces reluctantly supports them, knowing full well that domestic actors as well as international military donors consider direct military control to be illegitimate. The military furthermore prefers to have civilian governments because, if any crisis befalls the country, blame will rest on civilian leaders rather than the military, since civilians are seen as the face of the government. Civilian control in this model is medium to low, depending upon the level of pressure applied by the armed forces upon civilian actors at a given time. Sometimes, of course, the military might choose to do what the civilian government asks of it; this is a sign of confluence of interests rather than of control.

Siddiqa's (2007) 'parent-guardian military type' is also subsumed under this modified Janowitzian model. The parent-guardian describes militaries that preserve their power through constitutional/legal enactments. Thus, formally enshrined clout gives the armed forces legitimate authority to compete with or trump civilian actors. Such a situation is exemplified by Pakistan's military-dominant National Security Council (Siddiqa 2007: 54). Top-ranking officers are permitted to have leading, legally bestowed roles in preserving the political and developmental as well as the security dimensions of the state. Such arrangements can be found in *dwifungsi*, which describes the Indonesian military's dual political and security roles. Ultimately, the civil–military coalition variant combines the arbitrator and parent-guardian categories in that it de-

Table 1.3: Level of civilian control

Type of civil–military linkage	High	Med.	Low	Degree of civilian control over khaki capital
authoritarian-personal	X			Personalized, indirect control over certain aspects of khaki capital
authoritarian-mass party	X			Mass party control over certain aspects of khaki capital
(semi-) democratic-competitive	X	X		Civilian (semi-) monitoring and legally-enforced civilian control over khaki capital
parallel-state semi-democracy		X		Parallel state semi-control over khaki capital
civil–military coalition		X	X	Civilian appeasement of and acquiescence to the military
military oligarchy			X	Direct military control

scribes militaries that possess informal, back-seat-driver political powers as well as constitutionally-enshrined legal powers, a combination that allows them to behave as leading political actors in society. Yet the common denominator is that militaries in this variant prefer not to lead governments but rather to exercise formal or informal power in association with an elected civilian government. In this variant of civil–military relations, medium to weak civilian control compels governments to acquiesce in the insulation of military control over capital interests or appease militaries by granting them financial dividends, lucrative postings or legal corporations for military corporate benefits. On some occasions, senior military leaders may act as the patrons or partners of civilian politicians who work to expand the interests of khaki capital. In this sense, the civil–military coalition model is a favourite for militaries seeking to expand and sustain their interests but also hide behind the appearance of civilian control. Examples of camouflaged armed forces clout include Burma/Myanmar (1948–62; 2011–present); Turkey (1946–2002); and Pakistan (2007–present).

Military oligarchy

A final type of civil–military relations, in which military power is at its greatest and civilian control is non-existent, is what Janowitz refers to as military oligarchy. It can also be referred to as *Caesarism*. In this variant, which is synonymous to Perlmutter's (1981) 'ruler military', the armed forces directly rule the country and control all aspects of the economy. This variant includes regimes where an institutionalized military rules as well as those where a military strongperson is in charge. The category tends to develop in countries where, at independence, military development was far ahead of that of all other political institutions. Sometimes military leaders govern through political parties, but generally such parties are simple smokescreens behind which the military is fully in charge. Examples of this variant include Burma/Myanmar (1962–88; 1988–2011); Cambodia (1970–75); Indonesia (1965–98); and Thailand (1958–1968; 2014–present). Ultimately, as Table 1.3 shows, all six types of civil–military relations relate to levels of civilian control, especially in terms of the degree of civilian control over khaki capital.

Challenges to achieving civilian control over military economic influence

The historical legacies which entrench the type of political regime in question and the extent of military penetration across it tend to determine the extent to which militaries succeed in expanding their financial holdings or insulating themselves from attempts by civilians to control khaki capital. The strongest militaries can rule countries as oligarchies with the result that they are able to be the most powerful economic actors in the country. In civil–military coalitions, however, the armed forces can simply restrict any monitoring by civilians of khaki capital accumulation practices, or legitimize greater forms of khaki capital within constitutions, or simply ignore civilian monitoring efforts altogether. As for militaries in parallel-state semi-democracies, the armed forces are beholden to the dictates of the overarching, informal power structure rather than any elected government. Thus, any controls on khaki capital must come from the parallel state itself. It is with the remaining three types of civilian-military relations where civilian control of khaki capital is strongest. In authoritarian-personal systems, a charismatic, authoritarian dictator (or almost-dictator) exerts personalistic control over most, if not all of a military's economic activities. As for authoritarian-mass party regimes, the single dominating party is the predominant source of military funding, though militaries in such states are often able to obtain much of their own capital from alternative sources (e.g. timbering and mining). Finally, in democratic-competitive or semi-democratic competitive systems, elected civilians are most likely to effectively monitor a military's economic activities and ensure that khaki capital (usually in the form of budgeting) is essentially under civilian control.

In brief, the study contends that the capacity for the armed forces to obtain different degrees of formal and/or informal khaki capital is a function of how such political systems and degrees of military penetration across them evolved. Historical legacies translate to create path dependencies that are difficult to break in the lifespans of countries. Thus, any critical juncture that alters civil–military relations can have enormous impacts on the ability of civilians to influence khaki capital.

Organization of this book

This study seeks to understand the political economy of khaki capital of Southeast Asia by comparing and contrasting the experiences of seven countries in the region. Each country chapter in this volume generally analyses the civil–military relations and relative degree of khaki capital for the country under analysis. The author(s) of each chapter have been given free rein to apply concepts developed in the introduction in ways that make sense to the country they discuss. For some countries (e.g. Laos) not as much information is available as in other countries (e.g. Philippines).

Following their Chapter 1 exploration of theory, Napisa Waitoolkiat and Paul Chambers continue in Chapter 2 to look at the evolution of khaki capital in Thailand. They argue that generally since 1957, Thailand's monarchy and military, as the leading political institutions in the country, have possessed a mutuality of economic interests. The armed forces have specifically acted as the palace guardian. In this role they have accumulated capital possessions both formal and informal in nature. The pattern of arch-royalist military political-economic clout was again reflected in the 2014 military putsch and the dictatorship that has followed. Thailand today is a palace-centred military oligarchy where the armed forces possess expanding economic interests at the institutional, factional and individual levels. Turning to Chapter 3, Marco Bünte examines the trajectory of military control and khaki capital in Burma/Myanmar. Historically, Myanmar has possessed an extremely powerful military. Once a military dictatorship, he argues that civil–military relations in the country today are of the parent-guardian type. However, he says, there is so much military influence that it might be deemed to be an 'ultra-parental guardian relationship'. Today it maintains enormous formal and informal political power which cannot be checked by elected civilians. Such political power has gone hand-in-hand with large amounts of economic clout and indeed the lion's share of the country's economic pie. For the future, in the aftermath of the 2015 electoral victory by the National League for Democracy (NLD), he stresses that the military will remain a leading political and economic institution.

Meanwhile, in Chapter 4, Carlyle Thayer analyses changes in khaki capital in Vietnam. He posits that Vietnam represents a distinctive case of Southeast Asia's authoritarian-single party regime. He identifies three critical junctures that have punctuated the evolution of Vietnam's khaki capital. Since 1954, and especially since 1975, Vietnam became united under the Vietnamese Communist Party. Civil (party) and military roles became fused, making the notion of purely civilian control over military funding inapplicable. After 1989, several military bodies were demobilized and converted into corporation under the purview of the Ministry of Defence, where they could compete in the marketplace. He concludes that the military has gone largely unchallenged as it has carved out a corporate role in Vietnamese society for its enterprises and other interests.

In Chapter 5, Paul Chambers looks at the history of khaki capital in Cambodia. He contends that Cambodia since independence has historically been dominated by one personality after another, though usually legitimized through a monopolizing political party. Especially since 1997, the country has possessed a form of authoritarian-personal control, bolstered upon the trappings of democracy. Prime Minister Hun Sen, through his ruling party, has co-opted the country's security forces. Yet in becoming vassals in support of his singular supremacy, these forces have enjoyed the economic fruits of collaboration. He concludes that without some political opening, the continuing personalized collusion between the Prime Minister and his security forces could well lead to the increased concentration of capital in their hands, via the political status quo or a pro-Hun Sen military putsch.

Turning to Chapter 6, Hans Lipp and Paul Chambers scrutinize the evolution of khaki capital in Laos. They argue that the Lao PDR, since 1975, has become, like Vietnam, a single party authoritarian regime. At the same time, like Vietnam, the mass party structure is more elitist than Leninist. Yet though the communist party monopolizes formal politics, it is the Lao People's Army (LPA, born out of the Lao People's Liberation Army) which has been at the forefront of development and national unity. The political economies of Lao militaries throughout history have involved financial dependence upon a foreign patron: Siam (Thailand), France, the United States, and the Soviet Union/Vietnam. However, since the 1980s, the LPA has increasingly engaged in business ventures to support itself. They conclude that the party's continuing need for the LPA is ensuring the military's own growing political and economic empowerment.

Looking next at Chapter 7, Rosalie Hall examines changes in khaki capital in the Philippines. She argues that, though the country today can be considered democratic-competitive, civilian control over the military remains problematic. In the field, the military is often autonomous of civilian control. Though post-1986 regulations were installed to curb military autonomy in its economic practices and ensure accountability, there remain several parts of the military budget and grey areas that have eluded monitoring efforts. The military's principal role in internal security has also expanded its capital on the frontline. Indeed, its expanded non-combat role, particularly in construction and civil–military operations (CMOs) has given it access to unregulated pools of money. She concludes that effective civilian control over the Philippine military both politically and economically is in drastic need of improvement.

In Chapter 8, Jun Honna analyzes khaki capital in Indonesia. He contends that the military has always been the bulwark of Indonesia's polity, through dictatorship and democracy. From Suharto's military authoritarian polity until the post-1998 political transition to a nascent democracy, the armed forces have remained politically powerful. The historical evolution of the military ensured that such power translated into khaki capital as well. Suharto's military possessed numerous economic enterprises unregulated by civilian control. Since democratization, however, the military has maintained economic clout though it is less. The military has also increasingly competed with the police, both politically and economically. He concludes that Indonesia has witnessed a 'ceremonialized' form of civilian supremacy in which the armed forces have re-legitimized their role in internal security and thereby secured their continuing economic interests.

Lastly, in Chapter 9, the study concludes with a brief comparison of the country cases. It compares the historical evolution of the militaries in the Southeast Asian cases examined, their political perseverance, and what effects these had on the political economy of security.

In sum, we argue that though there are six forms of civil–military relations which correspond with variants of khaki capital, the only type which most assuredly maintains civilian supremacy as well as civilian control over the military economy is the democratic-competitive model of civil–military relations. That being said, there are few cases of this model in Southeast Asia. And where such a model formally exists (contemporary Philippines, East Timor and Indonesia), the military has often found informal means of either manoeuvring around the civil-ianized 'rules of the game' or finding formal exceptions to derive profits from specific sectors of the economy. In the end, the power of the armed forces lies not only in force of arms but also in the formal or informal acquisition of khaki capital.

Economic holdings by militaries will probably continue where security forces are already deeply embedded in society, external or in-ternal security problems persist, the military perseveres in spearheading development projects, civilian groups are deeply divided, corruption abounds across politics, weak civilian governments seek to placate powerful militaries with material benefits, or unofficial alliances exist between militaries and other political institutions (e.g. monarchies, political parties). Such financial dividends both lead to and result from the build-up and perpetuation of power. Militaries achieve such power and khaki capital because of historically-embedded path dependence of entrenched power, their ability to use coercion, alliances with other powerful entities, organisational clout, state moneys and knowledge of internal state secrets. Because of their capacity to advance linkages between political and economic interests, militaries become entrenched as dominant societal actors. As the chapters in this volume illustrate, demilitarizing the state – diminishing the political and economic power of militaries relative to civilians – so that the armed forces is completely under civilian control, represents at the very least a difficult challenge for every country in Southeast Asia.

Bibliography

Agüero, Felipe (2001) *Soldiers, Civilians, and Democracy: Post-Franco Spain in Comparative Perspective*. Baltimore und London: Johns Hopkins University Press.

Akin Rabibhadana (1969) *The Organisation of Thai Society in the Early Bangkok Period, 1782–1873*. Ithaca: Cornell University, Southeast Asia Program, Data Paper 74.

Alagappa, Muthiah (2001) 'Investigating and Explaining Change: An Analytical Framework', in Muthiah Alagappa (ed.) *Coercion and Governance: the Declining Political Role of the Military in Asia*. Stanford: Stanford University Press: 29–66.

Battye, Noel A. (1974) 'The Military, Government and Society in Siam; 1868–1910: Politics and Military Reform During the Reign of King Chulalongkorn', Ithaca, New York: Cornell University, Ph.D. Dissertation.

Beeson, Mark and Alex. J. Bellamy (2008) *Securing Southeast Asia: The Politics of Security Sector Reform*. London: Routledge.

Berlin, Donald L. (2008) *Before Gringo: History of the Philippine Military 1830 to 1972*. Manila: Anil.

Bottomore, Tom (ed.) (1991) *A Dictionary of Marxist Thought*. 2nd ed. Oxford and Cambridge, Mass.: Blackwell.

Briscoe, Ivan. (2008) 'The Proliferation of the "Parallel State"'. Madrid: FRIDE, October, Working Paper 71, http://www.fride.org/publication/511/the-proliferation-of-the-, accessed 17 April 2016.

Brömmelhörster, Jorn and Wolf-Christian Paes (eds) (2003) *The Military as an Economic Actor: Soldiers in Business*. London and New York: Palgrave/Macmillan.

Bruneau, Thomas and Florina Cristiana (2008) 'Towards a New Conceptualization of Democratization and Civil–military Relations', *Democratization* 15(5) (December).

Callahan, Mary (2002) 'State Formation in the Shadow of the Raj: Violence, Warfare and Politics in Colonial Burma', *Southeast Asian Studies* 39(4) (March).

Capoccia, G. and R. D. Kelemen (2007) 'The Study of Critical Junctures: Theory, Narrative and Counterfactuals in Historical Institutionalism', *World Politics*, 59, 3: 341–69.

Clapham, Christopher and George Philip (eds) (1985) *The Political Dilemmas of Military Regimes*. London: Croom Helm.

Collier, Ruth and David Collier (1991) *Shaping the Political Arena: Critical Junctures, the Labor Movement and Regime Dynamics in Latin America*. Princeton: Princeton University Press.

Colton, Timothy (1979) *Commissars, Commanders, and Civilian Authority: The Structure of Soviet Military Politics*. Cambridge, MA: Harvard University Press.

Cottey, Andrew, Tim Edmunds and Anthony Forster (2000) 'The Second Generation Problematic: Rethinking Democratic Control of Armed Forces in Central and Eastern Europe', Transformation of Civil–Military Relations Paper 1.7 (December).

Cribb, Robert and Audrey Kahin (2004) *Historical Dictionary of Indonesia*. Lanham: Scarecrow Press.

Croissant, Aurel, David Kuehn, Phillip Lorenz and Paul W. Chambers (2013) *Democratization and Civilian Control in Asia*. Basingstoke: Palgrave Macmillan.

Day, Tony (2002) *Fluid Iron: State Formation in Southeast Asia*. Honolulu: University of Hawaii Press, 2002.

Edmonds, Martin (1988) *Armed Services and Society*. Leicester: Leicester University Press.

Edmunds, Timothy (2003) *Security sector reform: Concepts and implementation*. Geneva: Geneva Centre for the Democratic Control of the Armed Forces (DCAF).

Evans, Grant (2002) *A Short History of Laos: The Land in Between*. Crows Nest, NSW: Allen & Unwin.

Finer, Samuel (1962) *The Man on Horseback: the Role of the Military in Politics*. London: Pall Mall.

Forster, Anthony (2002) 'New Civil–Military Relations and its Research Agendas', *Connections: The Quarterly Journal* 1(2) (Summer).

Hall, Peter and Rosemary Taylor (1996) 'Political Science and the Three Institutionalisms', *Political Studies*, 44: 936–57 (July).

Huntington, Samuel (1962) 'Patterns of Violence in World Politics' in Huntington (ed.) *Changing Patterns of Military Politics*. New York: Glencoe: 32–33.

Huntington, Samuel P. (1957) *The Soldier and the State*. Cambridge, MA, and London: Harvard University Press.

Janowitz, Morris (1988) *Military Institutions and Coercion in the Developing Countries*. Expanded edition of *The Military in the Political Development of New Nations* (1964). Chicago: University of Chicago Press.

Kohn, Richard (1997) 'How Democracies Control the Military', *Journal of Democracy* 8(4).

Lee, Yunkyong (2011) *Militants or Partisans: Labor Unions and Democratic Politics in Korea and Taiwan*. Palo Alto: Stanford University Press.

Levi, Margaret (1997) 'A Model, a Method, and a Map: Rational Choice in Comparative and Historical Analysis', in Mark I. Lichbach and Alan S. Zuckerman (eds) *Comparative Politics: Rationality, Culture, and Structure*. Cambridge: Cambridge University Press: 19–41.

Mahoney, James (2000) 'Path Dependence in Historical Sociology', *Theory and Society* 29: 507–548.

Mahoney, James and Dietrich Rueschemeyer (eds) (2003) *Comparative Historical Analysis in the Social Sciences*, New York and Cambridge: Cambridge University Press.

Mahoney, James and Kathleen Kathleen 2010 'A Theory of Gradual Institutional Change', in James Mahoney and Kathleen Thelen (eds) *Explaining Institutional Change: ambiguity, agency and power*. Cambridge: Cambridge University Press.

Mani, Kristina (2011) 'Military Empresarios: Approaches to Studying the Military as an Economic Actor', *Bulletin of Latin American Research*, 30 (2) (April): 183–97.

Martinussen, John (1996) *Society, State and Market: An Analysis of Competing Theories of Development in the Third World*. London: Zed Books.

Moe, Terry (2005) 'Power and Political Institutions', *Perspectives on Politics* 3(2): 215–33.

Ngunyi, Mutahi and Musambayi Katumanga (2014) *From Monopoly to Oligopoly of Violence: Exploration of a Four-Point Hypothesis Regarding Organized and Organic Militia in Kenya*. New York: United Nations Development Programme.

Nordlinger, Eric (1977) *Soldiers in Politics: Military Coups and Governments*. Englewood Cliffs, NJ: Prentice-Hall.

Page, Scott (2006) 'Path Dependence', *Quarterly Journal of Political Science* 1: 87–115.

Perlmutter, Amos (1980) 'The Comparative Analysis of Military Regimes: Formations, Aspirations, and Achievements', *World Politics* 33: 96–120.

Perlmutter, Amos (1981) *Political Roles and Military Rulers*, London: Frank Cass.

Pierson, Paul (2000) 'Increasing Returns, Path Dependence, and the Study of Politics', *The American Political Science Review*, 94(2): 251–67.

Pierson, Paul (2004) *Politics in Time*. Princeton: Princeton University Press.

Pierson, Paul and Theda Skocpol (2002) 'Historical Institutionalism in

Contemporary Political Science', in Ira Katznelson and Helen V. Milner (eds) *Political Science: State of the Discipline*. New York: W.W. Norton: 693–721.

Pion-Berlin, David (1992) 'Military Autonomy and Emerging Democracies in South America', *Comparative Politics* 25(1): 83–102.

Pion-Berlin, David (2010) 'Informal Civil–military Relations in Latin American: Why Politicians and Soldiers Choose Informal Venues', *Armed Forces and Society* 36(3): 526–44.

Reid, Anthony (1988) *Southeast Asia in the Age of Commerce: 1450–1680*, Vol. 1: 'The lands below the Winds'. Chiang Mai: Silkworm Books.

Siddiqa, Ayesha (2007) *Military Inc.: Inside Pakistan's Military Economy*. Oxford: Oxford University Press.

Tarling, Nicholas (1999 [1992]) *The Cambridge History of Southeast Asia*, Vol. 4: 'From World War II to the Present'. Cambridge: Cambridge University Press.

Thayer, Carlyle (2003) 'The Economic and Commercial Roles of the Vietnam People's Army', in Jorn Brommelhorster and Wolf-Christian Paes (eds) *The Military as an Economic Actor: Soldiers in Business*. London and New York: Palgrave-Macmillan: 74–93.

Thelen, Kathleen (2003) 'How Institutions Evolve. Insights from Comparative Historical Analysis', in James Mahoney and Dietrich Rueschemeyer (eds) *Comparative Historical Analysis in the Social Sciences*. Cambridge: Cambridge University Press: 208–40.

Thelen, Kathleen and Steinmo, Sven (1992) 'Historical institutionalism in comparative politics, in ´Sven Steinmo, Kathleen Thelen and Frank Longstreth (eds), *Structuring Politics: Historical Institutionalism in Comparative Analysis*, Cambridge and New York: Cambridge University Press.

Thucydides (1982) *The Peloponesian War* (transl. by T.E. Wick). New York: The Modern Library.

Tilly, Charles (1985) 'War Making and State Making as Organized Crime', in Peter Evans, Dietrich Rueschmeyer and Theda Skocpol (eds) *Bringing the State Back In*. Cambridge: Cambridge University Press: 169–91.

Tilly, Charles (1983) 'War and the Power of Warmakers in Western Europe and Elsewhere, 1600–1980', *CRSO Working Paper* /I287 (May): 1–35.

Transparency International (2015) 'Government Defence Anti-Corruption Index, 2015'. http://government.defenceindex.org/#close, accessed 11 May 2016.

Trinkunas, Harold (2000) 'Crafting Civilian Control in Emerging Democracies: Argentina and Venezuela', *Journal of Interamerican Studies and World Affairs* 42(3): 77–109.

Vickers, Adrian (2003) 'Two Historical Records of the Kingdom of Vientiane', in Christopher E. Goscha and Sören Ivarsson (eds) *Contesting Visions of the Lao Past: Lao Historiography at the Crossroads*. Copenhagen: NIAS Press.

———— (2005) *A History of Modern Indonesia*. Cambridge: Cambridge University Press.

Wallerstein, Immanuel (1974) 'The Rise and Future Demise of the World Capitalist System: Concepts for Comparative Analysis', *Comparative Studies in Society and History* 16(4) (Sept): 387–415.

Welche, Claude (1976) 'Civilian Control of the Military: Myth and Reality', in Claude Welche (ed.) *Civilian Control of the Military: Theory and Cases from Developing Countries*. Albany: State University of New York Press.

CHAPTER 2

Arch-Royalist Rent
The Political Economy of the Military in Thailand

Napisa Waitoolkiat and Paul Chambers

Introduction

The history of Thailand's military since its establishment as a permanent standing force in 1852 – but especially since 1957 – has represented its evolution as the principal guardian for the monarchy.[1] The military has been a crucial actor in the formation, expansion and consolidation of the Thai kingdom as it stands today. Relying on the palace for maintaining the legitimacy for an ever-greater political role, Thailand's military has been monarchised in the sense that it has generally acted as the junior partner to a palace-led parallel state: both throne and sword exert tutelage over Thailand's interrupted democratization (Chambers and Waitoolkiat 2016). During periods of semi-democracy, a parallel state of monarchy and military has informally dominated the country. When Thailand has existed under military oligarchy (as it has since 2014), the monarchy has retained the upper hand in what might be called a khakistocracy (military plus aristocracy). As such, the Thai military has comfortably transformed its political clout into an economic empire that in turn serves as a self-enduring force to maximize its political power. The symbiosis of monarchy and military has created a sense of entitlement among the armed forces, especially to its right to influence decision-making regarding national security and national development. Under the rubric of these responsibilities, and given its legal monopoly over the instruments of violence, the Thai military has over time ac-

---

1. The authors wish to thank Dr. Takahashi Katsuyuki for his assistance and comments.

cumulated sufficient power to become the strongest institution in the country – behind the monarchy.

Based upon these historical legacies, Thailand's developmental path has become dependent on a collection of formal and informal institutions, through which the Thai military has persisted in possessing enormous political influence while enjoying the economic privileges of power. This chapter examines the formal and informal elements of the Thai military's economic holdings as a function of its political leverage. It argues that the military today perseveres as a prominent economic actor in Thailand because of its history in 'developing' the countryside, its role in combating counter-insurgency and its close relationship with the monarchy. The dividends from such 'khaki capital' are alive and well today. The historical legacy of palace–military authoritarianism and armed forces' unity behind a highly-esteemed monarchy[2] has so far prevented any disruption from the path dependence of military prowess.

What is the history of the Thai military's political economy? What are the formal and informal elements of Thai khaki capital today? How might the military's vast economic influence affect Thai democratization? This chapter addresses these questions.

The study is organized into four parts. It first looks at the history of Thailand's military political economy until the 2014 coup. Second, in the aftermath of the coup, it examines the formal parts of Thai khaki capital today, including direct military enterprises, land, sinecures and the budget. Third, it scrutinizes informal dimensions of khaki capital such as indirect influence in business. Finally, the chapter provides a conclusion that offers predictions for the future.

The history of Thai khaki capital until the 2014 putsch

The onset of the path of a powerful Thai military began in 1852,[3] when Siam's absolute monarchy commenced the process of creating a permanent standing army upon which the kingdom soon became dependent

---

2. King Bhumiphol Adulyadej ruled for 70 years, from 1946 to 2016. His only son, Maha Vajiralongkorn Bodindradebayavarangku, accepted the throne on 1 December 2016 and will probably be crowned in December 2017.

3. King Mongkut (Rama IV) established a small though permanent army in 1852 and a police force in 1862, while his son King Chulalongkorn (Rama V) created a navy in 1875.

for its security. However, the armed forces were completely dependent upon the throne for their budgeting and economic wherewithal. As with other ministries at the time, the Defence Ministry competed for favour and thus funding from the Thai kings of the time. It was generally successful in obtaining large budgetary allocations; at one point the observation was made that the palace was willing to sacrifice economic reform in order to guarantee a 'strong war machine.'[4]

By the end of the 1920s, Siam was suffering from a severe economic crisis and then-King Prajadhipok sought to maintain a balanced budget. As such, he ordered large cutbacks in all of the ministries, including the Defence Ministry. Several bureaucrats were dismissed to save money. In 1931, during the annual military reshuffle, the cabinet vetoed the promotions of 92 army officers. Incensed, Minister of Defence Prince Boworadej submitted his resignation. On 24 June 1932, junior officers staged a 'coup' that terminated the absolute monarchy. One of the main motivations for the coup was the disappointment among soldiers about their salaries and careers, the military's declining economic share of the budget (Chai-Anan 1987: 29–31), and particularly that these sacrifices were part of a self-conscious policy by a monarchy focused on economic expedience. Following the putsch, the new National Assembly, controlled by the military-dominant People's Party, was henceforth responsible for the budget and could override any royal veto.

The 1932 coup represents a critical juncture in many ways. First, the centre of political power moved from monarchy to the bureaucracy. Second, military bureaucrats quickly came to dominate civilian bureaucrats. Third, the pre-1932 social order, which had been based around the feudal holdings of monarchy, now gave way to an economy dominated by the military. This last factor was cemented by the defeat of a royalist rebellion in 1933. Ultimately, absolute monarchy was completely abolished and Siam (now called Thailand) witnessed the dawn of a new era in 'institutional flux' (Ferrara 2015: 77) characterized by rapidly changing political structures and unheralded military clout.

The new political authority translated into enhanced military-economic might especially in the area of military budgeting, which was doubled between 1933 and 1938. By the time he became Prime Minister in 1938, Gen. Phibun Songkram had gained personal control over the

---

4. See Graham 1924: 317–18, cited in Wilson 1962: 171–2.

greatly expanded military purse, ensuring not only that the Defence Ministry was once again second to none in budgetary allocations, but also that he could use funds for political patronage (ibid.: 104). Defence spending remained a top priority during Phibun's 1938–44 authoritarian regime as it subsidized a brief 1940–41 war against France as well as Thailand's participation in World War II.

With Phibun's fall from power in 1944, a civilian regime came to office and sought to enact reforms that would weaken the armed forces as a political force. Indeed, the 1946 constitution forbade active-duty soldiers from simultaneously serving as elected representatives or cabinet ministers. Prime Minister Pridi Panomyong even reduced the defence budget. However, the 1947 military coup resurrected military power (Chambers 2013: 128). The military's corporate interest in re-establishing a high defence budget as well as reinstating military officials dismissed from service contributed to the putsch (Suchit 1987: 52).

From 1947 until 1957, the Soi Rajakru faction of the army dominated Thai politics. Four generals lorded over the country – Prime Minister Phibun Songkram, Army Chief Phin Chunhavan (1947–54), his successor in 1954, Army Chief Sarit Thanarat, and Police Chief (and Phin's son-in-law) Phao Siyanond. During this period, the Thai military budget again soared. In 1950, with the inception of US military assistance and grant aid, Washington came to bankroll a great deal of the Thai defence budget, which continued to grow. From 12.8 million US dollars in 1951, it expanded year by year, reaching $1,469 million in 1982 (Surachart 1988: 195).

A second area saw an expansion of khaki capital: military business and military sinecures on the boards of both state and, to a lesser extent, private enterprises. Indeed, from 1932 onward, but especially after the 1947 coup, state enterprises became the military's chief breadmaker. Coinciding with growing anti-Chinese sentiment, economic nationalism was promoted, formally seeking to stymie the growth of Chinese and other foreign capital throughout the country – which competed with local firms. But policies tied to this goal eventually were subverted to the purpose of accumulating wealth for state officials, especially leaders in the post-1947 junta.

Riggs (1966) finds a direct correlation between the number of board of directors slots (sinecures) held by cabinet politicians and their status as leaders of coups in 1932, 1947 and 1957. The leading generals (who simultaneously served as political leaders) during each of these periods (e.g. Phibun, Phin, Phao, Sarit) held varying numbers of board postings (Riggs 1966, pp.257–98). As a result, the acquisition of sinecures can be said to have become institutionalized for senior military figures.

During this time, Chinese businesspeople and bankers (who were dominant actors in the Thai economy) invited senior Thai military officials to sit on their boards of directors. Kunio Yoshihara (1988) conceptualized this practice as part of 'ersatz capitalism', defined as a distorted form of capitalism propagated by state officials and entrepreneurs (Yoshihara 1988). Before this, under the pre-1932 absolute monarchy, Chinese entrepreneurial families had worked directly with the royal family. In the post-1932 environment, Chinese entrepreneurs 'sought patronage from the revolutionary government...' (Suehiro 1992: 42). Despite the ostensible interest in economic nationalism, the military was not averse to engaging with and enriching the Chinese community when doing so would also serve the military's financial interests. Several state enterprises were created (e.g. Siam Cotton Mill was established by the Ministry of Defence in 1935). It has been estimated that the 1947–57 Soi Rajakru military dictatorship controlled 10 companies in the banking and finance sector, 15 companies in the industrial sector, and seven companies in the commercial sector (Chai-Anan 1982: 16). The Taharn Co-operation Company and the National Economic Development Corporation were set up by Gen. Phin Chunhavan as military holding companies for several state enterprises designed to monopolize control over such sectors as the distribution of rice, timber, gunny sacks, liquor and tobacco (ibid.: 46). In one particular case, the Bank of Ayudhya was transferred in 1947 from private control to ownership by the Soi Rajakru military clique, only to be transferred to control by the Sarit group following the 1957 coup. For Chinese entrepreneurs, Thailand's economic nationalism meant that deals lucrative to military officials would have to be made to ensure that the Chinese would be guaranteed access to the Thai economy and not be harassed by police or legal actions. For Thai military officials, they needed the business skills of the Chinese who came to manage and sit on the boards of state corporations. Soldiers also coveted the enormous salaries drawn from sitting on the boards of directors of private, Chinese-owned corporations (Skinner 1958: 192, 244).

Aside from budgets, ownership of businesses and sinecures, Thai security forces in 1950 engaged in informal khaki capital, earning profits from the opium and heroin trade. This was not then illegal as opium was not banned until 1959. The origins of modern military involvement in this trade date from 1943, when it appeared increasingly certain that Japan would lose the Second World War. Prime Minister Phibun ordered Thailand's Northern Payap Army to open a channel of communication with units of the Chinese Kuomintang (KMT) Army alongside which it had been fighting. To help raise financial resources, China's 93rd Division and the Payap army began working together, peddling opium from Yunnan through northern Burma and into Thailand (Scott 2010: 69–70). As years went by, this drug commerce became increasingly profitable. But with the end of World War II, the Payap Army returned to Thailand and the KMT's 93rd focused its attentions on the civil war in China. Thus, in 1945, their narcotics network was temporarily abandoned. The Payap Army was at the time led by Phin, but also included Phao, Sarit, Thanom and Praphas, as well as later Thai generals Krit Sivara, Kriangsak Chomanand and Prem Tinsulanonda. Many senior Payap officers had profited from the drug trade and stood to gain if it was recreated again. Thailand's 1947 coup, led by Phin, helped to facilitate the resurrection of the narcotics trafficking network between the KMT and the Thai army and each was able to profit thereafter.

In 1949, following the Chinese communist revolution, elements of the 93rd Division fled into Burma to escape imprisonment or execution by the communists. In northeastern Burma, they received income through their continuing opium trade with the Thai military. In addition, beginning in 1950, the United States Central Intelligence Agency began to fund many of their needs through 'Operation Paper.' The purpose of 'Paper' was for the KMT units in Burma to launch CIA-financed incursions into southern China as a new front in the Cold War. Though several such strikes were attempted throughout the 1950s, none was ever successful in terms of taking territory in China. In the end, Burma appealed to the United Nations for the United States and Taiwan to withdraw the KMT soldiers from Burmese soil. Many were flown to Taiwan and, in 1963, Thailand officially accepted thousands of KMT soldiers who had settled in Thailand, in return for their help in fighting Thai communist insurgents.[5] However, in northern Thai mountain settlements such as Doi Mae Salong, the Thai army continued to allow KMT soldiers to market opium in exchange for their help with guarding the border and fighting communists. Corrupt elements of Thai security forces (lower-ranking officers siphoning profits from generals) profited in the production and distribution of opium and heroin (Chouvy 2009: 110–11). In sum, this episode illustrates that the Thai military utilized its political clout to engage in the informal business of trafficking drugs. Although the sale of narcotics became illegal in 1959, both the trade and the military's involvement in it persisted thereafter.

The double military coups of 1957 and 1958 represent a second critical juncture in the history of the political economy of the Thai military. The 1957 coup, like the 1947 putsch, partly occurred because of military corporate interests. This time, however, the clash occurred between two competing factions representing rising stars in the Thai security apparatus – Army Chief Gen. Sarit Thanarat (leading the *Sisao Thewes* military faction) and Police Chief Gen. Phao Siyanond (of the *Soi Rajakru* faction). Each sought to expand his political and commercial interests at the expense of the other. Meanwhile, Phibun tried to prevent any ministers from holding positions on the boards of state-owned as well as private-owned enterprises. In this regard it affected Sarit because he held the board chairmanship of the Government Lottery Office. This was a motive for Sarit's 1957 coup (Ashida 1957: 2; Thak 2007; Takahashi 2014: 121–2, 140). In terms of budgeting, there developed a competitive struggle between the army and police for security appropriations. Sarit's successful putsch (and a second one in 1958) reflected the army's victory in this matter (Suchit 1987: 52–3). Control over the opium trade was another area which Phao and Sarit were in contention (McCoy *et al.* 1972: 90). According to the US government, Phao possessed enormous clout through his personally lucrative control over the opium trade after 1952 (Johnson 1959). Competition over control over opium and heroin commerce continued for the next five years. Sarit's 1957 and 1958 coups (which forced Phibun and Phao to flee the country) cemented his control over the trade. In 1959, a US embassy official

---

5. For a detailed description of Operation Paper and the KMT in Doi Mae Salong, see Gibson 2011.

warned that Sarit's 'military group [is] now more dependent than ever on the profits from opium exports,' (Bowles 1952).

In addition to using brutal repression to cement himself in power, Sarit resuscitated the role of the monarchy as a crucial ally in power. Military and monarchy entered into a symbiotic relationship that augmented the political influence of each. The responsibility of monarchy was to provide legitimacy to the ruling junta. In exchange, the new junta increased the economic authority of monarchy in various ways. First, it increased the annual amount of money available to the monarchy by 28 billion baht, with the amount increasing every year. Second, it restored several palaces and other holdings of the royal family. Third, it returned ownership of royal properties (which had been seized after 1932) to the Crown (Handley 2006: 174). Fourth, the junta allowed the palace, via the Crown Property Bureau, to grow and extend its enterprises and ventures (Hewison and Kengkij 2010: 186).

Sarit's regime furthermore established the Bureau of the Budget in 1959 as an independent department that was intended to thoroughly centralize control over budgeting, and reported directly to the Prime Minister. This budget system was oriented towards serving the administration of the military government with no elected politicians involved in the budget process (Kriangchai 2009: 65). With help from Sarit and the military, the king furthermore embarked upon many new 'Royal Projects' to help 'develop' rural areas and also increase connections between the monarch and the people (Waitoolkiat and Chambers 2013: 79). Ultimately, following the dual coups of 1957 and 1958, the monarchy and military came increasingly to share political and economic power. The putsches thus represented a second critical juncture for the evolution of Thai khaki capital.

Thailand's armed forces had four missions which legitimized its central role on the political stage. First, it spearheaded national security needs for the kingdom. Second, it saw to it that the monarchy was completely protected. Third, it led counter-insurgency efforts, especially amidst the 1965–85 communist insurrection. Finally, it brought development to the countryside by building roads, bridges and related infrastructure, acquiring extensive rural landholdings, and implementing development programmes. In this way, affixing itself as the necessary support for the kingdom, the military acquired vast amounts of khaki

capital. The United States was a principal ally in ensuring financial support for Thailand's military as it sought to fulfil these roles.

Following Sarit's natural death in 1963, his Sisao Thewes minions,
Gens. Thanom Kittikachorn and Praphas Charusatien – along with the
palace – dominated Thailand. During this time, US military assistance
to Thailand reached its apex and domestic military budgeting remained
high. Meanwhile, Sisao Thewes controlled approximately 12 companies
in the banking and finance sector, 15 in the industrial sector and 10 in
the commercial sector. Indeed, from 1963 until 1973, Thanom, Praphas
and Thanom's son Narong were involved in as many as 137 private
enterprises (Chai-Anan 1982: 17). Praphas himself held sinecures
on the boards of five commercial banks (Suehiro 1992: 50). In 1969,
Thailand held its first elections in 12 years with Thanom becoming the
elected Prime Minister. However, in 1971, several elected Members of
Parliament threatened to diminish the defence budget. This was one
factor that led Thanom to lead a coup against his own government and
clip the wings of his country's fledgling democracy (Neher 1976: 16).

Not until 1980 did Thailand's monarchy become the senior partner
in a power-sharing arrangement with the military. The fall of dictators
Thanom and Praphas in 1973 dulled the traditional prowess of the
armed forces. A short period of civilian rule commenced, albeit with
a dominant ally in the monarchy and alongside an acquiescent armed
forces. Nevertheless, growing political chaos by 1976 had increasingly
turned both monarchy and military against the government. In addition,
the military leadership became miffed by elected civilians' interventions
in military promotions and cancellation of military acquisitions from
abroad. Moreover, by 1976, the military had found itself with decreas-
ing economic dividends, and US military aid diminished after 1975. As
such, to some extent, the military coup of 1976 was partly intended to
consolidate military interests (Suchit 1987: 53). Following the coup, the
military immediately moved to re-enhance its political and economic
interests. The putsch brought to power a coalition of monarchy and
military, with the king's representative, Thanin Kraivichien, appointed
Prime Minister. However, a military coup in 1977 jettisoned Thanin
and brought Gen. Kriangsak Chomanand to the mantle of power.

In 1978, the Thai military found itself publicly embarrassed when a
drug kingpin situated in Thailand bragged about his personal ability to

stop the drug trade. The previous year, Prime Minister Kriangsak had agreed to allow the Shan United Army (SUA) of Khun Sa (an opium warlord on the Thai–Burma border) to enjoy unrestricted rights to traffic heroin into Thailand in recognition for SUA's help in fighting the Burmese Communist Party (Chouvy 2009: 111). Some suggested that Kriangsak himself had profited from the narcotics trade (Booth 2013: 275). Regardless, when Gen. Prem Tinsulanonda became Prime Minister in 1980, the Thai military launched a campaign to dislodge Khun Sa from Thai territory – something that was finally accomplished when Khun Sa moved his operations across the border into Burma in 1982 (Chouvy 2009: 110–11).

The 1980 to 1988 premiership of Gen. Prem Tinsulanonda survived because of his alliance with the popular monarch, his clever strategy of maintaining an unelected Prime Minister and Senate, and the increase in the military's total share of the budget under his leadership. Indeed, it increased from 17 per cent in 1975 to 22 per cent in 1985 (Baker and Pasuk 2009: 244). Some senior military officials also were granted business board position sinecures, though fewer than before. However, during the 1988–91 administration of elected Prime Minister (ret. Gen.) Chatchai Chunhavan (son of Gen. Phin), civilian politicians cut the military budget, clamoured for a more transparent one and criticized arms purchases proposed by the armed services (ibid.: 245). The senior military brass, led by the Class 5 army faction, soon became convinced that their corporate privileges were under threat from both Chatchai and the Lower House. Eventually, they found support in their antipathy for Chatchai from the palace, which was increasingly irritated by Chatchai's attempts to favour corporations that competed with those belonging to the palace, such as Siam Cement. The final straw came when Chatchai appointed to a cabinet position a military officer who had earlier attempted a coup against Prem – something taboo to both the military and palace. In 1991, the military carried out a coup that was endorsed by the king (Handley 2006: 329–30; 338–9).

The junta that came to power lasted only one year. In May 1992, amidst rising popular discontent, soldiers fired into a crowd of peaceful demonstrators and thus earned the Thai military the scorn of Thais and the international community alike. When, shortly thereafter, the king compelled Prime Minister Gen. Suchinda Kraprayoon (who had manipulated his ascension from junta chief) to resign in favour of a return to civilian rule, the military was left with a weakened, tainted image. In addition, with the Cold War having ended in 1991, the armed forces seemed to have lost their rationale for playing an enormous role on the political stage. Finally, the 1997 financial crisis forced a reduction in the military budget.

Despite the military's post-1992 weaknesses, it remained powerful (and its economic activities remained profitable) along Thailand's borders with Myanmar, Laos and Cambodia. One such military profiteer was Gen. Chavalit Yongchaiyudh. One of the longest serving army leaders in recent Thai history, Chavalit rose to be Thailand's army commander (1986–90) and then supreme commander (1987–90). Chavalit's name has long been connected with timber. In 1987, as army chief, he led forces in support of Thai logging companies that had been attacked by Lao forces for encroaching across an ill-defined portion of the Thai–Lao border. The fighting ended with 1,000 deaths, a stalemate and finally a negotiated settlement. But according to one account, the altercation was not about a border dispute. 'Basically, a Thai company was harvesting timber in this area, having facilitated this by paying off both Thai and Laos army personnel. The fighting flared when the company, on Thai army advice, stopped paying the Laotians. It ended when they started paying again,' (Robert Karniol, cited in Roughol 2008). Following this Thai–Lao frontier friction, Laos allowed several Thai logging companies to cut timber in Laos, though these ventures were discontinued in 1991 amidst Lao concern for potential Thai support for Hmong insurgents along the Thai–Lao border.

Meanwhile, in December 1988, Gen. Chavalit visited Burma with a group of over 80 military officers, businessmen and journalists to negotiate timber concessions with the military regime. As a result of the meeting, 35 Thai companies were bestowed 47 logging concessions, an event that sparked the beginning of unprecedented Thai logging within Burma (Global Witness 2003). Chavalit was delighted with the deal, especially as he had inside knowledge that would affect market values: the Thai government soon would impose a moratorium on logging within Thailand. This moratorium commenced in January 1989. Moreover, the lucrative nature of these interests for military-connected logging companies contributed to a shift in Thai foreign policy from backing anti-regime ethnic armies to greater support for the Burmese military regime (Lewis 2007: 50). Almost all of the companies benefiting from the deal were owned or partially owned by military officers close to Chavalit. These executives were also promoters of Chavalit's New Aspiration Party, established in 1990 (Chang Noi 1998) as Chavalit retired from the military. He persisted in his logging interests while also serving as an elected politician, including as interior minister, labour minister, defence minister, deputy prime minister and finally prime minister in 1996–97. He returned again in the 2000s as defence minister and deputy prime minister.

Though Laos and Burma have been important (especially for Chavalit), Cambodia has been a sizeable foreign source of Thai military capital, at least since the 1979 Vietnamese overthrow of the Khmer Rouge regime and Hanoi's occupation of Cambodia, and until the Paris Peace Accords of 1991. Thai security forces immediately joined an effort by China and the United States to organize and fund Cambodian resistance forces, including the Khmer Rouge. Thai military units were created to directly liaise with, train and assist all those who resisted the Vietnamese, but especially the Khmer Rouge. Special Warfare Unit 315 funnelled weapons and other assistance to the Khmer Rouge. Serving 315 was Unit 838 which directly collaborated with the Khmer Rouge.[6] Meanwhile, Taskforce 80 of the Supreme Command sought to unify all resistance groups together (Human Rights Watch 1995: 115; see Conboy 2013).

Thailand's Second Infantry Division, called *Buraphapayak* (Tigers of the East), was charged with protecting Eastern Thailand, but also spearheaded coordination along the eastern border with the Khmer Rouge and other anti-Vietnamese insurgents. Buraphapayak spawned an extraordinary number of senior leaders. Military officials who served in Buraphapayak at this time include Gen. Chettha Thanajaro (later Army Commander), Chainarong Noonpakdee (later First Army Commander), Prawit Wongsuwan, later Army Commander), Anupong Paochinda (later Army Commander), Prayuth Chan-ocha (later Army Commander),

---

6. Col. Surayud Chulanond commanded Unit 838 during the mid-1980s. Serving under him was Lt. Col. Sonthi Boonyaratklin. The two men's destinies would later again coincide when Sonthi staged a coup in 2006, after which Surayud was appointed Prime Minister.

Udomdej Sitabutr (later Army Commander), and Teerachai Nakwanich (later Army Commander).

By 1990, after over a decade of Thai Army–Khmer Rouge cooperation, the Thai military's objective of supporting the Khmer Rouge to bolster national security along the Thai–Cambodian border appeared to be giving way to more material interests. Even before that, in 1988, allegations emerged that Thai military personnel had skimmed 3.5 million US dollars from the United States CIA financial assistance programme for Cambodian insurgents (Erlanger 1988). Other reports surfaced that Thai army and police officials serving on Thailand's eastern border with Cambodia had engaged in profitable ventures with Khmer Rouge leaders, notably in cross-border trade in timber and gems, which generated earnings of upwards of $10 million. In 1992, though the Vietnamese occupation army had withdrawn three years previously, Thai soldiers were still operating along the border, reportedly still profiting from business with the Khmer Rouge, according to a 1992 Thai intelligence report (Shenon 1993). Senior Thai military officials – specifically members of Unit 838 – earned fortunes from kickbacks on the cross-border movement of lumber, gems, cars and other items from such Khmer Rouge-held areas in Cambodia as Pailin, into eastern Thailand (ibid.). The gem trade between the Khmer Rouge and Thai military/businesspeople was reportedly quite lucrative, earning 120 million dollars per year in revenue since the Khmer Rouge's capture of Pailin. Gem trade profits were divided 50:50 between the Khmer Rouge and Thai businesspeople, after paying 10 per cent to the Thai military units that controlled the border (Puangthong 2011).

The interests of Thailand's business-military nexus came to a head in Cambodia on 2 July 1994. On that day, Cambodian politician Gen. Sin Song attempted to overthrow the government of his arch-enemy, Second Prime Minister Hun Sen (and also First Prime Minister Norodom Ranariddh). The coup attempt was supported by Thai military officials and businessmen (including Thaksin Shinawatra) who were incensed that they had been deprived of profitable business deals by the Cambodian government (Adams 2014). In the end, as many as 33 Thais connected to Thailand's security forces were arrested in Phnom Penh following the attempted putsch (Thayer 1995). It took several months before Cambodia and Thailand were able to resume semi-cordial relations, and only after a visit to Phnom Penh by then-Foreign Minister Thaksin.

Ultimately, from 1979 until at least 1996, Thailand's military support for the Khmer Rouge helped to enrich many of the leaders of the Buraphapayak military faction. A Thai army official admitted in 1996 that, along the eastern border, 'rich illegal deals' were 'still being made between Thai army officials, the Khmer Rouge, and even the Royal Cambodian armed forces (Grainger, 23 August 1996). Aside from Buraphapayak, however, retired Gen. (and Defence Minister) Chavalit Yongchaiyudh sought to assist Thai timber companies seeking profits in Cambodia. Officially on behalf of 11 Thai enterprises, he signed a 'million meter' timber deal in 1996 with Cambodia's then-two prime ministers, Norodom Ranariddh and Hun Sen. However, there was an implicit understanding that Chavalit himself would financially benefit, as he was at the time collecting finances to campaign for the Thai premiership (Grainger, 20 September 1996).

Despite dividends generated from ventures along the border with Cambodia, Myanmar and Laos, Thailand's military hit a rough patch in income generation thanks to the 1997 financial crisis. Army Chief Gen. Surayud Chulanond transferred many military officers considered to be connected to the mafia to inactive positions and engaged in other security sector reforms designed to reduce the size and improve the efficiency of the armed forces. Surayud's action indicated the difficulty of 'the military' to control its own officers (some were funnelling profits from informal khaki capitalist activities to their own pockets instead of toward 'institutional goals').

In 2001, incoming Prime Minister Thaksin Shinawatra personalized control over military financing and attempted to carve a faction from the military and police that would be primarily loyal to him. During this time, military involvement in commercial enterprises declined markedly. Military-owned enterprises were now few and far between. The army now owned far fewer shares than previously in the Thai Military Bank. But it still controlled the War Veterans' Organization of Thailand and held shares in the national lottery quota.

Perhaps only in the telecommunications sector did the military hold real sway. The Army-owned TV Channel 5 and leased out TV Channel 7 through a concession. Meanwhile, the military controlled 245 out of

524 radio stations: 127 were owned by the Army, 21 by the Navy, 36 by the Air Force, 44 by the Police, 3 by the Ministry of Defence and 14 by the Supreme Command (Ubonrat 2002: 10).

Following Thaksin's elevation of his cousin Chaiyasit to the post of army commander in 2003, his administration made efforts to privatize and list TV Channel 5 on the SET (Stock Exchange of Thailand) (Lewis 2007: 109–11). The manner in which this would be accomplished led to some discontent among some senior Thai military officials who felt that civilians were wrongly seeking to exercise power over the armed forces. The 2006 coup, which deposed Thaksin, ended any efforts at privatizing military enterprises.

The 2006 putsch also affected military budgeting. Indeed, following the coup, the defence budget saw its first increase since before 1997, with the highest draw by ministry at 28 per cent. Moreover, on the day of the coup itself, an additional one billion baht was withdrawn from the military's slush fund account (Ukrist 2008: 137).

In 2007, following the 2006 coup, the military-backed Surayud government tightened laws on the state-supported broadcasting sector, enacted 'one of the world's harshest' internet crime laws and sought to manipulate the media to influence the result of the 2007 general election (Freedom House 2008). In late 2007, the military-sponsored National Legislative Assembly passed a Broadcasting Act which continued to grant broadcasting concessions to military vested interests (Ubonrat 2008).

Though democracy returned to Thailand in 2008, the military budget continued to grow. The 2007 constitution included a new charter clause (Section 77) that required the state to provide the armed forces with a sufficient (though unspecified) amount of money to guarantee national security. Then, in 2009, during the 2008–11 democratic government of anti-Thaksin Prime Minister Abhisit Vechachiwa, Defence Minister Prawit Wongsuwan enacted a 10-year military procurement programme, ensuring that the armed forces would have a fixed upward budget and additional grants to obtain new military hardware (Kocak and Kode 2014: 94). Thus, from 2007 until 2011, the military managed to guarantee for itself continued increases in defence allocations. Indeed, the defence budget rose from 3.3 billion US dollars in 2007 to $5.6 billion in 2011 (IISS 2011). By 2013, under the Puea Thai-led government of

Prime Minister Yingluck Shinawatra (Thaksin's sister), it had spiralled to $6.1 billion (Campbell, 10 December 2013).

In sum, the political economy of Thailand's military before the latest 2014 putsch represented the historical evolution of military influence and khaki capital—though it changed in significant ways. The 1932 demise of absolute monarchy, the first critical juncture, allowed for the armed forces to become independent of any palace resistance to increases in the military's economic power. Sarit's 1957–58 coups, the second critical juncture, facilitated a partial resurrection of monarchical influence such that military and monarchy (with connected aristocrats) partnered together in dominating the country's economy. By 1980, the monarchy overshadowed the military in influence, but both institutions possessed vast amounts of economic resources. Though civilian governments tried to keep the military under political and economic control (e.g. 1988–91; 2001–06), putsches by the armed forces undid all such attempts.

The military coup of 22 May 2014, terminating six years of frail democracy, also ensured that the Puea Thai government would not mark a critical juncture that entrenched Thai democratization. Rather, it opened the door to the resurrection of khaki capital in Thailand. The next section explores this period.

Khaki capital after the 2014 putsch

The incoming National Council for Peace and Order (NCPO) junta was led by Army Commander Gen. Prayuth Chan-ocha and his mentor, former Army Commander Gen. Prawit Wongsuwan, who became NCPO deputy leader, both of whom rose up through the Buraphapayak, the aforementioned army division that had profited along the Thai–Cambodian border during the 1980s and 1990s. Since the advent of the NCPO junta, military control over khaki capital has grown, especially in terms of sinecures (see below). There are three levels at which the military can exert its influence: institutional (e.g. land), factional (e.g. the Five Provinces Bordering Forest Preservation Foundation), and individual (e.g. illicit business such as human trafficking). In this section on post-2014 Thailand, these different types of khaki are examined.

Of course, one could argue that in reality, there is always a mix between these categories. We try to conceptualize the way in which the military has been engaged in economic activities based upon the 'principal-agent' model. This model takes as its starting point the idea that a structure acts as a contextual constraint. As a result, the tendency to change can be seen as the most difficult strategy, and thus the least likely outcome. Although military cohesion serves as a prerequisite for the proliferation of khaki capital in general, we often witness infighting among soldiers and factions that compete to gain control of military businesses. Moreover, military officials often engage in this economic activity under the façade of institutional interest. Thus, our conceptual types can be of value in that they can unmask various interests of different layers behind the interest of military organization. Our prototype is not rigid. Rather, it serves as an analytical tool to glean a deeper understanding of complex relations among khaki officials, factions and the military as a whole. In other words, these three conceptual prototypes are adopted as a conceptual lamp that can illuminate the military's overt or clandestine activities.

There are both formal and informal varieties of khaki capital. This study examines both.

Khaki capitalism and Thai governance
Within Thailand's formal governing structure, some aspects of khaki capitalism fall at least partially within the purview of civilian governing authorities, while others do not. Among the areas where civilian leaders exercise some control, the two most important are the allocation of budgetary resources and providing a legal framework that governs sinecures. National Security is today the fifth largest destination of all state budgetary allocations (Bureau of the Budget 2016: 29). In fact, the Thai military has possessed one of the most sizeable allocations of the annual budget since the 1868–1910 reign of King Chulalongkorn (Rama V). Up until today, the budget for defence has remained one of the top recipients of the annual budget. The post-1932 advent of military strongmen simply heightened the trend of military budgetary monopoly. Though the period 1992–2006 witnessed a budgetary drop in khaki clout, the 2006 military putsch reasserted the commanding position of budgetary allocations for the military (second to the monarchy). In Thailand's post-2014 coup era, the military has seen a resurgence of political power that rivals the days of the 1991–92 junta period. Paralleling this trend has been a resurrection in defence expenditures. While spending per capita

may not be remarkable, the amount of capital itself is breathtaking. The figures below and table overleaf offer a glimpse of Thailand's growing military budget. To be noted are the large, yet separate, areas of spending for 'national security', 'defence', 'public security and order', and the 'Ministry of Defence' (Bureau of the Budget 2016). In addition, beyond these immense reserves of funds, various security agencies also have access to slush funds (available amounts of state capital unmonitored by elected civilian officials) which are carte blanche accessible to the commander of a particular unit. Moreover, one can see in the table that

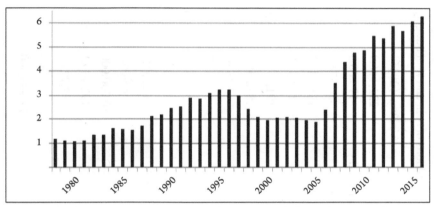

Figure 2.1: Thai military expenditure (1979–2016) (in US$ millions)

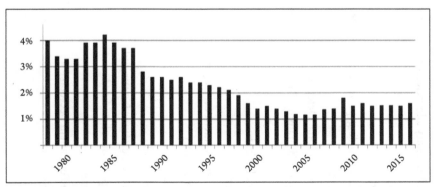

Figure 2.2: Thai military expenditure (1979–2016) (per cent of GDP)

Sources (both figures): Data for 1978–87 and 2004–07 derived from *IISS Military Balance*, International Institute for Strategic Studies, London, Routledge, various years. Data for 1988–2003 and 2008–16 derived from Stockholm Institute for Strategic Studies (SIPRI), Stockholm, various years.

Table 2.1: Thai budgetary allocations on security, 2015–16 (millions of baht and % of budget)

	Amount (2015)	% (2015)	Amount (2016)	% (2016)
National Security	222,116.9	8.6	239,034.3	8.8
a. Programme on upholding, protecting and preserving the monarchy	17,268.3		18,861.5	
b. Reconciliation	376.5		182.7	
c. Programme on National Defence	188,832.3		201,933.9	
d. Programme on Maintaining Order [since the coup]	16,016.3		18,056.3	
Defence	191,640.0	7.4	205,375.8	7.5
a. Total Military Defence	187,248.8		200,566.6	
b. Civil Defence	3,255.5		3556.9	
c. Research & Development on Defence	1,135.7		1,252.3	
Public Safety and Order	157,365.5	6.1	175,077.4	6.4
a. Police Services	94,668.3		106,899.5	
1. Police Slush fund	1,000,000		1,000,000	
Internal Security Operations Command	8,906.5		8,10,201.0	
Deep South Operations slush fund	20,000,000		20,000,000	
Ministry of Defence	192,949.1		206,461.3	
a. Office of the Permanent Secretary	7,771.2		8,675.0	
1. For royalty	NA		1,039.3	
2. Slush fund	12,193,000		12,393,000	

	Amount (2015)	% (2015)	Amount (2016)	% (2016)
b. Royal Aide-de-Camp Department	619.5		742.3	
1. For royalty	NA		742.3	
2. Slush fund	12,000,000		12,000,000	
c. Royal Thai Armed Forces Headquarters	14,779.7		15,822.9	
1. For royalty	NA		56.7	
2. Slush fund	54,422,000		44,422,000	
d. Royal Thai Army	95,485.6		101, 426.8	
1. For royalty	NA		306.0	
2. Slush fund	290,046,000		290,046,000	
e. Royal Thai Navy	37,522.2		40,395.4	
1. For royalty	NA		12.2	
2. Slush fund	42,698,000		42,698,000	
f. Royal Thai Air Force	35,700.2		38,208.6	
1. For royalty	NA		23.4	
2. Slush fund	30,000,000		30,000,000	
g. Defence Technology Institute	1070.7		1,190.3	

Sources: Bureau of the Budget 2016: 24–6; 25–7; 57–8; Government Gazette (2015) 'Budget Act for Fiscal Year 2016', 25 September: 22–3; *Naew Na*, 13 April 2016.

each military service allocates a certain portion of its budget to royalty. For the Royal Aide-de-Camp, this amount for royalty represents 100 per cent of its budget (Government Gazette 2016: 22–3) – though it also has access to a slush fund.

We classify military sinecures on political bodies and state-owned enterprise boards within the formal structure because the law allows security officers to have them. One type of sinecure can be found in post-2014 political bodies. These include the junta (NCPO) itself, the National Legislative Assembly or NLA (which passes laws) and the National Reform Steering Assembly or NRSA (recommends reforms to the NLA, cabinet, NCPO or related government agencies). Regarding the NCPO, 12 out of its 15 members (80 per cent) are military officials (Government Gazette 2016: 32). Each appointee is given a monthly salary of $3,464 (*Thaipublica* 2014). NCPO head Gen. Prayuth's salary is even higher. As for the NLA, through five shake-ups since the 2014 coup, the proportion of military officials to civilians has hovered over 50 per cent. Currently, 145 out of 250 NLA members (58 per cent) are military personnel, 90 (62 per cent) of whom are still active-duty (Ilaw 2017). Finally, regarding the NRSA, 65 out of its 200 members (33 per cent) are military personnel (Government Gazette 2015: 1–9). The military members of the NLA and NRSA each receive a monthly salary of $3,280 (*Thaipublica* 2014). Perhaps more than anything, the sudden sinecures made available to military officials through the creation of these three bodies represent the most obvious growth of khaki capital since the 2014 coup.

Yet appointees to any of these three bodies rarely rely on its formal salary alone. Take, for example, the case of Gen. Ekachai Chanchan Mongkol, Thailand's Under-Secretary of Defence. His total annual income per year comes to 1,470,000 baht from his membership salary on the NCPO, 1,440,000 baht salary as the director of CAT Telecom Ltd., 410,000 baht salary from being on the board of the Sports Committee of Thailand, 192,000 baht salary as the Director of the Institute of Defence Technology, 128,000 baht salary as a Board Member of the National Broadcasting and Telecommunications Commission, and finally 60,000 baht and a 1,360,000 baht salary as an NLA member, for a grand yearly total of 5,060,000 baht or 144,469 US dollars (*Khaosod* 2016).

Positions on boards of directors and boards of administration represent other methods through which the Thai military as an institution and also senior military officials as individuals economically benefit from the success of state-owned enterprises. Of course, this is nothing new to Thailand. Such positions require little or no work and yet bestow financial benefits upon the post's holder. Sinecures date back to the days of absolute monarchy, when members of the royal family were granted positions on trusts or enterprises to ensure the royals' financial security. As we learned in the first part of this chapter, generally from 1932 until 1988, senior military officials held a certain quota of seats on such boards, enriching themselves through sinecure income. The soldiers were often loyalist business buddies, golfing pals or even relatives of the Sino-Thai businesspeople who actually ran the corporations. Then came the 1997 Asian financial crisis, which was partly blamed on such opaque, corporate crony capitalism. Since then, the notion of 'Independent Directors' has been seen as the needed medicine for corporate reform. Independent Directors, according to the Stock Exchange of Thailand and the Securities Exchange Commission, are not allowed to hold shares of more than 0.5 per cent in a respective company, an affiliated company, associated company or related company, inclusive of the shares held by blood relatives. Independent Directors only receive incomes for sitting on a board.[7] Though the number of military officials sitting on State-owned Enterprise boards has diminished since 1997, most of them who still do are classified as 'Independent Directors'. Moreover, it seems that crony capitalism involving these board members has continued. Most lack the expertise to monitor any illegal misconduct by the corporate leadership (e.g. insider trading), and others might not want to or even engage in conflict-of-interest behaviour themselves (Fernquist, 12 April 2016). In all, Thailand's state-owned enterprises (SOEs) have combined assets of 360 billion US dollars, and they amount to 20 per cent of Thailand's stock market capitalization (Watts and Nopparat 2014). This is a powerful shield for khaki capital: The fact that these SOEs with their huge amounts of assets provide a feeding trough for senior military brass through sinecures demonstrates the financial importance of these postings for the military as an institution.

Under the administrations of Thaksin Shinawatra (2001–06) and Yingluck Shinawatra (2011–14), many individuals considered loyalists

---

7. See for example, Intouch Company, 'Definitions and Qualifications of Independent Directors', Enclosure 6.

to these governments were placed on SOE boards and attempts were made to privatize many such enterprises. Following the 2014 coup, corporate board members who were considered allies of the Shinawatra clan were replaced by people considered friends of the new military junta (ibid.). In shaking up the boards' compositions, NCPO head Prayuth, alongside his Deputy and junta Chief of Economic Affairs ACM Prajin Jantong, established a super-board to coordinate reforms in the state enterprises. Prayuth also took the helm of a newly revamped Board of Investment (BOI) as well 11 other board chairmanships in addition to his roles as NCPO head, Prime Minister and Army Commander (Prachatai 2014).

At the time of writing and as can be seen in Table 2.2 (overleaf), in 2017, three years after the latest coup, there were 57 SOEs in Thailand, though only 56 appear to be active. Of these, 14 did not have any military officials on their boards of directors, indicating that they either required substantial expertise of their directors or that the respective corporations were devoid of enough pecuniary interest for the military officials. Meanwhile, when comparing boards of directors to boards of administrators, one finds that there were many more soldiers on the former type of board. This owes to the fact that administrators are the ones who actually do the work of operating the corporations, which requires technical knowledge. In the end, only 13 SOEs had any military officials on their administrative boards. Table 2.2 does not include the Thai Military Bank (TMB) or TV Channel 5, which have been much more thoroughly controlled by the armed forces and discussed elsewhere in this section. One significant trend following the 2014 coup has been a jump in the number of military personnel who are eligible to sit on the SOE boards of directors across the country. In 2015, twelve names were added to the list.[8] Ultimately, in 2017, sinecures continued to be important cash cows for the intermediate- and top-level military officers who had them. Moreover, because the sinecures helped both these officials and associated entrepreneurs, they could provide a positive nexus between the particular corporation and the junta.

---

8. Calculated from the 'Pool of Names Eligible to Sit on the SOEs from 2008 until 2015', Ministry of Finance website.

Some elements of khaki capitalism exist entirely outside the purview of civilian governmental control. Among these, we present case studies of two areas: land ownership and military-owned enterprises.

Out of the total amount of land in Thailand (around 320 million rai, or 51 million hectares; ASTV 2015), the Thai military owns approximately 5 million rai (800,000 hectares), which accounts for 1.6 per cent of the total. Of this, the armed forces has formal land title to 460,000 rai (73,600 hectares; Kanda, 1 June 2015). The military does not actively use most of this land, yet prohibits private citizens from using it. Hence, it brings little or no productivity for the Thai farming population. This crucial factor has contributed to a sharp increase in inequality within the country (Krisada 2013). The military justifies its continued ownership on the basis of decades of legal precedent: Army Regulation regarding Land Administration and Management (18 January 1966); the State Land Act (5 March 1975); and the Ministry Announcement regarding Measures on Administrative Methods to preserve and maintain State Property (8 August 2002).

Indeed, former Prime Minister Thaksin Shinawatra had tried to minimize the gap between rich and poor through land redistribution by asking all government agencies (including the military) to relinquish their unused lands to the people. However, though other state agencies complied with Thaksin's requests, the government received only lukewarm cooperation from the military regarding the use of its lands to facilitate his land redistribution policy (Kanda 2015).

The military has used both direct and indirect methods to maximize profits from the land holdings it has chosen to develop. Plots are leased directly to other state agencies or private companies, just as a regular landlord would.

As for the indirect method, the military as an institution can and has benefitted from its initiation of development projects, such as highly subsidised housing developments for its soldiers, thus directly benefitting lower-ranking soldiers. Since those lands belong to the military, the land deeds cannot be transferred (except that land deeds can be transferred to other state agencies). Yet, the deeds to property (typically houses) that rest on the land can be transferred, typically to the person who resides in the house. In the first instance, this person is always a military official. But what if that person dies or wants to sell

Table 2.2: Military sinecures on Thailand's state enterprises (2016)

#	SOE	BoD*	BoA*
1	MCOT Public Co., Ltd.	2/13	0/23
2	Police Printing Bureau, Royal Thai Police	5/7	0/12
3	The Bangkok Dock Co., Ltd.	8/10	4/7
4	Thailand Tobacco Monopoly	3/12	0/32
5	Government Lottery Office	5/12	2/6
6	Playing Cards Factory, Excise Department	0/9	0/5
7	Liquor Distillery Organization, Excise Department	1/10	0/14
8	Syndicate of Thai Hotels & Tourists Enterprises Ltd.	0/3	0/3
9	Krung Thai Bank Public Co., Ltd.	1/12	0/6
10	Government Savings Bank	0/10	0/47
11	Government Housing Bank	0/9	0/14
12	Bank for Agriculture and Agricultural Co-operatives	0/15	0/5
13	Export–Import Bank of Thailand	0/12	0/4
14	Small and Medium Enterprise Development Bank of Thailand	0/10	0/5
15	Secondary Mortgage Corporation	0/7	0/15
16	Thai Credit Guarantee Corporation	1/9	1/5
17	Dhanarak Asset Development Co., Ltd	0/10	0/5
18	Islamic Bank of Thailand	1/10	0/8
19	Sports Authority of Thailand	2/15	–
20	Tourism Authority of Thailand	1/16	0/9
21	National Housing Authority	2/9	0/42
22	Office of the Government Pawnshop	3/11	0/33
23	Dairy Farming Promotion Organization of Thailand	0/13	0/22
24	Rubber Estate Organization	NA	NA
25	Marketing Organization for Farmers	1/10	0/4
26	Fish Marketing Organization	1/7	0/11
27	Office of the Rubber Replanting Aid Fund	0/14	0/6
28	Airports of Thailand Public Co., Ltd.	4/14	8/38
29	Port Authority of Thailand	2/10	12/30
30	State Railway of Thailand *(latest figures 2010)*	2/8	1/40
31	Bangkok Mass Transit Authority	2/10	0/8

#	SOE	BoD*	BoA*
32	Aeronautical Radio of Thailand, Ltd.	4/9	3/19
33	Thai Maritime Navigation Co., Ltd.	1/2	–
34	Thai Airways International Public Co., Ltd.	6/15	1/5
35	The Transport Co., Ltd.	2/9	0/14
36	Civil Aviation Training Center	5/11	5/15
37	Mass Rapid Transit Authority of Thailand	2/14	1/13
38	Expressway Authority of Thailand	5/14	0/5
39	Wastewater Management Authority	1/14	0/14
40	Botanical Garden Organization	0/6	0/8
41	Zoological Park Organization under Royal Patronage of H.M. the King	3/9	0/19
42	Forest Industry Organization	2/9	0/14
43	TOT Public Co., Ltd.	1/11	0/43
44	CAT Telecom Public Co., Ltd.	4/13	1/9
45	Thailand Post Co, Ltd.	1/6	0/6
46	Electricity Generating Authority of Thailand	2/11	0/45
47	PTT Public Co., Ltd.	2/14	0/10
48	Public Warehouse Organization	2/9	1/7
49	Metropolitan Electricity Authority	1/7	0/12
50	Provincial Electricity Authority	2/13	0/18
51	Metropolitan Waterworks Authority	3/13	0/10
52	Provincial Waterworks Authority	2/9	0/26
53	Market Organization	0/3	1/14
54	Thailand Institute of Scientific and Technological Research	1/11	0/8
55	National Science Museum	0/9	–
56	Government Pharmaceutical Organization	1/12	0/24
57	Industrial Estate Authority of Thailand	3/11	0/59

Notes: BoD = Proportion of military officials to all persons on Board of Directors; BoA = Proportion of military officials to all persons on Board of Administration.

Sources: Websites of each SOE.

his property? It turns out that some housing development projects have become very controversial because the property on lots (not the land itself) has been transferred to civilians. These development projects were originally meant for the welfare of soldiers; however, when some of the houses were transferred to private individuals, then the welfare of those soldiers meant to enjoy this housing becomes compromised. Alternatively, sometimes further down the road, senior military officers might attempt to transform properties (already transferred to civilians) into completely different projects, thus harming the civilian property. In this way, economic activities that were intended by some generals to generate military-institutional benefits have been redirected toward personal benefits for officers farther down the chain of command. In some cases, the military officials openly and publicly sell the land (including under housing developments), examples of which have occurred in Nakorn Ratchasima, Phathum Thani, and Nakorn Sawan (Kanda 2015; *Teedin2*, 14 May 2013).

Regarding individual benefits, high ranking military officials have reaped rewards by secretly using the military as guarantor for specific land deals. For example, a case came to light in 2011 in which the second wife of a former head of the army (Gen. Sonthi Boonyaratklin) illegally bought some land plots from another former head of the army (Gen. Surayud Chulanond) who is currently a member of the Privy Council; the price was not revealed. Other land plots she bought were similarly non-transparent, illegal purchases: it was found in the land-deed that the Royal Thai Army had secretly acted as a guarantor of another previous buyer who had also been a military official (*Isranews*, 29 May 2012). In short, in an illegal acquisition of military land, it would also be illegal to use the military as guarantor, hence the secrecy surrounding the role of military insiders. This example illustrates how senior military brass (and military relatives) can maximize benefits from their high-level positions by surreptitiously utilizing the military as an institution to guarantee land acquisitions.

With regard to the land use, the military has invested in several business ventures, including golf courses, hotels, sports stadiums, rice mills, restaurants and auditoriums-for-rent. For example, Rachanavy-Plutaluang Golf Course in Chonburi province earns a generous income for the navy in terms of profits from golfing fees and other related expenses (*Manager Online* 2012). In many cases, the military leases parts of its land to business entrepreneurs. Although some categories of dividends which the military derives from land are more profitable than others, overall they provide a stable income for the armed forces.

Ultimately, land has become the main source of income for the military especially more so for personal gain among the intermediate to high ranking military officials. When compared with the total amount of land owned by the top ten largest landowners in the country other than the military, Thai military land is more than five times greater than all those combined: 5,000,000/958,400 rai (800,000/153,344 hectares; *Prachachat Turakij* , 18 June 2014). Land is thus the nest-egg of khaki capital in Thailand.

A second area of khaki activities that is entirely beyond the purview of civilian control involves actual ownership of economic enterprises by the military. Among the sectors in which the military has expressed an interest, telecommunications, sports and banking stand out.

The Royal Thai Army Radio and Television Station (currently Channel 5) has become one of the major sources of income for the Royal Thai Army (RTA). It was first established as a property of the army in 1958 (under the name of Royal Thai Army Radio and Television Station, Channel 7) under Field Marshal Sarit Thanarat, who was then head of the army.[9] Indeed, several key characteristics of its business reflect the complete dominance of the army up until today. First, it is exclusively owned by the army. Unlike other military businesses, the army has not permitted shareholders from the private sector or even those from khaki counterparts such as the Royal Thai Navy and Royal Thai Air Force (Kanda, 25 April 2012). Interestingly, this is a change from Thailand's first experiment in television broadcast, in 1955 under Prime Minister and Gen. Phibun Songkram, when its shareholdings had been held jointly by several state agencies.

The RTA has traditionally possessed the monopoly on telecommunications and it can thus give out concessions in this area to those members of the private sector who want to do this type of business. When looking at the composition of the Army TV Channel 5 board of directors, all eight are high ranking RTA officials, and the head of the

---

9. See Royal Thai Army Radio and Television Station http: //app.tv5.co.th/history/, accessed 9 May 2016.

RTA is always the chair of the board. In this regard, any concession involving Channel 5 given to the private sector would not have to be done in a transparent manner since all eight board members are senior army officials. The khaki influence upon Channel 5 has permeated other TV channels as well. For example, Gen. Praphas Charusatien (commander of the RTA 1963–73) gave a TV concession in 1967 (the country's first colour TV – Channel 7) to his cronies (in this case, his wife's sister's husband), a concession that persists until today (ibid.). Nevertheless, Channel 7 is still beholden to the directives of the RTA. The individuals who directly run Channel 7 gain benefits from RTA patronage and they would never oppose RTA directives. Ultimately, ever since 1967, the RTA has maintained complete control over TV channels 5 and 7. Today the RTA perseveres as the telecommunications gatekeeper for potential concessionaires.

Third, guns, power and money are all intertwined. This can be seen in the case of the establishment of the Television Pool of Thailand (TPT), composed of four TV channels (including 5 and 7) in 1968, which has allowed the business of the RTA to grow unchecked. The fact that the head of TPT will always be the head of the Royal Thai Army Radio and Television Station creates an unequal playing field in the television business.

Fourth, the Royal Thai Army Radio and Television Station can become a last resort whenever the business of the RTA is threatened. There was a case where the Royal Thai Army Radio and Television Station became the exclusive lender to the newly established Royal Thai Army Holding Company in 1997, which was created to help mitigate the financial crisis of the Thai Military Bank. Basically, the RTA became the owner of the holding company. As such, the Royal Thai Army Holding Company became a principal economic arm of the RTA.[10]

The RTA currently controls 126 radio stations nationwide (Kanda 2012). These are overseen by the National Broadcasting and Telecommunications Commission (NBTC). Since the coup of 2014, senior RTA security officials have held a majority (six out of 10 members) on this commission, leaving the civilian members powerless (ONBTC 2016). The four civilians are tasked with doing the legwork of the NBTC while the military representatives simply enjoy their sinecures.

---

10. See ibid.; RYT9.com, September 29, 2004.

The RTA receives substantial benefits through its control over tele-communications. These can be divided into two dimensions. The first is acquiring direct profits by promoting favoured companies and advertising sales. The second is boosting up the image of the military through the media. As part of this, the RTA can advertise its work in support of monarchical 'Royal Projects.' Altogether, the TV and radio business serves as an economic and propaganda mechanism.

The military has a history of interest in promoting sport – and in using sport to promote itself. Soccer (football) and boxing have been particularly high on the military agenda. Regarding soccer, Army United Football Club is owned by the RTA and has existed since 1916 (*thaifussball* 2016). The team uses the Thai Army Sports Stadium, capacity 20,000, as its hub of activities. The RTA receives a share of stadium and advertising revenue from the activities of Army United Football. In 2011, when Gen. Prayuth Chan-ocha had just become Army Commander, there was a sudden accumulation of at least 60 million baht in state and private funds to support the team. By 2015, following the 2014 coup, then-Army Commander Gen. Udomdej Sitabutr had assured people that the amount of money going to the team had risen to approximately 120 million baht. Among the business sponsors were Beer Chang, Charoen Phokpand Group, King Power, Acer Computer, Pan Limited, Thai Life Insurance and Army TV Channel 5. The Army Commander is always president of the Army United Football Club board and most other members are senior army officers. Interestingly enough, in 2011, Col. Pongpan Wongsuwan (the brother of the current Defence Minister and a key member of the NCPO, ret. Gen. Prawit Wongsuwan) served as the President of technical development for the club (*Siam Sport*, 15 February 2011; *Thairath*, 11 February 2015).

Meanwhile, Lumpini Boxing Stadium was first established on 8 December 1956, long before soccer in Thailand began to boom, and is owned by the RTA. The project was initiated under Gen. Praphas Charusatien with the profits to be used mainly to provide welfare benefits for army officials and facilitate the works of other units in the RTA (Lumpini Boxing Stadium). The new boxing stadium, built in 2012 and located at Ramintra, also in Bangkok, is estimated to hold up to 5,000 seats and can potentially draw in up to 10 million baht per fight (*Thairath*, 10 March 2014).

The Lumpini Boxing Stadium board is composed of 16 members, and they are all military. The appearance of interest in army welfare has been institutionalized: the head of the Army Welfare Department is also the chief of the boxing stadium board, and other individuals have dual affiliations. The stadium's director is always the current army commander. All of these positions are purely and simply sinecures, though military officers with sinecures sometimes actually exercise certain influence across the enterprise. In those cases, sinecures can become positions of power.

Thailand's private sector has long supported the Lumpini Boxing Stadium. This can be seen by the advertisement of business sponsors such as Beer Chang, Twins Special and Thai Life Insurance. Indeed, there is a symbiotic relationship between the military and the business sector, leading to a commercialization of power. For example, Gen. Winai Pattiyakul (the former secretary general of the Council for National Security [2006–08] and Permanent Minister of Defence [2006–08] who was said to be the next head of the army after Sonthi Boonyaratklin) is currently on the board of directors, a sinecure position of Thai Life Insurance Public Company Limited (Thai Life Insurance).

Finally, the RTA has a long history of direct involvement in Thai financial institutions, most notably the Thai Military Bank (TMB).[11] Exploring the evolution of the TMB can shed light on the severely limited ability of civilian leaders to control the military. Through the TMB, the Royal Thai Army (as part of the Royal Thai Armed Forces, has been able to exert control over civilian leaders in the realm of political and economic activities for the interest of its institution while bypassing any accountability mechanisms.

The TMB initially was established under the regime of Gen. Sarit Thanarat in 1957 to help out and look after the welfare needs of military officials. Later on, it came to play the role of a 'cash cow' for the military, especially after Sarit issued the Commercial Bank Act (1962), which allowed his military regime to act as a gatekeeper for commercial bank investors. This Act in effect legitimized the military monopoly over commercial banking in Thailand (Kanda 2012). This Act also paved

---

11. We use TMB as an acronym for Thai Military Bank during the period 1957–97. In 2005, the bank officially changed its name to TMB Bank Public Company Limited (TMB).

the way for the bank eventually to become a full commercial bank in 1973.[12] In 1983 TMB became publicly listed on the Stock Exchange of Thailand.

Though being listed on the Stock Exchange, the way that the TMB had operated was quite market-averse. For instance, the Thai military remained the largest institutional shareholder of the bank (35–36 per cent until the mid-2000s), and senior military personnel with no bank experience were guaranteed seats on the board of directors: the supreme commander, the head of the army, navy, air force, the director of Channel 5, the first army region commander, and military personnel from finance departments were always included. There were also end-less renewals of khaki personnel and their civilian partners sitting on the board of directors, which created an *ersatz* capitalist environment because capitalism was distorted to favour the military. Indeed, a decade after being listed on the Stock Exchange, the Thai military and one of its business allies (Thai Life Insurance Co. Ltd) still held around 45 per cent of the total shares of the Bank.[13] In addition, it was found that the Thai military made at least one billion baht (~US$2.8 million) from 1983–90. Finally, the TMB, besides being a powerful economic source for the military, is also a financial safe house for military slush funds (*Manager Magazine*, July 1992).

Eventually, due to Thailand's 1997 financial crisis and poor banking management, TMB underwent major internal reforms and organiza-tional restructuring to ensure continued efficiency and profitability. Among these included changing its name in 2005 from Thai Military Bank to TMB Bank Public Company Limited in order to attract foreign investors. Along with this reform came the diversification of its share-holders by selling some shares to foreign investors such as the Dutch ING Bank in 2007. Since that year, the Ministry of Finance has become the bank's largest shareholder, taking the place of the RTA.[14] Indeed, the

---

12. In addition, regarding the composition of commercial bank boards, military of-ficers held sinecure seats on the boards of every commercial bank in Thailand from the 1940s until the 1960s, when military power was at the height. Military personnel comprised between 33 and 80 per cent (the latter in the case of TMB) of the boards of every commercial bank in Thailand (Riggs 1966: 298–9).

13. See Report of Meeting of the Bank on shareholders 1999, 2000.

14. See TMB; Annual Report of Meeting among the shareholders of TMB 1999: 26.

attempt to renew TMB's image can be seen in the recomposition of its Board of Directors as well as its executive board over time (see Table 2.3 opposite). Since 2007, only one military official sits on the board of directors (except for the years of 2012–14) and the executive board has no military officers at all.[15]

The structural reforms initiated by TMB do not mean that the Thai military has no influence on the bank.[16] Although the Ministry of Finance is now the largest shareholder and the Royal Thai Armed Forces has only 1.25 per cent of total shares, the head of the army remains on the Board of Directors. Besides being a sinecure position, the fact that the head of the RTA sits on the TMB's Board of Directors reflects how much influence that the military possesses, since the head of the army is known to be more powerful than any elected civilian prime minister of the country. So, any activities by the board can be monitored or even influenced by the Thai armed forces anyway.[17] In addition, the most recent chair of the TMB's Board of Directors (who previously served as the permanent secretary of the Ministry of Finance between 2013 and 2015) is concurrently the PM's advisor, as well as a member of the National Reform Steering Assembly. In this way, even more than a mere sinecure, the current chair of the TMB Board of Directors can act as the 'eyes and ears' of the Thai military in terms of ensuring the military's financial interests. From the economic institutional level, these military-dominated business interests have remained powerful pre- and post-2014 coup. Yet, what is unique about the 2014 coup situation is that the number of sinecures has expanded while the influence of the armed forces is intensifying across new areas of interest.

Informal channels of economic–military power in Thailand
As mentioned in the theory section above, there are three levels of interest (institutional, factional, individual) where the military can exert its influence. We turn now to the level of factions within the military and how they influence both the military as a whole and, especially, their effect on khaki capitalism. The individual level will be discussed

15. See Annual Report of Thai Military Bank, 2003–15. https://www.tmbbank.com/ir/fin_info/annualreport, accessed 8 March 2016.

16. See detailed discussion by Kanda Naknoi, 25 March 2012.

17. For example, it was the army chief who ordered TMB organizational restructuring in 1999–2000.

Table 2.3: Military influence on TMB Boards (2003–15)

Year	BoD*	Name	BoE*	Name
2003	5/14	Gen. Chaisit Shinawatra; Admiral Chumpol Pachu-sanond; Gen.Somtad Attanand; Air Chief Marshal Kongsak Vantana; Gen.Pang Malakul	2/7	Gen. Chaisit Shinawatra; Gen. Pang Malakul
2004	3/17	Gen. Chaisit Shinawatra; Gen.Pang Malakul; Air Chief Marshal Kongsak Vantana	1/7	Gen. Pang Malakul
2005	2/15	Gen. Chaisit Shinawatra; Gen. Pang Malakul	1/6	Gen.Pang Malakul
2006	2/13	Gen. Sonthi Boonyaratglin; Gen. Pang Malakul	1/6	Gen. Pang Malakul
2007	3/13	Gen.Sonthi Boonyaratglin; Gen.Pang Malakul; Gen. Anupong Paochinda	1/5	Gen. Pang Malakul
2008	1/12	Gen. Anupong Paochinda	0/7	–
2009	1/12	Gen. Anupong Paochinda	0/7	–
2010	1/12	Gen.Prayuth Chan-ocha	0/7	–
2011	1/12	Gen.Prayuth Chan-ocha	0/7	–
2012	2/12	Gen. Prayuth Chan-ocha; Gen.Kamol Saenissara	0/7	–
2013	2/12	Gen. Prayuth Chan-ocha; Gen. Kamol Saenissara	0/8	–
2014	2/11	Gen. Weeran Chantasatkosol*; Gen.Kamol Saenissara	0/7	-
2015	1/12	Gen.Teerachai Nakwanich	0/5	-

*Note: It is an unwritten rule that the head of the army will have a "guaranteed seat" on the Board of Directors. However, it was only in the year 2014 that the head of the army (Gen.Udomdej Sitabutr) did not sit on the Board of Directors.

below. The principal types of military factions have been based upon academy graduating class, unit within which officers have served, military personality and proximity to certain royal family members. These types sometimes overlap. In the aftermath of the 2014 coup, the junta leadership was based around pre-cadet academy class 12; the leading unit since 2007 – Buraphapayak (representing the First Army Region, Second Division), within which was the factional core Taharn Sua Rachanee or Queen's Tiger Guards (representing the 21st Regiment); the personalities of Gen. Prayuth Chan-ocha, Gen. Anupong Paochinda and Gen. Prawit Wongsuwan. The royal patron for this leading faction was Queen Sirikit. Since 2016, at the dawn of the rule of King Rama X, the leading classes are 16, 18 and 20. Class 18 was the first military class under which Princess Sirinthorn was the military academy teacher (*Matichon* 2017:16). It could thus be assumed to be close to her. In 2017, with regard to unit factions, Buraphapayak continues to be the leading one but it is challenged by others: Wongthewan (representing the 1st Regiment, First Army Region) and to a lesser extent the Special Forces faction. The personalities of Prayuth and Prawit are dominant in the military junta but Privy Council Chair Prem Tinsulanond makes his influence felt through the current Army Commander Gen. Chalermchai Sittisart (a member of Special Forces faction). Another military personality is Gen. Apirat Kongsompong who is the First Army Commander and leading member of Wongthewan faction. Chalermchai and Apirat are also thought to be close (ibid.). Apirat himself is allegedly a favourite of the new king (Crispin 2017). Yet because Buraphapayak (as dominated by the personalities of Prayuth and Prawit) has held the most senior positions in the army since 2007, it (and its members) today holds the most khaki capital relative to other factions.

The realm of the Five Provinces Bordering Forest Preservation Foundation (FPBFP) clearly shows how the profits of one faction within the military can be maximized, even at the expense of other factions. The FPBFP foundation was established in 2006 following a predecessor project, the Natural Environment and Wildlife Preservation of Five Provinces Project, which was initially funded by the Queen of Thailand. The foundation was initiated under the care of the RTA. The total area, which covers land in the five eastern provinces of Chonburi, Rayong, Chantaburi, Chachaengsao, and Srakaeow, contains approximately 1.2 million rai

(192,000 hectares) and is believed to have great socio-economic significance and biodiversity. This region covers the area of military responsibility of the Buraphapayak, which was introduced above. Table 2.4 (overleaf)
shows that half of the military personnel on the FPBFP board belong to
the Buraphapayak faction, while other board members have individual
connections with one or another of the Buraphapayak generals: Prawit
Wongsuwan, Anupong Paochinda or Prayuth Chan-ocha.

It is convenient in terms of power that the office of the FPBFP foundation is located in the 1st Infantry Regiment 'King's Own Bodyguard'
in Bangkok – a centre of army clout in the capital city. Though the
initiative of the Foundation is to preserve the natural environment and
wildlife, one can see that FPBFP has over time become the powerhouse
for the grand alliance among elites in Thailand, including the military,
business sector, senior bureaucrats. Although FPBFP is not a formal
institution for khaki capital, it has served as a ticket to big money and
senior promotions – power.

For example, among those sitting on the Board of Directors, only six
out of the 26 are civilians who are either wealthy businessmen or senior
bureaucrats. In other words, 77 per cent of the board members are high
ranking military personnel. Interestingly enough, some of the military
men who sit on the foundation board are concurrently sitting on other
Boards of Directors in the private sector (this will be explained in detail
below).

Why would any military personnel want to be part of this powerful
faction-led foundation? Businesspeople can benefit from close contact
with senior military men who have the authority to decide on any business pertaining to the military. Indirectly, they are also often informed
of things their competitors do not know about. For example, in a 1992
incident, Gen. Chavalit (who then led a powerful faction) cautioned
one entrepreneur to abstain from quarrying in a certain area, giving the
man insider information that the RTA would soon be closing off that
land (*Manager Magazine*, July 1992).

Buraphapayak's economic empire revolves around the linkages of its
three leading personalities: Gens Prayuth, Anupong and Prawit. Retired
generals benefit from links with the business sector, which can provide
them with economic 'goodies.' For example, Pattana Puttananon, a retired general and former deputy army chief, is concurrently a manager of

Table 2.4: The Five Provinces Foundation's Board of Directors

#	Name	Position	Pre-Cadet Class # (if any)
1	Ret. Gen. Prayuth Chan-ocha*	Honorary President	12
2	Mr. Jaroen Jareewatanapakdi	Honorary Advisor	Owner of Beer Chang
3	Ret. Gen. Prawit Wongsuwan*	President	6
4	Ret. Gen. Pathana Pathananon	Vice President	Chulachomklao Class 11
5	M.R. Pridiyathorn Devakul	Vice President	Close w/Prawit: Saint Gabriel's College
6	Ret. Gen. Anupong Paochinda*	Member	10
7	Ret. Gen. Udomdej Sitabutr*	Member	14
8	Mr. Pattawat Suksiwong	Member	Close link w/Prawit: CEO of Comp. Link Connection
9	Ret. Gen. Noppadol Inthapanya*	Member	6
10	Mr. Satit Sowintorn	Member	Close link w/Prawit: Member of NLA; candidate of Pracharat Party 2007; former head of Department of Forestry
11	Ret. Gen. Lertlit Vechasawan	Member	6
12	Mr. Kamol Iaosiwikul	Member	Link w/Anupong
13	Mr. Bamrung Lawjaroenwattanachai	Member	Link w/Prawit: head of Chamber of Commerce in Srakeow
14	Ret. Gen. Kittipong Kesgowit*	Member	8

#	Name	Position	Pre-Cadet Class # (if any)
15	Ret. Gen. Appichai Songsin	Member	10
16	Ret. Gen. Wit Thepsudin na Ayuthaya	Member	11
17	Ret. Gen. Kanit Sapitak*	Member	13
18	Ret. Gen. Sirichai Disakul	Member	13
19	Gen. Teerachai Nakwanich*	Member	14
20	Gen. Walit Rojanapakdi*	Member	15
21	Ret. Maj. Gen. Sawang Damnernswatranit	Member and Financial Officer	6
22	Col. Jaggrit Srinon	Member and Assistant Financial Officer	32
23	Col. Chinasorn Ruangsuk	Member and Assistant Financial Officer	32
24	Ret. Gen Surat Worarak	Member and Secretary	11
25	Ret. Gen. Anan Kanjanapan	Member and Assistant Secretary	13
26	Brig. Gen. Nat Indharajaroen*	Member and Assistant Secretary	20

Note: indicates members of Buraphapayak faction.

Source: Five Provinces Bordering Forest Preservation Project, http://www.5provincesforest.com/index.php?lay=show&ac=article&Ntype=4&Id=538680558, accessed 9 March 2017.

Beer Tip Brewery (which is a subsidiary of Thai Bev. Co. Ltd owned by Beer Chang) and is the vice chair of the FPBFP board of directors. His donation of two million baht to FPBFP was received personally by ret. Gen. Prawit, the Buraphapayak faction leader who was not only FPBFP chair, but also deputy junta leader and deputy prime minister (Thai Bev 2014).

Turning to another example, Gen. Peeraporn Sripanthawong, a member of the Board of FPBFP (and close associate of Prayuth and Prawit) is also on the Board of RTA Entertainment. His friend, Gen. Surawat Butarawong, the head of the Board of Directors of RTA Entertainment Ltd., gave a donation to the FPBFP Foundation. Though RTA Entertainment Ltd had already diversified itself from the RTA Channel 5, RTA Channel 5 nevertheless continued to hold at least a 50 per cent share of RTA Entertainment. Interestingly, this new military-led joint venture company received a concession to do public relations for several governmental agencies. During 2011–12, this concession made profits for RTA Entertainment of 97 million baht (~$2.7 million) while it received the concession from the Office of the Army Secretary to make army advertisements worth one million baht (~$28,500) (*Isranews*, 29 June 2013).

In still another example, the civilian head of PTT Global Chemical Ltd gave a donation of approximately two million baht to the chair of the Board of Directors of FPBFP foundation. This is actually not surprising. A close crony of this civilian director as well as Prime Minister Prayuth, Col. Nithi Jeungjareon, is part of the working team of the Prime Minister while sitting on the Board of Director of PTT Global Chemical Ltd. The current Prime Minister is actually sitting on the Board of Directors of FPBFP foundation and Col. Nithi began sitting on the Board of PTT Global Chemical Ltd. a few months after the coup in 2014.

In a final example, Lt Gen. Phichit Boonyatikarn, administrative director of the RTA Sports Centre (Ramindra) who is close to Prime Minister Prayuth and Prawit, made a donation equivalent to 490,000 baht to the FPBFP foundation. Incidentally, the Board of Directors of the RTA Sports Centre is composed of all five senior-most army officials (the 'Five Tigers': army commander, deputy commander, chief of staff, and two assistant army commanders), two of whom are members of the

Buraphapayak faction (*PimThaiOnline*, 17 February 2016).

༫

Finally, we address how individual military leaders have shaped khaki capitalism in Thailand. This level reflects the personal engagement of khaki capital under the façade of military necessity. Three military officials sit on the eleven-chair Administrative Board of the War Veterans' Organization of Thailand (WVOT). Formally, this organization operates under the Royal Patronage of his Majesty the King, but in fact its operations are financed via the sale of lottery tickets to sell across Thailand. It is responsible for distributing 2,350,000 out of the 27,753,300 tickets produced each year; only two organisations have a larger quota (*Thaipublica*, 11 June 2015).

But what makes this more interesting is that the lottery business in Thailand is essentially controlled by five big private enterprises, one of which has recently been taken over by Capt. Thammanas Phrompao, a former plainclothes military man. Lottery tickets officially cost around 80 baht each, but the street value averages in the area of 100–130 baht. So, these big five organizations, like the WVOT, make a profit of around 30–50 baht per ticket (*TNews*, 5 May 2015). The lottery business has thus become a major lucrative enterprise in the country, especially when the level of transparency and accountability is low.

Aside from the lottery, there has been evidence of senior level military officials engaging in other informal economic ventures. Indeed, some military officers have utilized the Rajadamnern and Lumpini boxing stadium businesses in Bangkok personally and illicitly to accrue unauthorized benefits.[18] Further, in 2016, the nephew of NCPO junta leader Gen. Prayuth Chan-ocha obtained business concessions for army construction projects. The nephew's company, Contemporary Construction, was reportedly involved in army contract bidding worth 26.9 million baht (*The Nation* 2016). Meanwhile, there is evidence of military participation in shady human trafficking syndicates. In 2013, reports surfaced that the Thai Navy was involved in the illegal trafficking of Rohingya refugees (CNN 2013). An even more elaborate human trafficking network targeting Rohingya was exposed in 2015, with the

---

18. See *Thai Post*, 9 May 2009; Lumpini Boxing Stadium; MuayThai 2000.

alleged ringleaders including a senior Thai army official, Gen. Manat Kongpaen (Chambers 2015).

Military corruption in terms of procurement overruns, undeclared assets and kickbacks is another contemporary element of informal khaki capital. For example, in 2009, the Thai army purchased an overpriced (350 million baht [US$11.4 million]), substandard surveillance blimp as well as 700 GT200 bomb detectors 'that turned out to be ... lumps of plastic with no working mechanical parts (Ahuja 2010).' Then, in October 2014, members of a new National Legislative Assembly (NLA) were appointed to office. The appointment required them to reveal their assets to ascertain whether they were 'unusually rich.' Appointees who stood out included: Admiral Kamthorn Pumhiran, who possessed approximately 800 million baht; Police Commander Somyos Pompangmuang, with around 375 million baht; Somyos' successor as Police Commander, Chakthip Chaichinda, reported 963.8 million baht; and Prime Minister Prayuth's brother, Gen. Preecha Chan-ocha, was reported to hold about 90 million baht (*Political Prisoners in Thailand* 2014). For civil servants, these declared assets appear to be overly substantial in proportion to their official salaries. The implication is that some assets might have been earned in a malfeasant manner. Under the current ruling junta, however, it is unlikely that monitoring agencies will fairly scrutinize the source of these appointees' assets. Indeed, in 2015, Thai newspaper *Thairath* reported the appointment of five new commissioners to the National Anti-Corruption Commission. Yet all were considered pro-junta and thus unlikely to raise a hand against any potential corruption by the regime or the military (*Thairath*, 21 October 2015).

Perhaps the most remarkable instance of military corruption under the NCPO junta is the malfeasance that occurred in relation to the construction of Rajabhakti Park, which seeks to honour seven past Thai kings. Rajabhakti Park as part of a Royal Thai Army Project was built on Thai Army property in 2015, with approximately one billion baht (~$28 million) in funds donated by the public and private sectors. Army Commander Gen. Udomdej Sitabutr at that time was in charge and oversaw the project that was strongly supported by Buraphapayak. Thailand's then-Crown Prince (now King Rama X) presided over the park's opening ceremonies. The park's large plaza of 91 rai (145,600 m2), is used by the military for parades, ceremonies welcoming foreign dignitaries, and other special events. There are allegations that at least one military official (and also an amulet dealer) were involved in a scandal centring upon kickbacks related to the building of the statues. Apparently, the official extracted a 10 per cent commission from five foundries, each of which was tasked with constructing one 40 million baht statue, for a total bribe of 20 million baht (Draper 2015; Bangkok Post 2015; New Democracy Movement 2015; Takahashi 2016: 56–9).

Meanwhile, in terms of abuse of power, in May 2013, evidence came to light that an army general and a police general held private interests in Tongkah Harbour Public Company Limited. Thung Kham Limited, a subsidiary of Tongkhah, has intimidated local villagers in Loei Province, forcibly evicting them to facilitate access to mining interests. Pol. Gen. Somyot Prueksakasemsuk held a position on the board (Asian Human Rights Commission 2014). Following the 2014 coup, he was elevated to become Thailand's Police Chief and carries on close, friendly ties with NCPO Deputy Chief Prawit Wongsuwan. For this reason, despite attempts by local people in Loei province as well as the Asian Human Rights Commission to prevent illicit mining activities by Tongkah, the NCPO is unlikely to react in support of action to help Loei province villagers any time soon.

A further example of informal khaki capital revealed itself in Bangkok, where some mafia military-men have continued to engage in extortion for profit. One army general (with no close ties to the army commander) was arrested in 2014 and accused of taking 'protection money' from vendors in the night market of Patpong, Bangkok. He and his accomplices allegedly required monthly fees of 10,000 baht from watch dealers on the street, 5,000 baht from bag and leather products venders, and 2000 baht from stalls selling other goods (*Bangkok Post* 2014).

A final instance of indirect military economic power-seeking is NCPO Act 17/2015, under the purview of the Ministry of Natural Resources and Environment. The Act, designed to enhance investment and border trade along 10 of Thailand's border provinces, mandates through the use of Article 44 that 10 Special Economic Zones (SEZs) be created along Thailand's boundaries in the provinces of Tak and Kanchanaburi along the Thai–Myanmar border; Chiang Rai on the Thailand–Laos–

Myanmar border; Mukdaharn, Nong Khai and Nakhon Phanom on the Thailand–Laos border, Trat and Srakaeow on the Thailand–Cambodia border, and Songkhla and Narathiwat in Thailand's Deep South near the Thai–Malaysian border. All land necessary for the SEZs would become state-owned property (NCPO Order no.17/2015). In some cases (e.g. Srakaeow), the SEZ exists on land already owned by the RTA (*Bangkok Post* 2015). In other cases, the land for SEZs would informally come under the control of the military, at least while the junta continues to rule. Promises of industry deregulation, cheap labour and tax cuts are being used by the junta to lure investors. Finally, as a means of attracting mega-projects to Thai rural areas, the junta has halved the EIA (Environmental Impact Assessment) process, diminishing it from approximately 22 months to nine months (*Prachatai* 2015).

The regime's order regarding SEZs allows for the expropriation of land from Thai farmers (as well as their eviction) in areas intended to become economic zones to make way for agri-industrialists in the private sector (*Prachatai* 2016). Act 17/2015 gives individuals dispossessed of their land and livelihood little means of legal recourse except by a committee appointed by the junta, the decision of which is final. The junta decides which investors can 'develop' the land, which tends to limit the competition to junta cronies – foreign[19] or domestic – and junta members themselves. Rather than using Thais, companies in SEZs could outsource their labour to low-cost migrants – akin to contract farming. In the end, the strategy amounts to a form of regime-inspired land grabbing for investor profit.

In sum, in post 2014 Thailand, khaki capital continues to operate successfully across three different levels: institutional, factional, and individual. Perhaps, given the continuity of military rule, its involvement in the economy is likely to persist for years to come.

Conclusion

Though the age when Thailand's military controlled the commanding heights of the Thai economy are long gone, the post-2014 period has to some extent seen the resurgence of the armed forces' economic clout.

---

19. In this sense, foreign allies of the junta refer to those countries such as China, whose investors have become quite chummy with Thailand's military regime since 2014.

Indeed, khaki capital is alive and well in contemporary Thailand, and it shows no signs of dissipating under the current military rule.

At the beginning of this chapter, three questions were asked. What is the history of the Thai military's political economy? What are the formal and informal elements of Thai khaki capital today? How might the military's vast economic influence affect Thai democratization? In answer to the first question, the mission of the military since 1852 and especially since 1957 has been as a guardian and consolidator of the kingdom, protector in every way of the monarchy, champion against insurgency, and developer of the countryside. But over the years the military evolved in power, displacing the monarchy as the most prominent institution from 1932 to 1944, and from 1951 to 1957. In fact, 1932 marked a critical juncture – a booming upturn – for khaki capital. Then, in 1957, the coup by Sarit Thanarat facilitated a second critical juncture in political economy – a move along the path to a mutualization of economic interests between monarchy and military. Indeed, since 1957 and especially after 1973, a partnership between monarchy and military (with the latter as the junior partner) has ensured enormous political power for the armed forces. Though after 1992 it appeared that the military's clout had faded, the 2006 coup disrupted this downswing, embedding it again on an upward trajectory. The 2014 putsch has further entrenched the path of a powerful political economy for the Thai military. In answer to the second question, the formal elements of Thai khaki capital include the defence budget, sinecures, land, and military-owned enterprises. As for the informal dimension of khaki capital, there has been involvement by certain Thai security figures in mining, human trafficking, and other ventures, including corruption. Regarding the last question, the military's vast economic interests may have effects on Thai democratization. This might occur in two ways. First, given the dividends currently being enjoyed by senior military officials, the latter may seek to hinder a return to democracy – where opportunities for enhanced monitoring by elected civilians might lead to the weakening of military power. Second, under the current junta, less budgeting may be apportioned for the funding of any future political party, NGO, and other elements of civil society.

In 2016, junta deputy leader Prawit Wongsuwan declared that 'the military under the Defence Ministry gets revenue from people and we must repay people with our intellect and sacrifices to protect the country,' (Wassana, 17 March 2016). Yet the NCPO junta is a dictatorship. It usurped power from a government elected by a majority of Thai people and it rules Thailand with legal impunity. In fact, Thailand's military today is only beholden to the palace. Junta chief Prayuth recently stated that Thailand 'has seen so much trouble because we have had too much democracy,' (*Khaosod* 2015). His logic makes economic sense for the military: unlike dictatorships in Thailand, some Thai elected governments have tended to reduce the economic holdings of the military, creating troubles for it. However, the post-2014 Thai military needs not worry. Its path dependence of control over multiple economic privileges remains largely unrestrained. For the future, it is highly likely that its khaki capital will continue to grow, becoming the envy of other militaries in the region and beyond.

List of Acronyms

BOI	Board of Investment
FPBFP	Five Provinces Bordering Forest Preservation Foundation
KMT	Kuomintang
NBTC	National Broadcasting and Telecommunications Commission
NCPO	National Council for Peace and Order
NLA	National Legislative Assembly
RTA	Royal Thai Army
SEZ	Special Economic Zone
SOE	State-owned Enterprise
TMB	Thai Military Bank
TPT	Television Pool of Thailand
WVOT	War Veterans' Organization of Thailand

References

Adams, Brad (2014) 'Marking the Anniversary of the Cambodian Coup Attempt', *The Cambodia Daily* (2 July). https://www.cambodiadaily.com/opinion/marking-the-anniversary-of-the-cambodian-coup-attempt-62966/, accessed 2 August 2014.

Ahuja, Ambika (2010) 'Analysis: Thailand struggles against tide of corruption', *Reuters* (28 September). http: //mobile.reuters.com/article/idUS-TRE68R0RZ20100928, accessed 14 July 2016.

Ashida Sadao (1957) 'Is the Sarit administration secure? The General election in Thailand today', *Mainichi Shimbun* (15 December): 2.

Asian Human Rights Commission (2014) 'Thailand: Protect Human Rights Defenders Fighting Mining in Loei Province', 17 May 17, http: //protectionline.org/2014/05/17/thailand-protect-human-rightsdefenders-fighting-corporate-mining-in-loei-province, accessed 14 November 2015.

ASTV ผู้จัดการสุดสัปดาห์ [Manager Weekend] (2015) 'ตั้งหลักลุยต่อ "ภาษีที่ดิน" คนจน-เศรษฐี ยังมีหนาว [Reaching a Settlement of the 'Land Tax' Poor-Weathy Still have a Chill]' (21 March (http://www.manager.co.th/AstvWeekend/ViewNews.aspx?NewsID=9580000032947, accessed 2 January 2016.

Baker, Chris and Pasuk Pongpaichit (2009) *A History of Thailand*. Cambridge: Cambridge University Press.

Bangkok Post (2014) 'Seh James charged in Patpong case', (6 August). http: //www.bangkokpost.com/news/politics/425211/seh-james-charged-in-patpong-case, accessed 8 August 2014.

——— (2015) 'Rajabhakti Park figure 'flees country'', 12 November , http://www.bangkokpost.com/archive/rajabhakti-park-figure-flees-country/761924, accessed 2 January 2016.

Booth, Martin (2013) *Opium: A History*. New York: St. Martin's Griffin.

Bowles, Chester (1952) 'Top Secret Telegram from US Ambassador to India Chester Bowles to the Department of State', *Foreign Relations of the United States 1952–1954*, Vol. XII, Part 2, 'East Asia and the Pacific' (in two parts), Document 17 (19 March). https: //history.state.gov/historical-documents/frus1952-54v12p2/d17, accessed 14 March 2016.

Bureau of the Budget (2016) 'Thailand's Budget in Brief Fiscal Year 2016', Bangkok: Bureau of the Budget.

Chai-Anan Samudavanija (1982) *The Thai Young Turks*, Singapore: Institute of Southeast Asian Studies.

——— (1987) 'Political History', in *Government and Politics of Thailand*. Oxford: Oxford University Press.

Campbell, Charlie (2013) 'How Thailand's Meddlesome Military Got Tired of Meddling', *Time* (10 December). http: //world.time.com/2013/12/10/how-thailands-meddlesome-military-got-tired-of-meddling/, accessed 2 January 2016.

Chambers, Paul (2013) 'A Short History of Military Influence in Thailand', in Paul Chambers (ed.) *Knights of the Realm: Thailand's Military and Police, Then and Now*. Bangkok: White Lotus Press.

——— (2015) 'Thailand Must End its Own Rohingya Atrocity', *The Diplomat*,

October, http: //thediplomat.com/2015/10/thailand-must-end-its-own-rohingya-atrocity/, accessed 1 December 2016.

Chambers, Paul and Napisa Waitoolkiat (2016) 'The Resilience of Monarchised Military in Thailand', *Journal of Contemporary Asia* 46(3). https: //journalofcontemporaryasia.wordpress.com/2016/03/23/mon-archised-military-in-thailand/, accessed 8 September 2016.

Chang Noi (1998) 'The Nation: Chavalit and the Salwee', (12 March). http: //www.burmalibrary.org/reg.burma/archives/199803/msg00122.html, accessed 2 February 2016.

Channel Five, http://www.tv5.co.th/web-2015-07-RES2/index.php, accessed 7 January 2016.

Channel Seven, http: //www.ch7.com, accessed 7 January 2016.

Chouvy, Pierre-Arnaud (2009) *Opium: Uncovering the Politics of the Poppy.* Cambridge, MA: Harvard University Press.

CNN (2013) 'Thai navy sues Phuketwan journalists over Rohingya trafficking report', (23 December). http: //edition.cnn.com/2013/12/22/world/asia/thailand-media-defamation, accessed 12 January 2014.

Conboy, Kenneth (2013) *The Cambodian Wars: Clashing Armies and CIA Covert Operations.* Lawrence, Kansas: University Press of Kansas.

Crispin, Shawn (2017) 'New Reign Takes Hold in Thailand', *Asia Times* (25 January). http://www.atimes.com/article/new-reign-takes-hold-thailand/, accessed 2 February 2017.

Draper, John (2015) 'Prem Calls for "Optimum Benefits" from Military Budget', *Prachatai* (26 November(. http://prachatai.org/english/node/5642.

Erlanger, Steven (1988) 'Thai Army Denies Skimming Sihanouk Fund', *The New York Times* (2 November). http: //www.nytimes.com/1988/11/02/world/thai-amy-denies-skimming-sihanouk-fund.html, accessed 19 November 2015.

Fernquist, John (2016) 'Independent Directors and Failure of Corporate Governance', *Bangkok Post* (12 April). http: //www.bangkokpost.com/learning/learning-from-news/929753/independent-directors-failure-of-corporate-governance, accessed 2 May 2016.

Ferrara, Federico (2015) *The Political Development of Modern Thailand.* Cambridge: Cambridge University Press.

Five Provinces Bordering Forest Preservation Project, http://www.5provincesforest.com/index.php?lay=show&ac=article&Ntype=4&Id=538680558, accessed 9 March 2017.

Freedom House (2008) 'Press Freedom: Thailand'. http: //www.freedom-house.org/template.cfm?page=251&year=2008, accessed 3 March 1015.

Gibson, Richard Michael (2011) *The Secret Army: Chiang Kai-shek and the*

Drug Warlords of the Golden Triangle. Hoboken, New Jersey: John Wiley & Sons.

Global Witness (2003) 'A Conflict of Interests: the Uncertain Future of Burma's Forests', (October). https://www.globalwitness.org/en/archive/conflict-interest-english/, accessed 12 April 2017.

Government Gazette (2015) Announcement of the Prime Minister's Office, 'The Members of the National Reform Steering Assembly', Book 3, Vol. 239 (5 October). http://www.ratchakitcha.soc.go.th/DATA/PDF/2558/E/239/3.PDF, accessed 2 January 2017.

———— (2015) 'Budget Act for Fiscal Year 2016', Vol. 132, Number 91 (25 September). http://www.ratchakitcha.soc.go.th/DATA/PDF/2558/A/091/17.PDF, accessed 17 March 2016.

———— (2016) Announcement of the NCPO Number 1/2016, 'The Appointments of the NCPO', Book 133, Vol. 221 (30 September). http://www.ratchakitcha.soc.go.th/DATA/PDF/2559/E/221/32.PDF, accessed 2 November 2016.

Graham, W.A. (1924) *Siam.* London: Alexander Moring, Ltd.

Grainger, Matthew (1996) 'Chavalit factor mooted in timber politics', *Phnom Penh Post* (20 September). http://www.phnompenhpost.com/national/chavalit-factor-mooted-timber-politics, accessed 14 October 2015.

———— (1996) 'Thais Forced to Play Key Role in Breaking the KR', *Phnom Penh Post* (23 August). http://www.phnompenhpost.com/national/thais-forced-play-key-role-breaking-kr, accessed 13 October 2015.

Handley, Paul (2006) *The King Never Smiles.* New Haven: Yale University Press.

Hewison, Kevin and Kengkij Kitirianlarb (2010) 'Thai-Style Democracy: The Royalist Struggle for Thailand's Politics', in Soren Ivarson and Lotte Isager (eds) *Saying the Unsayable: Monarchy and Democracy in Thailand.* Copenhagen: NIAS.

Human Rights Watch (1995) Cambodia at War (Asia/Arms Project) (1 March) http://www.refworld.org/docid/3ae6a7dd8.html, accessed 2 February 2017.

IISS (International Institute for Strategic Studies) (2011) *Military Balance.* London: Routledge.

Ilaw, (2017) 'ใครออกกฎหมาย? 1: สภาทหาร-สภาผลประโยชน์» เมื่อคนใกล้ชิดผู้นำประเทศ อยู่เต็ม สนช' [Who issued the law? 1: 'Assembly of Soldiers-Assembly of Interests' when the Premier's Close Circle sits in the National Legislative Assembly'] (5 February) https://ilaw.or.th/node/4407, accessed 3 March 2017.

Isranews (2012) 'เปิดหลักฐาน'องคมนตรี-กองทัพบก'โยงขายที่ดิน'บึกบัง-เมียคนที่ 2', (29 May). http: //isranews.org/lastest-news/71-investigate/6935--2--sp-1972874329.html, accessed 1 August 2015.

————— (2013) 'เจาะขุมทรัพย์ 'ททบ.5' โดยประชาสัมพันธ์หน่วยงานรัฐ 97 ล้าน', (29 June). http: //www.isranews.org, accessed 5 May 2015.

Intouch Company (n.d.) 'Definitions and Qualifications of Independent Directors', Enclosure 6, http://www.intouchcompany.com/IR/shin/agm_shin/agm_shin_2551/Enclosure%206-%E0%B8%81%E0%B8%A3%E0%B8%A3%E0%B8%A1%E0%B8%81%E0%B8%B2%E0%B8%A3%E0%B8%AD%E0%B8%B4%E0%B8%AA%E0%B8%A3%E0%B8%B0-E-Tim-20-3-2008.pdf, accessed 14 February 2016.

Kanda Naknoi (2012) 'เศรษฐศาสตร์สามัญสำนึก 55 ปีทุนกองทัพไทย (ตอนที่ 1)', (25 March). http: //www.matichon.co.th/news_detail.php?newsid=1332607776, accessed 16 May 2016.

————— (2012) 'เศรษฐศาสตร์สามัญสำนึก 55 ปีทุนกองทัพไทย (ตอนที่ 2)', *Prachatai* (25 April). http: //www.prachatai.com/journal/2012/04/40226, accessed 16 May 2016.

————— (2015) 'ทุนกองทัพไทย (3) : ที่ดินกองทัพบก', *Prachatai* (1 June). http: //prachatai.com/journal/2015/06/59565, accessed 3 June 2015.

Khaosod (2016) 'ป.ป.ช. เปิดบัญชีทรัพย์สิน 3 สนช.เข้ารับตำแหน่งใหม่ "บิ๊กช้าง" แจ้งรายรับอู้ฟู่ปีละ 5 ล้าน' ['National Anti-Corruption Commission reveals the accounts/assets of the three new National Legislative Assembly members taking the new positions; 'General Chang' declares his enormous income of five million baht per year'], (5 April). https://www.khaosod.co.th/featured/news_285231, accessed 19 May 2016.

Khaosod (2015) 'Junta Leader Blames Thai Crisis on "Too Much Democracy"', (23 March). http: //www.khaosodenglish.com/detail.php?newsid=1427094707, accessed 2 April 2015.

Kocak, Dennis and Johannes Kode (2014) 'Impediments to Security Sector Reform in Thailand', in Felix Heiduk (ed.) *Security Sector Reform in Southeast Asia*. London: Palgrave/Macmillan.

Kriangchai Pungprawat (2009) 'Budgeting system and bureau of the budget in Thailand', *Chulalongkorn Journal of Economics* 21(1): 9–71.

Krisada Suphawattanakul (2013) จำแหละที่ดินเมืองไทยวันน้อยอยู่ในมือใคร ไม่ใช้ประโยชน์-เสียหายปีละ 1.3แสนล้าน, *TCIJ*, (17 September). http: //tcijthai.com/tcijthainews/view.php?ids=3085, accessed 20 September 2013.

Johnson, (1959) 'Letter From the Ambassador in Thailand (Johnson) to the Director of the Office of Southeast Asian Affairs (Kocher)', *Foreign Relations of the United States 1958–1960*, Vol. XV, South and Southeast Asia, Document 522, Department of State, Central Files, 892.53 (29 June). https: //history.state.gov/historicaldocuments/frus1958-60v15/d522#fn1, accessed 17 August 2015.

Lewis, Gwen (2007) *Virtual Thailand: The Media, and Cultural Politics in Thailand, Malaysia and Singapore*, London: Routledge.

Lumpini Boxing Stadium, http: //www.muaythailumpinee.net/history.php, accessed 8 April 2016; http: //www.muaythailumpini.com/Index-th. html, accessed 8 April 2016.

Manager Magazine (1992) 'ทำไม! กองทัพในแบงก์ทหารไทยไม่มีวันแยกจากไปเด็ดขาด', (July). http: //info.gotomanager.com/news/details.aspx?id=6700, accessed 8 February 2014.

Manager Online (2012) 'ราชนาวีพลูตาหลวง สนามคลาสสิกฝั่งทะเลตะวันออก' ['Plutaluang Navy Classic Golf Course on the East Coast], 14 June, http://www.manager.co.th/Golf/ViewNews.aspx?NewsID=9550000073108, accessed 9 April 2017.

Matichon (2017) 'สแกนจุดอ่อน 'บิ๊กป้อม' กลางศึก รอบทิศของ 'บิ๊กตู่' กับ ภารกิจร้อนๆวัดฝีมือบิ๊ก เจี๊ยบ และความหวังของตท.18' ['Scan the Weakness of Gen. Prawit in the Middle of Omni-Directional Battles of Gen. Prayut, the Performance of Gen. Chalermchai and Prospects of Military Pre-Cadet Class 18'], Number 1903 (3–9 February): 14–16.

Maikaew, Piyachart (2015) 'SEZ Welcome, with Reservations', *Bangkok Post* (19 October). http: //www.bangkokpost.com/print/734912/, accessed 17 January 2017.

McCoy, Alfred, with Cathleen B. Read and Leonard P.Adams II (1972) *The Politics of Heroin in Southeast Asia*. New York: Harper & Row.

Ministry of Finance (Thailand) 'Pool of Names Eligible to Sit on the SOEs from 2008 until 2015'. http: //www2.mof.go.th/, accessed 5 February 2016.

MuayThai 2000, 'Rajadumnern boxing stadium'. http: //www.muaythai2000. com/muaythai2000/rachadumnern.php, accessed 5 April 2013. *Naew Na* (2016) 'A Dissertation about Slush Funds', 13 April, http: //www.naewna. com/politic/columnist/18937, accessed 19 April 2016.

Neher, Clarke, ed. (1976) *Modern Thai Politics: From Village to Nation*, Cambridge, MA: Schenkman Publishing Co.

New Democracy Movement (2015) 'Moving Beyond', (November).

ONBTC (Office of National Broadcasting and Telecommunications Commission) (2016) https://broadcast.nbtc.go.th/home/, accessed 8 January 2017.

Order of the Head of the National Council for Peace and Order (NCPO) (2015) no.17/2015 on the Expropriation of Land for the Development of Special Economic Zone, (May 5).

PimThaiOnline (2016) 'สกู๊ปเด่นประจำสัปดาห์ 'ศูนย์พัฒนากีฬากองทัพบก' รามอินทรา' [Scoop of the Week: 'Royal Thai Army Sports Center' Ramindra', 17 February, http://www.pimthaionline.com/html/modules.php?name=hots&file=popup&asid=152, accessed 8 May 2016.

Political Prisoners in Thailand (2014) 'Protecting the Corrupt', (11 October). https: //thaipoliticalprisoners.wordpress.com/2014/10/11/protecting-the-corrupt/, accessed 15 December 2015.

Prachatai (2014) "บิ๊กตู่ Big Ass' สำรวจเก้าอี้ที พล.อ. .ประยุทธ์ ดำรงตำแหน่งอยู่' [Big Tu, Big Ass: Surveying the Chairmanships Given to Gen. Prayuth'], (23 August). https://prachatai.com/journal/2014/08/55196, accessed 17 June 2015.

——— (2015) 'Thai government to cut short EIAs for mega projects', (11 April). http://www.prachatai.com/english/node/5585, accessed 14 March 2016.

——— (2016) 'Thai junta to push eviction for special economic zones on northern border', (22 September). http: //www.prachatai.com/english/node/5483, accessed 29 October 2016.

Prachachat Turakij (2014) 'เปิดตระกูลดังตุนที่ดินทั่วไทย 'เจริญ'อู้ฟู่6.3แสนไร่ ระทึกคลังชง เก็บภาษี', (18 June). http: //www.prachachat.net/news_detail.php?newsid =1403008576, accessed 14 January 2015.

Puangthong Rungswasdisab (2011) *Thailand's Response to the Cambodian Genocide*, Cambodian Genocide Program, Yale University. http: //www. yale.edu/cgp/thailand_response.html, accessed 19 April 2013.

Riggs, Fred (1966) *Thailand: The Modernization of a Bureaucratic Polity*. Honolulu: East-West Center Press.

Roughol, Isabelle (2008) 'Border Standoff Echoes 1980s Thai-Lao Conflict', *The Cambodia Daily* (28 October). https: //www.cambodiadaily.com/archives/border-standoff-echoes-1980s-thai-lao-conflict-62276/, accessed 13 March 2009.

Royal Thai Army Radio and Television Station, http: //app.tv5.co.th/history/, accessed 9 May 2016.

RYT9.com (2004) 'รายงานผลการสอบข้อเท็จจริงกรณีสถานีวิทยุโทรทัศน์กองทัพบก ช่อง 5, (ททบ.) 5', (29 September). http: //www.ryt9.com/s/cabt/153128, accessed 2 February 2015.

Scott, Peter Dale (2010) *American War Machine: Deep Politics, the CIA Global Drug Connection, and the Road to Afghanistan*. Lanham, Maryland: Rowman & Littlefield Publishers.

Shenon, Philip (1993) 'Pol Pot & Co.: The Thai Connection – A Special Report – In Big Threat to Cambodia, Thais Still Aid Khmer Rouge', *The New York Times* (19 December). http: //www.nytimes.com/1993/12/19/world/pol-pot-thai-connection-special-report-big-threat-cambodia-thais-still-aid-khmer.html?pagewanted=all, accessed 8 April 2015.

Siam Sport (2011) 'อาร์มีเปิดตัวเปลี่ยนฉายาสุภาพบุรุษกงจักร', (15 February). http: //www.siamsport.co.th/Sport_Football/110215_001.html, accessed 14 September 2016.

SIPRI (Stockholm International Peace Research Institute) (2016) 'Sipri Military Expenditure Database'. Stockholm, various years (Excel Sheet), http: //www.sipri.org/research/armaments/milex/milex, accessed 20 January 2017.

Skinner, G. William (1958) *Leadership and Power in the Chinese Community of Thailand*. Ithaca: Cornell University Press.

Suchit Bunbongkarn (1987) 'Political Institutions and Processes', in Somsakdi Xuto, ed., *Government and Politics of Thailand*. Singapore: Oxford University Press: 41–74.

Suehiro, Akira (1992) 'Capitalist Development in Postwar Thailand: Commercial Bankers, Industrial Elite and Agribusiness Groups', in Ruth McVey (ed.) *Southeast Asian Capitalists*. Ithaca: Cornell University Press.

Surachart Bamrungsuk, (1988) *United States Foreign Policy and Thai Military Rule 1947–1977*. Bangkok: Editions Duang Kamol.

Takahashi, Katsuyuki (2014) *The Peace Movement During the Early Cold War Years in Asia*. Tokyo: Waseda University Press (in Japanese).

———— (2016) 'The Ratchapak Park Scandal that Shocked the Thai Junta', *Taikoku Joho*, 50(1):49–59 (in Japanese).

Teedin2 (2013) 'Land Sale Announcement', (14 May). http://www.teedin2.com/detail/2614.html, accessed 5 February 2015.

Thai Bev (2014) 'ไทยเบฟสนับสนุนมูลนิธิอนุรักษ์ป่ารอยต่อ 5 จังหวัด' [Thai Bev supports the Five Provinces Bordering Forest Preservation Foundation], (25 August). http://www.thaibev.com/en08/detailnews.aspx?ngID=1032&tngID=2, accessed 12 March 2015.

thai-fussball (2016) 'Army United'. http://www.thai-fussball.com/en/Content-Army-United-item-17.html, accessed 3 January 2017.

Thai Life Insurance, http://www.thailife.com/, accessed 10 April 2016.

Thai Military Bank, https://www.tmbbank.com, accessed 7 March 2016.

Thai Military Bank, Annual Report of Meeting among the shareholders of TMB, Annual Report of Thai Military Bank, 2003–2015. https://www.tmbbank.com/ir/fin_info/annualreport, accessed 8 March 2016.

Thai Post (2009) 'Mafia Soldiers never die', (9 May). http://www.thaipost.net/news/090509/4390, accessed 30 September 2013.

Thaipublica (2014) 'เปรียบเทียบเงินเดือน "คมช. – คสช." หลังรัฐประหาร 2549/ 2557 นายกรัฐมนตรี-ประธาน สนช. ได้เท่ากัน 125,590 บาท' ['Comparing Salary of Council of National Security and the National Council for Peace and Order post-coup 2006/2014 Prime Minister-Head of National Legislative Assembly receive equal amounts of salary 125,590 baht'], 14 November, http://thaipublica.org/2014/11/personal-income-in-thailand-3/, accessed 1 April 2017.

Thaipublica (2015) 'เปิดรายชื่อ โควตาคนขายหวย ฉบับสมบูรณ์', (11 June). http://thaipublica.org/2015/06/lottery-16/, accessed 6 July 2015.

Thairath (2014) 'สนามมวยลุมพินี รามอินทรา' เลือด ศักดิ์ศรี และชัยชนะ!', (10 March). http://www.thairath.co.th/content/408786, accessed 8 April 2014.

————(2015) 'บิ๊กโด่ง' ทุ่มงบ 120 ล้าน ดัน 'อาร์มีๆ' ยึดแถวหน้าไทยลีก 2015', (11 February). http://www.thairath.co.th/content/480614, accessed 13 February 2015.

———— (2015) 'Wissanu Views it as not Strange that Five New NACC Members are Close to the Regime', 21 October, http: //www.thairath.co.th/content/533949?utm_source=CPBee&utm_medium=twitter, accessed 23 October 2015.

Thak Chaloemtiarana (2007) *Thailand: The Politics of Despotic Paternalism.* Ithaca: Cornell Southeast Asia Program.

Thayer, Nate (1995) 'Cambodia: Asia's New Narco-State? Medellin on the Mekong', *Far Eastern Economic Review* (23 November). http: //www.nate-thayer.com/cambodia-asias-new-narco-state-medellin-on-the-mekong/, accessed 17 May 2015.

The Nation (2016) 'Preecha Stands Firm by Wife and Son Amid Controversies', (20 September) http://www.nationmultimedia.com/news/national/30295738, accessed 22 September 2016.

TNews (2015) 'เจาะลึก!!! โควต้าสลากกินแบ่งรัฐบาล 74 ล้านฉบับ', (5 May). http: //www.tnews.co.th/html/content/140905/, accessed 1 January 2016.

Ubonrat Siriyuvasak (2002) *Thailand Media Profile.* http://www.freedom.commarts.chula.ac.th/articles/FXSU02-Thailand_media_profile_2002.pdf, accessed 12 April 2017.

———— (2008) 'Media Reform in Thailand', *Campaign for Popular Media Reform*, 18 February, http: //www.media4democracy.com/eng/PDF_file/Media%20reform%202008.pdf, accessed 21 March 2009.

Ukrist Pathmanand (2008) 'A Different Coup d'Etat?' *Journal of Contemporary Asia* 38(1).

Waitoolkiat, Napisa and Paul Chambers (2013), 'Khaki Veto Power: The Organization of Thailand's Armed Forces', in Paul Chambers (ed.), *Knights of the Realm: Thailand's Military and Police, Then and Now.* Bangkok: White Lotus Press.

Watts, Jake Maxwell and Nopparat Chaichalearmmongkol (2014) 'In Thailand a Struggle for Control of State Firms', *Wall Street Journal* (17 June). http: //www.wsj.com/articles/in-thailand-a-struggle-for-control-of-state-firms-1402930180, accessed 19 June 2014.

Wassana Nanuam (2016) 'Prawit Says Defence Purchases Graft-Free', *Bangkok Post* (17 March). http: //www.bangkokpost.com/news/politics/900264/prawit-says-defence-purchases-graft-free, accessed 18 November 2016.

Wilson, David (1962) *Politics in Thailand.* Ithaca: Cornell University Press.

WVOT (The War Veterans' Organization of Thailand Under the Royal Patronage of his Majesty the King). http: //www.thaiveterans.mod.go.th/index_th.html, accessed 5 October 2017.

Yoshihara, Kunio (1988) *The Rise of Ersatz Capitalism in Southeast Asia.* Singapore: Oxford University Press.

CHAPTER 3

The NLD–Military Coalition in Myanmar
Military Guardianship and Its Economic Foundations

Marco Bünte

Not so long ago, Myanmar's military regime was widely regarded as an exception.[1] Whereas military regimes worldwide were giving way to multi-party democracies in the 1980s and 1990s, the military regime in Myanmar, ruling directly since 1988, withstood that trend. Although far from being considered legitimate internally or internationally, the military junta remained unusually stable. Myanmar's armed forces (Tatmadaw) were often described as a 'state within a state' (Steinberg 2001: 74) or as a 'garrison state' following Harold Laswell's concept of militaries as 'masters of violence' usurping state power (Laswell 1941). Some scholars went even further and portrayed Myanmar's military as *the* state, given its deep penetration of the regime, the economy and the society (Steinberg 2007). Steinberg once suggested that Myanmar might even be 'the most militarized society in the contemporary world' (ibid.: 127). The presence of men in uniform in the regime's top decision-making positions, and the military as an economic actor with a huge share in the national economy (including companies, factories, land titles and investments), with ownership of monasteries, schools and charities – all this illustrates the deep permeation of the military into fundamental aspects of the state and the society. The many Western observers who see the military's deep penetration as an anomaly fail to acknowledge that this situation might be the result of decades of anti-colonial struggles and efforts at nation building – struggles that often led

---

1. Burma was renamed in 1989. The chapter uses 'Burma' to refer to the country before 1989, Myanmar thereafter.

to an interventionist military, if we think for instance of Indonesia before 1998, Pakistan, Thailand or Myanmar (Chambers 2013; Koonings & Kruijt 2002; Rüland, Manea & Born 2012; Mietzner 2012).

Yet, since 2011 we have also witnessed astonishing reforms in Myanmar. After 22 years of direct military rule, the junta (the State Peace and Development Council) formally handed over power to a 'civilian' government in March 2011. To the surprise of many, President Thein Sein (previously a high-ranking member of the former military junta) introduced a far- reaching liberalization of the political system: political prisoners were released, censorship was abolished and new political freedoms were established. These reforms culminated in the free and fair elections of 8 November 2015, in which the oppositional National League for Democracy (NLD) under the leadership of Aung San Suu Kyi won a landslide. Though some of these reforms were planned well before, to facilitate an exit for long-term strongman Senior General Than Shwe and to ease the competition in the upper echelons of the military (Bünte 2014), the extent of these reforms surprised many. The International Crisis Group already speculated that the military's reform path might lead to its 'return to the barracks' (ICG 2014).

How real are these changes and how far do they go? How could the military become so entrenched in politics, the economy and society? How can we characterize civil–military relations today, six years after the introduction of reforms? What are the economic foundations of military rule and to what extent have these been reformed? I argue that the military has established a guardianship over the political system, shielding and protecting its political power. Although the military is not ruling directly and has withdrawn from certain segments of the government and administration, it is guarding the political system from a position of strength. Still a vital part of the political game, it is providing checks on civilian politicians and has shored up its position in the economy. During the past two decades, the military has been able to dominate the political system and, in so doing, has generated valuable income for both military modernization and personal enrichment of senior military officers. This coercion-intensive period has not only allowed the military to build up institutions that provide it with tools to monitor and influence elected politicians, but also to stifle the growth of counterweight forces in civil society. Additionally, the military has consolidated its dominant position in the economy to meet its corporate needs and, thus, potentially profit from the current economic opening.

This study follows Siddiqa's understanding of guardianship as a form of military capital that is used for military benefit. Accordingly, the military has 'carved out a permanent role for itself in governance and politics' (Siddiqa 2008: 69). The study is organized into four parts: First, it outlines the evolution of military rule and its economic foundations throughout the country's most important critical junctures. Second, it gives an overview over the changes that happened since the transition to civilian rule since 2011, in order to characterize the current state of civil–military relations and discuss whether these reforms represent a new critical juncture. Third, it looks into the formal and informal sources of 'khaki capital' before and after the transition to civilian rule in 2011, in order to show how the military institutionalized its control of the Myanmar economy and reformed it since then. Finally, the chapter concludes by discussing several scenarios on the future of military guardianship.

The path towards military control in Burma/Myanmar

The trajectory of civil–military relations in Burma/Myanmar has been shaped by several critical junctures which have not only brought an overall dominance of the military in politics and the economy, but also affected the military's mindset and willingness to share power and resources with civilians. These critical junctures help also to explain why and how the military institutionalized its control of Myanmar's economy. Three critical junctures, defined as 'short, time-defined periods, where antecedent conditions allow contingent choices that set a specific trajectory of institutional modification that is difficult to reverse' (Page 2006: 8), have shaped the country's institutional development: the formation of the modern Tatmadaw (Burmese army) and the fight for national independence from the British, the outbreak of regionalist rebellions in the early post-independence period, and the breakdown of the civil–military coalition leading to General Ne Win's coup in 1962. The period that followed with the rise and fall of Ne Win's socialist military regime (1962–88) does not represent a critical juncture but a continuing involvement of the military in political affairs, albeit under a different institutional environment and economic foundation. The period between 1962 and 1988 also witnessed the deepening of civil war between the military and the ethnic rebel armies and the nationalization and isolation of the Burmese economy. After the 1988 student demonstrations, the regime evolved into a military oligarchy. The period from 1988–2011 was characterized by a deepening of the military's role in the political and economic spheres. At the same time, the military was able to come to an agreement with some of the ethnic armed organizations. Before we start to discuss, whether the changes 2011 represent another critical juncture, let us take a closer look at these critical periods and how they have affected the military as an institution as well as how they have shaped civil–military relations.

The birth of the modern army, rebellion and the demise of the first civil–military coalition
The first critical juncture can be seen in the struggle for national independence, which laid the groundwork for a political and military role of the army. Aung San and a group of young nationalists founded the army in 1941. Originally trained and supported by the Japanese, the Burmese Independence Army (BIA) was involved in the Japanese invasion of Burma in 1942, but turned their back against its sponsors later and fought a guerrilla war against Tokyo (Callahan 2001). After the return of the British, the BIA was integrated into the Burma Army under British control. Although offered a senior position in the army, Aung San declined in favour of becoming the president of the Anti-Fascist People's Freedom League (AFPFL), an umbrella organization of diverse nationalist groups and parties, and the military leader of the People's Volunteer Organisation. He was able to control a huge number of loyal soldiers and armed volunteers and to maintain pressure on the British colonial administration, which finally retreated and granted Burma independence in 1948. As the formation of the Burmese Army preceded the existence of an independent state and the officer corps was politicized as a liberating force during the struggle for national independence, the army could retroactively claim the role of a guardian of the Burmese state and bulwark of national independence (Callahan 2001; 2003). The overlap of politics and military affairs continued during the immediate post-independence period, since many officers were affiliated with the AFPFL. Others were closely attached to the Communist Party, which also had a mixed civilian-military leadership. The rebellions of

the Arakanese Mujahidin, the Karen and the communist group after the departure of the British hit the young army unprepared. Being organised along ethnic lines, the armed forces lost a huge number of troops and much of its territory beyond Rangoon. Both army and state nearly collapsed. The outbreak of these insurgencies had devastating consequences and triggered the institutional modernization of the armed forces, imbued soldiers with a praetorian ethos and led to an increasing centralization of political power and capital in military realms (Taylor 1985; Callahan 2001; 2003). However, the union government gradually expanded its territorial control beyond Rangoon and strengthened its command structure under the leadership of General Ne Win. Although the weak state became dependent on the army, the military accepted the supremacy of the U Nu government and the 1947 constitution, which enshrined civilian control over military expenditures, security policies and senior promotions (Callahan 2001: 414). However, unlike its Thai or Indonesian counterparts, the Burmese army did not develop its own business network at this point in time (Taylor 1985: 28).

In the early 1950s, the external threat posed by Kuomintang troops intruding from China triggered the modernization and further strengthening of the army. Also, democratic civilian control gave way to what Janowitz calls a civil–military coalition. The military increasingly took over administrative and civilian functions and claimed one-third to one-half of the national budget for internal security. New organs such as the Military Planning Staff, the Defence Service Institute (DSI) and the Psychological Warfare Directorate were created. These organizational reforms brought about improvements in military doctrine, training, logistics and welfare (Callahan 2003: 159). The Defence Service Institute was established to provide consumer goods to members of the armed forces. This business slowly extended to include a range of other economic activities such as banking, shipping, trading, publishing and retail businesses, leading Aung Myoe to conclude that the DSI became 'the largest commercial enterprise in Myanmar' as early as the end of the 1950s (Myoe 2009: 174). The income generated from these businesses was utilized for the welfare of soldiers and their families.

The political role of the military widened gradually until 1958, when the civil–military coalition broke down. Increasing factionalism within the ruling AFPFL led to a split between the new 'Clean AFPFL' led by

Prime Minister U Nu and the 'Stable AFPFL' faction led by Ba Swe and Kyaw Nein. Both factions launched fierce campaigns to rally supporters and local militias behind them. This split also led to growing parliamentary instability; U Nu barely survived a no-confidence motion in the Constituent Assembly in June 1958. When polarization increased and spilled over into the army, General Ne Win urged the civilian government of Prime Minister U Nu to transfer power temporarily to the armed forces. Although the Ne Win's 'Caretaker Government' returned power back to civilians in February 1960, the General staged a coup in March 1962, which brought army leaders back into power and 'eliminated their civilian counterparts once and for all' (Callahan 2001: 422). According to the official army rhetoric, U Nu's decision to make Buddhism the state religion, along with the calls by ethnic groups for greater autonomy and secession from the union prepared the groundwork for the 1962 military intervention. During this period, the officer corps developed a praetorian ethos, grounded in the belief that it was more effective than its civilian counterparts. The deeply rooted beliefs that civilian politicians are untrustworthy and the military is above disruptive 'party politics' have been among of the most important and recurrent narratives of the military leadership to this day.

The rise and fall of Ne Win's military–socialist regime
In 1962, General Ne Win formed a 17-man Revolutionary Council of senior military officers, which ruled the country by fiat until 1974. It abolished the 1947 Constitution, dissolved Parliament, banned all political parties and barred civil organisations (with the exception of religious organisations). Under the banner of the 'Burmese Way to Socialism', the military nationalized the economy and expropriated private industries and businesses. It set up its own Leninist party, the Burmese Socialist Programme Party (BSPP), which ran the country unchallenged for over 25 years. The military became the backbone of the socialist one-party state (1974–88). It permeated both party and civil bureaucracy: all save one of the members of the BSPP Central Executive Committee from 1971 to 1985 were active or retired military officers (Nakanashi 2013: 167). Ne Win was both party chairman and president. Based on his personal influence in the army and the party, he kept his subordinates divided and controlled all potential rivals through regular purges. Formally, the party controlled the military institution.

However, through informal channels Ne Win controlled both party and the military by providing retiring military officers with positions in the BSPP or civilian ministries. Party and civilian bureaucracy in this way extended the career paths of retired military officers, thus easing generational pressures within the army and laying the foundation for its extraordinary stability (Nakanashi 2013).

In the socialist era, the military was required to refrain from commercial activities. It nonetheless continued on a very small scale, in order to address the welfare needs of soldiers and their families. Individual units engaged in the production of basic commodities. For instance, battalions grew rice and vegetables and raised poultry and fish, and ran cottage industries (Myoe 2009: 175). However, it was only after the military's takeover of the state in September 1988 that its commercial interests were revived on a larger scale.

The harsh economic and political measures introduced by the Ne Win regime in the 1960s further exacerbated ethnic conflicts. While the Tatmadaw was able to reassert some control over the heartland, communist and ethnic insurgencies spread rapidly in the rest of the country. The army fought relentless counterinsurgency campaigns, often brutally effective, and drove ethnic rebel groups closer to the border regions (Smith 1999: 261). In the 1970s and 1980s, much of the borderlands continued to be controlled by ethnic armies, since these terrains often proved to be inaccessible for the Tatmadaw. The army's offensive arrived at a deadlock and, as a consequence, combat fighters developed the perception that the army was left with insufficient resources to fight these insurgencies. Moreover, for its part, the 186,000-strong national army was regarded as insufficiently equipped, trained and poorly funded (Callahan 2003: 210).

Ne Win's military-backed, socialist one-party regime crumbled from within during 1987–88, when the country was facing a severe economic crisis. In order to stop inflation and put an end to black market activities, the government decided overnight to devalue the country's 25, 35 and 75 kyat currency notes in September 1987. Ne Win introduced 45 and 90 kyat notes, which were multiples of 9, which was his lucky number and which was astrologically assured to enable him to live up to 90. The devaluation came without warning or compensation and rendered more than 70 percent of the country's currency worthless. Further economic mismanagement led to massive student demonstrations in 1988, which forced General Ne Win to resign as party chairman in July of that year. The protests escalated into a broad-based countrywide movement that continued until September 1988, when the military reorganized itself, staged a coup and brutally cracked down on the movement, killing thousands of demonstrators (Steinberg 2001: 3–12; Lintner 1990). The State Law and Order Restoration Council (SLORC) coup re-established direct military rule on 18 September 1988. Under the leadership of Saw Maung, the military revoked the 1974 Constitution, dissolved parliament and concentrated all executive, legislative and judicial powers in the hands of the SLORC. When seizing power, the junta promised to hand over control after holding fresh multi-party elections. Although elections were called for May 1990, the military council failed to acknowledge the results, which had ended in a landslide victory for the oppositional NLD. Acting in the manner of a caretaker government, the military argued that the country lacked a constitution for transferring power to a new government. The junta, led after 1992 by a new strongman, Senior General Than Shwe and renamed State Peace and Development Council (SPDC) in 1997, stayed in power until March 2011.

Militarization of the state and economy: military oligarchy 1988–2011
SLORC's coup was followed by direct military rule for more than two decades. It continued Ne Win's military government without the civilian and socialist veneer (Prager Nyein 2012: 26). SLORC's first announcement in September 1988 laid out its long-term vision to stage multi-party elections 'after peace, order and the economy had been restored' (SLORC 1988). However, the junta leadership saw the Tatmadaw as ill equipped to achieve these goals. Feeling threatened by an urban democracy movement that might collaborate with ethnic insurgent groups and foreign powers, the junta felt a strong need to modernize the armed forces, or, as Selth has stated, 'to take whatever measures were required to recover and consolidate its grip on government' (Selth 2002: 33). In other words, the junta's strategy in the 1990s was guided by its corporate interest in securing its future predominance. Although the policies of the military regime were often shrouded in secrecy and used opaque language, we can identify five broad reforms to achieve the self-proclaimed goals of 'non-disintegration

of the union', 'non-integration of national-solidarity' and 'perpetuation of national sovereignty' (SLORC 1988). These policies included:

- the modernization of the armed forces,
- the deepening of the military's involvement in the economy,
- the signing of ceasefires with 17 ethnic-armed organizations, and
- the attempt to establish a political order, which allowed for a future political role for the armed forces.

These 'policies' were not formalized and were often influenced by personal interests of members of the military regime. They also were highly interrelated, opaque and often implemented at a glacial pace. They led to an increasing militarization of the state, a huge degree of coercion and the increasing dominance of the military over the economy, which aggravated economic malaise and starvation. At the same time, the limiting and policing of social spaces deprived actors of any room for independent action (Bünte forthcoming).

▷ *Modernization of the armed forces*
After 1990, the military embarked on a massive state-building programme, which has concentrated on modernizing the country's weak infrastructure (construction of roads, bridges, hospitals, etc.). As in the early 1950s, the modernization of the coercive apparatus was at the heart of this state-building programme. This entailed an expansion of the armed forces from 186,000 to more than 370,000 soldiers (Callahan 2003; Selth 2002). The military subsequently enhanced its territorial representation in the country and increased its surveillance capacities. The reasons for this have to be seen in the military's unique threat perception: its fear of armed dissidents and insurgents within the country as well as foreign forces outside the country. Moreover, the impression prevailed that the counteroffensives of the 1970s and 1980s had not been successful because the military had lacked strength. Consequently, the military allocated huge sums for defence expenditures throughout the 1990s: the junta spent more than one billion US dollars on 150 new combat aircraft, 30 new naval vessels, 170 tanks and 2,500 armoured personnel carriers, as well as rocket-launching systems, infantry weapons and other hardware (Callahan 2001: 424). It also stirred up nationalism in order to achieve a rally-around-the-flag effect; moreover,

it continuously pointed out its historical role as builder of nation and state (Steinberg 2007: 102–10; Taylor 2009).

▷ *The deepening of the military's role in the economy*
To fund the expansion of the military, the SLORC/SPDC opened up the economy and started to build up its business empire. It discarded the socialist economy of the Ne Win era and adopted a market economy. This set the context for a transition from state-socialism to state-mediated capitalism (Jones 2014b). The military managed to build up an effective monopoly in economic affairs. It dominated the economy through a large complex of investment rules and economic initiatives, which gave military companies a central position.[2] The 1990s also saw the creation and expansion of a number of companies or conglomerates with direct links to the military junta. A new form of 'crony capitalism' evolved that was based on wealthy businessmen's access to patrons in the military regime.

Due to weak economic conditions and a lack of finances to develop a proper defence industry, the military started to build up the most important conglomerates in the country in the 1990s: the Union of Myanmar Economic Holdings Limited (UMEH) and the Myanmar Economic Corporation (MEC). They were given licences in diverse businesses such as construction, hotels, tourism, transport, gem and jade extraction and agriculture. UMEH, founded in 1990, is a military-managed business engaged in small and medium-sized commercial enterprises and industries. Its main objective was to support welfare organizations of the regime, veteran organizations and retired military personnel. As a pension tool for retired officers it provides a yearly return normal retirement schemes can only dream of. MEC was founded in 1997 to give the mili-

---

2. Liberalization remained rather limited, partly as a consequence of Western sanctions and the US investment ban, and partly due to a lack of access to capital through the banking sector for the foundation or expansion of business. Additionally, conservative generals, ministers and officials blocked liberalization, fearing the loss of revenues, rents and control over employment decisions. The consequence of these developments was manifold: First, a new form of 'crony capitalism' evolved around the top military generals and their families. To take advantage of the state's opening the private sector required access to the military leadership. Consequently, only a few 'cronies' of top military generals were able to secure monopolies and contracts to expand their wealth (Ford *et al.* 2016; Jones 2014b). Second, formal state monopolies were retained in many sectors. Some sectors, such as defence industries, were completely controlled by [[or restricted to]] the state.

tary access to supplies of important material, in order to build up heavy industry. By 2009, it had an insurance monopoly as well as 21 factories, including four steel plants, a bank, a cement plant. MEC is operated under the Ministry of Defence's Directorate of Defence Procurement and all of its private shares are owned by active-duty military personnel. The corporation's capital was established through revenue generated from the public auctioning of state-owned enterprises in the 1990s (Ford *et al.* 2016: 26; Aung Myoe 2009: 201). Through joint ventures with foreign companies and mergers with smaller companies, MEC has become one of Myanmar's largest companies. MEC is widely seen as generating most of the military's operating revenue, together with UMEH. The most lucrative sectors in the economy, such as rice trading and imports of vehicles, refined petroleum and edible oils, continue to be reserved for the latter (ICG 2014: 9).

Apart from these activities, the military engages in a wide range of decentralized commercial interests and enterprises. Economic opportunities opened particularly at the local level due to the evolving ceasefire economies (see below). Consequently, many regional officers who engaged in these businesses became unusually rich. Such extra-legal activities and abuses of power damaged the reputation of the military; people began to see the commercial activities as being above the law (Prager-Nyein 2012: 40).

▷ *Ceasefires with the ethnic armed groups*
During the 1990s, a series of ceasefires negotiated between the military and ethnic insurgent groups significantly reduced the internal armed threat the Tatmadaw faced. General Khin Nyunt, SPDC secretary-1 and head of military intelligence, signed ceasefires with 17 armed groups, in order to avoid a collusion between the ceasefire groups and the pro-democracy movement (Callahan 2007; Zaw Oo & Win Min 2007; Smith 2007). The ethnic armed groups were permitted to retain their weapons and exercise control over their territories. This included the right to trade, often bartering for illicit commodities such as weapons and narcotics (Callahan 2007; Smith 1999; Smith 2007; Zaw Oo & Win Min 2007).[3] Woods has rightly pointed out that the military engaged

---

3. Callahan calls this evolving governance structure a 'mosaic' with varying degrees of autonomy ranging from devolution to full autonomy.

in private-military partnerships with ethnic elites and traditional businessmen and managed to achieve significant progress in state-building. The ceasefires allowed an increasing military territorialization in some parts of the country, in which military commanders and relevant state agencies gave out licenses to extract the region's natural resources. Ethnic leaders often acted as middlemen or brokers to Chinese investors (Woods 2011; Lee 2014b).

The ceasefires were not formal; they were 'gentlemen's agreements' between Khin Nyunt and leaders of the ethnic groups, which had different reasons for accepting this form of ceasefire, even if it precluded their long-term goal of federalism or greater autonomy. Some groups suffered from a general war fatigue; others faced pressure from their grassroots communities, the drying up of financial support from China and Thailand, or new business opportunities and prospects for economic development under a ceasefire (Zaw Oo & Win Min 2007; Callahan 2007). Altogether, these ceasefires were integral to co-optation of the armed ethnic groups, as they gave political actors in the regions some breathing room, which they used for local economic development (Jones 2014a: 792). Apart from rent-seeking opportunities, ceasefires gave the military regime the chance to fight specifically those groups which continued their active resistance, such as the Karen National Liberation Army and the Shan State Army South.

▷ *The creation of a new political order under military guardianship*
The military ended direct rule in March 2011 only after it had managed to design a political system that institutionalized the formal political role of the military. Consequently, it is fair to say that the reforms after March 2011 do not represent another critical juncture and the military retained its capacity to control large parts of the economy, despite a considerable transfer of formal power to a civilian government. The transition to quasi-civilian rule was introduced from a position of strength: having consolidated its position internally and weakened the opposition movement severely, the military regime started to entrench its political prerogatives. The most important phases of formal institution-building were the drafting of a new Constitution by National Conventions (1993–96; 2003–07), the holding of the referendum about the new Constitution (2008), the creation of the regime-sponsored Union

Solidarity and Development Party (USDP) and the conducting of (heavily scripted) elections in November 2010 – won by the USDP in a landslide.

The praetorian strategy from 1988 to 2011 did not represent any form of liberalization or a genuine democratic transition, since the military controlled every step, political spaces were restricted to a minimum and state repression was at its tightest (Pederson 2011; Prager-Nyein 2009). To achieve the first three of the four stated objectives (see p. 101), the SLORC/SPDC military oligarchy ruled with an iron fist and exercised a high degree of repression, manifested in the taking of a high number of political prisoners and the continuous neglect of basic freedoms and political liberties. According to Amnesty International and other human rights groups, there were more than 1500 political prisoners during the 1990s, and Myanmar was constantly ranked among the lowest countries in democracy by organisations such as Freedom House and the Bertelsmann Transformation Index. Anti-government protests were cracked down on vehemently, including the student demonstrations in 1988 and 1996, and the peaceful protest of Buddhist monks in September 2007. Opposition politicians suffered under severe state repression: NLD leader Aung San Suu Kyi famously spent more than 16 years under house arrest. The high level of repression and huge number of human rights abuses sparked not only a wave of international criticism but also a number of punitive economic sanctions, such as travel bans against senior members of the regime, export and investment bans (Pederson 2008).

Arguably, these measures impaired the economic opening and also aggravated the security concerns of the ruling junta. In the wake of Cyclone Nargis in 2008, when the inability of the military junta to provide aid effectively became very clear, the international community even loosely discussed an external intervention under the banner of the United Nations' 'responsibility to protect' (Bünte 2008; Haacke 2009; Selth 2008). Although a US invasion was never a real prospect, the hostility shown towards the SLORC and the SPDC by Western powers between 1988 and 2011 – George W. Bush's inclusion of Burma as an 'outpost of tyranny' felt very threatening, indeed – encouraged military leaders to believe that Myanmar faced an existential threat (Selth 2015: 9). The regime was only liberalised after President Thein Sein assumed office in March 2011: he freed political prisoners, ended press censorship and opened up political spaces for opposition and civil society. Thus began a 'protracted transition' that culminated in the free and fair elections of November 2015 (Bünte 2016b).

Military guardianship: The civil–military coalition since 2011

When the military junta transferred power to the quasi-civilian government of President Thein Sein and dissolved the SPDC in March 2011, Myanmar's military oligarchy transformed itself into an electoral-authoritarian regime ruled by a civil–military coalition under the leadership of the military proxy party USDP (Janowitz 1964; 1988: 81). After the 2015 elections and election victory of the NLD, Myanmar can be classified as a tutelary democracy with fragile civil liberties and political rights (Bünte 2016b). Myanmar's political history is consistent with Siddiqa's 'parent–guardian military type', since the military has taken over the role of a guardian, institutionally secured a number of veto positions and further deepened its involvement in the economy. The whole political system is infused with military checks on civilian politicians. This section looks at the legal foundations of military guardianship and describes the first six years of the civil–military coalition, while the following section looks at the economic foundations of military guardianship.

The military as guardians: legal foundations

The Tatmadaw has secured its political influence and veto position through a number of legal safeguards. Section 6(f) of the 2008 constitution gives the military a role in 'the national leadership of the state' and Section 20 makes it the principal safeguarding force for the constitution. Section 17(a) and (b) specify that the military is given a role in both the executive and legislative affairs at Union and at regional levels. According to Article 232(ii) of the 2008 constitution, the Minister of Defence, the Minister of Home Affairs and the Minister of Border Affairs are appointed from serving officers by the Commander in Chief. The Ministry of Home Affairs is particularly important: the Head of the General Administration Department for a region or state, who ultimately reports to the Minister of Home Affairs, is deemed to be secretary of the region or state government (section 260). As a result, the Minister of Home Affairs, and through him the military, plays a significant role in state and regional government administration in addition to the powers granted to appoint state and region ministers (sections 262(a)(ii), (n) (ii), 276(d)(ii)).

Moreover, six out of 11 seats on the powerful National Defence and Security Council are filled with serving military officers. The body meets weekly to discuss security issues and has the authority to decide about amnesties, the appointment of the commander-in-chief and states of emergency.[4] Additionally, the military has a 25 per cent representation in all national parliaments (Upper House, Lower House and regional parliaments). These representatives are appointed by the Commander in Chief of the Armed Forces (as laid down in articles 109(b), 141(b) and 161(b)). Since a quorum of 75 per cent in the legislature is needed to change the constitution (Article 436), the military has a de facto veto power over any future constitutional changes. All these provisions are basically guarantees that core military functions will not be touched by the civilian government (ICG 2014: 10).

What is even more important is that the military has complete autonomy in regard to security-related issues. Article 20 of the 2008 constitution gives the commander-in-chief autonomy over the management of intra-military affairs. Article 20(b) guarantees 'the Defence Services the right to independently administer and adjudicate all affairs of the armed forces'. Guardianship becomes fully visible in the case of an emergency. According to Chapter XI of the 2008 constitution, the President and the National Defence and Security Council have the powers to impose martial law, disband parliament and rule directly, if the president declares a state of emergency. This provides a legal channel for the military to reimpose direct military rule. We consequently see that the military has created a 'praetorian constitution' (Egreteau 2017a: 124) to influence the political process, safeguard its own interests and guard civilian politicians (Egreteau 2016; Kamerling & Croissant 2013). If the military leadership sees a failure of civilian politicians, evidenced for example by increased separatism, ethnic violence or any measures that put the Tatmadaw's corporate interests at stake, then the

---

4. The National Defence and Security Council consists of the president, the two vice presidents, the speakers of the Upper and the Lower House, the commander-in-chief and his deputy, and the ministers of Defence, Home Affairs, Border Affairs and Foreign Affairs.

civilian–military coalition might break down again and the military might reverse the reforms. To be sure, the threshold is low, given the country's history of civil war and the military's unique threat perception and deep involvement in the economy. The military is also much more than a normal guardian (Bünte 2014) or arbitrator (Egreteau 2015: 30). Let us take a closer look at how the military has interpreted its role during the first years of quasi-civilian rule.

Military guardianship in practice: the first six years of the civil–military coalition

The military is still deeply entrenched in the political arena, although it has made room for civilian politicians to debate and decide in certain policy arenas. As Selth rightly points out, the military has never seen itself as having separate political and military roles (Selth 2015: 12). Seeing itself above politics, the military imagines itself to be guiding civilian politicians and 'caretaking democratization' (Egreteau 2017b). This gives the military a deeply political role, which it has used to block further constitutional changes, restrain liberal freedoms, comment on the political role of politicians and negotiate the nation-state. The military is also protecting its own corporate interest and trying to delineate the contours of the evolving 'disciplined democracy' – a political system with an elected government but with restricted liberal freedoms and limited room to criticize the government.

During the first years of quasi-civilian rule the military attempted to keep a low profile, in keeping with the 2008 constitution, as it worked with elected politicians and participated in the leadership of the state. Moreover, even the 14 regional commanders (who held extensive military *and* administrative powers in their respective regions during the SPDC era) tended to exercise their authority only on military matters (Selth 2015: 12). There were hardly any open and disruptive conflicts between the quasi-civilian government of President Thein Sein and the military leadership. This is hardly surprising, since President Thein Sein has been a high-ranking member of the former military junta and is one of the key architects of the transition to disciplined democracy – the Burmese version of a tutelary democracy.[5] Moreover, parliaments were

---

5. A tutelary democracy is a regime with formally democratic institutions, but the armed forces retain the capacity to intervene to correct undesirable states of affairs.

dominated by the USDP, a proxy party of the military that was packed not only with former military officers but also with cronies of the former military junta. Most military appointees in parliaments were of lower rank, mere place holders who were regularly rotated. This was obviously a deliberate move to ensure that the military remained cohesive and under the strict control of the commander-in-chief, Senior General Min Aung Hlaing. Only after 2012 did he appoint more senior representatives (Egreteau 2015: 24). After the election victory of the NLD in November 2015, relations between the military bloc in Parliament and the government became more conflictive, despite military commander Min Aung Hlaing's promise to work *under* the president. Military representatives aimed to provide some checks and balances in order to equilibrate the predominance of the NLD in Parliament. To date, Aung San Suu Kyi has refrained from showing any open confrontation with the military, and she does not intend to push the military out of politics (interview with NLD speaker Nyan Win, December 2015). Knowing that any perceived challenges to Myanmar's unity, internal stability and sovereignty, or to the Tatmadaw's self-appointed national role might delay or even reverse the transition process, she approached the military cautiously and worked in cooperation with the military during her first year.

According to Egreteau's landmark study of military parliamentarians in the early years of the transition, the military guard has taken over the role of 'moderators' and 'arbitrators' in parliament (Egreteau 2015: 31; Egreteau 2017). While exercising oversight over civilian politicians, the military is trying to stand above 'party politics'. Army chief Min Aung Hlaing has repeatedly stressed the need for the army to play a political role. On the 71st Armed Forces Day in March 2016, he reiterated that the army had to assume the role of shepherding the democratization process until a stable multi-party system and the rule of law evolved (Pyae Thet Phyo 2016). In an interview with the *Washington Post*, he indicated that the military might be willing to turn more authority over to the civilian government, but that 'it would depend on the stability of our country and people understanding the practice of democracy (Weymouth 2015). Arguably, this seems to indicate that the military intends to retain its role as guardian. Already in June 2014, military representatives blocked constitutional changes that would lower the

75 per cent threshold for constitutional change to 70 per cent, which would have reduced the veto power of the military. This is a clear sign that it wants to retain its role as guardian of the 2008 constitution, and of the political order more generally. Moreover, the military bloc also prevented changing Article 59(f), which bars Aung San Suu Kyi from the presidency. The military does not seem to trust civilian politicians at this point in time, especially one with such huge popularity as Aung San Suu Kyi (Selth 2015: 13). When the NLD changed the institutional setup of the administration to introduce the powerful position of State counsellor for Aung San Suu Kyi in April 2016, the military representatives staged a boycott to demonstrate their dissatisfaction with the decision. One of the military legislators stated: 'as the Hluttaw [legislature] did not consider our proposed amendments, we refused to vote on the bill' (NLM 2016: 3). At the end of the session, the bloc stood in silent protest and subsequently denounced the passage of the bill as 'democratic bullying' by the majority. Since the NLD appointed all members of the Constitutional Tribunal, the military likely felt a formal legal challenge would be unsuccessful and risked further demonstrating its legislative impotence. Instead, the military appointed Myint Swe, a well-known hardliner and close confident of former general Than Shwe, as vice president. All of this underlines the military's discomfort in working with civilian politicians at such an early stage of the civil–military coalition.

The military has not only devised the new political order, it is also actively guarding and restraining the extent of democratization. To the surprise of many, military representatives have supported President Thein Sein's liberalization. The military did not block the release of political prisoners, the liberalization of the press or the relaxation of the freedoms to protest (Bünte 2016a). It also allowed the elections in November 2015 to run freely, fairly and smoothly (Bünte 2016b). However, at the same time, the military is actively engaged in restraining some of the new democratic freedoms. The press is not allowed to criticize the military as an institution or write negatively about military projects. If some press outlets cross the line, they are approached by the military and told to watch their reporting (personal interview with an editor of *The Myanmar Times*, December 2015). The military is also not comfortable with the rising wave of protests since 2011. These protests are often triggered by land-grabbing or military development projects. The USDP government drafted a new restrictive Assembly law to stifle some of these protests. Once elected into office, the NLD has continued to use these laws to stifle criticism as well (Bünte 2016a, Bünte forthcoming). Similarly, direct military representatives in parliament voted against the repeal of various repressive laws on the grounds of national security. For instance, when the NLD repealed the Emergency Provisions Act in October 2016, military representatives tried to block it. Since they form a minority in the newly elected parliament, they could not prevent this legislation to sail through. Yet, the military representatives sent a strong signal to elected politicians that a far-reaching liberalization is too early at this point. In a similar vein, military representatives in Parliament staged a protest in February 2016, when a NLD MP openly criticized alleged misconduct by local authorities involved in the Letpadaung copper mine project – a controversial enterprise with heavy involvement of a military conglomerate. This symbolic and theatrical behaviour by military representatives bluntly shows that the military disapproves of being criticized for its involvement in commercial activities, including land grabbing and natural resource-related projects. Any future NLD moves against the military's business interests might lead to open conflict between the NLD government and the military.

The military has also played an important, though not uncontroversial, role in the peace process. Here, it is a veto-player par excellence. The commander-in-chief, Aung Min Hlaing, supported President Thein Sein's peace initiative, and military generals actively participated in peace negotiations with rebel groups since 2011. Their aim was to end 60 years of civil war through ceasefires followed by a political dialogue. Of the 15 groups included in the peace process, eight groups signed the National Ceasefire Agreement (NCA) on 15 October 2015; seven refused to do so, including the United Wa State Army (UWSA) and the Kachin Independence Army (KIA). Together with a number of smaller ethnic armed groups, these seven continue to pose a challenge to the central government.

The peace process directly involves the military, which is in a position to provide security guarantees and must agree on whatever future political order emerges from the dialogue. High-level military representatives have actively participated in all talks so far. Although military generals and rebel group leaders eyed each other with suspicion during the initial rounds in 2012 and each side blamed the other for past hostilities, the general atmosphere improved significantly during subsequent rounds. The military generally was well prepared and actively participated in the discussions (personal interviews at the Myanmar Peace Centre, November 2014 and December 2015). At the same time, the military continues to insist that only those ethnic groups that have signed the NCA should be allowed to participate in the upcoming political dialogue. This is a major obstacle for a solution of the protracted conflict.

Yet, the military seems to have agreed on some sort of federalism, although it shuns this specific word. A few years ago, the military vehemently opposed any move towards federalism, which it saw as an initial step towards the break-up of the country. The military seems willing to talk with some rebel groups about a future political order and is now willing to enter into a dialogue with civilian politicians and ethnic group leaders to achieve this end (personal interviews at the Myanmar Peace Centre, November 2014). The military leadership, however, will not allow Aung San Suu Kyi to take the lead on federalism and the establishment of a new political order (Min Zin 2016: 128). On the other hand, the Tatmadaw leadership hopes that Aung San Suu Kyi can bring the non-signatory, armed ethnic organizations into the peace process. The most promising example has been the peace talks with the oldest insurgent group, the Karen National Union. After agreeing to enter peace talks, both sides have further agreed on an early warning mechanism, and both sides are having monthly meetings at the highest level with both the President and the Commander in Chief to debate critical issues of the peace process (personal interviews at the Myanmar Peace Centre, December 2015).

Whereas the military seemed supportive of this process in some parts of the country, its conduct on the ground in other parts gave rise to scepticism about its real commitment to peace, especially during the resurgence of conflicts in Kachin State and Shan State. Although President Thein Sein issued an order in 2011 that the Burmese army should cease all offensive campaigns against the KIA, the Burmese Army continued to move in troops into Kachin State and the war has escalated since then (for a background, see Sadan 2015). The Tatmadaw claimed that it was only acting to protect its supply lines at a time when the KIA ambushes were increasing (personal interviews at the Myanmar Peace Centre, November 2014). Despite the rhetoric of a new peace process, the military continues to be involved heavily in fighting the KIA. The NLD government of Aung San Suu Kyi revived the peace process in 2016, but fighting in northern Myanmar continues. In October 2016, thousands of Kachin State residents held protests calling for an end to the military's offensives against the KIA. They also criticized the NLD government for being silent on the renewed military offensives (Nyein 2016). The military's rhetoric of commitment seems to contradict its behaviour on the ground, and the new NLD government seems unable to control the military. Arguably, the war is driven by illicit enterprises such as the lucrative jade business. According to research reports by Global Witness, both sides are profiting immensely from this business (Global Witness 2015a). Consequently, some authors argue that renewed fighting was driven by regional commanders with interests in rent seeking, who might have acted on their own in order to derail the peace process (Jones 2014a). The situation in Shan State is similar: major fighting resumed between the Myanmar National Democratic Alliance (MNDAA) troops and the army in the Kokang Self-Administered Zone since February 2015. Elsewhere, in Shan State, we have seen sporadic clashes between the army and the Ta'ang National Liberation Army (TNLA). In 2016 these groups joined forces with the KIA and formed the Northern Alliance, which launched joint military operations against the Myanmar army. The group maintained that the attacks were an inevitable response from constant military pressure from the Tatmadaw.

All in all, we can say that during the first five years of quasi-civilian rule, the military provided guardianship over what it hopes will become a disciplined democracy. It is actively involved in all national affairs, while trying to protect its interests and shield the political order. It also has attempted to restrain democratization of the country. Its involvement in the peace process is ambivalent. On the one hand, it supported the negotiations with various rebel organizations. On the other, it acts as veto-actor over the path to a political dialogue and increased its offensives against those groups which have rejected the NCA. The next section turns to the economic foundation of the military, which has been largely untouched during the transition to disciplined democracy.

Military capital in the semi-democratic era

Military guardianship is not limited to the political system. It is backed by formal and informal control of the country's economic capital. For more than two decades, the military was responsible for both the formulation and the implementation of economic policy (Steinberg 2005: 60). Military-owned conglomerates dominated the economy. As a consequence, the military managed to obtain a huge volume of economic rent, and a 'crony capitalism' evolved that favoured the military's business interests. Moreover, some retired high-ranking generals have been able to siphon off enormous wealth during this period. The transition to quasi-military rule is gradually transforming the military's role in the economy. It is affecting not only formal defence spending but also the military's conglomerates and its land holdings. This section focuses on military-economic developments from 2011 to 2016 and concludes with prospects for the NLD-led government to change the militarization of the economy.

Defence spending

Andrew Selth, an astute observer of the security sector in Myanmar, has repeatedly warned us of the intricacies of estimating Myanmar's annual defence spending (Selth 2002: 130; 2009). Neither the government nor the military has defined 'defence spending', nor is it really clear what calculations are taken into account. Since budgets were not published at all for many years, it is not clear what share the military received. Even now, data from 2006 to 2011 is not available and data from 2011 onwards is not comparable with earlier figures. This should caution us in our analysis. The analysis that follows is based on secondary-source estimates until 2005; data from 2011 onwards are taken from budgets as disclosed by the military.

Data from the Stockholm International Peace Research Institute (SIPRI) indicate that Myanmar's defence spending has seen a steady rise from the early 1990s to the late 2000s. While these figures are difficult to verify given the weakness of Myanmar's currency and high inflation rates, the relation of defence spending to the GDP reveals a slightly different pattern: we see a slow increase in defence spending from 2.1 per cent of GDP in 1988 to a peak of 3.7 in 1995, after which defence spending decreased to a low of 1.6 per cent of GDP in 2005. The figures

Table 3.1: Military spending in Myanmar

Year	Spending by calendar year (in billion kyats)	Spending (in constant [2014] USD millions	% of GDP	% share of government spending
1988	1.6	242	2.1	–
1989	3.7	430	3.0	–
1990	5.2	511	3.4	–
1991	5.9	443	3.2	–
1992	8.4	514	3.4	–
1993	12.7	591	3.5	–
1994	16.7	628	3.5	–
1995	22.3	668	3.7	–
1996	27.7	713	3.5	–
1997	29.8	593	2.7	–
1998	37.7	489	2.3	9.7
1999	43.7	484	2.0	9.2
2000	58.8	653	2.3	10.7
2001	63.9	585	1.8	9.6
2002	73.1	426	1.3	8.9
2003	148	634	1.9	13.9
2004	173	708	1.9	11.8
2005	192	716	1.6	9.6
2011	973	NA	2.6	18.0
2012	1,902	2969	4.6	17.6
2013	2,210	3269	4.7	16.3
2014	2,336	3276	4.3	12.9
2015	2,549	3187	3.9	13.3

Note: The figures for Myanmar (Burma) are presented in kyat owing to the extreme variation of unstated exchange rates between the kyat and the US dollar. Stated exchange rates vary from 6.076 to 960 kyat/US$ (2003). The figures for 2011–13 are from the official state budget, and may not be directly comparable with earlier figures, which are from secondary sources.

Source: SIPRI 2016.

together reflect the massive modernization of the armed forces from the 1990s to the early 2000s. Though SIPRI lists the military's share of government expenditures as between 9 and 18 per cent, it is a well-known fact that generally 30–40 per cent of the national budgets were spent on the military until 2011 (Selth 2002: 134), and even more after extra-budgetary sources are included.

The military tried to insulate itself from budgetary uncertainties and scarcities by developing its own military enterprises. These ensured cheap and constant supplies of basic commodities such as steel, cement and vehicle tyres. After the transition to a civilian–military coalition, official spending remained high. According to data from SIPRI, Myanmar spent 4.6 per cent and 4.7 per cent of its GDP on defence in 2012 and 2013. With civilian oversight over the budget being a mere façade or meaningless ritual, there is no corrective against high military spending. During a discussion on the annual defence budget in March 2013, some military appointees approached their civilian colleagues behind closed doors to convince them not to vote against the budget prepared by the Ministry of Defence. They maintained that the budget for the armed forces was one of the lowest in Southeast Asia and a drastic reduction would hurt the country's 'national security' (Egreteau 2015: 39). While this is certainly true, this line of argumentation refers to the official state budget only. Much of the income is not derived from official state sources. Moreover, a special funds law (enacted in March 2011) permits the Tatmadaw to access additional funds without parliamentary oversight (Selth 2015: 11).

In 2014, overall spending increased to 2,336 billion kyat. Due to a much higher budget, this was only 13 per cent of the overall budget. In 2015, the spending increased to 2,549 billion kyat. The Defence Minister was quoted in the press as saying that half of the budget was for salaries and allowances, while 29 per cent of the budget was earmarked for a further modernization of the army, including heavy weapons (Htoo Thant 2015). This trend has continued under the NLD government, which also earmarked 13 percent of its overall budget to the Ministry of Defence (Irrawaddy 2017). Consequently, the budget allocations for the military were hardly reduced after the transition to the democratic era. Such high military spending can be interpreted as a payoff for military officials stepping back from day-to-day politics (Selth 2015: 11).

The NLD's refusal to cut the military's budget in 2017/18 supports this interpretation.

The military's economic holdings

The military conglomerates, the Union of Myanmar Economic Holding Limited (UMEH) and the Myanmar Economic Corporation (MEC), provide the backbone of military dominance in the economy. Although some observers see a 'significantly diminished role' for these enterprises due to a loss of government monopolies and licensing practices (ICG 2012: 6; 2015: 10), there is strong evidence that the military companies have been left unharmed so far and that the military can still extract significant rents from these businesses. Admittedly, the military has lost its dominant role in policy formulation, and consequently military conglomerates are facing growing competition from wealthy business-men (cronies of former generals) and their companies. Also, there is enhanced control and oversight through governmental consultation and increased cooperation with international organizations such as the IMF and the World Bank (ICG 2015). Yet, during the last six years, military conglomerates benefitted immensely from diverse rounds of privatiza-tion, and they continue to make significant footprint on Myanmar's economy. Military companies also have started to modernize in order to being able to compete in the modern era.

Under direct military rule (1988–2011), military businesses profited from the decisions by the Trade Council, which was responsible for issu-ing import and export licenses and was chaired by an army commander. In the past, decisions on government contracts were made in secrecy and without outside control. Often, the main beneficiaries were the military conglomerates, MEC and UMEH. Founded in 1997 to establish profit-able heavy industries to give the military access to supplies of important materials such as cement and rubber, MEC's operations were shrouded in secrecy. In 2009, MEC owned 21 factories, including 4 steel plants, a bank, a cement plant and an insurance monopoly. It is operated under the Ministry of Defence's Directorate of Defence Procurement, with its private shares exclusively owned by active-duty military personnel. The corporation's capital was established through revenues generated from the public auctioning of state-owned enterprises in the end of the 1990s (Ford *et al.* 2016: 26). Through joint ventures with foreign companies and mergers with smaller companies, MEC has become itself one of

Myanmar's largest companies. MEC is widely seen as generating most of the military's operating revenue – together with UMEH. The most lucrative sectors in the economy were reserved for the latter, such as rice trading and imports of vehicles, refined petroleum and edible oils (ICG 2014: 9). Accordingly, it is believed that UMEH controls 70 per cent of all major businesses in the country.

After 2011, the Trade Council was abolished. Military enterprises have lost some of their monopolies and their status as tax free bodies. Consequently, it is questionable whether these companies will be profitable in the future or remain a drain on the military's budget. There is now greater competition and disclosure, although e.g. UMEH's monopoly in the gems sector is unbroken. Some observers have come to the conclusion that the role of military conglomerates has been reduced, and the military has lost its gatekeeper function in the economy (ICG 2014: 9). Although the conglomerates have lost their exclusive access to preferential contracts with foreign firms, they are still profiting from ongoing monopolies and contacts in the bureaucracy. In the most recent rounds of privatization, military companies were again among the main beneficiaries (Ford *et al.* 2016: 31). Most of the heavy industries owned by the Ministry of Industry have been transferred to the MEC via a privatization scheme (Min/Kudo 2014: 154). Even shortly before the handover of power to the NLD government at the end of February 2016, another round of privatization spurred the anger of the NLD parliamentarians. The NLD openly criticized the government's handling of new projects (such as dams and new hospitals) and the military's involvement in resource extraction, which led to the military's show of open defiance in parliament (see above, Htoo Thant 2016).

However, Ford *et al.* also point to the political salience and increasing autonomy of wealthy domestic businessmen with connections to military patrons. These 'nascent oligarchs' started to appear on the scene in the 1990s, have shown increasing signs of autonomy since the transition period, and are increasingly challenging military businesses (Ford *et al.* 2016: 33). Some of these cronies even met with Aung San Suu Kyi in 2015 in order to get her ideas about future economic development. Despite facing much more competition from these cronies, military businesses remain powerful and deeply entrenched in the overall economy. UMEH, for instance, has 51 subsidiaries throughout the country.

It is active in mining, banking, livestock and fisheries, trading and transportation, food and beverages, steel, and pharmaceuticals. Moreover, UMEH and the military elite control the prime real estate in Yangon and can extract millions from the capital's property boom. In June 2016, UMEH announced in a military-run newspaper that it will become a public company and is preparing an initial public offering (Mahtani 2016). This major turnaround underscores the military conglomerate's efforts to be attractive to foreign partners. The loss of its tax-exempt status has put pressure on the conglomerate and their subsidiaries to modernize and be more competitive. The reforms of the conglomerate are also a pre-emptive measure to survive in the future, since the NLD won the election based on the promise to create a transparent economy and modernize ailing state enterprises (Matsui 2016). Despite these reform steps, the military remains in control of the company. As a retirement scheme for soldiers and their families, the conglomerate plays an important role for the military. The other conglomerate, MEC, has 31 subsidiaries in the country and is active in fields such as transportation, hotels and tourism, construction, tradition, banking and resource extraction (gas, gems and metals), steel and coal, and manufacturing (Ford *et al.* 2016: 36). Both companies not only provide lucrative career channels for retired army personnel but active members of the military can also extract significant rents from these businesses.

The jade industry may serve as a good illustration of the military's involvement in one of the most profitable parts of Myanmar's economy. Jade production is primarily centred in Kachin State. Driven by the demand from China, the jade industry has boomed since the late 1990s. It is estimated that Myanmar provides more than 70 per cent of the world's supply of high quality jadeite (Egreteau 2012: 93) with an estimated annual production value of between 12 and 31 billion US dollars, and companies from the military are among the main beneficiaries (Global Witness 2015a).[6] According to official sales records, army companies made a profit of US$180 million in 2014 and US$100 million in 2013 (ibid.: 11). UMEH and MEC share their profits from this industry with families of senior generals of the former military junta or families of senior USDP party officials, cronies and drug lords, who

---

6. Twelve billion US dollars is a figure derived from Chinese import data, whereas Global Witness includes figures from the domestic market and the black market.

are notorious for their local involvement in this business (ibid.). The new NLD-government has announced plans to reform the jade sector and has stopped giving out new licences to operate in Kachin State. We can conclude that the military companies retain a significant portion of Myanmar's economy, which provides important off-budget finances for military projects and income for retired military officers. The current economic opening is putting economic conglomerates under pressure to modernize and remain competitive. Of particular importance is the military's ongoing involvement in a number of resource-related projects, such as the country's jade or copper mines, which has started to trigger resistance on the ground, often due to its seizure of farmland and environmental problems caused by extraction and processing.

The military and land grabbing
The foundation of military power also rests on its seizure of farmland. In a country with a long history of 'nationalized' land, followed by a military-directed state and, recently, transition to quasi-civilian rule, the issues of land seizure and ongoing ethnic conflict raise important questions regarding rent-seeking and the role of the army (Ferguson 2014). In the 1990s, land grabbing became a common and largely uncontested practice. Military units seized large tracts of farmland, usually without paying compensation. While some of the land was used for the expansion of military bases, new government offices or infrastructure projects much of it was utilized either by military units for their own commercial purposes or sold to private companies (McCartan 2013). Burmese agribusinesses with close affiliations to the military government could access land with hardly any costs. Land confiscations peaked in 2006 under the veneer of a countrywide privatization programme. According to a study cited in the Global Witness report, by 2013 approximately 5.3 million acres – 35 times the size of Yangon – had been awarded to domestic companies with close connections to the government and military officials, predominantly for agriculture. As much as 1.5 million acres of this land was earmarked for rubber plantations, as in neighbouring Cambodia or Laos (Global Witness 2015a: 8). The appropriation of land builds one of the economic foundations of the political power of the military. The symbiotic relationship between serving and retired military officers and private businessmen that flourished under the previous military regime remains largely unchanged under the semi-

civilian administration. In 2012, parliament set up the Farmland Investigation Commission to investigate the problem. In May 2013, this commission submitted its first report, which reveals that between late July 2012 and January 2013, the Commission had received more than 585 complaints alleging that the military had confiscated 247,077 acres (~100,000 hectares) of land. The report outlines six reasons for the confiscation of farmland: the expansion of urban areas, the expansion of industrial zones, the expansion of army battalions and military units, the construction of state-owned factories, the implementation of state-run agricultural projects and land allocation to private business-men linked to the military. The Commission recommended that land which had not yet been developed by the military be returned to the farmers. Where land had already been put to use, the military should pay adequate compensation to affected farmers (Htet and Aye 2015). In February 2014 the military announced a commitment to return 154,116 acres of confiscated land to its original owners (ICG 2014; Global Witness 2015b), which gives some indication of the vast scale of its previous land seizures. Following this announcement, national media reported that land is slowly being returned to landowners. At the same time, however, a new wave of land grabs was on the way. Whereas land grabs during previous periods were predominately conducted directly by military-state and non-state armed actors for their benefit alone, 'crony companies' with extreme wealth and political leverage have become the new driver of land grabs in different parts of the country, often financially backed by foreign investors. The semi-civilian USDP-government was working hand-in-hand with former military-favoured businessmen and their companies, enabling them to get legal access to one of the country's biggest and most promising assets: it has actively encouraged more investment in agriculture by promoting the country's former role as the rice bowl of Asia and highlighting its potential for commercial infrastructure (Woods 2014).

The NLD has avoided direct confrontation with the military and crony companies and shied away from placing any civilian control over military business and their activities in land grabbing. Nevertheless, it has promised the return of land and compensation of farmers and made this one of its priorities. It has formed a new committee in May 2016 to oversee the process and has promised to resolve all land disputes in one year, which would put Suu Kyi on a collision course with the generals and threaten Myanmar's fragile transition to democracy.

Conclusion and outlook: Military guardianship in Myanmar

Ruling directly or indirectly for more than four decades, Myanmar's armed forces have been allowed to permeate all of the country's main state institutions, the economy and the society. After governing the country directly between 1988 and 2011, the military has given way to a civil–military coalition in which the military has taken over the role of guardian of the political order. It continues to protect its interests from a position of strength while it secures the country's constitution and moderates civilian politicians. In a number of policy fields, such as defence and security, it still rules directly, without civilian oversight. During the first five years of guardianship, 2011–15, the military shared national leadership with elected civilians, although it still distrusts civilian politicians. It actively prevented meaningful constitutional change, in order to safeguard military primacy under the constitutional order devised by General Than Shwe's military regime a decade earlier.

In 2011, President Thein Sein embarked on a far reaching political liberalization that culminated in the historic November 2015 elections. Despite presiding over this liberalization, the military has continued to limit some of the new democratic freedoms. The press is not allowed to criticize the military as an institution or write negatively about military projects. If some press outlets cross the line, they are approached by the military to adjust their reporting. Press coverage of military behaviour in the field is still considered a taboo. The military is also not comfortable with the rising wave of protests since 2011. These protests have often been triggered by land-grabbing or military development projects. Since 2011, the quasi-civilian government (along with the USDP majority in parliament 2012-2015) has used the provisions in the new restrictive Assembly Law to stifle these protests. This policy is closely connected to the military's formal and informal predominance in the economy, which still allows the military to extract a huge volume of rents.

The real test for the military's willingness to initiate *real* reforms of its economic and political power is still out. So far, the NLD government under de facto leader Aung San Suu Kyi has avoided any open confrontation and attempted not to hurt the military's genuine interests.

It has neither encroached on military's businesses, nor reformed its grip on land or resource extraction. Since the establishment of a civil–military coalition budget allocations for the military have hardly been reduced. According to official data, budget allocations to the military have increased dramatically. High military spending is a payoff for its withdrawal from day-to-day politics. Over the past two decades, the military has also deepened its involvement in the economy, visible in the activities of the two military conglomerates, UMEH and MEC, and their involvement in land-grabbing, resource extraction and illegal trade. A crony capitalist economy is emerging, in which the military plays the role of gatekeeper. Several conglomerates with deep connections to the military rulers could get extremely rich. Since the military regime transformed into a civil–military coalition, military companies have retained control of a significant portion of Myanmar's economy, which provides important off-budget finances for military projects as well as income for retired military officers. At the same time, the economic opening is putting conglomerates under pressure to modernize and remain competitive. Of particular importance is the military's ongoing involvement in a number of resource-related projects, such as jade and copper mines. Since some of these projects are located in territories of ethnic minorities, the issue of their control is deeply connected to the overall peace process.

What is a realistic scenario for civil–military relations in Myanmar? Is the military withdrawing in the long term? Senior General Min Aung Hlaing has indicated his willingness to withdraw from politics in the future, subject to positive developments in peace, national reconciliation and democratic deepening. Consequently, Aung San Suu Kyi's ability to negotiate a long-term peace deal with *all* ethnic groups becomes imperative (see Jones 2014a). A positive scenario relies on lasting peace and increased gains in state building under the new NLD-led government. Critical questions, such as the involvement of the military in resource extraction and land grabbing, must be resolved in a way that suits both the civilian government (and the people it represents) and the military.

For this scenario to become a reality, the military leadership would have to learn that it can trust civilian politicians. From a foundation built on trust, the NLD government might be able to demilitarize politics and establish civilian control over the military in the medium to long-term.

At the same time, the economic interests of the military would have to be safeguarded from any intrusive civilian supremacy. The negative scenario, which revolves around increased fighting, the failure of the peace process and a growing polarization among political parties, might lead the military back to the helm of the government and oust the civilian leadership once again. Yet since the military seems genuinely to be interested in reforms and an international opening, this scenario is unlikely. What we might actually see in the near to medium future is a scenario of positive and negative steps, increasing collaboration between civilian and military actors, but also ongoing struggles and skirmishes, ongoing dissent between civilian politicians and military actors in a number of economic and political realms.

List of Acronyms

AFPFL	Anti-Fascist People's Freedom League
BSSP	Burmese Socialist Programme Party
DPP	Ministry of Defence Procurement
DSI	Defence Service Institute
KIO	Kachin Independence Organization
MEC	Myanmar Economic Cooperation
NLD	National League for Democracy
SLORC	State Law and Order Restoration Council
SPDC	State Peace and Development Council
UMEH	Union of Myanmar Economic Holdings Limited
USDP	Union Solidarity and Development Party

References

Aung Min and Toshihiro Kudo (2014) 'Business Conglomerates in the Context of Myanmar's Reforms', in H. Lim and Y. Yamada (eds) *Myanmar's Integration with Global Economy: Outlook and Opportunities*. Bangkok: Bangkok Research Centre, IDE-JETRO: 138–73.

Aung Myoe (2009) *Building the Tatmadaw: Myanmar Armed Forces Since 1998*. Singapore: Institute of Southeast Asian Studies.

——— (2014) 'The soldier and the state: The Tatmadaw and political liberalization since 2011', *South East Asia Research* 22(2): 233–49.

Bünte, Marco (2009) 'Myanmar und die Frage der externen Intervention: Von der Responsibility to Protect zum humanitären Dialog' [External Intervention in Myanmar: From Responsibility to Protect to Humanitarian Dialogue], *Die Friedenswarte* 84(1): 125–41.

—— (2014) 'Burma's Transition to Quasi-Military Rule: From Rulers to Guardians', *Armed Forces and Society* 40(4): 742–64.

—— (2016a) 'Myanmar's Protracted Transition: Arenas, Actors, and Outcomes', *Asian Survey* 56(2): 369–91.

—— (2016b) 'The End of Military-Guided Electoral Authoritarianism: The 2015 Elections in Myanmar'. Working Paper, No. 176, Southeast Asia Research Centre, City University of Hong Kong.

—— (forthcoming) 'Policing Politics: Myanmar's Military Regime and Protest Spaces in Transition', in E. Hansson and M. Weiss (eds) *Political Participation in Asia: Defining & Deploying Political Space*. London: Routledge.

Callahan, Mary (2001) 'Burma: Soldiers as State Builders', in M. Alagappa (ed.) *Coercion and Governance. The Declining Political Role of the Military in Asia*. Stanford: Stanford University Press: 413–33.

—— (2003) *Making Enemies. War and State Building in Burma*. Ithaca and London: Cornell University Press.

—— (2007) *Political Authority in Burma's Ethnic Minority States: Devolution, Occupation and Coexistence*. Washington D.C.: East-West Center.

Chambers, Paul (2013) *Knights of the Realm. Thailand's Military and Police: Then and Now*. Bangkok: White Lotus.

Croissant, Aurel and Jill Kamerling (2013) 'Why Do Military Regimes Institutionalize? Constitution-making and Elections as Political Survival Strategy in Myanmar', *Asian Journal of Political Science* 21(2): 105–25.

Egreteau, Renaud (2012) 'The Burmese Jade Trail: Transnational Networks, China and the (Relative) Impact of Sanctions on Myanmar's Gems', in N. Cheesman, M. Skidkmore and T. Wilson (eds) *Myanmar's Transition. Openings, Obstacles and Opportunities*. Singapore: Institute of Southeast Asian Studies: 89–119.

—— (2015) 'Soldiers as Lawmakers? Assessing the New Legislative Role of the Burmese Armed Forces (2010–2015)', in R. Egreteau and F. Robinne (eds) *Metamorphosis. Studies in Social and Political Change in Myanmar*. Singapore: NUS Press: 15–43.

—— (2017a) 'Embedding Praetorianism. Soldiers, States and Constitutions in Myanmar', in M. Bünte and B. Dressel (eds) *Politics and Constitutions in Southeast Asia*. London, Routledge: 117–39.

—— (2017b) *Caretaking Democratization*. London: Hurst.

Ferguson, Jane M. (2015): 'The scramble for the Waste Lands: Tracking colonial legacies, counterinsurgency and international investment through the lens of land laws in Burma/Myanmar', *Singapore Journal of Tropical Geography* 35: 295–311.

Ford, Michele, Michael Gillan and Htwe Htwe Thein (2016) 'From Cronyism to Oligarchy?' *Journal of Contemporary Asia* 46(1): 18–41.

Fuller, Thomas (2015) 'Aung San Suu Kyi and General meet, taking steps toward sharing power', *The New York Times* (2 December). http://www.nytimes.com/2015/12/03/world/asia/myanmar-aung-san-suu-kyi-meets-president-army.html.

Global Witness (2015a) *Jade – Myanmar's Big State Secret, Report Global Witness*, (October). https://www.globalwitness.org/documents/18095/Jade_full_report_online_hi_res.pdf.

——— (2015b) *Guns, Cronies and Crops. How military, political and business cronies conspired to grab land in Myanmar.* Report, (March). https://www.globalwitness.org/documents/17960/gunscroniescrops_lo-res_pages_-_FINAL.pdf, accessed 27 March 2017.

Haacke, Jürgen (2009) 'Myanmar, the responsibility to protect, and the need for practical assistance', *Global Responsibility to Protect*, 1 (2): 156–84.

Htet Naing Zaw and Aye Kyawt Khaing (2015) 'Military Involved in Massive Land Grabs: Parliamentary Report', *The Irrawaddy* (3 March). http://www.irrawaddy.com/human-rights/military-involved-in-massive-land-grabs-parliamentary-report.html, accessed 27 March 2017.

Htoo Thant (2015) 'U Thein Sein govt's last budget approved', *Myanmar Times* (2 April).

——— (2016) 'Govt and military clash with NLD over 'fire-sale' motion', *Myanmar Times* (29. February).

International Crisis Group, ICG (2012): *Myanmar: The Politics of Economic Reform*, Asia Report (27 July), Yangon/Brussels.

International Crisis Group, ICG (2014): *Return to the Barracks*. Group Asia Report, Yangon Brussels.

Janowitz, Morris (1964) *The Military in the Political Development of New Nations*. Chicago: University of Chicago Press.

——— (1988) *Military Institutions and Coercion in the Developing Countries*. Chicago: University of Chicago Press.

Jones, Lee (2014a) 'Explaining Myanmar's Regime Transition: the Periphery is central', *Democratization* 21(5): 780–802.

——— (2014b) 'The Political Economy of Myanmar's Transition', *Journal of Contemporary Asia* 44(1), 144–70.

Koonings, Kees and Dirk Kruijt (2002) *Political Armies. The Military and Nation Building in an Era of Democracy*. London: Zed Books.

Laswell, Harold (1941) 'The Garrison State'. *The American Journal of Sociology*, 46(4): 455–68.

Lintner, Bertil (1990): *Outrage: Burma's Struggle for Democracy*. Weatherhill.

Mahtani, Shibani (2016) 'Myanmar's Military's Vast Conglomerate Goes Public'. *The Wall Street Journal* (10 June).

Matsui, Motokazu (2016): 'Time to demilitarize Myanmar business', *Nikkei Asian Review* (19 April).

Mietzner, Marcus (2012) *The Political Resurgence of the Military in Southeast Asia. Conflict and Leadership*. London: Routledge.

Min Zin (2016) 'The new configuration of power', *Journal of Democracy* 27(2): 116–31.

McCartan, Brian (2013) 'Myanmar: Land Grabbing as Big Business', Cetri-Southern Global Newswire. http://www.cetri.be/Myanmar-Land-grabbing-as-big?lang=fr, accessed 27 March 2017.

Nakanashi, Yoshihiro (2013) *Strong Soldiers, Failed Revolution. The State and Military in Burma, 1962–1988*. Singapore: NUS Press and Kyoto University Press.

NLM (2016) 'State Counsellor Bill passed by Lower House', *Global New Light of Myanmar* (6 April).

Nyein Nyein (2016) 'KIA: Govt needs to control its military', *The Irrawaddy* (10 October). http://www.irrawaddy.com/burma/kia-govt-needs-to-control-its-military.html, accessed 27 March 2017.

Page, Scott (2006) 'Path Dependence,' *Quarterly Journal of Political Science* 1: 87–115.

Pederson, Morten (2011) 'The Politics of Burma's Democratic Transition: Prospects for Change and Options for Democrats', *Critical Asian Studies*, 40 (1): 49–68.

Pederson, Morten (2008) *Promoting Human Rights In Burma: A Critique of Western Sanctions Policy*, New York: Rowman&Littlefield.

Prager-Nyein, Susanne (2009): 'Expanding Military, Shrinking Citizenry, and the New Constitution in Burma', *Journal of Contemporary Asia* 39(4): 638–48.

——— (2012) 'The Armed Forces of Burma: The Constant Sentinel', in M. Mietzner (ed.) *The Political Resurgence of the Military in Southeast Asia: Conflict and Leadership*, London: Routledge: 24–44.

Pyae Thet Phyo (2016) 'Tatmadaw chief marks the 71st Armed Forces Day', *Myanmar Times* (28 March).

Rüland, Jürgen, Maria Gabriela Manea and Hans Born, eds (2012) *The Politics of Military Reform: Experiences from Indonesia and Nigeria*. Heidelberg: Springer.

Sadan, Mandy (2015) 'The ongoing conflict in Kachin', in D. Singh (ed.) *Southeast Asian Affairs 2015*. Singapore: Institute of Southeast Asian Studies: 246–59.

Scurrah, Natalia, Philipp Hirsch and Kevin Woods (2015) The Political Economy of Land Governance in Myanmar, MRLG Mekong Region Land Governance Working Paper, November 2015. http://www.burmalibrary.org/docs21/MRLG-2015-11-Political_Economy_of_Land_Governance_in_Myanmar-red.pdf, accessed 27 March 2017.

Selth, Andrew (2002) *The Power of Glory*. Norwalk: Eastbridge.

——— (2008) 'Burma's 'saffron revolution' and the limits of international influence', *Australian Journal of International Affairs*, 62(3): 281–97.

——— (2009) 'Known Knowns and Known Unknowns: Measuring Myanmar's military capabilities'. *Contemporary Southeast Asia* 31(2): 272–92.

——— (2015) 'Strong, Efficient, Modern: The New Look for the Armed Forces', *Regional Outlook Paper*, No. 49, Griffith Asia Institute, Brisbane.

Siddiqa, Ayesha (2008) 'Military's Economic Role and Beyond', *The RUSI Journal*, 152(6): 64–70.

SLORC (1988): State Law and Order Restoration Council Announcement 1/1988, 18 September 1988. http://www.burmalibrary.org/docs15/1988-SLORC_Announcement1988-01-Formation_of_SLORC.pdf, accessed 27 March 2017.

Smith, Martin (1999) *Burma and the Politics of Ethnicity*. London: ZED Books.

——— (2007) *State of Strife: The Dynamics of Ethnic Conflict in Burma*. Washington, D.C. East–West Center.

Steinberg, David (2001) *Burma: The State of Myanmar*, Washington: Georgetown University Press.

——— (2005) 'The Role of the Military in the Economy', *Burma Economic Watch* 1/2005.

——— (2007) 'Political Legitimacy in Myanmar/Burma', in N. Ganesan and Kyaw Yin Hlaing (eds) *Burma: State, and Society, Ethnicity*. Singapore: Institute of Southeast Asian Studies: 109–40.

——— (2014) 'The Persistence of Military Dominance', in D. Steienberg (ed.) *Myanmar: The Dynamics of an Evolving Polity*. Boulder, London: Lynne Rienner: 37–59.

Stockholm International Peace Research Institute (2016): Military Expenditure Database, Stockholm.

Taylor, Robert (1985) 'Burma', in Z. Haji and H. Crouch (eds) *Civil-Military Relations in Southeast Asia*: Singapore: Oxford University Press: 13–49.

——— (2009) *Burma: The State in Myanmar*. London: Hurst.

———— (2015) 'The Armed Forces in Myanmar Politics: A Terminating Role?' *ASEAN-Perspectives*, 2/2015, Singapore: ISEAS.

Weymouth, Lally (2015) 'Burma's Top General: I am prepared to talk and discuss and answer and discuss with Aung San Suu Kyi's government', *Washington Post* (23 November).

Woods, Kevin (2011) 'Ceasefire capitalism: military–private partnerships, resource concessions and military-state building in the Burma–China borderlands', *Journal of Peasant Studies* 38(4): 747–70.

———— (2014) 'A political anatomy of land grabs' *The Myanmar Times* (3 March).

Zaw Oo and Win Min (2007) 'Assessing Burma's Ceasefire Accords', *Policy Studies 39*, East-West Center: Washington.

CHAPTER 4

The Political Economy of Military-Run Enterprises in Vietnam

Carlyle A. Thayer

Introduction

This chapter presents an analysis of the extensive role of the Vietnam People's Army (VPA)[1] in the political economy of Vietnam. The VPA owns and operates numerous state enterprises including those with wholly commercial functions. This analysis confirms that Vietnam represents a distinct case of Southeast Asia's authoritarian-single party regimes. First, the Vietnam Communist Party (VCP) is an elitist and not a mass party modelled on Leninist lines. Second, civil and military roles are fused in Vietnam. Third, an examination of historical legacies reveals that the VPA has undertaken two distinct roles since its inception: national defence and socialist construction. Three critical junctures may be identified: (1) the period following partition in 1954; (2) the period after reunification in 1975–76; and the period after 1989 when *đổi mới* or renovation began to take hold. By the mid-1990s the military's role in running civilian enterprises had become so extensive that two waves of reform (1995–97 and 1998–2006) were carried out to restructure these enterprises to make them more efficient and profitable. Fourth, an examination of historical institutionalism in Vietnam reveals the salience of recent conflicts and external threats that have reinforced the VPA's two strategic tasks. A critical juncture was reached in 1989 when the VPA carried out a massive demobilisation of troops following Vietnam's

---

1. The VPA is also referred elsewhere in this volume as the PAVN or People's Army of Vietnam.

withdrawal from Cambodia; entire Corps and Divisions were converted into General Corporations under the Ministry of National Defence. They were given legal status equivalent to civilian enterprises. They competed in the market place and formed joint ventures with foreign investors. The most outstanding example is Viettel, a telecoms company that provides mobile phones around the world. Efforts to divest the Ministry of National Defence of all commercial enterprises in 2007 foundered when the Global Economic Crisis impacted on Vietnam and Vietnam's Gross Domestic Product (GDP) growth slumped.

Historical legacies

The VPA was founded by the VCP and led by 'political generals' until well after national reunification in 1975 (Turley 1977: 233). The political and economic roles of the VPA were shaped at the outset by Marxist-Leninist ideology. The armed forces were considered an instrument of the worker-peasant alliance led by the communist party against the capitalist class. But the Vietnamese military, in addition to suppressing class enemies, also had to fight against foreign intervention. The VPA led the armed struggle against French colonialism (1946–54), conducted a war of national liberation in South Vietnam (1960–64), and a war against American intervention (1965–73). In sum, both Marxist-Leninist ideology and the legacy of more than two decades of armed conflict provide the historical foundation for the VPA's contemporary role in national defence, internal security, political affairs and economic production. Vietnam represents a distinct case among Southeast Asia's authoritarian regimes.

In times of peace, such as the period following the establishment of the Democratic Republic of Vietnam in 1954 (first proclaimed in 1945) and the Socialist Republic of Vietnam in 1976, the VPA constituted one of the four main pillars of the communist political system. The other three pillars were the VCP, the state apparatus and the Vietnam Fatherland Front (an umbrella group of mass organizations). The VPA is accorded bloc representation on the party's Central Committee as well as in the National Assembly. Political and military roles are fused. Senior military officers are dual-role elites through their membership in the VCP. The highest-ranking military officer is simultaneously the Minister of National Defence and the only military representative on the Politburo. The other senior members of the military also serve on the party Central Committee and Secretariat.

The salience of conflict and external threats has contributed to historical institutionalism (see discussion in Chapter 1). For example, the VPA has been continually engaged in 'fighting and economic production' since it was founded in 1944. This was particularly the case during the eight-year war against the French. After the 1954 settlement at Geneva, which partitioned Vietnam, the VPA was regrouped to northern Vietnam and local and guerrilla forces were reorganized along regular military lines (Thayer 1985: 234–8). In this period, the army was given a dual role. In addition to its national defence mission, the army was assigned responsibilities for economic construction and production, including running state farms that produced industrial or non-food crops for manufacturing. This was a major economic undertaking because, up until the 1990s, the Vietnamese economy was mainly agricultural with the peasants organised into high-level agricultural producers' cooperatives in which the means of production were socialised.

Historical legacies also account for the VPA's engagement in economic production, socialist construction and other state-building activities. The VPA's engagement in economic activities evolved over time to embrace commercial and business activities from the 1990s to the present.

Because civil (party) and military roles are fused, the notion of purely civilian control over military funding is inapplicable. The key civil–military interface is the Central Military Party Committee chaired by the VCP secretary general. The deputy chair is the Minister of National Defence, who is also a Senior General and a member of the Politburo. Vietnam's budget process is opaque. It is not known with any degree of clarity how military budget allocations are made. It is also not known whether the official defence budget includes income generated from military-owned and operated enterprises. Vietnam never released details of its military budget before 2009, and since then only general figures have been given.

It is presumed that the military proposes a budget that is discussed by the Central Military Party Committee and approved by the Politburo. The chairman of the National Assembly's Finance and Budget Committee once revealed that he is not given a breakdown of

Table 4.1: Vietnam's official defence budget, 2005–08 (billion VND)

Year	GDP	Defence budget	Share of GDP
2005	839,211	16,278	1.872%
2006	973,791	20,577	2.194%
2007	1,143,442	28,922	2.529%
2008	1,490,000	27,024	1.813%

Note: VND = Viet Nam đồng, the unit of currency in Vietnam.

Source: Socialist Republic of Vietnam, Ministry of National Defence, *Vietnam National Defence* (Hanoi: December 2009), 38.

the total defence budget; he sees only the bottom line. Other sources have revealed that the military has made direct representations to the Prime Minister on an *ad hoc* basis to secure supplementary funds for arms purchases or other major projects (Thayer 2011b).

Evidence suggests that the military budget is tied to economic growth but is also related to assessments of external threat. There was a marked decline in defence spending as a percentage of GDP during the Global Financial Crisis and a rise that accompanied tensions with China in the South China Sea.[2] Defence spending as a percentage of total government spending declined between 2005 to 2014 when it fell to around eight per cent of total government expenditure.[3]

Table 4.1 above provides the only official figures for the defence budget that Vietnam has released. It shows that for the four-year period (2005–08) the defence budget was pegged at around two per cent of GDP (a distinct measure from government spending).

Two strategic tasks, 1975–86

In the period following unification in 1975, the military in the south was primarily involved in maintaining public order and security, including transporting war refugees back to their native villages, disposal of

---

2. Australia Government, Defence Intelligence Organisation, *2015 Defence Economic Trends in the Asia-Pacific*, Defence Reference Aid 15-003. http://www.defence.gov. au/dio/documents/DET_15.pdf, accessed 26 January 2017.

3. Ibid., p. 30, accessed 26 January 2017.

unexploded ordnance and running re-education camps.[4] The VPA's roles were gradually expanded to include building new economic zones in remote areas and taking part in capital construction projects. VPA units, for example, were given responsibility for building roads, railways, ports, pipelines, industrial plants, civil installations and airports.

The VPA was also assigned to carry out a number of economic construction tasks, such as afforestation, land cultivation, livestock breeding, and manufacturing consumer goods at national defence factories. The VPA Navy was tasked with the transportation of merchandise between north and south, repair of commercial freighters, developing a fishing fleet, and participating in oil and gas exploration (*Vietnam Courier* 1976: 8–9).

In order to accommodate the growing demand for manpower in civilian reconstruction, military conscription was broadened to include service with labour brigades. These developments provoked dissent among middle and high-ranking military officers, who objected to the diversion of the VPA from defence tasks. They argued that continued VPA involvement in reconstruction would degrade combat readiness, erode discipline and delay the process of regularization and modernization. According to one Hanoi-based observer at the time, 'some officers point to the already demonstrated threat to the southern border' and argue that it [is] dangerous to reduce the military's combat readiness and effectiveness' (Ray 1979: 24).

In May 1976, Defence Minister Võ Nguyên Giáp responded to these concerns by arguing that the tasks of national defence and economic construction are interdependent (Giáp 1976: 13–45). In October, the party's Politburo reaffirmed the military's involvement in economic work by stressing that it was 'a fundamental and urgent demand of the revolution' (Ray 1979: 24). One indication of this new priority was the establishment of a General Directorate for Economic Development within the VPA to oversee the efforts of army units in civilian economic reconstruction tasks in four main areas: agriculture, industry, communications and transport and capital construction.

---

4. For an overview of this period, see Thayer 1985: 250–4, 256–62.

5. The threat to the southern border refers to incidents instigated by the Khmer Rouge regime in Cambodia.

In late 1976, the matter of the VPA's involvement in economic construction was endorsed as a national policy priority by the VCP's Fourth National Party Congress. According to a resolution adopted by this congress: 'our armed forces have two tasks: always to stand ready to fight and to defend the fatherland and to actively participate in economic construction' ('General Resolution of the Fourth Party Congress', Vietnam News Agency, 24 December 1976).' In a speech delivered to the congress, Senior General Văn Tiến Dũng elaborated that the VPA would continue to assist in redistributing the work force throughout Vietnam and consolidate strategic areas that were important for both the economy and national defence. General Dũng then described the army's other roles:

> In addition to the aforementioned tasks, the party entrusts the army with the duty to act as one of the great schools to train hundreds of thousands of our youths as new socialist human beings who are resolved to defend the fatherland and are at the same time, skilled labourers enthusiastically engaged in building the fatherland and socialism (Hanoi Radio Domestic Service, 16 December 1976).

Finally, the Fourth Congress resolution also approved the continuation of military service and importantly called for the development of a national defence industry.

The decision of the Fourth Congress to intensify the VPA's involvement in economic tasks resolved a major dilemma facing party leaders: whether to maintain a large yet economically unproductive standing army or to sanction a massive post-war demobilisation. The Fourth Congress chose a middle path. According to a foreign journalist based in Hanoi:

> The case for participation by the armed forces in the economic recovery program was strong. A generation of war had left the army with a near monopoly of resources for certain types of construction and it was by far the largest single source of trained cadres. Disciplined, politicised and often possessing important technical skills, the troops were best equipped to meet reconstruction needs on an emergency basis (Ray 1979: 24).

In the months following the Fourth Party Congress, twenty thousand army personnel were given specialized training as district-level economic managers (Thayer 1985: 253). Army units were assigned a variety of specialized tasks including the upgrading the strategic road network along the Hồ Chí Minh Trail, running state farms, constructing large-scale irrigation works and hydroelectric power stations, and engaging in land reclamation and other major projects. Other military units continued to train and maintain their combat proficiency to ensure national defence, but they too were required 'to devote a fixed amount of time to stepping up production and making full use of waste and fallow land... to produce grain and food' (Thayer 1985: 254).

Vietnam's efforts to recover from the devastation of nearly thirty years of war and begin the task reconstruction were curtailed by a growing conflict with the Khmer Rouge regime in neighbouring Cambodia. In 1978 large-scale fighting broke out, inaugurating a decade-long conflict known as the Third Indochina War (1978–89). Vietnam invaded Cambodia in December 1978 and China retaliated by attacking Vietnam's northern border in early 1979. During the Third Indochina War the VPA rapidly expanded in size through national conscription. Main force strength jumped from 615,000 in 1978 to 1.26 million in 1987 (Thayer 1985: 254–6).

The sudden escalation of conflict on Vietnam's south-western and northern borders raised a conundrum for VPA leaders who debated whether or not to curtail the VPA's continued engagement in domestic reconstruction. The debate was resolved by re-emphasizing that the VPA would continue to undertake two strategic tasks simultaneously. According to party secretary Lê Duẩn speaking in July 1981:

> Our entire party, army and people will have to carry out two strategic tasks simultaneously: successfully building socialism and being constantly ready to fight and firmly defend our socialist fatherland and resolutely defeat every scheme and act of aggression of Chinese expansionism and hegemonism and international reactionary forces... It is necessary for the people's army to undergo intensive training in order to become a mighty and increasingly modern and regularized revolutionary army... *while at the same time participating in production and economic development in appropriate ways* [emphasis added].[6]

In the late 1970s and early 1980s, Vietnam experienced an economic crisis of mammoth proportions brought on by a number of factors:

---

6. Le Duan's speech was carried in instalments on Hanoi Radio Domestic Service, 26–30 June and 1 July 1981.

repeated natural disasters, the withdrawal of foreign aid and economic isolation, the costs of conflict, and the failure of Soviet-styled central planning that resulted in a grain deficit of nearly three million tons. Shortages of all types – food, medicine, clothing, and consumer goods – became pervasive.

Lê Duẩn informed Vietnam's National Assembly that the country's socio-economic plan for the 1980s would have to be reformulated. Priority was given to emergency measures to overcome the economic crisis. Lê Duẩn outlined three national objectives that had to be achieved:

1. To stabilize and take a significant step forward in improving the people's material and cultural life – first and foremost, definitively to solve the grain and food problems and meet the basic clothing needs of the entire society.

2. To overcome the most serious economic imbalances, create considerable sources of accumulation from within the national economy and establish the key features of the material and technical infrastructure for socialism.

3. To fully meet the needs of national defence and maintain national security (Broadcast on Hanoi Radio Domestic Service, 26–30 June and 1 July 1981).

In March 1982, the VCP's Fifth National Congress reviewed Vietnam's domestic and international situation three years after Vietnam's invasion of Cambodia and the imposition of aid and trade embargoes by countries within the region and around the world. Vietnam's economy was in a parlous state, the VPA was bogged down in a protracted counter-insurgency conflict in Cambodia, and Vietnam's northern provinces were kept in a constant state of tension by Chinese sabre-rattling. The Fifth Congress once again assigned the VPA two strategic tasks: building socialism and defending the fatherland (Thayer 1983: 299–324).

The effects of Vietnam's economic crisis were manifest in society at large. 'Negative phenomena' such as smuggling, stealing, hoarding, speculation and draft evasion, became widespread. Food riots occurred in central Vietnam. These conditions only reinforced the VCP's determination to employ the VPA in economic production activities. Under the task of building socialism, the VPA was now expected to contribute to economic development by taking part in a wide range of production activities in the agricultural and industrial sectors. Specialized military economic construction units continued to participate in 'productive labour and economic development.' The bulk of these units were stationed between Hanoi and the China border.

Under the national defence task, which also included internal security duties, the VPA was expected to carry out its internationalist duties in Cambodia and Laos, and stand ready to repel a second Chinese attack in the north. Vietnam's national defence strategy was redrawn to give emphasis to the military's enhanced role in economic development. Individuals who completed their military service were discharged and assigned to their former work place, a new economic zone or to a vocational school for specialized training. These individuals constituted the core of the ready reserves and were expected to play key leadership roles in local militia and self-defence forces.

In the decade up to 1986, Army units of corps (*binh đoàn*) size were assigned to new economic zones, state farms and forests, hydroelectric and water conservancy projects, building roads, and oil and gas exploration (Thayer 2000: 98). One unit of roughly 12,000 men was given responsibility for completing the Hòa Bình hydroelectric project northwest of Hanoi. Brigades and smaller sized units planted rubber, tobacco, coffee and tea.

Economic renovation and its impact on the military

In December 1986, the VCP's Sixth National congress adopted a major economic reform programme known as *đổi mới*. This had a major impact on the VPA and its roles (*Quân Đội Nhân Dân*, 12 May 1991). In 1987 Vietnam initiated a major strategic readjustment of its armed forces (Thayer 1995: 185–201). VPA units were withdrawn from Cambodia and Laos. The size of the VPA's main force was cut from 1.26 million (1987) to less than half a million in a six-year demobilization programme (Thayer 2000: 199–219). Renovation also resulted in the VPA becoming involved in commercial activities. This was a marked change from the VPA's previous involvement in economic construction and production tasks.

In March 1989 the Council of Ministers issued Directive 46, a major new policy document regarding the military's role in economic activities. This directive required all VPA units and defence enterprises involved in production and economic construction to conduct their affairs under an 'independent economic accounting system.'[7] Legal status was gradually extended to other military enterprises were now able to open foreign currency bank accounts, form legal associations, and enter into joint ventures with Vietnamese or foreign partners

This was a critical juncture for the VPA's economic role. Nine major VPA economic construction units were converted into legal entities – corporations (*công ty*) and general corporations (*công ty tổng cục*) – that remained under military control but were now subject to the same state laws as civilian enterprises Dau 1989). By August 1989, so many military enterprises had become involved in economic activities that the table of organization of the Economic General Department had to be redrawn four times. By the end of the year even more army units were transformed into corporations, general corporations or other types of legal entities (Nghĩa 1990: 67).

Military-run enterprises continued to be involved in economic construction and production such as constructing houses, hotels, roads, bridges and ports; managing coffee, tea and rubber plantations in the Central Highlands; mining coal, tin and precious stones; catching and processing seafood; transporting oil workers to off-shore rigs by helicopter; producing cement and asphalt; and operating joint ventures with foreign companies (Branigin 1993). Military units were also involved in large-scale construction projects such as the Yali, Phả Lại and Vĩnh Sơn power projects; the Vũng Tàu oil and gas exploration zone; the Trường Sơn north-south highway; and the Hải Phòng export-processing zone (Vietnam News Agency 30 January 1994).

Because army enterprises had land-use rights, disciplined labour and strategic location, they quickly expanded their economic and commercial activities. One military commentator revealed that almost all enterprises and factories under the VPA's Technical General Department 'produced economic goods which have accounted for 40–50 per cent of their production output' (Dau 1989). Another source estimated that the army raised twenty per cent of its revenue from internal sources (Senior General Lê Trọng Tấn, cited by Hiebert 1991: 24).

The case of Technical Application and Production (Tecapro) is instructive. Tecapro was established in 1990 by the Military Technology

---

7. See Biến 1991. This system converted accounting methods to reflect profit and loss.

Institute to specialize in computer science and environmental solutions. It won a number of contracts with Vietsovpetro, the Soviet-Vietnamese petroleum joint venture, and with Petrolimex, Vietnam's national petroleum company. It then set up two joint ventures with overseas partners. It was estimated that only ten percent of Tecapro's business activities were related to contracts with the VPA (Thayer 2003: 201).

The commercial activities of these diverse military-run enterprises were breathtaking in scope. According to one report, 'army factories, which began to produce consumer goods in the 1980s on a small scale, massively broadened their production in 1991 and 1992' (Vietnam News Agency, 21 February 1993). Among the consumer items produced were paper, ready-made garments, raincoats, electric fans, bicycle and motorcycle parts, oil cookers, fluorescent bulbs, televisions, radio-cassette recorders and computers. Army enterprises also provided services such as real estate development and running hotels and nightclubs. Other army factories manufactured industrial goods such as jute polishers, hydraulic presses, lathes, detonators, electricity meters, transformers, buses and heavy trucks.

Military enterprises that were given legal status were now able to open foreign currency bank accounts, form legal associations, and enter into joint ventures with Vietnamese or foreign partners. In 1993, the VPA set up its first joint stock commercial bank (*Asian Defence Journal* 1994: 97 and Vietnam News Agency 8 December 1994). The VPA also set up a consulting firm that specialized in international law and accountancy (Cleary 1995). By 1995 there were forty-nine army-run joint enterprises with foreign partners, this number rose to fifty-six in 1997[8] and sixty-seven by 2003 (*Quân Đội Nhân Dân* 7 January 2003). They were mainly engaged in consumer goods, garment industry, automobile manufacturing, construction work, ship and plane repair, hotels and real estate, and mechanical engineering (Thayer 1996, p. 18).

When military-run enterprises were first established in the late 1980s, they were created from defence industries or existing military

---

8. Vietnam News Agency, 20 February 1996; Vietnam News Agency, 12 May 1996; 'Vietnamese Army Streamlines Businesses', *Jane's Defence Weekly*, 24 September 1997, p. 13; and Nguyen Nham, 'Money the new target for army', *Vietnam Investment Review*, 15–21 June 1998, p. 11.

units.[9] These corporations originally provided employment to army personnel and their families. It was not anticipated at the time that they would grow so large. In 1993 the total number of army-run commercial enterprises was put at 300 employing 70,000 soldiers or 12 per cent of the entire standing army.[10] The VPA main force alone had nearly sixty organizations legally classified as corporations, general corporations, scientific and production federations engaged in economic activities. Production on behalf of these organizations was assigned to more than 200 primary level enterprises (*Quân Đội Nhân Dân* 12 May 1991). Local militia units were reported to have set up at least 160 enterprises.

Four giant military-run general corporations stood out as especially successful in the marketplace:

1. *Trường Sơn Construction General Corporation* (12th Corps). This unit once built and maintained the Hồ Chí Minh Trail (Nghia, 1990:67–69). It was involved in the construction of every major road project in Vietnam, including National Route 1. It has been a successful bidder for major infrastructure projects including the North-South power line, Hòa Bình hydroelectricity plant and international construction projects. The corporation has also branched out into such areas as rail repair, coal and export, coffee growing, goods transport and general support service provision (*Voice of Vietnam* 2 February 1992). In the early 1990s the corporation employed 7,000 persons (four-fifths of whom were military personnel) in nineteen enterprises (Hiebert 1991: 26).[11]

---

9. Some units kept their original designation. For example, *Binh đoàn* 15, the 15th Corps that operated in the Tây Nguyên or Central Highlands, was designated Corporation 15.

10. See Hiebert 1991: 26–7; Branigin 1993; and Hiebert 1993: 40. According to Lt. Gen. Phan Thu (1994: 18), the director of the National Defence Industry and Economic General Department, 'since 1976 the army has assigned a large force to engage in economic construction. A total of 280,000 soldiers in 29 divisions are participating in almost every economic sector.' Phan Thu's figure apparently includes the number of soldiers engaged in all types of economic activities and not just those involved in the operation of 300 or so army-run enterprises.

11. These included nine corporations, six enterprises, one state farm, one state forest unit, one bridge and road construction unit and a vocational middle school; see also Tuyen and Anh 1991: 34–36.

2. *Flight Service Corporation.* It is equipped with military aircraft including helicopters. The Corporation provides services for aerial surveys, tourism, medical emergencies, maintenance of the trans-Vietnam electricity line, and searches for U.S. service personnel missing-in-action during the Vietnam War. The southern branch of this company runs a helicopter service for eight foreign oil and gas exploration companies.

3. *Tây Nguyên Corporation* (15th Corps). This company manages rubber, coffee, wet rice and timber production in the central highlands.

4. *Thành An Construction and Assembly Corporation* (11th Corps). It was formed in 1997 and has eleven affiliates engaged in such key sectors as construction, mineral exploration, coal mining and training.

At the VCP's first Midterm Conference in January 1994, the party decided that Vietnam's main development objectives would be the industrialization and modernization of the economy. This had important implications for industries that came under the direct control of the Ministry of National Defence. Military-owned enterprises were now tasked with developing and acquiring advanced technology with a dual civil–military application. Army-run enterprises became heavily involved in such new sectors as electronics, computing and telecommunications.

In May 1994, for example, Prime Minister Võ Văn Kiệt ended the telecommunications monopoly exercised by the Directorate General of Posts and Telecommunications. The Ministry of National Defence was now permitted to offer services in this sector. The Military Electronics Telecommunications Company (METC) entered into a joint venture with the American company NewTel to manufacture telephones, fax machines, pagers and consumer electronic products such as circuit boards for CD players (Lam 1996: 15). In 1998, the Military Telecommunications General Corporation (Viettel) was approved as Vietnam's fifth internet service provider.

The first wave of reforms, 1995–97

In 1995–96 the VPA launched the first wave of a major reform drive to restructure its expanding network of enterprises and corporations. The National Defence Industry and Economic General Department was charged with responsibility for reorganizing existing enterprises, streamlining top echelons, merging businesses in the same sector, and dissolving a number of loss-making enterprises. Particular attention was paid to merging small and medium enterprises in the same line of business in order to strengthen their domestic competitiveness against local firms, joint ventures and foreign businesses. By May 1996 the number of military-run enterprises had been reduced from 335 to 193 (Vietnam News Agency 12 May 1996). As was to be expected, the restructuring programme achieved some successes and ran into a number of difficulties. On the plus side, a number of army-run enterprises were able to accumulate capital, reduce their workforce, improve competitiveness and remit increased revenue to central government coffers. In some cases, restructuring led to the creation of new jobs.

The greatest success was achieved in reforming those industries and trades in which the army already enjoyed an advantage: capital construction (building and infrastructure), flight and maritime services, mining, engineering, industrial explosive materials and garment manufacture. As a result, the already strong role of army businesses in these areas was strengthened. According to the editor of the *Military Industry Magazine*, the following enterprises emerged as the seven largest military-run companies after restructuring: Trường Sơn Construction General Corporation, Thành An Construction and Assembly Corporation, Garment Export Company 28 (*Vietnam Business Journal*, October 1996: 5; and *The Saigon Times*, 17 November 1998), Đông Bắc (East–North) Coal Company,[12] Military Commercial Joint Stock Bank, Chemical Export Company 21 and Chemical Company 76.

Many military-owned enterprises suffered from the same ills as their civilian-run counterparts in the state sector. In several instances, mergers were merely formalistic paper exercises. According to one report, 'Worse still, some units have simply combined several enterprises and imposed a newly created corporate apparatus on them, thus only streamlining the top echelon while inflating the indirect apparatuses and making them even more cumbersome and inefficient' (Đỗ Phú Thọ, *Nhân Dân*, 13 September 1997 quoted in Thayer 2003: 88). The same account also

---

12. For details on the operation of the Đông Bắc Coal Company, formed after the merger of thirteen coal mining enterprises under the control of various military zones and units, see: Vietnam News Agency, 20 February 1996.

revealed that 'in addition, when restructuring their productive forces, a number of enterprises have failed to reorganize their redundant personnel, giving rise to negative phenomena.'

In 1993, it was reported that half of the army-run enterprises were small companies with outdated equipment and limited amounts of subscribed capital (newly issued securities that an investor had expressed an intent to purchase). The Air Defence Cement Company, for example, was reportedly given only 250 million VND in capital, enough to meet only 5.6 per cent of its needs. Finally, the restructuring programme uncovered another basic problem: many military-run enterprises were owed unrecoverable debts.

Some military-run enterprises maintained a huge stockpile of goods that they could not sell. Although these firms faced competition in the market and were economically unviable, they were kept afloat by subsidies from the Ministry of National Defence. Also, it was discovered that army-run enterprises tended to spend their profits on luxury items rather than reinvesting in capital stock. Luxury items included new automobiles, renovated guesthouses, new conference halls, modern interior equipment and expensive imported appliances for use by the enterprise. In June 1997, for example, a commentary in *Quân Đội Nhân Dân* warned that more needed to be done to eliminate wastefulness and corruption. The commentary noted that some army units incurred 'big losses' as a result of casual spending hosting guests, ceremonies and parties (quoted in Thayer 1998: 57). Losses were also due to weak financial management in army construction projects. A thrift campaign was launched to discourage these practices.

In 1997, military-run companies were divided into three main types: defence-economic enterprises (*doanh nghiệp kinh tế quốc phòng*) that produced and repaired weapons and military equipment, undertook special defence duties, and also produced commercial goods as a sideline; national defence economic enterprises (*doanh nghiệp quốc phòng*) that produced and traded civilian products, provided daily logistics support, or participated in economic development in remote areas; and exclusive economic enterprises (*doanh nghiệp chuyên làm kinh tế*) that specialized in producing and trading in commercial products. Of the three categories, the exclusive economic enterprises accounted for more than half of the army's business interests. These corporations were involved in the full spectrum of commercial activities from the most basic services (laundry and food processing) to the highly advanced manufacturing (computers and telecommunications).

Vietnam has never released a set of comprehensive official figures on the contribution of military-owned enterprises to the national economy. What figures have been released are vague and contradictory some figures refer to production, others to revenue. But it is clear from comments made by official spokespersons that military-run companies have been increasingly successful. In 1996, for example, it was reported that the army's national defence enterprises achieved a 25 per cent increase in production over 1995. The following year, it was reported that army-run enterprises had achieved an increase of 30 per cent in revenue over 1996. Figures for 2002 also indicate an increase in revenues (*Quân Đội Nhân Dân* 7 January 2003). Other sources indicate a twenty-four-fold increase in revenue over a nine-year period from US $25 million in 1990 to US $600 million in 1998 (Thayer 2000: 108).

Military earnings were reportedly higher than enterprises run by central ministries or other sectors. Military enterprises under the General Logistics Department alone earned record revenues of US $83 million in 1997, while the Trường Sơn Construction General Corporation increased its earnings 40 per cent over 1996. The average wages in this sector were 70 dollars per month against the national average of 40 dollars.

Vietnam's military enterprises pay taxes like any other legal business. The military is permitted by law to engage in commercial ventures because it earns funds to support genuine military activities that the state budget does not meet. According to the head of the VPA's Economics Department, 'There is a conflict of interest here: defence activities cost a lot of money, while business means profit. So the army is engaged in business not just to make money, but for the sake of national security. If we put the profit motive first, we would be making a big mistake' (quoted in Dung 1999: 23).

The second wave of reforms, 1998–2006

In 1998–99 military-run enterprises were subject to further reforms and the VPA was given the additional responsibility of administering economic-defence zones in remote areas (Lê Hữu Đức, 2014).

According to Hanh Dung (1999), the Ministry of National Defence 'is structured like a real, if miniature, government'. According to another observer, it was difficult to conceive of any industry in which the military was not involved as its tentacles reached into every corner of the economy. Of the 164 corporations under the control of the Ministry of National Defence, four were under the direct control of the central ministry while the remaining 160 were under the control of ten subordinate departments, including foreign joint ventures.[13] Over half of the military-run enterprises were small companies that were unable to compete effectively in the market due to limited prescribed capital and outdated equipment (Đỗ Phú Thọ, *Nhân Dân*, 13 September 1997 quoted in Thayer 2003: 88).

In May 1998, the Central Military Party Committee issued a directive launching a second wave of reforms for army-run enterprises in order to improve their business efficiency and ability to take on major projects. The Ministry of National Defence was ordered to adopt firm measures to dissolve loss-making military companies. The directive also prohibited army divisions, provincial units, and specialized departments within the defence ministry from setting up and operating commercial enterprises.

Later in 1998, Prime Minister Phan Văn Khải announced that military-run enterprises would be required to rationalize their commercial activities. In order to implement these new reforms, the Economics Division, formerly under the General Department of National Defence Industry and Economics, was upgraded to the status of an independent Economic Department under the direct control of the Ministry of National Defence (Vietnam News Agency 28 April 1999).

Most army-run enterprises could not stay solvent by fulfilling their military contracts alone. They had to seek outside work. Army enterprises therefore came under increasing pressure to concentrate on finding a permanent niche in the economy for themselves. At the end of 1999, for example, it was reported that a fourth army corps, *Binh đoàn 16*, had been converted into a general corporation with responsibility for fertilizer production in central Vietnam. National Defence Ministry figures showed that up to 80 per cent of the army's contracts came from

---

13. There was a reduction in the number of foreign-partner joint ventures. Some military joint ventures that did not perform well were sold to foreign investors.

the civilian sector (Dung 1999: 22). The number of army personnel engaged in economic activities rose steadily since *đổi mới* was adopted. It was estimated in 1999 that the number of army personnel employed in military-run enterprises had risen to 100,000 (Watkin 1999). Given the decline in main force numbers, this represents one-fifth to one-quarter of the standing army.

According to one observer, the second wave of reforms was aimed at 'cutting down the number of small-scale enterprises, concentrating on key strengths, promoting co-operation between army enterprises to win state contracts and making their products more competitive' (Dung 1999: 22). In 1999, the army had the smallest number of businesses in Vietnam running at a loss. By 2006, military-run firms earned US two billion dollars in revenue, or approximately 3.6 per cent of Vietnam's GDP (Thayer 2011a: 75).

The second major development in 1998 that affected the role of the VPA was the decision to give the military responsibility for the setting up of special economic-defence zones or *khu kinh tế-quốc phòng* (Agence France-Presse 1998). The programme was promulgated by the prime minister's Decision 135/1998/QD-TTG that instructed each military region to establish one or two economic-defence zones to promote economic activity and national defence. By the end of the following year, 13 economic-defence zones with total investment of US $215 million had been set up in strategic areas along borders with China, Laos and Cambodia. The VPA was given the responsibility for 'mobilizing the masses and building political bases' (Phạm Thanh Ngân, 1999: 20) and thus reinforcing ties between the military and society.

According to Defence Minister Phạm Văn Trà, 'an economic and military combination enhances fighting capacity, improves the defence industries, allocates soldiers in key areas and, perhaps most importantly, balances the budget for all military activities' (quoted in Hanh Dung 1999: 23) Vice Minister of Defence Nguyễn Văn Rinh stated that the programme was aimed at 'fewer numbers but greater proficiency' (Hanh Dung 1999: 23). The objective was to combine economic activities with defence capability in remote and relatively under-populated areas. Funding for this new initiative came from both the Ministry of National Defence and provincial governments, but because of insufficient revenue, the VPA was given permission to mobilize funds from international organizations as well as domestic sources. In addition, proposals for foreign investment projects were now evaluated for their impact on national defence (Dung 2000: 6).

In the new economic-defence zones, the VPA was assigned the task of assisting in the relocation of families from highly populated provinces to mountainous areas and islands. The military was also assigned to build the infrastructure for settlers.[14] An estimated 84,000 families had been resettled in these areas when the project was completed in 2013.

The Tây Nguyên Army Corps opened thousands of hectares of new land for the growth and production of rubber, coffee, wet rice, fruit and industrial crops as well as livestock breeding. Its units constructed industrial processing plants, schools, cultural centres, sports complexes, and amusement facilities. Elsewhere, military units engaged in dual civilian-military tasks. Naval patrols were involved in offshore fishing, border guard units were assigned afforestation tasks, the Flight Service Corporation combined its commercial operations with pilot training, army hospitals offered services to civilian patients, and military research centres were authorized to sign contracts with non-military bodies to use their specialised services.

The VPA also assumed responsibility for the implementation of social welfare projects in remote areas that no other ministry wanted to undertake. Military groups became the driving force behind road and dyke construction, planting new forests, relocation of ethnic minorities,[15] and provision of newspapers and television services. The VPA inaugurated a new programme, the Army and People Healthcare Corporation, with agreement of the Ministry of Public Health. Border troops became involved in an anti-illiteracy campaign. Border guards not only constructed new schools, but also provided the teachers for an estimated 80,000 pupils. The military worked closely with community elders and religious leaders and cooperated with state agencies in social welfare activities in remote mountain areas and islands where govern-

---

14. For an overview see Hồ Quốc Toản , 'Xây dựng khu kinh tế-quốc phòng trên các địa bàn chiến lược (Building national-defence zones in strategic areas)', *Tạp chí Quốc phòng toàn dân*, No. 7, July 2001: 34–36.

15. The VPA was also involved in resettling so-called nomadic ethnic minorities into permanent villages. Security officials were concerned that ethnic minorities were abandoning traditional ancestor worship to follow 'other religions' (Christianity) and thus contribute to social unrest.

ment officials seldom ventured. As a result of its active involvement, the VPA had a say in local government decisions and, in effect, acted as an arm of the government in remote economic-defence zones (Tran Le Thuy 1999: 25).

Divestiture of commercial enterprises

The military's growing economic and commercial interests directly clashed with the imperatives of global economic integration when Vietnam became a member of the World Trade Organization in January 2007. At that time, the VPA ran 140 enterprises and held shares in another 20 companies. The army's commercial enterprises were engaged in an incredibly diverse range of moneymaking activities from coffee production, coal mining and garment manufacture to stock broking, telecommunications and health services.

In order to comply with Vietnam's WTO obligations, the VCP Central Committee adopted a resolution at its fourth plenum directing the army, police and regime-sponsored mass organisations to divest themselves of all commercial enterprises that they currently owned and operated. This resolution was intended to end state subsidies and make these enterprises competitive against foreign companies. Divestiture of these enterprises was an extremely sensitive issue because the VPA would lose an important source of income. The fourth plenum's resolution specified, however, that the VPA could retain ownership and control over companies that were directly related to national defence and security.

The process of handing over ownership was due to begin before the end of 2007 and conclude by 2012 (*People's Army Newspaper Online*, 2007; Nhung 2007; *Viet Nam News*, 4 April 2008). In December 2007, Defence Minister General Phùng Quang Thanh stated that his ministry would hand over around 140 military-owned commercial enterprises to the state by 2012 and 'focus on training and building up a regular modern army' (*Quân Đội Nhân Dân*, 19 December 2007). Both Viettel and the Military Commercial Joint Stock Bank were slated to be handed over.

In 2007 inflationary pressures that had been building up rose to an all-time high. Senior military officers, in a sign of foot-dragging, signalled that the transfer of military-owned businesses would take many years (*Thanh Niên* 20 December 2007). In 2008, the then-global economic crisis 'had a great impact on army businesses', a conference to review the activities of army enterprises was told, and this slowed the pace of divestment. The official defence budget dropped noticeably from 2.2 per cent of GDP in 2007 to 1.8 per cent in 2008. Nevertheless the army-run Viettel Corporation and the Vietnam Service Flight Company both reported profits (*People's Army Newspaper Online* 19 February 2009).

In 2008, the National Assembly adopted the Ordinance on Defence Industry that provided the legal basis for the transfer of military-run businesses and set out the principles and legal framework for national defence industries to be retained by the Ministry of National Defence. Plans to divest the Defence Ministry of its business enterprises appeared to gather steam in April, when the Prime Minister issued instructions for the divestiture of one hundred and thirteen military-owned enterprises (*Viet Nam News* 2008). While the initiative led to the divestment, restructuring or breakup of small military businesses, it allowed the VPA and the Defence Ministry to hold on to their most precious asset, Viettel, and nine other major general corporations (see Table 4.2 opposite).

The VPA's Defence Industry General Department also reported that despite facing 'numerous economic difficulties and negative impacts during the year' it had 'surpassed all of 2008's set plans' (*People's Army Newspaper Online* 11 February 2009). According to a report in the army's newspaper, 'factories and plants under the General Department proactively sought out orders and contracts, extending both domestic and international markets in order to maintain a stable production schedule and pay raises for its workers' (ibid.).

In late 2009, Vietnam released a Defence White Paper that for the first time listed ten major general corporations owned by the Ministry of National Defence (see Table 4.2). This list confirmed that neither Viettel nor the Military Commercial Joint Stock Bank had been privatized. In addition, the Defence White Paper noted, 'there are 98 VPA businesses at present operating in various fields of the economy, such as flight services, seaport services, telecommunications, and ship-building industry. Their export commodity and service turnover is ever increasing' (Socialist Republic 2009: 69).[16]

---

16. On seaports, see 'Sông Thu corporation hailed for business achievements', *People's Army Daily Online*, 17 April 2014. The Sông Thu Corporation is under the General Department of Defence Industry.

Table 4.2: Major military-owned general corporations, 2009

Name of Corporation	Founding Date	Main Headquarters
Trường Sơn Construction General Corporation	19.5.59	Hanoi
Military Petrol General Corporation	30.9.65	Cầu Giấy, Hanoi
General Corporation No. 28	9.5.75	Hồ Chí Minh City
Thành An General Corporation	11.6.82	Đống Đa, Hanoi
General Corporation No. 15	20.2.85	Pleiku, Gia Lai province
Tân Cảng General Corporation	15.3.89	Hồ Chí Minh City
Flight Service General Corporation	1.6.89	Đống Đa, Hanoi
Viettel – Military Telecommunications General Corporation	1.6.89	Ba Đình, Hanoi
Military Bank (Military Commercial Joint Stock Bank)	4.11.94	Ba Đình, Hanoi
Northeast General Corporation	24.12.94	Hạ Long, Quảng Ninh province

Source: Socialist Republic of Vietnam, Ministry of National Defence, *Vietnam National Defence* (Hanoi: December 2009).

Case study: Military Telecommunications General Corporation (Viettel)

The Military Telecommunications General Corporation was originally founded on 1 June 1989 and is wholly owned and operated by the Ministry of National Defence. Today the Vietnam Military Telecommunications Group is the parent company of the Viettel Group (*Tập đoàn Viễn thông Quân đội*), which was founded in 2004. The Viettel Group comprises a number of companies, including Vietnam Distribution (also known as Viettel Import and Export Co.), Viettel New Service Development,

Viettel Post, Viettel Investment and Real Estate, Viettel International Investment and Viettel Football Training Centre.

Viettel produces for both the civilian and military markets. For example, Viettel quickly became Vietnam's largest mobile network operator. In early 2010 Viettel introduced 3G services including video call, mobile broadband 3G, TV mobile, video-on-demand, and online music (*The Saigon Times* 2010). In late 2012, Viettel severed its ties with China's Huawei and began producing mobile phones on its own (*The Saigon Times* 2012). In 2012 it was estimated that based on revenues Viettel had a market share in Vietnam of 40.6 per cent and 58.9 million customers (*Hàng Hóa Thông Hiểu* 2013). Viettel also expanded its commercial operations outside Vietnam and now claims to have 285 million customers in ten countries including Cambodia, Laos, Haiti, Mozambique, Peru, Cameroon, Tanzania and Timor-Leste.[17]

In 2013, Viettel began production of military equipment for the VPA such radar, airspace management systems, unmanned aerial vehicles and communications and information systems for military vehicles and the infantry (VietNamNet.Bridge 2014 and Grevatt 2015).

In May 2014, Senior Lieutenant General Lê Hữu Đức, Deputy Minister of National Defence, chaired a conference to review the financial work of Viettel in 2013. According to a press report,

> [Viettel] determined the level of spending, regulations on using budget to promptly ensure capital for production and investment in projects. *Its turnover, profit and contributions to the State budget exceeded set targets* [emphasis added].
>
> General Đức highly valued Viettel's achievements in doing business and social welfare, and improving its employees' living standards.
>
> He asked the unit to continue to effectively implement production activities and regulations on financial economic management and financial disclosure, fight against corruption and extravagance, and maintain its sustainable growth rate (*People's Army Newspaper* 2014).

In 2014 Viettel employed 80,000 persons worldwide (VietnamBreaking News, 2015). It reported total revenue of VND 196,650 billion (equivalent to US $9.36bn) and a pre-tax profit of VND 31,458 billion ($1.49 billion) resulting in a net profit of VND 2 trillion or US $0.11bn

---

17. On Timor-Leste, see 'Viettel brand brings services to Timor Leste's villages', *People's Army Daily Online*, 19 September 2014.

(VietnamNet 2014; Viettel.com.vn). But Viettel also released figures claiming that in 2014 it earned total revenue of VND 197,000 billion (representing 20 per cent growth over the previous year) and a profit of VND 42,000 billion before tax (a growth rate of 15 per cent; see Viettel. com.vn). In 2014, of one thousand state-owned enterprises, Viettel was the largest contributor to the state budget with remittances totalling VND 15,000 billion.

On 27 January 2015, the Ministry of National Defence held a conference to review the performance of military-owned enterprises in 2014 and their business targets for 2015 (Grevatt 2015). The conference was told that military-owned business companies accrued total revenue of VND 292 trillion ($13.7 billion) or nearly seven percent of GDP, a profit of VND 46 trillion (15 percent more than 2013), and contributed VND 41 trillion to the state budget (or 14 per cent of total revenue). These figures represented a year-on-year increase of 18, 15 and 12 per cent, respectively.

Viettel was the most successful military-run enterprise, while the Military Bank expanded to become one of Vietnam's largest commercial banks (*People's Army Newspaper*, 2015). The conference signalled out for praise the Saigon Newport Group (one of Vietnam's leading ports), Lũng Lô Construction Group, Corporation No. 319, Corporation No. 789, Đông Bắc Company, Housing and Urban Development Corporation, and the Aviation Construction Company.

Finally it was noted that during 2014, military-owned enterprises that were totally state-funded were reorganised and restructured to make them more efficient. These enterprises conducted commercial activities in 421 fields. In addition, some military-owned enterprises expended some of their funds on charity and welfare, including building two hundred houses for families of wounded or deceased soldiers in 2014.

Conclusion

This chapter presented a broad historical overview of the role of the VPA in economic production including commercial businesses activities. This chapter argues that trying to determine the extent of civilian (read Vietnam Communist Party) control over military financing, a major theme of this volume, is problematic in the Vietnamese context because of the dual role that senior party-military elites play in the country's political system.

This chapter touched on two major themes, historical legacies and historical institutionalism. The evolution of the military's involvement in economic production was historically shaped from the very foundation of the VPA. As a guerrilla force it was given responsibility for economic production to meet its material needs. The chapter also argued that prolonged armed conflict and the salience of external threats institutionalised Vietnam's historical legacies.

The military's role in economic production was reinforced by three critical historical junctures. First, after the partition of Vietnam in 1954, the VPA was gradually transformed into a regular conventional force. At the same time, it was assigned to run state farms that produced industrial crops. Second, after the reunification of Vietnam in 1975, the VPA was assigned wide-ranging responsibility for post-war reconstruction. Third, after the end of the Cambodian conflict in 1989–91, the VPA was demobilized and entire units ranging from divisions to corps were converted into military-owned and operated state enterprises. The legacy of the VPA's involvement in economic production became self-reproducing at it expanded from production to commercial operations.

In the 1980s, when Vietnam moved to reform its failed Soviet-style system of central planning, the combination of historical institutionalism and historical legacies shaped the path dependence of continued VPA involvement in the economy. At this critical juncture in 1989, military-owned enterprises were placed on the same legal footing as, and competed in the marketplace with, civilian-run state-owned enterprises.

While the chapter argued that it was difficult to separate civilian control over military funding because of the fused nature of dual role elites, it is clear that Vietnam's proactive efforts at global economic integration have affected military businesses. Military-owned enterprises were subject to two waves of institutional reform designed to weed out the inefficient and loss-making enterprises. The military generally complied with this policy direction.

In 2007, the VCP Central Committee directed the military (and other agencies) to divest itself of commercial enterprises; but this policy initiative foundered when the Global Financial Crisis struck Vietnam.

The military weathered this period and retained control over its most economically profitable enterprises, such as Viettel.

In the course of contemporary development, a bargain appears to have been reached between party and state leaders on one side and the military leadership on the other to link central funding for the military's budget to GDP growth. This figure became stabilized at around 2–2.5 per cent of GDP.

At the same time, it appears that military-owned enterprises were largely successful in the marketplace and supplemented central funding with their business profits. These funds were largely used to provide for the social welfare of soldiers and their families, veterans and their families, and war widows. Funds were also used to improve the living conditions of soldiers as well as the officer corps. In sum, the military has carved out a corporate role in Vietnamese society for its enterprises that has gone largely unchallenged. Although it was noted that the military was extravagant in purchasing luxury items for use by its members, there is no substantial evidence, such as court cases published in the Vietnamese media, that corruption in military-run enterprises is widespread. There have been occasional calls in Vietnamese social media for greater transparency, however.

In summary, Vietnam's military is extensively involved in generating formal military capital (defence budget, ownership of land, pensions and social welfare, and military-owned enterprises) but there is little evidence that the military is extensively involved in generating informal or illegal military capital. The VPA has carved out an institutional role in Vietnam's one-party political system through bloc membership on the VCP Central Committee that has not altered appreciably over the past three decades.

References

Agence France-Presse (1998), 'Vietnam's military should play vital role in economy: defense minister', 3 November.

Asian Defence Journal (1994) 'Vietnam Licenses First Military Bank', (November): 97.

Australia Government, Defence Intelligence Organisation (2015) *Defence Economic Trends in the Asia-Pacific.* Defence Reference Aid 15-003. http://www.defence.gov.au/dio/documents/DET_15.pdf, accessed 28 March 2017.

Biến, Thiều Quang (1991) 'How Can the Efficiency of the Army's Production and Economic Building by Correctly Assessed?', *Quân Đội Nhân Dân* (12 August) translated in U.S. Joint Publications Research Service, *East Asia Report* SEA-91-028, 20 November: 26–8.

Branigin, William (1993) 'Hanoi's Enterprising Army, Budget Cuts Put Soldiers in Business: From Fish to Hotels', *The Washington Post*, 17 October.

Cleary, Paul (1995) 'Plenty of Consultants, But Their Quality Varies Widely', *The Australian Financial Review*, 10 May.

Dau, Quang (1989) 'The Army on the Economic Building Front', *Quân Đội Nhân Dân* (13 August), translated in U.S. Foreign Broadcast Information Service, *Daily Report*, EAS: 89–157, 16 August: 71–3.

Đức, Lê Hữu (2014) 'Developing economic zones intertwined with national border protection', *Báo điện tử Quốc phòng*, 24 April.

Dung, Hanh (1999) 'Military Enterprises', *Vietnam Economic Times* (December): 23.

Dũng, Lê Văn (2000) '5 năm thực hiện Nghị định 19/CP của Chính phủ về công tác quốc phòng ở các bộ, ngành và các địa phương – Kết quả và Phương hướng' (5 years of implementing Government Decree 19/CP on national defence work in ministries, branches and localities – results and directions)', *Tạp chí Quốc phòng toàn dân* No. 5 (May): 6.

Giáp, Võ Nguyên (1976) 'Xây dựng nền quốc phòng toàn dân vững mạnh bảo vệ tổ quốc Việt Nam xã hội chủ nghĩa', (Build a strong national defense, Defend the socialist fatherland of Viet Nam)', *Học Tập* (Studies) (May): 13–45.

Grevatt, Jon (2015) 'Vietnam reveals the significant financial scope of military-run businesses', *Jane's Defence Weekly* (1 February).

Hàng Hóa Thông Hiểu (2013) 'Năm 2012 khó khăn của các mạng di động nhỏ', (2012 a year of difficulties for small mobile networks)', 28 March. http://hanghoavathuonghieu.com.vn/hoat-dong-doanh-nghiep/4-01-2013/nam-2012-kho-khan-cua-cac-mang-di-dong-nho.html, accessed 28 March 2017.

Hiebert, Murray (1991) 'Defeated by Victory', *Far Eastern Economic Review*, 13 June, p. 24.

―――― (1991) 'Soldiers of fortune', *Far Eastern Economic Review*, 13 June, pp. 26–7.

―――― (1993) 'Corps Business', *Far Eastern Economic Review*, 23 December: 40.

Jane's Defence Weekly (1997) 'Vietnamese Army Streamlines Businesses', 24 September: 13.

Lam, Huong (1996) 'Defence Ministry enters telecom fray', *Vietnam Investment Review* (22–8 July): 15.

Lê Duẩn's speech (1981) Carried in installments on Hanoi Radio Domestic Service, 26–30 June and 1 July.

Ngân, Phạm Thanh (1999) "'Xây dựng quân đội vững mạnh về chính trị trong thời kỳ phát triển mới của đất nước' (Build a politically strong military in the new stage of development of the country)', *Tạp chí Cộng Sản*, No. 23 (December): 20.

Ngân, Phạm Thanh (1993) 'Phát huy truyền thống "Bộ đội Cụ Hồ" xây dựng người chiến sĩ QĐND Việt Nam trong giai đoạn cách mạng mới', (Promote the tradition of 'Uncle Ho's soldiers' to build the VPA combatant in the new revolutionary period)', *Tạp chí Quốc phòng toàn dân*, No. 12 (December): 10–13.

Nghĩa, Trần Đức (1990) 'Trường Sơn Construction General Corporation: Program to Renew Technical Equipment in the Years 1990–1995', *Tạp chí Quốc phòng toàn dân* (All People's National Defence Journal), (October), translated in U.S. Joint Publications Research Service, *East Asia Report* SEA-90-034, 26 December: 36–8.

Nham, Nguyen (1998) 'Money the new target for army', *Vietnam Investment Review*, 15–21 June: 11.

Nhung, Tuyết (2007) 'Vietnam's army to hand over business enterprises', *Thanh Niên*, 20 December.

People's Army Newspaper Online (2007) 'Decree on reorganization of defence businesses', 19 December.

———— (2009) 'GGDI heading for higher objectives despite difficulties', 11 February.

———— (2009) 'Army businesses grew in 2008 despite economic difficulties', 19 February.

———— (2014) 'Song Thu corporation hailed for business achievements', 17 April.

———— (2014) 'Viettel urged to well implement financial work', 24 May.

———— (2014) 'Viettel brand brings services to Timor Leste's villages.' 19 September.

———— (2015) 'Defence businesses urged to give top priority to country's interest', 27 January.

Quân Đội Nhân Dân (1991) 'Defence Ministry Reports on Economic Activities', 12 May, translated in U.S. Publication Research Service, *East Asia Report*, SEA-91-018, 1 August: 27–8.

———— (2003) 'Vietnamese Military Industry Targets Revenue Increase of 8–10% This Year', 7 January, reproduced by Global News Wire – Asia Africa Intelligence Wire, Vietnam News Briefs, 7 January.

Ray, Chris (1979) *Vietnam: Reconstruction and the Chinese Invasion — An Eyewitness Account* (Forrest Lodge: Australian Radical Publications): 24.

Socialist Republic of Vietnam (2009) Ministry of National Defence, *Vietnam National Defence* (Hanoi: December): 69.

Thanh Niên (2007), 'Vietnam proposes cuts in army business', 31 January.

Thayer, Carlyle A. (1983) 'Vietnam's Two Strategic Tasks: Building Socialism and Defending the Fatherland', in Pushpa Thambipillai (ed.) *Southeast Asian Affairs 1983*. Singapore: Institute of Southeast Asian Studies: 299–324.

———— (1985) 'Vietnam', in Zakaria Haji Ahmad and Harold Crouch (eds) *Military-Civilian Relations in South-East Asia*. Oxford: Oxford University Press: 234–66.

———— (1995) 'Vietnam's Strategic Readjustment', in Stuart Harris and Gary Klintworth (eds) *China as a Great Power: Myths, Realities and Challenges in the Asia-Pacific Region*. New York: St. Martin's Press: 185–201.

———— (1996) 'People's Army gets in step with era of friendly reform', *The Australian* Special Survey, *The Australian*, 6 September: 18.

———— (1998) 'Marching Orders', *Vietnam Business Journal*, 6(4) (July/August): 57.

———— (2000) 'Demobilization but not Disarmament – Personnel Reduction and Force Modernization in Vietnam', in Natalie Pauwels (ed.) *War Force to Work Force: Global Perspectives on Demobilization and Reintegration*. Baden-Baden: Nomos Verlagsgesellshaft for BICC Schriften zu Abrüstung und Konversion: 199–219.

———— (2000) 'The Economic and Commercial Roles of the Vietnam People's Army', *Asian Perspective*, 24(2): 98.

———— (2003) 'The Economic and Commercial Roles of the Vietnam People's Army', in Jörn Brömmelhörster and Wolf-Christian Paes (eds) *The Military as an Economic Actor: Soldiers in Business*. London: Palgrave Macmillan: 74–93.

———— (2011a) 'Military politics in contemporary Vietnam: Political engagement, corporate interests, and professinalism', in Marcus Mietzner (ed.) *The Political Resurgence of the Military in Southeast Asia: Conflict and Leadership*. London: Routledge Taylor & Francis Group: 63–84.

———— (2011b) 'Vietnam's Defence Budget', *Thayer Consultancy Background Briefing*, 23 April; https://www.scribd.com/doc/53416310/Thayer-Vietnam-s-Defence-Budget, accessed 28 March 2017.

The Saigon Times (1998), 'Military Textile Enterprise starts operation', 17 November.

———— (2010) 'Viettel officially launches 3G network', 26 March.

———— (2012) 'Viettel joins phone production group', 2 November.

Thu, Phan (1994) 'The Army Engages in Economic and Productive Labour Activities', *Tạp chí Cộng Sản* (Communist Review), 18–20 December, translated in U.S. Foreign Broadcast Information Service, *Daily Report* EAS-95-037, 24 February 1995: 82–4.

Thuy, Tran Le (1999) 'On the home front', *Vietnam Economic Times*, December: 25.

Toản, Hồ Quốc (2001), 'Xây dựng khu kinh tế-quốc phòng trên các địa bàn chiến lược (Building national- defence zones in strategic areas)', *Tạp chí Quốc phòng toàn dân*, No. 7 (July): pp. 34–6.

Turley, William S. (1977) 'Origins and Development of Communist Military Leadership in Vietnam', *Armed Forces and Society*, 3(2): 218–47.

Tuyen, Lt. Col. Nguyen Duy, and Man Ha Anh (1991) 'About Organizing Party Leadership in an Army Unit Specialized in Economic Construction', *Tạp chí Quốc phòng toàn dân*, March, pp. 34–6, translated in U.S. Joint Publications Research Service, *East Asia Report* SEA-91-017, 29 July: 30–2.

VietnamBreakingNews.com (2015) 'Military group strives for VND 230 trillion in 2015', 25 January. https://m.vietnambreakingnews.com/2015/01/military-group-strives-for-vnd-230-trillion-in-2015/, accessed 28 March 2017.

Vietnam Business Journal (1996) 'Ministry of Defence Property JV Licensed', October: 5

Vietnam Courier (1976) 'New Important Task of the Viet Nam People's Army', No. 52 (September): 8–9.

VietNamNet.Bridge (2014) 'Viettel develops unmanned military aircraft', 25 February. http://english.vietnamnet.vn/fms/science-it/96281/viettel-develops-unmanned-military-aircraft.html, accessed 28 March 2017.

VietNamNet.com (2014) 'Three telecom giants earn over VND330 trillion in 2014', 26 December.

Viet Nam News (2008) (Reproduced in VietNamNet Bridge), 'Military enterprises await restructuring', 4 April 2008.

Vietnam News Agency (1976) 'General Resolution of the Fourth Party Congress', 24 December, Hanoi Radio Domestic Service, 16 December.

——— (1993) 'Army factories' consumer goods production', 21 February, translated in BBC, *Summary of World Broadcasts*, FE/W0271, 2 March 1993: A/12.

——— (1994) 'Report on Armed Forces Trade and Business Activities', 30 January.

——— (1994) 'Chairman Comments on Role of New Military Bank', 8 December.

——— (1996) 'Military Enterprises Active in Economic Development', 12 May.

———— (1999) 'Defence ministry opens economic department', 28 April.

Viettel.com.vn (2015) 'VIETTEL 2014: Spectacular Growth', 26 January. http://viettel.com.vn/61-83-2-2451-VIETTEL-2014-Spectacular-growth.html, accessed 28 March 2017.

Voice of Vietnam (1992) 'Army-run construction firm's plans for expansion', 2 February in BBC, *Summary of World Broadcasts*, Far East, FE/W0219, 26 February 1992: A/7.

Watkin, Wat (1999) 'Proud military slips into decline as aid dries up', *South China Morning Post*, 7 July.

CHAPTER 5

Khaki Clientelism
The Political Economy of Cambodia's Security Forces

Paul Chambers

The military in some places have been accused of abusing the land [rights] of the people ... it affects the dignity of the military and I can't accept it. You can't blame [the military] for what's not wrong ... the military is very disciplined and has the approval of the Government. – Prime Minister Hun Sen (Kyne 2000)

Introduction

In addition to the traditional armed forces, Cambodia's security forces include the police, the gendarmerie and several paramilitaries. Depending on the historical moment, some or all of these have been crucial actors tasked with maintaining national security. Four times they have been used to overthrow a sitting government (1945, 1970, 1979, 1997). On two occasions they were modified to act as a mechanism beholden to revolutionary party structures (1975, 1979). During 1992–93, the United Nations unsuccessfully sought to reform them into apolitical entities. Despite a disjointed history, the security forces today appear to be clients of Prime Minister Hun Sen and his Cambodian People's Party (CPP), and the corporations allied with it. While this has ensured civilian supremacy over security forces, it is in fact only personalized control under Hun Sen. The political economy of the military in Cambodia today is thus one of embedded, asymmetrical neopatrimonialism between a civilian prime minister and his security forces. Following Max Weber, Christopher Clapham (1985: 48) defines neopatrimonialism as

> a form of organisation in which relationships of a broadly patrimonial type pervade a political and administrative system which is formally

constructed on rational-legal lines ... [Relations are subsumed into] a pattern of pattern of vassal and lord, rather than the rational-legal one of subordinate and superior, and behaviour is correspondingly devised to display a personal status, rather than to perform an official function.

In such a situation, the patrimonial system deforms the logic of the formal state's functions. The formalized rationality of bureaucratic administration and democratic legitimation of electoral representation cloaks an informal series of personalist, patron-client relations which are the actual engine of state control. To some extent, an opaque, symbiotic relationship involving the politics of plunder unites elites together and creates obstacles for political and economic development.

Hun Sen's regime is neopatrimonial in character. It utilizes 'a melding of bureaucratic, military and economic power' (Heder 2005: 114) in a form of patronage politics that link Hun Sen and his party to 'voters', 'government officials and 'business tycoons' (Un 2005: 203). Hun Sen, as patron, personally dominates the Cambodian polity behind the façade of democracy through a mixture of material rewards ('carrots') and military repression ('sticks'). In this sense, a 'hybrid' regime of *authoritarian-personal control* – as elaborated upon in Chapter 1 – has acquired certain trappings of democracy while retaining specific auto-cratic features (ibid.)

The prime minister's relationship with the security forces has been both coercive and patron-clientelistic. The coercion involves the prime minister's use of (or threatened use of) non-promotions or purges against soldiers deemed as not sufficiently loyal. Such tactics can be applied because, over time, Hun Sen has created units, outside of the regular military, that come under his direct control. These units have to some extent offset the regular military and 'helped Hun Sen to en-sure his domination over all of Cambodia's security forces' (Chambers 2015: 189). Meanwhile, the *patronage* involves the centralization of power around 'an individual to whom all within the system owe their position' (Thomson 2004: 127). A patron-client relationship itself is an instrumental bond in which 'an individual of higher socioeconomic status (patron) uses his own influence and resources to provide protec-tion or benefits, or both, for a person of lower status (client) who, for his part, reciprocates by offering general support and assistance, including personal services, to the patron' (Scott 1972: 92). Hun Sen has used his control over state resources to transform the security forces into his personal vassalage. In this way, one can speak of Cambodia's security force as a political-economic 'client' of the prime minister and his party. In Cambodia today, Hun Sen has created a situation of security force clientelism whereby the prime minister has appeased a large number of security officials by offering them patronage in the form of material resources, positions and status in society. In return, they provide him with obedience and services in the form of maintaining internal security but also ensuring security for the CPP and corporations allied with it. In some cases, leading officers are granted mini-fiefdoms of their own. Such patronage has fostered a relationship of dependency. The combination of coercion and patron-clientelism has produced a political economy of the military in Cambodia today verging on embedded asymmetry between a civilian prime minister and his security forces. This form of civil–military relations merely repeats earlier variants of neopatrimonial personalism found in previous Cambodian regimes.

Yet how and why did such a political economy come about? How are Cambodia's security forces currently organized? How have Hun Sen and his party come to control the security sector? To what extent does it act as a vassal to the economic interests of the party and to corporate interests? To what extent do parts of the security sector have their own economic interests? How might security force clientelism in Cambodia affect the future of democracy there? This analysis attempts to answer these questions.

The study is organized into six parts. First, it examines the historical evolution of Cambodia's security sector economy. Second, it looks at the organization of Cambodia's security forces today. Third, it scrutinizes the means of Hun Sen's and his party's conditional control over the security sector. Fourth, it looks at security sector vassalage to the CPP and to corporations allied with Hun Sen. Fifth, it examines the extent to which parts of the security sector themselves possess economic interests. Finally, the study offers a conclusion.

Cambodia's security forces and their political economy

Cambodia has experienced a disjointed path in the evolution of its security forces. This trajectory has evolved from a legacy of entrenched authoritarianism, deep political divisions and long periods of external interference in Cambodia's internal affairs. Since the beginning of the military's existence, it has operated as both a political and economic vassal of those holding power. In pre-colonial, colonial and postcolonial Cambodia, finance has often been scarce and funding security services has been a challenge.

In pre-colonial Cambodia, most Cambodian kings had never possessed permanent standing armies, preferring to raise them as different crises arose.[1] Once the calamity passed, the army would be disbanded (Chandler 2007: 132). One rationale for temporary armies was insufficient capital to subsidize a permanent force. Indeed the palace relied on powerful lords, called *chaovay sruk*, to raise and maintain small, private armies that could not always be trusted to defend the sitting king (ibid.: 133). This gradually changed after 1863, the year in which Cambodia became a protectorate of France. Henceforth, Cambodia's security was guaranteed by France, but at the price of becoming a French colony (ibid.: 168, 185).

During the colonial period, security forces were necessary to pacify insurrections. It was at this stage that the onset of path dependence in the evolution of a permanent military occurred. At first, only small French forces existed. But in 1904, an indigenous gendarmerie or constabulary (the *Garde Nationale* or *Garde Indigène*) was established. However, this unit was not truly 'Cambodian' because many of the troops were Vietnamese. Within ten years, the French had set up a light infantry battalion (*Bataillon Tirailleurs Cambodgiens*). By 1941, three such battalions operated under a *Regiment Tirailleurs Cambodgiens* (RTC; see Forest 1987).

Organizationally, the RTC was composed of Cambodian soldiers and commanded by French officers. The unit ultimately formed part of a larger command force that was headquartered in Hanoi. The *Garde Indigene*, meanwhile, was a force of mostly Cambodians, but also some 2500 Frenchmen. Both the RTC and the *Garde Indigene* would typically pair up with soldiers temporarily raised by Cambodian kings to defend the colony against rebellions (ibid.: 135–41).

Meanwhile, French state salaries for Cambodia's colonial security forces tended to be both slow in coming and low – far lower than their

---

1. A clear exception was Jayavarman VII (1181–1218) of the Khmer Empire, who organized permanent forces in garrisons.

French counterparts. Finally, unlike French soldiers, local colonial soldiers received no pension upon retirement. This situation compelled many soldiers to live off the land, finding and extracting protection money from colonial subjects (Tatu 1987). Soldiers' incomes have continued to be paltry, and the tradition of troops making money off of the people has often become embedded within the mindset of many Cambodians – in terms of perceptions by soldiers and civilians alike. This heritage has persisted until today.

When Norodom Sihanouk became king in 1941, France expected him to be pliant to their continued colonial intentions. But during World War II, Japan occupied Cambodia and Tokyo made Cambodia an independent country in 1945, enabling the young king to experience what amounted to quasi-independent sovereignty. The Japanese allowed the retention of the Cambodian constabulary (which exists to this day) and the light infantry battalion (which was later incorporated into the Royal Khmer Army).

Amidst the end of World War II, Son Ngoc Thanh, a nationalist prime minister (August–October 1945) oriented toward republicanism, spearheaded a post-World War II movement among Cambodians for independence from France. The French exiled Thanh and replaced him with Sihanouk's uncle, Prince Sisowath Monireth. In late 1946, under measured pressure from Monireth, France and Cambodia signed two agreements that together paved the way for more autonomy for Cambodia in its military affairs. The first, the Franco–Cambodian Modus Vivendi of 7 January 1946, gave official recognition to the existence of a Cambodian army. The second, the Franco–Khmer Military Convention of 20 November 1946, elaborated the functions of the new military, one of which was to ensure domestic security. Yet this military (the Royal Khmer Army or *Armée Royale Khmère*, or ARK) was commanded by French officers and organized according to French military norms (Conboy 2011: 9). The ARK fought alongside other French forces and saw immediate action on the western frontier (against Khmer Issarak rebels, a fractious group that saw itself as patriotic) and on the eastern frontier (against the Viet Minh-directed Khmer People's Liberation Army), with both struggles happening simultaneously in the First Indochinese War (1946–54). Accordingly, ARK's size swelled to 47,000 soldiers, including the *Garde Nationale* and a growing number of battalions.

King Norodom Sihanouk returned from military training in France in 1948, and it was only then that he began to become involved in politics, supporting more independence for Cambodia – but as a kingdom and not a republic. In 1949, Cambodia was granted the status of self-ruled protectorate, though the French still controlled defence matters (Chandler 2007: 216). Yet partly because of the intensification of the First Indochinese War and defections of such senior Khmer Issarak leaders as Prince Norodom Chantaraingsey and Dap Chhuon, the French allowed Sihanouk greater control over ARK. By November 1953, France had succumbed to the king's demands for independence altogether.

The 9th of November 1953 marks Cambodia's first critical juncture, shifting the trajectory in the path of Cambodia's military. On that date, the military became the armed forces of an independent Cambodia. ARK was renamed FARK: the Royal Khmer Armed Forces (*Forces Armées Royales Khmères*; see Soonthornpoct 2005). Second, November 1953 saw the growth of Sihanouk's personal control over Cambodian politics.[2]

This domination was based upon his great charisma, his legitimacy as a popular king and his ability to hold leverage over Cambodia's unstable political parties (Chandler 2007: 228). At the 1954 Geneva Conference, and with an eye toward elections set for 1955, a July final declaration proclaimed that Cambodia (along with Laos) would be fully neutral in the Cold War. Sihanouk himself attempted to distance the country from US–USSR manoeuvring, but he did establish diplomatic relations with China in 1958 at least partly to offset Thai and Vietnamese pressures on Cambodia.

Sihanouk attempted to keep close personal control over Cambodia's military. The FARK was composed of three security services. The Royal Cambodian Army had been established in 1946 and became the core of FARK from the moment of independence. In 1955, a former governor of Kratie named Lon Nol, who had gained Sihanouk's trust, became its commander. Five years later, he was appointed commander of all FARK

---

2. Sihanouk never defeated the Khmer Issaraks but rather suppressed them with French assistance to his own security forces. After the 1954 Geneva Conference, many of the nationalist Khmer Issaraks cooperated with the government. However, many Viet Minh-influenced Khmer Issarak continued their struggle, turning the previous objective of achieving national independence into a fight for communist revolution.

forces. In 1954 the Aviation Royale Khmer (Royal Khmer Air Force) was created by royal decree. Sihanouk's personal physician and flying enthusiast Dr. Ngo Hou was appointed as chief, and his deputy was an inspector from the Department of Forestry. The Royal Khmer Navy was also created in 1954. Its commander initially was Captain Pierre Coedès, the half-French, half-Cambodian son of historian George Coedès, the French scholar on Southeast Asia. Both of these services received direction from the army (FARK). French and US military officers initially provided extensive advice to all three services. Meanwhile, Cambodia's colonial police and constabulary, like FARK, were used as tools through which Sihanouk could maintain control over the country outside of relying on FARK. In 1955, Sihanouk appointed Dap Chhuon as interior minister in charge of the police. Chouhan regularly used both the police and his own militia to beat and intimidate opponents of Sihanouk's regime. Yet as events would show, neither Dap Chhoun nor Lon Nol was actually loyal to the king.

Sihanouk's abdication in 1955 (his father ascended the throne) and successful contestation of the 1955 elections (totally undemocratic as a result of state intimidation and ballot fraud) brought to office the Sangkum Reastr Niyum (SRN) party. SRN won all seats in parliament in each of the Cambodian charade elections (held in 1955, 1958, 1962 and 1966 (Nohlen, Grotz and Hartmann 2001: 74). It also began a trend in Cambodian politics whereby the ruling party would dominate both Cambodian politics and the Cambodian armed forces. Not only was Sihanouk still palace-leader to Cambodians, but he also became 'a dictatorial Chief of State, with his policies ratified by a rubber-stamp National Assembly' and his SRN lorded over the country until 1970 (Vickery 1999: 252).

From 1946 until 1970, Sihanouk controlled the FARK – first as head of state (until 1955), then through his father (until 1960), and again as head of state (1960–70). During this time, the country's security forces became entrenched under his SRN government and Cambodia enjoyed civilian control over the military. This state of affairs was maintained through Sihanouk proxies with military training, such as Lon Nol and Nhiek Tioulong. Nevertheless, such supremacy was personalized in Sihanouk rather than any form of institutionalized control. From 1963 to 1969, most of the FARK's activities involved carrying out developmental projects in the economic sector, including construction of roads, dykes and dams, as well as spearheading the administration of provincial Cambodia (Kingdom of Cambodia 2000: 13). At the same time, on the Cambodian–South Vietnamese border, the FARK busied itself smuggling supplies to the Viet Cong while, on the Thai–Cambodian border, it entrenched itself amidst sabre-rattling between Sihanouk and Thai military leaders related to boundary disputes.

From 1956 until 1969, Son Ngoc Thanh led the US-assisted, anti-communist and republican Khmer Serei movement against Sihanouk. Because of Sihanouk's fears about this group, its defeat became a chief mission for FARK: it executed thousands of suspected Khmer Serei members, while the Khmer Rouge received much less attention. In 1969, around five hundred Khmer Serei insurgents defected to FARK and the Khmer Serei itself was dissolved. It has been speculated that this mass defection was orchestrated by the United States Central Intelligence Agency to reinforce then-Prime Minister Lon Nol and his loyalists, who were preparing a putsch against Sihanouk (Turkoly-Joczik 1988: 57). Many members of the Khmer Serei (including Son Ngoc Thanh) were of Khmer Krom ethnicity, and Khmer Krom soldiers also became Lon Nol loyalists (Lon Nol also was Khmer Krom). The 1969 integration of these soldiers into FARK worked to make the military much more divided.

By 1969, however, communist Khmer Rouge insurgents were starting to crystallize as a threat to Sihanouk's government. At about the same time, Vietnam's civil war, along with Viet Cong insurgents (informally recruited and taking orders from North Vietnam), uniformed North Vietnamese soldiers and United States forces expanded into Cambodia. As a result, as time went on, Cambodia's armed forces took a much larger role in directly controlling parts of Cambodia.

In terms of foreign aid, beginning in 1950 and especially since 1954, Cambodia's security forces increasingly depended upon United States assistance to fund its needs. From 1954 until 1959, the US allocated 84 million US dollars in military equipment and supplies for Cambodia. Of this, Washington bankrolled the FARK to the tune of approximately 62 per cent of the funds needed for the pay allowances and rations of Cambodian military personnel (United States 1960: 11, 21). In parallel with their engagement with the Royal Thai Army beginning in 1950,

Washington carried out studies of and attempted to work closely with and even manipulate the FARK. However, in 1959, Sihanouk's relations with Washington turned sour. This owed to a US-linked coup plot against him (purportedly led by Dap Chhoun) which was foiled in February, the refusal of the United States in June to oppose South Vietnamese incursions into Cambodia, and a bomb attack on the Cambodian palace in August (Osborne 1994: 110–11). Amidst his increasing suspicions of US intentions, Sihanouk immediately cut relations with Washington in 1965. In 1967, Sihanouk used his forces to crush the Samlaut peasant rebellion and, though he had been active in its repression since the 1950s, it is from this event that a Cambodian communist insurgency had begun to gather steam.

Ultimately, from 1953 until 1970, Norodom Sihanouk established a quasi-democratic regime that was both authoritarian and featured charade elections. For the most part, security forces became tightly linked to his ruling SRN.

In March 1970, a military coup ousted the princely Head of State from office and Prime Minister Lon Nol assumed control of Cambodia. Seven months later, Lon Nol made Cambodia into a Republic and gave himself two titles: president and commander-in-chief of the armed forces. He also cosmetically changed the name of the military from FARK to the Khmer National Armed Forces (*Forces Armées Nationales Khmères* or FANK). This proved, however, not to be a critical juncture. Instead, Lon Nol merely became Cambodia's new autocrat in control of a military which remained organizationally the same. In this sense, Lon Nol recreated for his regime the autocracy of the Sihanouk years, while further expanding the influence and size of security forces (though this is debatable, given Cambodia's massive loss of territory at the time). He did allow for one election, in 1972, in which his Social Republican Party won all of the seats in the legislature (IPU 1972). As with the Sihanouk period, soldiers were loyal first to Lon Nol (as well as to regional commanders and money) and only then to Cambodian democracy – if they supported that at all.

The period 1970–75 saw the newly renamed Khmer Republic become a virtual economic and military dependency of the United States (Clymer 2004: 58) as US military assistance to FANK reached more than $1.2 billion (United States 1977: 864). Corruption during this time was so rife that it is estimated that at least half of the 1974 $350 million in military aid to Cambodia was siphoned off for personal profit by Cambodian officers, other soldiers added extra names to unit payrolls in order to collect extra salaries ('ghost soldiers') and some officers were known to be selling weapons to the enemy (Slocomb 2010: 133–9). Lon Nol's autocratic regime finally collapsed in 1975, when Pol Pot's ultra-militant Khmer Rouge insurgents took over Phnom Penh.

Once in power, the Khmer Rouge established 'Democratic Kampuchea' (DK), destroyed the FANK and restructured its own insurgent Cambodian People's Liberation Armed Forces (CPNLAF) to create the Revolutionary Army of Kampuchea (RAK). This new force was placed under the control of the Communist Party of Kampuchea – the Khmer Rouge. The RAK spent the vast majority of its time either suppressing insurgencies launched from Thailand and Vietnam or purging zone or sector forces whose loyalty was in doubt. Internal security forces and district militias handled the majority of civilian intimidation. It was also closely connected with the Khmer Rouge-supported National United Front of Kampuchea (FUNK), the only organization allowed to contest the 1976 election. As with all previous elections in Cambodia, this one resulted in complete victory for the regime's party (IPU 1976). The FUNK-led Khmer Rouge regime relied mostly upon Chinese military and economic assistance, without which it could not have survived (Mertha 2014). Since there was no money in circulation, RAK soldiers relied on rations provided by the state. The allocation of rations could depend upon which zone or region that a soldier lived, since the DK was decentralized in administration (Vickery 1999: 68). Ultimately, the sudden 1975 regime change and transition in security force composition did not amount to a critical juncture in terms of military organization because the Khmer Rouge ruled Cambodia for less than four years. Nevertheless, it must be admitted that the Khmer Rouge's mass indoctrination of RAK troops to become ultra-nationalistic, anti-Vietnamese defenders of Cambodian territory left lasting imprints.

1979 brought sudden yet lasting change to the country. Following its intervention in Cambodia on 21 December 1978, the Vietnamese army succeeded in driving the Khmer Rouge regime out of Phnom Penh on 7 January and established on the following day both the People's Republic of Kampuchea (PRK) and the Kampuchean People's Revolutionary

Party (KPRP), and occupied much of the country.[3] Ostracized by the West, Cambodia's new pro-Vietnamese proxy government was dependent upon the Soviet Union and Vietnam for economic and military aid. In a 1981 election contested only by the KPRP, it won every legislative seat (Nohlen, Grotz and Hartmann 2001: 74). Though this was expected given that the PRK was a Communist state, the election shows that the model of one-party rule, established in 1955, continued to dominate Cambodia's parliament and politics.

The PRK's army was called the Kampuchean People's Revolutionary Armed Forces (KPRAF). Crafted with much direction from the Vietnam's senior brass, it was centralized, obedient to the leadership of the KPRP, which was pro-Vietnamese and shared ideological and organizational similarities with the Vietnamese military. Indeed, the current Royal Cambodian Armed Forces (RCAF) is a direct descendent of the KPRAF (Tatu 1987). 1979 represented Cambodia's second critical juncture – a historical point which saw the construction of a new lasting national military as an appendage of another communist ruling party akin to the Vietnamese model.[4] However, in one sense, the military was not completely restructured: its post-1979 leadership contained a few figures who had been Communist Party of Kampuchea insurgency leaders prior to 1975 (such as Bou Thong, who later served the Khmer Rouge regime as defence minister and deputy prime minister). But these cases were few and far between as Hanoi overshadowed the reconfigured military. From the beginning, the regime was factionalized among pro-Vietnam military cadres including Heng Samrin (KPRP secretary-general), Pen Sovann (prime minister 1981), Chan Si, Hun Sen and others. An early falling out that pitted Hanoi (with most KPRP leaders) against the forces of the PRK's first prime minister, Pen Sovann (who was removed as prime minister and imprisoned by the Vietnamese), led to the installation of Chan Si as prime minister (see Vickery and Amer 1996). Following Chan Si's death in 1984, then-foreign minister Hun Sen was elevated to the position of prime minister in 1985. Despite such

---

3. The RAK renamed itself the National Army of Democratic Kampuchea or NADK in December 1979. Its troops were mostly loyal ex-RAK soldiers, but also included conscripts who had been forced into service.

4. Personal interview with Dr. Stephen Heder, Phnom Penh, 7 November 2014.

instability, the path dependence of the powerful, post-1979 military has lasted (despite 1993 efforts at modifications) until the present.

Hun Sen's KPRP maintained political control over Cambodia until early 1993. Yet by 1989, Vietnamese influence had waned (they had been making incremental withdrawals since 1985) and Hun Sen only led one clique within the KPRP Indeed, it was really only in the late 1980s that Hun Sen gained military significance. Meanwhile, the KPRP (renamed the Cambodian People's Party or CPP in 1991) and the KPRAF (renamed the Cambodian People's Armed Forces in 1989) had become overwhelmed with prosecuting counterinsurgency. Backed up by Vietnam, Hun Sen's forces were at war against not only the Khmer Rouge but also Norodom Sihanouk's FUNCINPEC group (with its armed wing, the *Armée National pour un Kampuchea Independent* or ANKI) and Son Sann's Khmer People's National Liberation Front (KPNLF), which oversaw the Khmer People's National Liberation Armed Forces (KPNLAF). To boost unity, these groups, in 1982, together formed an insurrectionary, unwieldy alliance in exile called the Coalition Government of Democratic Kampuchea.

The 1991 Paris Peace Accord and the 1992–93 administration of Cambodia by the United Nations Transitional Authority in Cambodia (UNTAC) permitted these often-divided political actors (as well as the cliques within them) to start to share the political stage with the factionalized CPP. One major UNTAC objective was reform of the security sector. The goal was to disarm, demobilize and reintegrate (DDR) the forces of Cambodia's four disputing armies, transforming them into a new, united RCAF. Yet the Khmer Rouge in 1992 refused to participate, preferring to maintain their insurgency. Thus, UNTAC suspended the DDR and consequently the concept of UNTAC Security Sector Reform (SSR) died an early death. Moreover, the other warring factions thereupon re-armed and, though they merged to form the RCAF in 1993, quickly became divided into a pro- and anti-CPP grouping (Globalsecurity.org). Despite cosmetic change in the armed forces, the failure of DDR to take place in 1993 prevented any critical juncture from happening at this time along the trajectory of civil–military relations in Cambodia.

Elections were again held in 1993. The outcome for the first time gave defeat to the incumbent party, Hun Sen's Cambodian People's

Party (CPP). Indeed, CPP came in second to the FUNCINPEC party.[5] Yet CPP successfully pressured UNTAC to name Hun Sen as second prime minister and co-commander of the RCAF. Norodom Ranariddh, leader of FUNCINPEC and first prime minister, was the other RCAF co-commander. The duality of this arrangement produced a deep schism within the government. At the same time, there was factionalism within each party. The most remarkable example of such fission was the attempted coup in 1994 by CPP faction members against both prime ministers.[6] Turning to the military, not only was the RCAF divided because of the sharing of power over the military, it was further faction-alized given the UNTAC re-integrative formula for the armed forces' post-1993 re-creation: former KPRAF comprised 60 per cent, while 30 per cent and 10 per cent came from two former insurgent groups (Kingdom of Cambodia 2000: 6). Understandably, any loyalty of the ANKI and KPNLAF groups to 'the CPP-dominated majority' was 'paper-thin' from 1993 to 1997 (Grainger 1998). Moreover, each prime minister had his own security force.

By the mid-1990s, the new RCAF seemed to be motivated by four goals. First, it was tasked with dealing with those Khmer Rouge insur-gents who were still holding out. Second, it generated income and acted as a political machine, raking in profits for commanders. Third (in what would become much more significant later on), it came to the assistance of the ruling CPP during electoral campaigns. Fourth, it provided the jobless with an employment opportunity, which kept keeping men off the streets. International donors backed the first objective, but upon the Khmer Rouge's final defeat in 1999 (the last resistant senior Khmer Rouge leader, Ta Mok, was captured on 6 March), pushed hard to reform the security sector. The goals of SSR donors included the following: demobilization and reducing the size of the security sector, improving

---

5. *Front Uni National pour un Cambodge Indépendant, Neutre Pacifique, et Coopératif* (FUNCINPEC) translates as 'National United Front for an Independent, Neutral, Peaceful and Cooperative Cambodia.'

6. The leaders of the coup attempt, Prince Norodom Chakrapon, Sin Song and Sin Sen, were all CPP members. According to Brad Adams, over 70 generals and almost all of the CPP leaders knew of and backed the coup, including ex-Defence Minister Bou Thong and top members of the Chea Sim-Sar Kheng clique. In addition, Thai officials and businesspeople (including Thaksin Shinawatra) were supportive of the attempted putsch (Adams 2014).

its efficiency, enhancing professionalism, strengthening civilian control, increasing transparency, reducing corruption, diminishing human rights abuses and transferring more state funds meant for defence into social welfare and poverty alleviation programmes (Hughes 2009: 106–13). In the end, though security forces were downsized, the other SSR challenges have remained until this day. Perhaps SSR has only improved in terms of the RCAF's role in participating on United Nations demining and peacekeeping missions as well as a greater focus on disaster relief.

In 1997, Hun Sen led a military putsch (though CPP member and RCAF chief of staff Gen. Ke Kim Yan refused to back the coup; see Adams 1997). His lack of support owed once again to CPP factionalism rather than any opposition to the use of putsches as a political tactic.

Following the coup, the prime minister became acting armed forces chief, conducted numerous purges of security forces, and then oversaw the 1998 elections (in which there were irregularities), which the CPP won.

Hun Sen's 1997 victory prevented any further deviations from the continued path dependence of a strongly-entrenched and CPP-dominated Cambodian military and police. The CPP has won all three elections held since 1998. Past opponents, such as Norodom Ranariddh, had been effectively co-opted while current political foes such as Sam Rainsy and Kem Sokha, the Cambodian National Rescue Party (CNRP) leader and sub-leader, have either been forced into exile or charged with crimes. However, reflecting CPP factionalism, Gen. Ke Kim Yan was in 1998 appointed to succeed the prime minister as armed forces commander. It was Yan who, along with his deputy, Gen. Pol Saroeun, oversaw the state's defeat of the last remaining Khmer Rouge forces in 1999. That victory had involved granting numerous amnesties to non-leading Khmer Rouge cadres, including men such as NADK commanders Keo Pong, Sok Pheap and Y Chhien. But the amnesties also came with side benefits. In association with the CPP, Pong and Pheap were allowed to join the RCAF as officers and were promoted to the rank of four-star general in 2014 (*Radio Free Asia* 2014). In similar fashion, Chhien was permitted to serve as the Governor of Pailin province from 1996 until 2014, when he was replaced (Blomberg and Soenthrith 2014). Such senior postings were accompanied by lucrative economic benefits.

The government now embarked on a military demobilization pro-gramme. Employing 140,000 individuals (in 1999; World Bank 2001: 1), and consuming 49 per cent of the national budget (in 1998; Asian Development Bank 2000: 30) seemed to be a luxury at a time when Cambodia faced few domestic or external threats. This 49 per cent was for the Defence and Interior Ministries together; the formal military budget at the time was 18.2 per cent. Despite some financial assistance from donors, the downsizing of Cambodia's military never really got off the ground because of insufficient financing and the failure by donors and the government to agree on programme design, demobilized sol-diers' needs and land ownership, among other issues. By 2010, Prime Minister Hun Sen himself permanently shelved demobilization 'due to a lack of donor funding and the high level of tension along the border with Thailand' (Globalsecurity.com).

This decision more or less coincides with Hun Sen's solidification of his personal control over the armed forces after the 2008 election – though this control was conditional on Hun Sen continuing to appease the armed forces. Assisting him in consolidating power over the military is Tea Banh, Cambodia's deputy prime minister (since 2004) and min-ister of national defence (since 2006). Moreover, in 2009, armed forces chief Gen. Ke Kim Yan was finally dismissed and Hun Sen loyalist Gen. Pol Saroeun took charge in his place (Strangio and Sambath 2009). Under Saroeun, a coterie of Hun Sen loyalists was posted, including RCAF deputy commanders Meas Sophea (who is also army com-mander) and Kun Kim, (who is also the chair of the RCAF Joint General Staff). At the same time, Hun Sen began to receive support from two other powerful players: Deputy Prime Minister/Interior Minister Sar Kheng (who oversaw the police) and Deputy Prime Minister Sok An. Moreover, Hun Sen deploys the Cambodian police force, gendarmerie and various personalized security services (e.g. bodyguard units) as 'sticks' to maintain his personal control.

There are also 'carrots' to encourage civilian support for Hun Sen. One of these is the Naga Youth Federation, formed in 2015, with purportedly 30,000 active members. The organization 'devotes itself to demonstrating its love for the CPP by donating blood to hospitals and doing other humanitarian work' (Sony 2015). Nevertheless, in October 2015, this same group revealed a darker side when some of its members seriously beat up two opposition members of parliament in front of the country's national assembly (*Economist* 2015). Today, supported particularly by other powerful personalities within the CPP and the executive branch, Hun Sen is thoroughly dominant across the CPP and the military. His economic power in Cambodia dominates every sector.

Meanwhile, in order to curry favour with Hun Sen, leading Cambodian entrepreneurs (many of them *Oknha*[7]) have contributed money to the CPP, and Hun Sen can call on them to donate to charities and public works projects and to attract foreign investment for projects that the CPP can claim it has initiated. In return, these businesspeople are often favoured by Hun Sen (United States Embassy Cable 2007).

Meanwhile, since 1998, Hun Sen's wife Bun Rany has served as the president of the Cambodian Red Cross (CRC), succeeding Norodom Marie (wife of Norodom Ranariddh) in that position and symbolically identifying her as the designated successor to female Cambodian royalty.

According to an international watchdog NGO, the CRC 'functions as a microcosm of Hun Sen's patronage system and its central committee comprises many of the Hun family's business associates, CPP officials and their family members' (Global Witness, quoted in *South China Morning Post*, 7 July 2016). These include many powerful women who make up Bun Rany's close political entourage: Choeng Sopheap, Annie Sok An, Lim Chhiv Ho, Ouk Maly and Khuon Sudary.

In an attempt to further legitimize his rule, Hun Sen has sought to connect himself to the nation and royalty through ritual and ceremony in two ways. First, he has invoked the historical figure Sdech Kan, a commoner living in the 1500s who overthrew and killed a wicked monarch and then himself ruled as a benevolent king. Cambodian people perceive Sdech Kan as having great merit. By invoking Sdech Kan, Hun Sen promotes a counter-narrative to that of Cambodian royalists, who base their own leadership legitimacy to their blood connection to monarchy. He has supported research that locates Kan's ancient capital coincidentally close to his own birthplace, and Sdech Kan statues that have facial likenesses to Hun Sen have recently been erected across the country. Second, he has indirectly appeared to connect himself to the

---

7. A very high honorary title in Cambodia bestowed upon those who make large donations to the royal family, usually with the recommendation of the prime minister. Many *Okhna* are today tycoons closely connected to the CPP.

King Norodom Sihanouk. At the public ceremony of the King Norodom Sihanouk's cremation in 2013, Hun Sen appeared to be the only person who could effectively light the funeral pyre. Journalists later wrote that this was proof that Sihanouk had designated Hun Sen as his worthy heir (Noren-Nilsson 2016: 193).

Cambodia's historical legacies of volatility, autocracy and a strong security force have contributed to a non-transparent relationship of reciprocity between security officials and the CPP – a linkage lorded over by Hun Sen (Chambers 2015). Beyond the military itself, there have been fractious schisms among the military, the police (which was traditionally linked to the royal court before its 1979 reorganization) and the gendarmerie (which is a branch of the RCAF). Though an examination of this inter-service rivalry is beyond the scope of this chapter, the topic deserves further investigation. All senior officials in Cambodia's security agencies are members of the CPP. They depend upon Hun Sen not only to provide their extravagant salaries and promotions, but also to legitimize them. The CPP relies upon close connections with Cambodia's security forces to dominate the country. At the same time, average soldiers earn approximately $20 per month plus a 20-plus kilogramme rice allowance. This insufficient pay has led many state security officials to subcontract out their services to private organizations (Mead 2004). Meanwhile, security officials often commit human rights violations with legal impunity. Their insulation from the rule of law has helped to prevent the consolidation of Cambodian democracy. Finally, aside from missions in support of the United Nations, there tends to be little transparency or accountability in Cambodia's armed forces while corruption is often endemic.

The organization of Cambodia's security sector
(1993 to the present)

The current military hierarchy, as created by the 1993 constitution, is similar to that used by FARK in pre-1970 Cambodia. At the apex, the monarch is the supreme commander (Article 23) and chairperson of the Supreme Council for National Defence (Article 24), which is tasked with responding to potential national security emergencies – though in discharging this responsibility it can also shape politics, the economy and society. The king's authority is only ceremonial and effective power rests with the vice-chair of that council, who is the prime minister. Neither Norodom Sihanouk (as king 1993–2004) nor Norodom Sihamoni (who succeeded his father in 2004) has exerted any real influence on Cambodia's security.[8] Other members of this supreme council include the ministers of defence, foreign affairs, finance and interior, as well as the supreme commander of the armed forces. Under this council are the deputy supreme commanders, who double as commanders of their own respective units, as for example Deputy Supreme Commander Gen. Meas Sophea, who also directs the army. Below this is the joint general staff, whose duty is to coordinate between the services. The joint staff chief (currently Kun Kim) simultaneously serves as deputy commander of the RCAF. This joint staff sits directly above the four services: army, navy, air force, and gendarmerie (military police). Meanwhile, since their creation in 1979, the national police have also been under the direct purview of the ministry of the interior. However, neither Interior Minister Chea Sim nor his successors in this role, Ney Pena and then Sar Kheng, have had military backgrounds. However, their consecutive domination over the police has meant that they have not depended upon support from the RCAF to help guarantee their political standing or preserve their personal security needs. Nor are they necessarily reliant on Hun Sen for their rank in the CPP hierarchy, though the prime minister does dominate the party. All of the country's security forces have tended to be rather decentralized (with regional commanders exerting enormous influence) and subject to partisan interference. The commanders of these regular forces are all closely linked to the prime minister and CPP (*Phnom Penh Post*, September 21, 2006). Figure 5.1 loosely illustrates Cambodia's security forces and who commands which units.

As the figure demonstrates, aside from the regular forces of army, navy, air force and police, the prime minister has created special units which are considered the most loyal to Hun Sen. Among these are the Counter-Terrorism Unit (led by Hun Sen's US-educated son, Gen. Hun Manet), the Bodyguard Unit, Intervention Brigade 70 and the Paratrooper Special Forces Brigade 911 (ibid.) A much more recently created unit is the District Municipal Security Guards (DMSG). The

---

8. 1993 Constitution, Articles 7, 23, https://www.constituteproject.org/constitution/Cambodia_2008.pdf?lang=en.

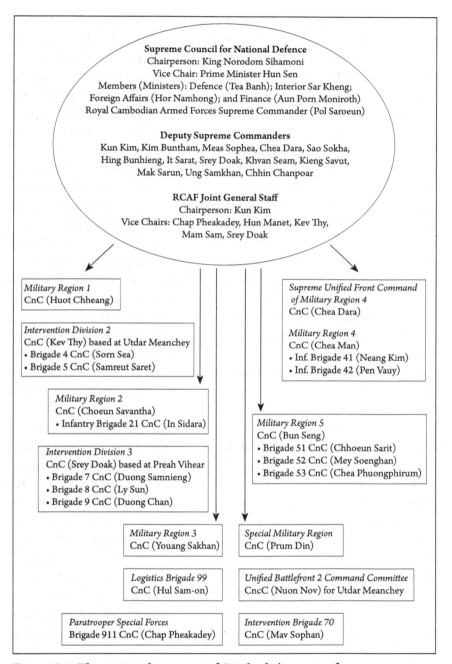

Figure 5.1: The principal structure of Cambodia's security forces

Source: Partly based upon HRH, 2015.

DMSG has been a principal unit involved in forcibly dispersing protestors from Phnom Penh's Freedom Park during 2014. The DMSG itself was formed in 2003 by Daun Penh District Governor Sok Sambat and his deputy Sok Penhvuth. Its members were drawn from the 'Pagoda Boys', an informally organized grouping of pro-CPP street youth and ruffians (Hunt 2014). Ultimately, though there is a regular military (the leaders of which are closely connected to the CPP via family ties, as party members, or informal clients of the party), including many units that circumvent the chain of command and report directly to the prime minister.[9] In fact the Bodyguard Unit, numbering around 10,000 troops, is precisely tasked with protecting Hun Sen and preventing attempted coups against him. Altogether, these units might be characterized as a form of praetorian guard for the premier.[10] As such, Cambodia's security forces today follow a balance of power between regular forces and the praetorian guard directly loyal to Hun Sen (other CPP bigwigs also have their own praetorian guards). There has been no negative public response by regular security forces to the establishment of these praetorian units. Given the overwhelming dominance of Hun Sen over the country, they simply would not dare. Only the parliamentary opposition, actors within civil society and certain foreign watchdog elements have shown criticism. Yet none of these three groups represent a challenge to Hun Sen.

Cambodia's defence budget reflects the needs of a relatively impoverished, dysfunctional state that has experienced the ravages of civil war. Defence expenditures skyrocketed in the 1990s, after Vietnamese soldiers withdrew from the country in 1989 and left Cambodia to wage counter-insurgency against the Khmer Rouge on its own. By 2000, defence spending had partially diminished, following Hun Sen's consolidation of in 1997 and defeat of the Khmer Rouge in 1999. Yet defence spending grew once again in 2009, following military clashes along the Thai–Cambodian border. Though funding allocated for defence diminished slightly in 2010, it began to grow again the following year, for two reasons: continuing instability along the Thai–Cambodian frontier (Vannarith, 2013), and because the CPP (and especially the

---

9. Personal interview with anonymous Western journalist who has long lived in Cambodia, 27 April 2014.

10. Ibid.

Table 5.1: Cambodia's military expenditure

Year	US$ millions	% of GDP	% of govt spending
1992	62.3	3.1	–
1993	44.6	1.8	–
1994	107.0	3.8	–
1995	123.0	3.6	–
1996	114.0	3.2	20.7
1997	103.0	3.0	24.2
1998	83.3	2.7	19.9
1999	88.2	2.5	18.2
2000	81.0	2.2	14.7
2001	70.8	1.8	11.7
2002	65.2	1.5	9.0
2003	67.5	1.4	9.2
2004	69.2	1.3	9.4
2005	71.0	1.1	9.1
2006	75.9	1.0	8.1
2007	79.0	0.9	6.4
2008	82.6	0.8	5.2
2009	137.0	1.3	6.6
2010	168.0	1.5	7.5
2011	192.0	1.5	7.6
2012	217.0	1.5	7.5
2013	243.0	1.5	7.7
2014	278.0	1.7	7.9

Source: Data from SIPRI, http://www.sipri.org/research/armaments/milex/milex_database.

Hun Sen faction) sought to economically appease Cambodia's military leaders so as to co-opt them, that is, to command their loyalty in support of the prime minister. Indeed, in 2014, as much as 22 per cent of the national budget informally was going to the military though the formal figure was 7.9 per cent (see figures above).[11] A final possible reason for

11. Ibid.

these defence budgetary increases was that the CPP leadership was using it to bankroll a new generation of executive leaders. Indeed, in 2014, ex-Defence Minister Bou Thong's son was appointed governor of Ratanakiri province, thus perpetuating the family's hold over this area and guaranteeing its loyalty (Soenthrith 2014).

As for military procurement, where countries provide helicopters and other materiel to the armed forces, civilians are not in a position to monitor what is received or how it is deployed. Other than the prime minister, who officially signs off on military acquisitions himself, and his closest advisors, there is little or no civilian control in this area.[12] Nor is there any transparency in such procurement.[13] Finally, the committees that officially oversee defence issues in the Cambodian legislature in reality tend to be unable or unwilling to scrutinize the armed forces either because of a lack of expertise about military affairs (for those truly civilian members of parliament), available information, cooperation from the executive branch, sufficient time or partisan connections to both the CPP and the military itself. The Defence Ministry, which contains mostly men in uniform faithful to the CPP, and has long been dominated by Hun Sen loyalist Tea Banh, is in charge of all aspects of the military budget.[14] However, the CPP has its own committee on defence within the party.[15]

The CPP's patronage of security forces

Elements of formalized as well as paramilitary security agencies have accepted clientelistic CPP payoffs or sinecures in return for acting as 'protection rackets' that safeguard the interests of senior CPP leaders and the party itself. The purge of Pen Sovann in 1981, followed by the coup of 1997, proved to be successive catalysts that transformed Cambodia's security forces into a loyal guard for the CPP, and eventually for Hun Sen alone. The putsch led to a deep purge involving torture and killings of those security officials who had supported FUNCINPEC

12. Ibid.

13. Personal interview with Executive Director of Transparency International Cambodia Preap Kol, 7 April 2014.

14. Personal interview with former Ambassador Po Sothirath, 19 May 2014.

15. Personal interview with anonymous Western journalist who has long lived in Cambodia, 27 April 2014.

and Norodom Ranariddh, as well as those troops who had supported Son Sann's KPNLF. The fact that Hun Sen carried out a coup (but was pressured to revert back to semi-democracy) ultimately helped him to personalize his power over the military and the country.[16] After 1997, Cambodia's security forces became a bastion in support of the CPP alone (Peou 2001).

Indeed, the security forces have acted to support the CPP prior to and during every election since 1998 (as they did for Sihanouk in the past). At the 1998 polls, the military used intimidation, violence and 'disappearing' people as well as intervention at polling stations to help ensure a CPP victory (ANFREL 1999: 30). Then, during the 2003 election, military commanders threatened several opposition political party activists with confiscation of property and even death if they did not stop working against the CPP. In addition, Cambodian police were reported to have illegally entered polling booths to count votes during the election (NICFEC 2003: 10, 17). During the 2008 election, senior police and military officials engaged in illegal political activities in support of the CPP, such as partisan campaigning and assisting in the building of CPP party structures. The military is also suspected of threatening assassination of opposition party activists and even the murder of an opposition-affiliated journalist (ACE 2008: 15). At the time of the 2013 election, the army, police and gendarmerie once again served the CPP by for example giving campaign speeches and intimidating voters to support the CPP. Security officials who engaged in these activities were on the CPP payroll (ERA 2013: 15).

The security forces actually became more tightly connected under the CPP (and Hun Sen) from 1997 until 2014. Indeed, after the 1997 coup, it could be argued that the closeness between Cambodian security forces and the CPP actually went full circle back to the pre-1992 period. Within almost all levels of Cambodia's security bureaucracies, pro-CPP partisanship is prevalent. According to Human Rights Watch, the CPP leadership has also granted high-level CPP postings to many senior officers within the police, navy, air force and gendarmerie (HRW 2015). Though this is illegal according to Article 15 of the Law on Political Parties, officers have persisted in their pro-CPP activities with legal impunity (ERA 2013: 15; HRW 2013). Moreover, opposition activists

---

16. Personal interview with Prof. Pou Souvachana, 7 May 2014.

continue to worry that security officials might continue to make arbitrary arrests and engage in extra-judicial killings (HRW 2013). The formal connections between security officials and the CPP are illustrated in appendices 3 and 4.

After thirty-five years of vertical control by a single party (except for the brief 1992–97 hiatus), Cambodia's security forces are almost completely under the thumb of the Cambodian People's Party. Such control is of course conditional on the amount of patronage that Hun Sen, who dominates the CPP, delivers to the RCAF. Those troops aligned with parties other than the CPP (such for example as those troops who supported army deputy chief ret. Gen. Nhiek Bunchhay before the 1997 coup and currently support his Khmer National United Party) are today a distinct minority and, since Hun Sen's 2009 consolidation of conditional control over the RCAF command structure, have generally stayed quiet.

As Deputy RCAF Commander Gen. Chea Dara said in July 2015, 'I speak frankly when I say that the army belongs to the Cambodian People's Party' (*Radio Free Asia* 2015). Yet military and police partisanship in favour of CPP has evolved into personalistic domination (especially since 2008) by Prime Minister Hun Sen. Hun Sen is well known for taking good care of his loyalists, although, as a pragmatist, he makes changes when needs demand. He rewards those who work with him. He rarely changes ministers and generally makes very few changes in personnel. He regularly increases the number of stars for his generals. This is why Cambodia has perhaps the most generals of any country in the world.[17] Neopatrimonial control by the prime minister over his military forces is so entrenched in Cambodia that it brings to mind the control over security forces by President Ferdinand Marcos of the Philippines (1972–86). But Hun Sen has not been as financially successful as Marcos in propping up his army. Thus, he has turned to a form of neofeudalism.

Security force vassalage to corporations

Despite apparent co-optation of Cambodia's security forces by the CPP and Hun Sen, the prime minister lacks one crucial asset to ensure adequate patronage-based and personalized control over the armed forces

---

17. Ibid.

and military: sufficient funding. It is in this light that he has enticed corporations to help pay the military in return for his personal attention to their specific needs. As a result, what Cambodia sees today is a form of political economy of military vassalage to corporations. Beginning in 1989, both foreign and domestic corporations have increasingly used security officials to enforce their legal claims to lands already in use, mostly by poor Cambodians – as well as to defend the property they hold from hostile rivals in the CPP.

Security forces have been regularly used by corporations to grab land forcibly in Cambodia. First, a corporation is given a concession and then soldiers are dispatched to shoot people. This has been going on forever.[18]

To understand these land conflicts, one must first comprehend the history of land titling in Cambodia. Traditionally, all land was owned by Cambodia's king; Cambodians have a customary right to 'possession', that is, to temporarily cultivate it on a first come, first serve basis. In 1920, French colonial Cambodia legalized private ownership via adoption of France's Civil Code. But both 'possession' and private ownership law were utilized side by side depending upon the case, though French authorities decided which code would be applied. This split land regime continued across independence in 1953 until the Khmer Rouge revolution in 1975, when private ownership was not only forbidden, but all land titles were destroyed. Farmers tilled the land in the status of usufruct under state ownership.[19] In 1989, as the Cold War was fast fading, Cambodia's government adopted the Instruction on Implementation of Land Use and Management and Policy. Under this law, the state recognized ownership of residential land and the right to possession on cultivated land. A 1992 Land Law explicitly allowed for private ownership. Finally, a 2001 law elaborated ownership into several types (Segikuchi and Hatsukana 2013: 438–9). Yet under this law, people who failed to prove they had tilled land for five years could be evicted. As in other countries, proof via paperwork was required; unlike other countries, virtually all such paperwork had been destroyed during the Khmer Rouge period.[20]

---

18. Personal interview with Mathieu Pellerin, LICADHO, 29 March 2014.

19. Personal interview with anonymous representative of ADHOC, 7 May 2014

20. Ibid.

By 1995, Cambodia had moved to a market economy, civil war had declined and the country was flooded in foreign aid. As a result, inflation fell, foreign investment began to pour into Cambodia, the economy expanded and rural land rapidly accrued value. Four-fifths of Cambodians still lived in rural areas, but their claims to land use were and remain almost entirely based upon the country's earlier informal system of 'possession'. Land developers with substantial finances, connections and knowledge about land law moved quickly to secure necessary documentation to gain title over much of Cambodia's increasingly valuable rural land. These entrepreneurs were assisted by both private and public security sector officials (Paling 2012: 2889–912). Meanwhile, during the mid-1990s, the Cambodian government awarded upwards of '40 logging concessions to Cambodian and foreign-owned companies' (Global Witness 2009: 13).

The civil war itself contributed greatly to the economic clientelism of Cambodian security forces. Khmer Rouge insurgents as well as government forces utilized extractive industries (logging, mining in gems) as well as casinos to subsidize their war efforts (Global Witness 2009: 13; Nette 2008). However, when civil war ended in 1999, soldiers on each side lost a rationale to earn money through these industries since there was no longer a war to subsidize. However, they still sought to improve their standard of living. The number of land disputes involving military officials dramatically increased after Khmer Rouge forces began to defect in 1996. Some soldiers and ex-Khmer Rouge simply took the land of local people (some of whom were also former members of the Khmer Rouge) for their own benefit or for that of local strongmen (Kimsong and Saito 1998).

Although Hun Sen's government was seeking to centralize CPP control over all of Cambodia's armed groups, many of which were merged into the state security forces, it lacked sufficient capital to satisfy the financial needs of this now-enlarged army and police. Hun Sen thus turned to corporate cash. By 2000, the insufficient salaries of security officials were increasingly being complemented by moneys from corporations that needed state connections and physical force to protect their investments, mostly in rural areas, or evict Cambodians from lands that they coveted. Though military personnel generally lack the legal authority to evict, they nonetheless have done so. As for evictions conducted by other agencies (police, military police, forest administration and so on), most of these are also unlawful since they are conducted without a court order and indeed there is no due process granted to affected families (LICADHO 2009: 21). Such legal impunity reflects the interventionist tendency of security forces across Cambodia's political landscape.

In 2000, evidence was collected showing that at least 133 Cambodian families had been forcibly evicted from rural lands by the military. Cambodian NGO LICADHO provided the *Phnom Penh Post* with a partial list of documented military-backed evictions. Said LICADHO NGO Director Eva Galabru, 'it's pretty clear the military will abuse its power and grab land,' (Kyne 2000). In many cases, RCAF officers (especially the army), police and gendarmerie worked with companies involved in the trafficking of narcotics or illegal logging. For example, the elite RCAF Brigade 70 has long operated an illegal timber and contraband trafficking operation worth 2–2.75 million US dollars annually (Global Witness 2007: 12, 67). But forced evictions really began in earnest in the year 2000.[21]

Over the next several years, the iron triangle of collaboration among private enterprises (especially those from Vietnam, China and Thailand), security forces and the Cambodian People's Party grew tighter and tighter. As of 2016, over 850,000 people or six per cent of the population have been pushed off of their lands in often violent circumstances – with the vast majority of evictions carried out by security forces (Rogers 2016). By the mid-2000s, it was becoming increasingly common to see land evictions of villagers being carried out by security forces.[22] The growth in such land grabbing has coincided with the intensifying consolidation by Hun Sen over other CPP faction leaders and Cambodia's military, police and military police. The prime minister acquiesced to allow an interventionist military to exert itself over Cambodian society – as long as he could 'personalistically assert control over all the security forces.'[23]

In May 2008, as tensions grew along the Thai–Cambodian border, large numbers of Cambodian security forces were sent to the northern frontier to help guarantee Cambodian territory there. Yet funding for

---

21. Ibid.

22. Personal interview with anonymous case worker, NGO 'Voice,' 29 March 2014; Personal interview with anonymous representative of ADHOC, 7 May 2014.

23. Personal interview with Prof. Pou Souvachana, 7 May 2014.

these troops was insufficient. By 2009, as frontier frictions persisted, the state began to encounter difficulties paying for the upkeep of these troops. It was at this stage that Hun Sen decided to enable private corporations to support separate Cambodian military units. His idea was to have private corporations help to 'sponsor' various units along the border and in other parts of the country. The informal understanding was then that the units could assist the corporations that had sponsored them, if the corporations found this useful. And they did. The new arrangement transformed parts of the state into 'vassals' for corporate 'lords' (Brady 2010). However, this collaboration was not altogether new. Indeed, this sort of situation had gone on informally at least since the Sihanouk period (1953–70).[24]

At first the prime minister privately encouraged businesses to become 'donors.' In February 2010, Hun Sen publicly urged businesspeople to give money for border security forces, praising those who already had. The request was legalized through the issuance of a sub-decree that year.[25] Moreover, though the prime minister's appeal to companies was for them to make 'voluntary' donations to military units, 'it was a request you cannot say no to.'[26] In other words, you could ignore the request, but at a financial and political cost. Indeed, on February 24, 2010, leaders of Cambodian divisions, brigades and other security force units along the Thai–Cambodian frontier met with leading entrepreneurs at the plush Cambodiana Hotel in Phnom Penh. The gala get-together, led by the prime minister, was meant to commence the '*Oknha* Alliance with the Frontline Soldiers.' The objective of setting up this alliance, involving initially 60 corporation-military unit pairings, was to harmonize and formalize military-business connections as legitimized by the CPP and government. Upwards of 300 businesspeople and *Oknha* attended the event. Participants included Royal Group chairman Kith Meng, Businessman Nang Sothy, president of Royal Phosphate Ltd, and the son of CPP Senator and commodities tycoon Mong Reththy. A president of

---

24. Personal interview with anonymous Western journalist who has long lived in Cambodia, 27 April 2014.

25. Sub-decree legalizing the sponsorship by corporations of security force units, Government Gazette; February 2010; Personal interview with anonymous representative of ADHOC, 7 May 2014.

26. Personal interview with former Ambassador Po Sothirath, 19 May 2014.

one attending 'donor' corporation, Khaou Chuly Group, revealed that in 2009 it gave $100,000 to Cambodian soldiers stationed on the Thai–Cambodia border. The money was apparently used to buy rice, noodles, mosquito nets, well-water and vehicles for the troops (Wallace 2010; see also Appendix 2 for a partial listing of corporation-unit alliances). The quid pro quo agreements of corporate lord and security force vassal formally arranged at this meeting have made it much easier for companies to use such units to physically enforce company land claims. For example, the conglomerate of one participant at the meeting, CPP Senator and tycoon Ly Yong Phat, provided finance to several units, including Battalion 42 and Battalion 313. These same units have been seen at forced evictions to push peasants off of lands for plantations that Ly Yong Phat owns (IDI 2014).

Since 2010, many corporations tightly connected with the CPP and Hun Sen have utilized the services of security sector units with increasing frequency. For example, in Kratie province, RCAF forces, in early 2012, subsidized by the agribusiness TTY Co. Ltd., opened fire on villagers protesting their eviction from 9000 hectares of land (Titthara 2012). In 2013, another agro-industry company, KDC Company, which had sponsored RCAF soldiers from a particular regiment, was found to have used these troops to forcibly evict villagers from lands coveted by KDC (Naren 2013). Pheapimex, yet another agribusiness close to the CPP and Hun Sen, holds 7.4 per cent of Cambodia's total land area, most notably a 316,000-hectare site in Pursat province's Krakor district. Armed gendarmerie troops have guarded the site from villagers protesting their eviction from these lands. In early 2013, hundreds of police, gendarmerie and RCAF troops were seen standing outside the mansion of Pheapimex's owners Choeng Sopheap and her husband, CPP Senator Lao Meng Khin (who are closely linked to Hun Sen). They were awaiting annual bonuses, which the couple have annually handed out to soldiers since 2013. One gendarmerie officer awaiting his bonus stated to a journalist, 'We are military forces and we are also assistants to her (Choeng Sopheap). We always help with whatever she needs help with,' (Pheap and Chen 2013).

Battambang province has witnessed a substantial amount of military-linked land grabbing. In one case, military units in the 5th Military Zone banned local people from ploughing land on which villagers possessed title. In this case, soldiers themselves were attempting to simply take control over 100 hectares of land. In a second case, ongoing since 2010, a corporation called Khla Five and a second corporation have been using 5th Military Zone forces to try to gain control over land held by Cambodians in Battambang's Thmor Puok district. The military evicted villagers, arguing that they did not have a proper license to own the land. The military helped these companies but also sought hectares of this land to build accommodations. The military also hoped to gain control over forest areas for logging and to dig a mine. Meanwhile, since 2010 there has been a dispute involving 280 hectares of land in the Konchang community in Phnom Srok district, Battambang province. A Cambodian businessman sold land already titled to villagers to a company called *Konchang*. When the villagers (over 300 families) protested, the military forcibly evicted them (Sun 2014).

Though most of these are domestic companies, some are international. For example, Vietnamese rubber firm Hoang Anh Gia Lai (HAGL), Vietnamese cartel Vietnam Rubber Group (VRG), Metfone (a subsidiary of Vietnamese telecommunications [military] corporation Viettel Group) and Mobitel (a joint venture between Kith Meng's Royal Group and Sweden's Millicom) have been sponsors of RCAF military units. An anonymous journalist in Cambodia opined that the corporate-military arrangement 'will be a detriment to national security as private sectors are not concerned about the interests of the nation, but about their interests only' (Bennett 2010). Meanwhile, in December 2009, VRG representatives, local authorities and armed forces forcibly evicted the villagers from their households at gunpoint. One VRG company in particular, *Tan Bien*, constantly uses violence, employing Cambodian soldiers and military police to forcibly remove villagers from their land (Global Witness 2013: 26). Also, during a village protest against evictions from their land by Heng Brothers (a subsidiary of HAGL) in 2012, military police (privately bankrolled by the company) opened fire on the villagers and threatened to punish them if they sought to reclaim their lands. (Global Witness 2013: 16). In addition, since 2013, units of the People's Army of Vietnam (PAVN) have taken control of 99-year leases of close to 40,000 hectares of land in Ratanakkiri province next to a 31-kilometre-long frontier between Cambodia and Vietnam. Though four agribusiness companies initially owned the lands separately, the holdings passed into the hands of Companies 72, 74 and 75 within Corps 15 of the PAVN. Logging in Cambodia appears to be the principal economic activity of Corps 15, and its own headquarters is just over the border in Vietnam. Rather than enforcing Cambodia's control over this area, Cambodia's military (and state) appear to have allowed Vietnam to carve out an entire enclave in this area (Blomberg and Roeun 2015). At the same time, the local Cambodian power holders are taking advantage of the Vietnamese labour and market. It could be viewed as economic rationalism from their perspective.

Chinese corporations have also used Cambodian troops to bolster their economic interests in Cambodia. In 2008, Phnom Penh signed a 99-year contract with the Chinese company, Tianjin Union Development Group Company Ltd, giving the company 36,000 hectares for the development of a commercial zone and resort area. With Cambodian military assistance, the state evicted at least 1000 families to make way for the project (Narim 2014).

Still another example of foreign corporations using the military for 'land grabbing' is also in Koh Kong province. Thailand's Khon Kaen Sugar Industry Plc, the Taiwanese company Vewong and Cambodian businessman and senator Ly Yong Phat have together, since 2006, operated sugar plantations on 20,000 hectares in southwestern Cambodia. According to rights groups and local people involved, these businesses have used Cambodian security forces to evict farmers from their lands (Tamayo 2011).

Security businesses are another area where active-duty soldiers have found employment. In 2015, pensions and salaries remain very small for lower-level security personnel with the Cambodian government unable to meet security officials' needs.[27] As a result, many soldiers and officers need part-time jobs to complement their insufficient salaries. Eighty per cent police and military officers took part-time private sector jobs. A lot of this is in the area of private security. At least 30 per cent of military and police are involved in private security.[28] One private security company even boasted that it could acquire active-duty security personnel to act as personal armed bodyguards, in this case from the Ministry of Interior, (Worrell and Chakrya 2014).

---

27. Personal interview with anonymous middle-level police officer, 25 March 2014.

28. Personal interview with anonymous senior police official, 27 March 2014.

Since the 2008 frontier frictions with Thailand, and especially since the February 2010 enactment of the sub-decree for corporate sponsorship of military units, patron-client relations between corporations and military units have become quite explicit.[29] The number of such deals and the amount of cases (involving reciprocity of corporate finance to a military unit in return for that unit's service to the corporation) has skyrocketed. Cambodia today reflects the case of positive-sum triangularity: CPP–military–corporations, all guaranteed by the indispensability of Hun Sen.[30] In July 2015, Defence Minister Tea Banh praised the continuing linkages between military units and corporations, saying 'It is a culture of sharing and contributing to our nation, between civil institutions and the RCAF, during a period in which the armed forces have faced difficult living conditions,' (Sokheng and Pye 2015).

Where security forces are master

The military does possess its own economic interests and there are military institutional holdings as well as holdings by individual security force commanders. For example, Cambodian Channel 5 TV is co-owned by the Royal Cambodian Armed Forces in a joint venture with MICA Media Co. Ltd. Also, the Ministry of Defence (in a joint venture with MICA Media Co. Ltd.) operates Radio Station 5 (Military FM, 98.0 MHz), which itself is owned by TV 5 (LICADHO 2009A).

Following the 1993 Cambodian general election, the armed forces took charge of all state lands for national security reasons. As civil war lessened, increasing numbers of civilians were given the right to settle on and till the land. Nevertheless, military officers continued to hold sizeable pieces of land, often located in forested areas. Military officers carried weapons and were the representatives of the state. They had power. But settlers' rights to land really only depended upon the age-old tradition of 'possessing a right to till', elaborated upon earlier in this chapter. Most villagers also either kept or tried to maintain positive linkages with local security strongmen as an informal protection guarantee. Yet in general, military officers tended to possess greater knowledge

---

29. Personal interview with anonymous Western journalist who has long lived in Cambodia, 27 April 2014.

30. Personal interview with Prof. Pou Souvachana, 7 May 2014.

about legal land rights than did villagers. Finally, officers tended to be allied with corporate interests and the ruling CPP (Grainger 1996). Though military-held lands have since 1993 mostly existed in the provinces of Kompong Speu, Koh Kong, Mondulkiri, Pursat, Ratanakiri, and Kompong Cham, military control is increasing throughout Cambodia, especially in provinces bordering Thailand. Such land holdings earn money for individual officers or local units because these lands are often leased to corporations in the form of economic land concessions.

In 1999, when Cambodia's civil war ended, military development zones were created (from tracts of land previously held by the Khmer Rouge) to provide jobs and land for demobilised soldiers (United Nations 2004: 3). Today these military development zones comprise an undisclosed portfolio covering 700,000 hectares – almost four per cent of Cambodia's land area (Global Witness 2009: 26). But there is little information about the location of or the exact extent of these zones. It is known, however, that the Ministry of National Defence has leased tracts out to corporations and that senior military officers close to the CPP have personally benefited from the zones (ibid: 6, 21).

Individual members of the military have invested in economic activities, at least since 1989.[31] Each province of Cambodia offers cases of active-duty military officials who own land. Legally, there can be no military businesses in Cambodia. But individual military personnel do informally open hotels, hospitals and so on.[32] In such endeavours, they often use the names of their spouses, children or other relatives. Today there are at least two known mining companies and swathes of land owned by powerful military men. The first, the Rattanak Stone Mine in Preah Vihear Province, is mostly owned by Gen. Pol Saroeun, commander-in-chief of the Royal Cambodian Armed Forces. Beginning its mining operations in 2004, soldiers guarding the site have reportedly harassed villagers who had been removed from the area to make way for the mine (Global Witness 2009: 21). Another mining company, the Southern Mining Project (SMP, in the Phnom Samkos Wildlife Sanctuary) is led by CEO Gen. Ouk Kosa, who is also the director of the Development Department under the Cambodian Ministry of National Defence). This department, not coincidentally, oversees the military

---

31. Personal interview with anonymous middle-level police officer, 25 March 2014.

32. Personal interview with anonymous senior police official, 27 March 2014.

development zones. Together with his deputy, Col. Aoch Chany, as Vice-Director, Gen. Ouk operates SMP and receives protection from RCAF infantry forces, even though it is located in a wildlife sanctuary and is thus to be an area protected from economic exploitation (Global Witness 2009: 25). In August, 2008, the Vietnamese firm Vinacomin bought a 70 per cent share of SMP. The corporation is connected to Gen. Meas Sophea, the commander of the RCAF infantry forces (Global Witness 2009: 26). In 2010, ethnic minority villagers were evicted from 225 hectares of land on which their families have long lived. Though they traced their legal residence in these areas back to 1979, an RCAF official connected to the CPP, one Hem Khorn, obtained the legal title deed over the lands in 2007. Since the lands were under the name of a military official (and military officials are much more influential than most civilians), the governor of the district in which the lands existed claimed that there was nothing he could do (Titthara 2010).

A principal new area of military holdings has been along the Thai–Cambodian border region, specifically in northernmost Cambodia. Following the build-up of Thai–Cambodian frontier tensions in 2008 and Hun Sen's aforementioned February 2010 donations announcement, the Cambodian military began constructing numerous bases in 14 provinces along the border with Thailand. To make way for these bases, the RCAF forcibly removed 938 families from 2000 hectares of land between 2008 and 2013 (Titthara, 2013). In addition, in Preah Vihear Province in 2012, soldiers burned houses to the ground and removed villagers to establish a 5,557-hectare Social Land Concession (SLC). This SLC was officially meant for handicapped and retired soldiers (Seangly 2012). Nevertheless, a great part of this land had been riddled with UXO (unexploded ordinance) and was thus unsuitable as a resettlement zone, especially for the disabled. The fact is that this military SLC could become developed for commercial use in the future. By 2013, bases were still being built in the provinces of Preah Vihear, Oddar Meanchey, Pailin, Pursat, Battambang and Koh Kong (Titthara 2013).

Three more cases will suffice. First, in 2010, Hun Sen's regime awarded the armed forces land on Koh Sla Island (also to be used as the Military Handicap Development Zone).[33] Moreover, the desire of Cambodian security forces to build more bases has now spread to

---

33. Anonymous interview with security sector official, 11 May 2014.

non-border provinces and its apparent need for land to have a base for purposes of national security has sometimes masked motives of economic gain. For example, in Siem Reap Province (which is not on a boundary), the military evicted a community from its lands purportedly to build a base. However, the RCAF then rented it to businesspeople to cultivate cassava (Titthara 2013). Second, in 2013 a thousand families were evicted from their land in Kratie province to make way for a giant new base for Unit 9 Royal Cambodian Armed Forces. The land for the base is in the middle of valuable cassava fields and is adjacent to a rubber plantation (Titthara and Seiff 2013). Finally, in 2014, following massive evictions from the Boeng Kak neighbourhood inside Phnom Penh, it was announced that a base for either military police or District Municipal Security Guards would be built in part of that area (though other areas would be retained for commercial use). Cambodians refusing to be evicted from this zone allege that the construction of the base is meant to house troops tasked with repressing demonstrators in order to control their activities (Dara and Peter 2014).

All in all, though Cambodia's security forces have generally acted as political proxies of the CPP and the economic vassals of major corporations, they themselves are increasingly gaining their own economic dividends in terms of businesses, lands and other investments. However, much of the economic clout of the military (and other security agencies) is in the hands of individual officers rather than in the form of institutionalized economic influence. Perhaps in the future, if the military manages to use possible threats from Thailand, Vietnam (or perhaps even Laos) to rationalize the need for more land and business holdings then their role in the Cambodian economy may become even stronger.

Conclusion: Cambodia's security forces – purged, pliant and partisan

This chapter has argued that security forces in Cambodia have, throughout the country's history, tended to be proactive clients of powerful, personalist political leaders. As a price for their support, they have enjoyed the 'carrots' of economic gain. Since 1997, the military and other security services have tended to assist Hun Sen, the CPP and CPP-favoured corporations. Troops have often evicted people from their homes and land, despite lacking any legal authority. These forces today are hierarchically integrated under Hun Sen and his allies. Military and police units are politicized, but they are also up for hire.

At the beginning of this study, six questions were asked. I address them now, in turn. First, how and why did a political economy of neopatrimonial relations between prime minister and security forces come to evolve across Cambodia's history? One could argue that it was the nature of Cambodia's evolution that has ensured the ascendance of personalist authoritarianism backed up by military might. Cambodia has followed a historical path that has been highly chaotic, witnessing two critical junctures in the development of its military: 1953, when it gained independence, and 1979, when it saw the last enormous change in the structure of its military. It has experienced some level of war continuously from 1941 until 1999 which, in combination with seemingly constant regime changes (1944, 1953, 1954, 1970, 1975, 1979, 1992, 1993, 1997), has led to an entrenched instability from which it is still climbing out. It has long been regionally subservient to its neighbours (Thailand and Vietnam) while suffering interference from global powers (the United States, Russia and China). It has been occupied by the Vietnamese (1979–89) as well as the United Nations (1992–93). It is a nation of extreme poverty and nationalism, and successive variants of neopatrimonial, personalist regimes have predominated (e.g. Sihanouk, Lon Nol, Pol Pot, Hun Sen). The societal dislocation brought about by war and occupation provided the space for Hun Sen and his CPP to seek control over Cambodia in a post-1993 equilibrium. The 1997 coup helped Hun Sen to begin to solidify his personal power through the CPP over Cambodia's security forces and over Cambodia. He has since established a form of control over the RCAF partly through the use of coercion. However, such control has been conditional upon his patron-clientelistic appeasement of the military. In some ways, his style of governance is akin to that of former Prime Minister Norodom Sihanouk – also a populist leader who deformed democratic structures through intimidation and electoral fraud – and centralized power in himself. By 2010, Cambodia's security forces had become the junior partner of the prime minister in an asymmetrical alliance of control over the country. In addition, the military as an institution but more prominently through individual military commanders had gained its own military capital as 'payback' for its loyalty to Hun Sen and CPP.

Second, how are Cambodia's security forces currently organized? It appears as though Cambodia's security forces are organized such that, in addition to a regular military under the formal control of the king, an informal grouping of security units act as a sort of praetorian guard to Prime Minister Hun Sen. All commanders and sub-commanders simultaneously hold positions in the CPP.

Third, how has Hun Sen and his party come to control the security sector? Prime Minister Hun Sen and his CPP have come to dominate Cambodia's security forces by following a combination of strategies. That is, the civilians have acquiesced to security forces' influence over parts of Cambodian society, co-opted the security force leadership, purged potentially malcontent security officials, promoted proven Hun Sen loyalists to senior postings, counterbalanced security bureaucracies off of one other, and finally built up a group of defence units personally loyal to Hun Sen himself rather than society at large.

Fourth, to what extent does it act as a vassal to the economic interests of the party and to corporate interests? Salaries and pensions of security forces are under the total control of Hun Sen. The prime minister and CPP allow security officials close to the party to informally assist corporations, even if these activities were illegal. After 2008 and especially during 2010, military units became formalized vassals to corporate lords through an elaborate system of corporate sponsorship of military units. The danger of this situation is that military units might become 'mercenary-ized' – more loyal to the highest bidder rather than to the country.

Fifth, to what extent do parts of the security sector have their own economic interests? While the military is formally barred from economic activities, the CPP has long allowed military officials to engage informally and illegally in profit-making activities, some of which were criminal in nature. Since 2008, the CPP legalized the right of the military units and individual active-duty soldiers to obtain land concessions. As a result there, have been increasing numbers of properties or businesses owned by security forces.

Sixth, how might security force clientelism in Cambodia affect the future of democracy there? The current state of relations between Cambodia's political leaders and its security forces might be termed security force clientelism. As long as Hun Sen successfully maintains supremacy over security forces, such clientelism is likely to continue. This of course does not bode well for the future of democracy in Cambodia. Today, Cambodia is ruled by a neopatrimonial hybrid regime that incorporates and integrates the various security bureaucracies. There is civilian control over the military and other security forces. Yet Cambodia has no institutionalized civilian control. If Hun Sen's party is not victorious in the next election, it would be no surprise if the armed forces supported a Hun Sen-led coup. With such a history of political pandemonium, regime change and transformations of military structures, there has been little time to really entrench the security sector under democratic civilian control. Instead, Cambodia is a case of illiberal civilian control – personalized under Hun Sen and his CPP. In terms of classifying Cambodia's form of civil–military relations, it should be viewed as an example of authoritarian-personal control. In other words, though Cambodia possesses the trappings of procedural but unconsolidated democracy, power is hierarchically diffused from Hun Sen. He alone personally controls the political dimensions of Cambodia's polity, and the security force that ostensibly serves it.

Yet only time will tell how long Hun Sen and the CPP can depend upon such contracted loyalty. For the future, Hun Sen's Cambodia could become the Philippines of the 1972–86 dictatorship of Ferdinand Marcos, whereby an elected leader distorted (or terminated) democracy, ruled through martial law and brought in the military as a junior partner in his rapacious autocratic regime. However, the close 2013 election results do tell us that, to some extent, the CPP has been playing by the rules and there is no guarantee that the CPP will win the 2018 or 2023 elections. If the CPP loses, would it abide the electoral decision? What would Cambodia's security forces do in such a scenario? Would security forces be willing and ready to serve the CNRP's Sam Rainsy and/or Kem Sokha? Such questions have implications for the business and political interests of Hun Sen and his allies as well as the political economy of security forces themselves. Most likely, Hun Sen and his CPP would not support such a result because doing so would likely mean the demise of his vast political and economic pyramid of power. Given his enormous influence over security forces, if Hun Sen does not accept an election result, it is likely that the majority of security officials will not accept it, either. Such a situation would effectively bring Cambodia to a 'Marcos future.' There is also the possibility that, in exchange for credible promises of substantial economic and political benefits from a party other than the CPP (should that other party win), security forces would support this winning party, regardless of its identity. The plausibility of such a scenario also does not bode well for the ability of Cambodian-style democracy to serve the needs of Cambodian citizens. Alternatively, regular security services like the army might support the electoral outcome, while praetorian elements like Hun Sen's bodyguard unit would not. Such well-armed disunity could spark a bloody clash, turning into civil war. Yet if Cambodia's security forces support a 'Marcos future,' then they are liable to gain increasingly sizeable portions of economic booty in return for helping Hun Sen sustain his rule. As throughout Cambodia's history, the symbiosis between a personalist patron and the military will likely be entrenched for years to come.

List of Acronyms

ANKI	*Armee National pour un Kampuchea Independent*; armed wing of FUNCIPEC
ARK	Royal Khmer Army or *Armée Royale Khmère*
CNRP	Cambodian National Rescue Party
CPNLAF	Cambodian People's Liberation Armed Forces
CPP	Cambodian People's Party
CRC	Cambodian Red Cross
DDR	disarm, demobilize and reintegrate (UNTAC operation)
DK	Democratic Kampuchea
DMSG	District Municipal Security Guards
FANK	Khmer National Armed Forces (*Forces Armées Nationales Khmères*)
FARK	Royal Khmer Armed Forces (Forces Armées Royales Khmères)
FUNCINPEC	National United Front for an Independent, Neutral, Peaceful and Cooperative Cambodia
FUNK	National United Front of Kampuchea
HAGL	Hoang Anh Gia Lai (a Vietnamese rubber company)
KPNLAF	Khmer People's National Liberation Armed Forces

KPNLF	Khmer People's National Liberation Front
KPRAF	Kampuchean People's Revolutionary Armed Forces
KPRP	Kampuchean People's Revolutionary Party
LICADHO	Cambodian Leagure for the Promotion and Defence of Human Rights
NADK	National Army of Democratic Kampuchea (RAK, as renamed in 1979)
PRK	People's Republic of Kampuchea
RAK	Revolutionary Army of Kampuchea (becomes NADK in 1979)
RCAF	Royal Cambodian Armed Forces
RCAF	Royal Cambodian Armed Forces
RTC	*Regiment Tirailleurs Cambodgiens*
SLC	Social Land Concession
SRN	*Sangkum Reastr Niyum* (political party)
SSR	Security Sector Reform (UNTAC operation)
UNTAC	United Nations Transitional Authority in Cambodia
VRG	Vietnam Rubber Group (cartel)

Bibliography

Personal interviews (all undertaken in Phnom Penh)
Anonymous Cambodian Senate official (13 May 2014).

Anonymous CICP academic (13 April 2014).

Anonymous middle-level police officer (25 March 2014).

Anonymous representative of ADHOC (7 May 2014).

Anonymous security sector official (11 May 2014).

Anonymous senior police official (27 March 2014).

Anonymous Western journalist who has long lived in Cambodia (27 April 2014).

Heder, Dr. Stephen, Phnom Penh (7 November 2014).

Kheum Sucheat, case worker, NGO Voice (29 March 2014).

Nan Ony, Housing Rights Task Force (18 May 2014).

Pellerin, Mathieu, LICADHO (29 March 2014).

Pou Sothirath, Pou, Ambassador (19 May 2014).

Pou Souvachana, Prof. (7 May 2014).

Preap Kol, Executive Director of Transparency International, Cambodia (7 April 2014).

Sun, Kim, personal interviews with VSGs (Village Support Groups) (13–15 May 2014).

Tippens, Toy Neil, US Embassy Cambodia (15 May 2014).

Secondary Sources

ACE (Administration and Cost of Elections) European Union Election Observer Mission. The Committee for Free and Fair Elections in Cambodia (2008) '2008 National Assembly Elections', (27 July). acepro-ject.org/eroen/regions/asia/KH/Cambodia...on...2008.../file, accessed 10 March 2017.

Adams, Brad (1997) 'Cambodia: July 1997: Shock and Aftermath', *Human Rights Watch*. http://www.hrw.org/news/2007/07/27/cambodia-july-1997-shock-and-aftermath, accessed 10 March 2017.

—— (2014) 'Marking the Anniversary of the Cambodian Coup Attempt', *The Cambodia Daily* (2 July). https://www.cambodiadaily.com/opinion/marking-the-anniversary-of-the-cambodian-coup-attempt-62966/, accessed 10 March 2017.

ANFREL (Asian Network for Free Election) (1999) 'Cambodia: Struggling for Justice and Peace – Report of Missions on the 1998 Elections'. http://anfrel.org/wp-content/uploads/1998/09/1998_cambodia.pdf, accessed 10 March 2017.

Asian Development Bank (ADB) (2000) Country Economic Review, ADB, Cambodia.

Bennett, Jody Ray (2010) 'Cambodia: Military, Inc', *The International Relations and Security Network* (ISN) (16 August). http://www.isn.ethz.ch/Digital-Library/Articles/Detail/?lng=en&id=120178, accessed 10 March 2017.

Blomberg, Matt and Van Roeun (2015) 'Grand Concessions', *The Cambodia Daily* (24 December). https://www.cambodiadaily.com/grandconces-sions/, accessed 10 March 2017.

Blomberg, Matt and Saing Soenthrith (2014) 'Y Chhien Quits Pailin Council Despite Show of Support', *The Cambodia Daily* (10 October). https://www.cambodiadaily.com/archives/y-chhien-quits-pailin-council-de-spite-show-of-support-69520/, accessed 10 March 2017.

Brady, Brendan (2010) 'The Cambodian Army: Open for Corporate Sponsors', *Time Magazine* (9 June). http://content.time.com/time/world/arti-cle/0,8599,1995298,00.html, accessed 10 March 2017.

CMND (Cambodian Ministry of National Defense) 'Structural Chart'. http://www.mod.gov.kh/kh/org_chart.php, accessed 10 March 2017.

Chambers, Paul (2015) 'Neo-Sultanistic Tendencies: The Trajectory of Civil–military Relations in Cambodia', *Asian Security* 11(3): 179–205.

Chandler, David (2007) *A History of Cambodia* Boulder Colorado: Westview.

Clapham, Christopher and George Philip, eds (1985) *The Political Dilemmas of Military Regimes.* London: Croom Helm.

Clymer, Kenton (2004) *The United States and Cambodia, 1969–2000: A Troubled Relationship.* London and New York: Routledge.

Conboy, Ken (2011) *FANK: A History of the Cambodian Armed Forces, 1970–1975.* Djakarta, Indonesia: Equinox Publishing (Asia).

Dara, Mech and Zsombor (2014) 'City Builds Military Police Base Amid Activist Neighborhood', *The Cambodia Daily* (24 June). http://www.cambodiadaily.com/archives/city-builds-military-police-base-amid-activist-neighborhood-62576/, accessed 10 March 2017.

Economist (2015) 'Assault on CNRP a turning point in rapprochement with CPP', (29 October). http://country.eiu.com/article.aspx?articleid=2003634584&Country=Cambodia&topic=Politics&subtopic=Forecast&subsubtopic=Political+stability&u=1&pid=384721022&oid=384721022&uid=1, accessed 10 March 2017.

ERA (Electoral Reform Alliance) (2013) 'Joint Report on the Conduct of the 2013 Elections', (November). nationalrescueparty.org/wp.../2013/11/FINAL-ERA-REPORT.NDI_.pdf, accessed 10 March 2017.

Forest, Alain (1987) *Le Cambodge* et la colonisation française: Histoire d'une colonisation sans heurts (1897–1920) Paris: Harmattan.

Globalsecurity.org, 'Cambodian Royal Armed Forces—Demobilization'. http://www.globalsecurity.org/military/world/cambodia/army-demobilization.htm, accessed 10 March 2017.

Global Witness (2007) *Family Trees: Illegal logging and the stripping of public assets by Cambodia's elite.* https://www.globalwitness.org/sites/default/files/pdfs/cambodias_family_trees_low_res.pdf, accessed 10 March 2017.

——— (2013) 'Rubber Barons, How Vietnamese Companies and International Financiers are Driving a Land Crisis in Laos and Cambodia', (26 May). http://bit.ly/1ar7lKn, accessed 10 March 2017.

——— (2009) *Country for Sale: How Cambodia's Elite has Captured the Country's Extractive Industries.* file:///C:/Users/AcerM/Downloads/country_for_sale_low_res_english%20(2)pdf, accessed 10 March 2017.

Grainger, Matthew (1998) 'RCAF's Fractured Past Points to Future', *The Phnom Penh Post* (19 June). http://www.phnompenhpost.com/national/rcafs-fractured-past-points-future, accessed 10 March 2017.

—————— (1996) 'Army Land Deals Cut Across Budget', *The Phnom Penh Post* Issue 5/11, May 31 – June 13. http://www.phnompenhpost.com/national/army-land-deals-cut-across-budget, accessed 11 March 2017.

Heder, Stephen (2005) 'Hun Sen's Consolidation: Death or beginning of reform?' in *Southeast Asian Affairs*. Singapore: Institute of Southeast Asian Studies.

Hourn, Kao Kim (2003) *Civil–military relations in Cambodia*. Phnom Penh: Cambodian Institute of Cooperation and Peace.

HRW (Human Rights Watch) (2013) 'Cambodia: Army, Police Campaign for Ruling PartyPartisanship Intimidating Voters, Threatening Fair Elections', (22 July). https://www.hrw.org/news/2013/07/22/cambodia-army-police-campaign-ruling-party, accessed 10 March 2017.

—————— (2015) 'Cambodia: Party Extends Control of Security Forces', (4 February). https://www.hrw.org/news/2015/02/04/cambodia-party-extends-control-security-forces, accessed 10 March 2017.

Hughes, Caroline (2009) *Dependent Communities: Aid and Politics in Cambodia and East Timor*. Ithaca: Cornell Southeast Asia Publications Program.

Hunt, Luke (2014) 'Spotlight on Cambodian Government Brutality', *The Diplomat* (5 May). http://thediplomat.com/2014/05/spotlight-on-cambodian-government-brutality/, accessed 10 March 2017.

IDI (*Inclusive Development International* [blog]) (2014) 'ANZ Bankrolls Massive Land Grab in Cambodia', (22 January). http://www.inclusivedevelopment.net/anz-bankrolls-massive-land-grab-in-cambodia/, accessed 10 March 2017.

IPU (Inter-parliamentary Union) (1972) '1972 elections', Cambodia. http://www.ipu.org/parline-e/reports/arc/KHMER_REPUBLIC_1972_E.PDF, accessed 10 March 2017.

IPU (Inter-parliamentary Union) (1976) '1976 elections', Cambodia. http://www.ipu.org/parline-e/reports/arc/CAMBODIA_1976_E.PDF, accessed 10 March 2017.

Kimsong, Kay, Saito, Mhari, (1998) 'Battambang Officials Pledge to End Land Grab', *The Cambodia Daily* (27 November). http://www.cambodiadaily.com/archives/battambang-officials-pledge-to-end-land-grab-11985/, accessed 10 March 2017.

Kingdom of Cambodia (1993) *Constitution*. https://www.constituteproject.org/constitution/Cambodia_2008.pdf?lang=en, accessed 10 March 2017.

—————— (2000) 'Defending the Kingdom of Cambodia: Security and Development'.

Kyne, Phelim (2000) 'RAC booted, RCAF boosted, by Hun Sen', *The Phnom Penh Post* (7 July). http://www.phnompenhpost.com/national/rac-booted-rcaf-boosted-hun-sen, accessed 10 March 2017.

Law on Political Parties (1997) 'Cambodia: Law of 1997 on Political Parties', Refworld, http://www.refworld.org/docid/3ae6b51414.html.

LICADHO (Cambodian Leaugre for the Promotion and Defense of Human Rights) (2009) *Land Grabbing & Poverty in Cambodia: The Myth of Development: A LICADHO Report.* http://www.licadhocambodia.org/reports/files/134LICADHOREportMythofDevelopment2009Eng.pdf, accessed 13 April 2013.

———— (2009A) 'Restrictions on the Freedom of Expression in Cambodia's Media', Phnom Penh: (May). www.licadho-cambodia.org/.../130LICAD HOFreedomofExpressionBrief, accessed 10 March 2017.

Mead, Col. David (2004) 'Reforming the Royal Cambodian Armed Forces: Leadership is the key', *Phnom Penh Post* (30 January). http://www. phnompenhpost.com/national/reforming-royal-cambodian-armed-forc-es-leadership-key, accessed 10 March 2017.

Mehta, Harish and Metha, Julie (2013) *Strongman: The Extraordinary Life of Hun Sen—From Pagoda Boy to Prime Minister of Cambodia.* Singapore: Marshall Cavendish Editions.

Mertha, Andrew (2014) *Brothers in Arms Chinese Aid to the Khmer Rouge, 1975–1979.* Ithaca, NY: Cornell University Press.

Naren, Kuch (2013) 'Military Denies Troops Posted to Protect KDC Companys Land...Guns for Hire', *The Cambodia Daily* (15 May). http://khamerlogue.wordpress.com/2013/05/15/military-denies-troops-posted-to-protect-kdc-companys-land-guns-for-hire/, accessed 10 March 2017.

Narim, Khuon (2014) 'Villagers Claim Soldiers Hired to Prevent Planting', *The Cambodia Daily* (14 June). https://www.cambodiadaily.com/archives/villagers-claim-soldiers-hired-to-prevent-planting-61420/, accessed 10 March 2017.

NICFEC (Neutral and Impartial Committee on Free and Fair Elections in Cambodia) (2003), http://www.licadho-cambodia.org/reports/files/39NICFEC%202003%20report.pdf, accessed 5 November 2016.

Nohlen, D., F. Grotz and C. Hartmann (2001) *Elections in Asia: A data hand-book*, Volume II. OUP Oxford.

Noren-Nilsson, Astrid (2016) *Cambodia's Second Kingdom: Nation, Imagination, and Democracy*, Ithaca, New York: Southeast Asia Program Publications, Cornell University.

Osborne, Milton (1994) *Sihanouk: Prince of Light, Prince of Darkness.* Honolulu: University of Hawaii Press.

Paling, Willem (2012) 'Planning a Future for Phnom Penh: Mega-Projects, Aid Dependence and Disjointed Governance', *Urban Studies* 49(13): 2889–912.

Peou, Sorpong (2001) 'Hun-Sen's Pre-emptive Coup: Causes and

Consequences, Causes and Consequences', in Peou, Sorpong, *Cambodia: Change and Continuity in Contemporary Politics*. Farnham, UK: Ashgate.

Pheap, Aun and Dene-Hern Chen (2013) 'Senator's Wife Showers Police with New Year Cash', *The Cambodia Daily* (12 February). http://www.cambodiadaily.com/archives/senators-wife-showers-police-military-with-new-year-cash-9831/, accessed 10 March 2017.

The Phnom Penh Post (2006) 'Thai Coup Sends Few Ripples Through Cambodia', (21 September). http://www.phnompenhpost.com/national/thai-coup-sends-few-ripples-cambodia, accessed 10 March 2017.

Radio Free Asia (2014) 'Cambodian PM Promotes 29 to Four-Star General', (5 February). http://www.rfa.org/english/news/cambodia/promotion-02052014165509.html/, accessed 10 March 2017.

———— (2015) 'Cambodia's Armed Forces 'Belong' to The Ruling Party: Four-Star General', (29 July). http://www.rfa.org/english/news/cambodia/military-07292015145855.html, accessed 10 March 2017.

Rogers, Richard (2016) 'ICC will investigate environmental destruction as well as war crimes', *Open Democracy* (blog), (19 October). https://www.opendemocracy.net/openglobalrights/richard-j-rogers/icc-will-investigate-environmental-destruction-as-well-as-war-crim, accessed 10 March 2017.

Scott, James (1972) 'Patron-Client Politics and Political Change in Southeast Asia', *The American Political Science Review* 66(1).

Seangly, Phak (2012) 'Preah Vihear Villagers Protest Soldiers', *The Phnom Penh Post* (7 August). http://www.phnompenhpost.com/national/preah-vihear-villagers-protest-soldiers, accessed 10 March 2017.

Sekiguchi, M. and N. Hatsukano (2013) 'Land Conflicts and Land Registration in Cambodia', in J. Unruh and R.C. Williams (eds) *Land and Post-Conflict Peacebuilding*. London: Earthscan.

Sithol, Im and Chap Sotharith (2008) 'Role of Parliament in Defence Budgeting in Cambodia'. http://ipf-ssg-sea.net/userfiles/Explanatory%20Background%20Note%20Cambodia%20.pdf, accessed 10 March 2017.

Slocomb, Margaret (2010) *An Economic History of Cambodia*, Singapore: NUS Press.

Soenthrith, Saing (2014) 'Governors of Preah Sihanouk, Ratanakkiri and Pursat Replaced', *The Cambodia Daily* (9 May). https://www.cambodiadaily.com/archives/governors-of-preah-sihanouk-ratanakkiri-and-pursat-replaced-58415/, accessed 10 March 2017.

Sokchea, Meas (2014) 'Talks ongoing, still no Accord', *The Phnom Penh Post* (11 March). http://www.phnompenhpost.com/national/talks-ongoing-still-no-accord.

Sokheng, Vong and Daniel Pye (2015) 'In Praise of RCAF Inc', *The Phnom Penh Post* (30 July). http://www.phnompenhpost.com/national/praise-rcaf-inc, accessed 10 March 2017.

Sony, Ouch (2015) 'CPP, CNRP Groups in "Lightning Oath" Swearing Competition', *The Cambodia Daily* (22 June). https://www.cambodia-daily.com/archives/cpp-cnrp-groups-in-lightning-oath-swearing-competition-86077/, accessed 10 March 2017.

Soonthornpoct, Punnee (2005) *From Freedom to Hell: A History of Foreign Intervention in Cambodian Politics and Wars*. New York: Vantage Press.

South China Morning Post (2016) 'Cambodian Red Cross playing by the party's rules, watchdog says', (7 July). http://www.scmp.com/news/asia/southeast-asia/article/1986859/cambodian-red-cross-playing-partys-rules-watchdog-says, accessed 10 March 2017.

Strangio, Sebastian, and Thet Sambath (2009) 'Party factionalism looms behind Ke Kim Yan sacking: observers', *The Phnom Penh Post* (19 February). http://www.phnompenhpost.com/national/party-factionalism-looms-behind-ke-kim-yan-sacking-observers , accessed 10 March 2017.

'Sub-decree legalizing the sponsorship by corporations of security force units', *Government Gazette* (February 2010).

Tamayo, Jingo (2011) 'Bittersweet Harvest: Thai sugar company on land grab in Cambodia?' (September). http://farmlandgrab.org/post/view/19264, accessed 10 March 2017.

Tatu, Frank (1987). 'National security', in Russell Ross (ed.) *Cambodia: A Country Study*. Washington: Library of Congress Federal Research Division.

Thomson, Alex (2004) *An Introduction to African Politics*, London: Routledge.

Titthara, May (2010) 'Cambodia: Tribal land protest crushed, land owned by general-PPP', *The Phnom Penh Post* (15 June). http://facthai.wordpress.com/2010/06/18/cambodia-tribal-land-protest-crushed-land-owned-by-general-ppp/, accessed 10 March 2017.

———— (2012) 'Protestors Injured as Soldiers Fire', *The Phnom Penh Post* (19 January). http://www.phnompenhpost.com/national/protesters-injured-guards-fire, accessed 10 March 2017.

———— (2013) 'RCAF Evicting for Bases: NGO', *The Phnom Penh Post* (28 October). http://www.phnompenhpost.com/national/rcaf-evicting-bases-ngo, accessed 10 March 2017.

Titthara, May and Abby Seiff (2013) '"Separatist" Farms Replaced by RCAF base', *The Phnom Penh Post* (6 February).

Turkoly-Joczik, Robert L. (1988) 'The Khmer Serei Movement', *Asian Affairs* 15(1).

Un, Kheang (2005) 'Patronage Politics and Hybrid Democracy: Political Change in Cambodia, 1993–2003', *Asian Perspective* 29(2).

United Nations (2004) 'Land Concessions for Economic Purposes in

Cambodia: A Human Rights Perspective', Mission of the Special Representative of the Secretary-General for human rights in Cambodia, Office of the High Commissioner for Human Rights, 7–14 November.

United States Department of Commerce (1977) *Statistical Abstract of the United States,* Foreign Commerce and Aid, Table 1467, Washington, D.C.

United States Embassy Cable (2007) 'Cambodia's Top Ten Tycoons', Ref: 07PHNOMPENH1034, (9 August). https://wikileaks.org/plusd/cables/07PHNOMPENH1034_a.html, accessed 10 March 2017.

United States Operations Mission to Cambodia (1960) 'U.S. Economic Aid Program to Cambodia 1955–1959', Phnom Penh: International Cooperation Administration, January.

Vannarith, Chheang (2013) 'Cambodian security and defence policy', Security Outlook of the Asia Pacific Countries and Its Implications for the Defense Sector, Tokyo:NiDS.

Vickery, Michael (1999) *Cambodia: 1975–1982.* Chiang Mai: Silkworm.

——— (1999a) 'Kambodscha', in Bernhard Dahm and Roderich Ptak (eds) *Südost Asien Handbuch.* München: Verlag C.H. Beck.

——— (2007) *Cambodia: A Political Survey.* Phnom Penh, Funan Press.

Vickery, Michael and Ramses Amer (1996) 'Democracy and Human Rights in Cambodia'. http://michaelvickery.org/vickery1996democracy.pdf, accessed 10 March 2017.

Wallace, Julia (2010) 'Business, Border Military Units to Attend Networking Event', *The Cambodia Daily* (24 February). http://www.cambodiadaily.com/archives/business-border-military-units-to-attend-networking-event-2840/, accessed 10 March 2017.

World Bank (2001) *Cambodia-Demobilization and Reintegration Project.* Report No. PID10234.

Worrell, Shane, and Khouth Sophak Chakrya (2014) 'In Capital, Protection Still a Thriving Business', *The Phnom Penh Post* (8 November). http://www.phnompenhpost.com/post-weekend/capital-protection-still-thriving-business, accessed 10 March 2017.

Appendices

Appendix 5.1: Military officers in key CPP positions

Officer	Position
Gen. Ke Kimyan	CPP Standing Committee
Gen. Pol Saroeun	CPP Standing Committee
Gen. Kun Kim	CPP Standing Committee
Gen. Meas Sophea	CPP Standing Committee
Gen. Net Savoeun	CPP Standing Committee
Gen. Prum Din	CPP Central Committee
Gen. Chea Dara	CPP Central Committee
Gen. Ma Chhoeun	CPP Central Committee
Gen. Mao Chandara	CPP Central Committee and vice-chairman of a CPP work team assigned to Sihanouk province.
Gen. Sao Sokha	CPP Central Committee
Pol Gen. Mok Chito	Chair of CPP Work Team
Gen. Hing Bunhieng	Vice-chair of CPP Standing Committee of Kandal Province Committee for Grassroots Strengthening vice-chairman of a CPP work team assigned to Samlaut district in the brigade's Battambang province
Gen. Hun Manet (first son of Hun Sen)	Vice-chairman of the CPP Centre-Level Work Team for Kampong Cham Province
Gen. Hun Manit (second son of Hun Sen)	led a CPP delegation to Kandal province
General Kim Bunthan	Vice-chairman of the CPP Work Team for Going Down to Help Oddar Meanchey Province
General Chea Man	Chair of the CPP Center-Level Work Team Group for Going Down to Assist Trapeang Prasat District of Oddar Meanchey Province
General Bun Seng	Advisor to CPP Party
General Huy Piseth	Chair of a grassroots work group for CPP election activities in a part of Kandal province

Officer	Position
Pol. General Suos Angkear	Chair of a CPP work team assigned to 'grassroots strengthening' at the village and sub-district level of Thmar Korl district of Battambang province
Pol. General Touch Narot	Vice-chair of a CPP work team for strengthening the party in the Peareang district of Prey Veng province
Pol. General Dy Vicchea	Vice-chair of the CPP Federal Youth Union and chairman of its Svay Rieng province organization
Pol. General Keo Vanthan	Vice-chair of a CPP work team for election campaigning in Svay Antor district of Prey Veng province
Pol. General Dul Koeun	Vice-chair of a CPP grassroots strengthening committee for Kandal province
Brigade 52 Commander Heng Bunhieng	Vice-chair of a CPP work team assigned to Samlaut district in Battambang province
Gend. Commander Rat Sreang	Member of the CPP Standing Committee for Banteay Meanchey and responsible for 'party strengthening' in localities in its Mongkolborei district
Gend. Commander Local Commander Men Siborn	Kampong Speu province openly active in praising the CPP and criticizing the opposition leadership in public CPP meetings in Kamong Speu Province
Police Commissioner Chuong Seanghak, Kratie province	Member of the provincial CPP Standing Committee and chairman of a party work team for strengthening its organization in Prek Prasap district
Police Commissioner Eav Chamraoen, Kandal province	Chair of a CPP grassroots strengthening committee in S'ang district of Kandal Province
Police Commissioner Chhay Keumson, Kampong Cham province	Chair of a CPP work team operating in Steung Trang district of Kampong Cham province

Source: HRW, 2013.

Appendix 5.2: Partial list of security force unit alliances with corporations in Cambodia (2014)

Military

▷ **Army Region I** *[Stung Treng, Ratanakkiri, Mondolkiri Provinces]*
- Region I headquarter + MoSAVY + Chamkar Adong Rubber Company
- Regiment 42 + MoAgriculture + Pean Cheang Rubber Company
- Battalion 101,102,103 + MoWA + Try Pheap Company

▷ **Army Region II** *[Kampong Cham, Prey Veng, Svay Rieng, Kampong Thom Provinces]*
- Border Battalion 201,202,203,204 + MoJ + Koh Pich Development Company
- Brigade 21 + MoFA + AZ Group

▷ **Region III** *[Kampong Speu, Takeo, Kampot, Preah Sihanouk, Koh Kong Provinces]*
- Region III headquarter + MoLMUP + Anko (អង្គរ) Company
- Border Battalion 301,302,303 + MoAFF + Koh Kong Casino (Ly Yong Phat)
- Battalion 313 + Phnom Penh Autonomous Port + Kampong Speu Sugar Company (Ly Yong Phat)

▷ **Region IV** *[Siem Reap, Oddar Meanchey, Preah Vihear Provinces]*
- Region IV headquarter + MoTourism + Aspara Authority + Mobitel 012
- Brigade 41 + MoPTelecommunication + Chub Rubber Company
- Brigade 42 + Electricite du Cambodge + O'Smach Casino (Ly Yong Phat)
- Border Unit 401 + MoF + Bayon TV/Radio
- Border Unit 402 + MoPWTransport + CTN
- Border Unit 403 + MoPWTransport + Cambodiana Hotel
- Border Unit 404 + prime minister Cabinet + Canadia Bank

▷ **Intervention Division 2**
- Division 2 headquarter + Custom Department + Tela Company
- Brigade 4 + Preah Sihanouk Provincial Cabinet + Memot Rubber Company
- Brigade 5 + Siem Reap Provincial Cabinet + Spark Nightclub
- Brigade 6 + Kampong Cham Provincial Cabinet + *Okhna* Lao Meng Kim & Lok Chumtiev + *Okhna* Siv Kong Triev & Lok Chumtiev + *Okhna* Ving Hour

▷ *Intervention Division 3*
- Division 3 headquarter + prime minister Cabinet + Kreak Rubber Company
- Brigade 7 + MoLV Training + Men Saron Company
- Brigade 8 + Phnom Penh Water Supply + ANZ Royal Bank
- Brigade 9 + Phnom Penh Municipal Cabinet + NCX Honda Company + Nhok Phaon Group

▷ *Army Region V [Battambang, Pursat, Bantey Meanchey, Pailin Provinces]*
- Region V headquarter + Fishery Department + Sokimex Company
- Brigade 51 + MoH + Sokha Resort & Hotel
- Brigade 52 + MoRuralD + *Oknha* Som Ang & Lok Chumtiev Chhun Leng
- Brigade 53 + National Treasury Department + *Oknha* Som Ang & Lok Chumtiev Chhun Leng
- Brigade 14 + MoIME + Canadia Bank
- Border Unit 501 + Tax Department + Som Ang & Chhun Leng Company
- Border Unit 502 + Dry Port + Soriya Mall
- Border Unit 503 + Camcontrol/MoC + Sovanna Mall
- Border Unit 504 + Civil Aviation Department + Independence Hotel
- Division 11 + MoC + Boeung Ket Rubber Company

▷ *Other Units*
- Ream & Benda Koh + Preah Sihanouk Autonomous Port + Metfone 097
- Division (aka Brigade) 31 + MoWRM + Metfone 097
- ACO Tank Unit + Neak Lueung Ferry + Roath Sopheap Company
- Brigade 1 + National Bank + Attwood Company
- Artillery Unit + Transport Department/MoPWT + Foreign Trade Bank
- Transmission Unit + MoRCults + Mong Rithy Group
- Air Force headquarter + FA + Thary Pinex Company

▷ *Special Region [Kandal, Phnom Penh, Kampong Chhnang Provinces]*
- Border Unit 601 + Kandal Provincial Cabinet + Heng Development Company
- Special Commandos Paratrooper Unit 911 + MoEY Sports + Suy Sophan Company

Police

▷ *Region 3*
- Battalion 827 + MoNASR Inspection + Mong Rithy Group
- Battalion 269 + MoNASR Inspection + Khou Houlong Company

▷ *Region 4*
- Battalion 105 + MoF + Bayon TV/Radio
- Battalion 793 + Phnom Penh Municipal Cabinet + Mobitel 012
- Battalion 795 + MoCFArts + Tela Company
- Battalion 905 + MoCFArts + ANZ Royal Bank
- Battalion 702 + Electricite du Cambodge + Ly Yong Phat Company

▷ *Region 5*
- Battalion 807 + MoInformation + OMC Group
- Battalion 911 + MoInformation + Foreign Trade Bank
- Battalion 891 + Bantey Meanchey Provincial Cabinet + Ly Chhoung Company
- Battalion 815 + Bantey Meanchey Provincial Cabinet + Canadia Bank
- Battalion 817 + Battambang Provincial Cabinet + Sokimex Company
- Battalion 819 + Battambang Provincial Cabinet + Sokimex Company
- Battalion 821 + Pailin Provincial Cabinet + Chiv Leng Company
- Battalion 823 + MoPlanning + Navy Garment
- Battalion 310 + MoPlanning + Saom Sophal Company
- Battalion 825 + MoIME + Try Pheap Company

Source: LICADHO.

Appendix 5.3: Map of Cambodia with concessions, including those of the RCAF

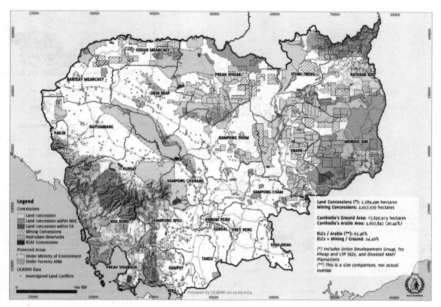

Source: LICADHO.

Appendix 5.4: Connections between military officials and the Cambodian People's Party

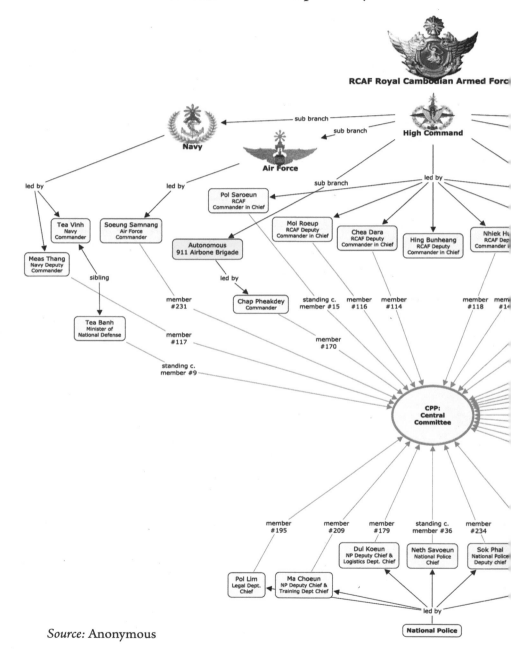

Source: Anonymous

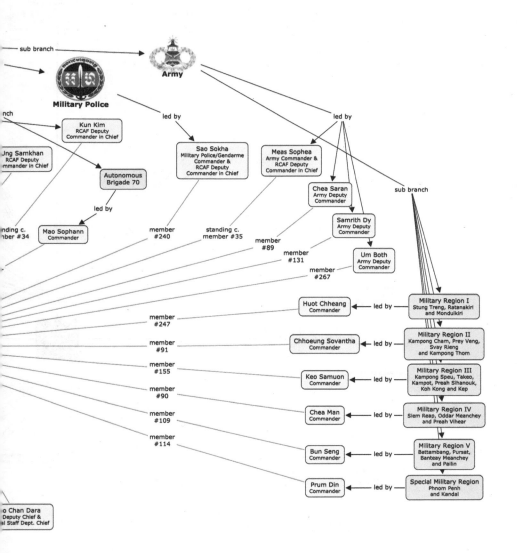

Appendix 5.5: Connections between key government positions, CEOs and the CPP

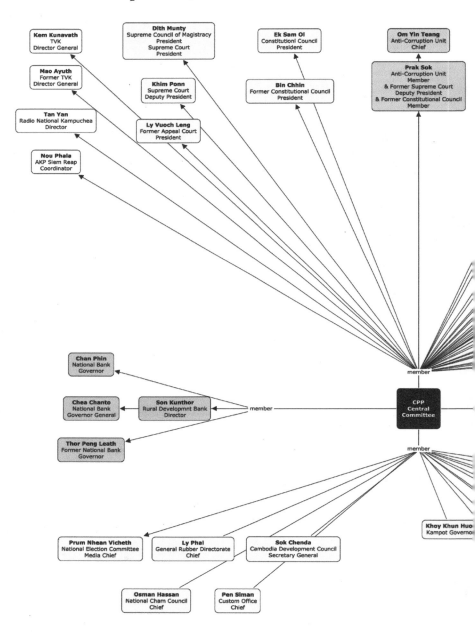

Source: Anonymous

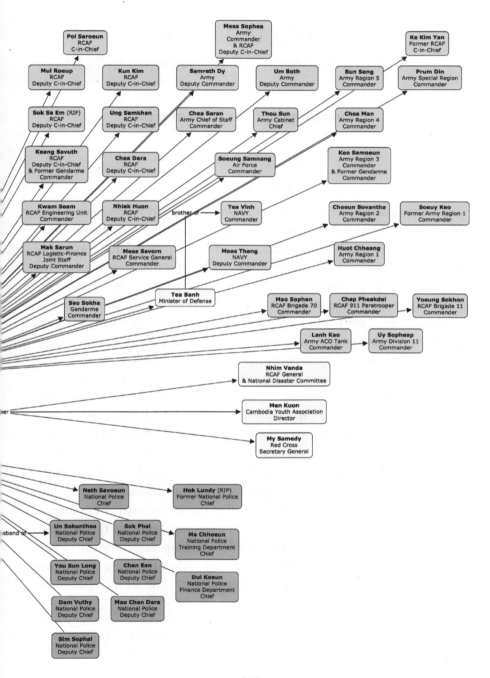

CHAPTER 6

Earning their Keep
The Political Economy of the Military in Laos

Hans Lipp and Paul Chambers

Introduction

This study examines the political economy of security forces in contemporary Laos (Lao PDR [People's Democratic Republic]).[1] Impoverished, landlocked, regionalized and centrally situated in mainland Southeast Asia, Laos has existed as a political and economic dependency of one external power or another since 1707. For Siamese, Chinese or Vietnamese monarchs as well as French colonizers, or United States cold warriors, Laos was rarely more than a buffer or proxy state, to be used as a vassal to collect tribute or a tool for great power designs. Laos's 1975 Revolution brought to power the Lao People's Revolutionary Party (LPRP),[2] which was greatly influenced by the Communist Party of Vietnam. The LPRP remains dominant over Lao PDR, yet Southeast Asian political geography has undergone historical changes and so has development in Laos. In 2017, 26 years since the end of the Cold War and 64 years after France granted Laos its independence in 1953, the country is experiencing rapid economic growth amidst even stronger state control over society. Such growth has mainly been fuelled by the exploitation of natural resources as well as foreign investment in megaprojects. Yet Laos, with a dearth of infrastructure, remains the poorest country in Southeast Asia. Naturally, it has been necessary for the LPRP to guarantee security and stability for all state-supported economic projects. For this task it relies on the Lao military. This study argues that

---

1. This chapter uses the terms 'Laos' and 'Lao PDR [People's Democratic Republic]' when referring to the country and 'Lao' as the adjective describing the country.

2. A complete list of acronyms is provided at the end of the chapter.

in Laos today, an authoritarian mass party exercises control over society – including the military – though the armed forces are allowed to find additional funding not covered by the national budget. Lao security forces, fused under the LPRP, have become sometimes-unmonitored political and economic drivers of development, with the party helping influential security officials to acquire pieces of the nation's economic pie. The study scrutinizes the historical evolution of the Lao military as an institution of security, development and business. It also looks at the nexus between the LPRP and Lao security forces. Next, it examines the organization of Lao security forces today. Then it turns to scrutinize the political economy of these forces. Finally, it offers a conclusion regarding the prospects for the Lao military's political economy.

Early Lao military history

Lao history is rich in tragedy. The kingdom (or sometimes kingdoms) was frequently in a struggle with powerful neighbours (Burma, Vietnam, China, Siam/Thailand) that were only too ready to exploit it. By 1707, the Lan Xang kingdom had been divided into Luang Prabang in the north, Vientiane in the centre and Champasak in the south, plus the quasi-independent principality of Xieng Khouang (Muang Phuan). In 1778 and later in 1828, Siamese troops invaded southern and central Laos. In the latter instance, Siamese troops crushed the 'Anuvong Rebellion', Vientiane King Anuvong's failed attempt to break free from (or even topple) the young Chakri dynasty in Bangkok. Following the 1828 capture of Vientiane, Siam initiated a scorched-earth policy that left Laos largely depopulated. Siam also incorporated Vientiane as a part of its territory. In pre-colonial Laos, there was generally no permanent standing army (with the exceptions of Lan Xang kings Fa Ngum and Xetthathirat). In fact the political economy of security during this period was always unstable, because kings had to raise militias and such armies could only be raised when the monarchy had enough capital (e.g. tributes) to support training, provisioning and weaponry for either offensive or (mostly) defensive measures (Stuart-Fox 1998: 169, note 105).

In 1893, the kingdom of Luang Prabang and Xieng Khouang accepted French protectorate status, while Vientiane and Champasak became French colonies (Xieng Khouang became a colony in 1899). The French preserved the Lao aristocracy in positions of superficial power and the colony of Laos was administered as part of French Indochina by only a few French bureaucrats and many more colonized Vietnamese. French rule lasted until 1953, though the process of downsizing the French administrative presence began in 1949. During this period, French regular troops were responsible for Indochina's external security.

Colonial security forces within French colonial Laos initially consisted of a poorly trained and armed *Garde Indigène* (founded in 1895). This force was officered by the French themselves while and enlisted personnel were mostly (three-quarters) Vietnamese troops. The purpose of this unit was internal security, and it quashed numerous revolts in southern, northern and central Laos throughout its existence. The *Garde* itself was under the authority of French Indochina's governor-general (who was based most of the time in Hanoi) through the *résident supérieur* in Laos (this post eventually was situated in Vientiane). French officers were paid much higher wages than indigenous soldiers (by the decree of the governor-general) from the local Laos budget and the staggering difference in income eventually created frictions (sometimes leading to violence) between French officers and Lao enlisted soldiers (Womack 2009: 117–21). The *Garde*'s local budget derived partly from French colonial infusions as well as subsidies from the royal house of Luang Prabang. In fact, *Garde* members took oaths of loyalty to the Lao monarchy, which initiated a connection of legitimacy between the Lao military and monarchy that lasted until the 1975 revolution. In 1941, as pressures from World War II were engulfing France, the French established a completely Lao-staffed military unit called the *1er Bataillon de Chasseurs Laotiens* (First Lao Rifle Battalion or BCL). As with the earlier *Garde*, it was tasked with protecting internal security but never saw action until after Japan's 9 March 1945 intervention in Laos, when it acted as a guerrilla force (Auclair 1994a: 263–4). With war's end in 1945, the French incorporated the 1er BCL into a newly created French Union Army (FUA). The FUA, led by French officers, engaged in battles against the Lao Issara (Free Lao) Army (which dissolved in October 1949), eventually re-establishing French control over most of Laos. Yet intent on creating a local force to carry on counter-insurgency operations, the French formally established the *Armée Nationale Laotiènne* (Lao National Army or ANL) in July 1949. Most of its leading officers had left the Lao Issara army and now supported a Laotian constitutional monarchy within the French Union. Among this generation of leaders were Sing Rattanasamai, Ouane Rattikone, Oudone Sananikone and Phoumi Nosavan; the latter became army Chief of Staff in 1955. Yet from the beginning, the Lao armed forces were weakened by personal disputes, kinship competition and military factionalism (Conboy 1995: 14). Some Lao Issara members who opted for revolution with support from Hanoi, such as Prince Souvannavong and Phoumi Vongvichit, formed the genesis of the newly resurgent *Pathet Lao* army.

Lao military influence, 1953–75

With Laos' formal (though not completely sovereign) independence in October 1953, the ANL changed its name to the Royal Lao Army (RLA) and, with the Royal Lao Navy (RLN) and the Royal Lao Air Force (RLAF), came to be incorporated under the overall *Forces Armées du Royaume* (Royal Lao Armed Forces or FAR) in 1959. Following France's signing of the Geneva Accord in 1954, French colonialism over all parts of Indochina ceased, though Paris continued to provide military missions, government advisors and teaching personnel to newly independent Cambodia and Laos. The year 1954 found Laos lodged at the crossroads of Cold War dividing lines in Southeast Asia: a United States-led power bloc that included Thailand and South Vietnam versus a Soviet Union-led power bloc that included the People's Republic of China and North Vietnam. The post-1954 Royal Lao Army relied upon training from a small French military mission with offices in Vientiane, Pakse and other cities, as well as funding from the United States. The mid-1950s saw Washington begin to send millions of dollars in aid to Laos to support the Lao government, particularly the military. Beginning in 1955, the US also maintained in Vientiane a 'Programs Evaluation Office', which was actually a covert military mission. From 1955 onward, through this mission, the US 'was paying the entire cost of the Royal Lao Army's salaries' (ibid.: 266; Stuart-Fox 1997: 91).

Yet US military funding, directed primarily toward right-wing military elements, contributed to corruption, as senior Lao officials began embezzling parts of these funds to private bank accounts (Stuart-Fox 1997: 91). Moreover, the RLA soon degenerated into a decentralized group of self-interested warlords who prioritized the securing of personal power over maintaining any form of military efficiency or professionalism. Given that the French had always held the officers' positions in the previous Lao security forces and that Vietnamese soldiers filled most enlisted posts, there was little military leadership experience among Lao soldiers. It was thus a giant leap for them to move from the status of colonial enlistees to suddenly serving as officers or even commanders in the RLA. Meanwhile, from 1953 until the early 1970s, Lao elites cultivated often pre-existing ties with the fledgling Lao military leadership. The result was that Lao officers tended to prioritize politics and economic plunder over preserving national security (Anthony and Sexton, 1993: 11–14). This state of affairs climaxed during the years 1959–65. Malfeasant or disenchanted Royal Lao security units sometimes cooperated with Pathet Lao insurgent forces and desertion rates were rife. Laos' five military regions were decentralized under the control of commanders in league with 'his' region's local elite families. There were also subregional fiefs controlled by junior officers (majors and colonels) (Anthony and Sexton 1993: 5). Table 6.1 illustrates the regionalized connections between Lao military leaders and local economic elites before the 1975 Revolution.

Meanwhile, an insurgency was brewing. In August 1950, Prince Souvannavong and his supporters merged together with Lao-Vietnamese members of the Indochinese Communist Party (such as future revolutionary leader Kaysone Phomvihane) to form the Neo Lao Issara (which then became the Lao Communist Party in 1955). The Neo Lao Issara's 'armed wing' was referred to as the Pathet Lao, 'which became synonymous with both the Communist Lao military resistance and its associated political front.' The armed wing was renamed as the Lao People's Liberation Army (LPLA) in October 1965 and was trained and financed by Vietnam and China. However, like soldiers of the FAR, Lao communist forces generally lived off the land, depending on subsistence and 'taxes' in areas under their political control. In the image of Vietnam, the LPLA was tightly incorporated as an arm of the Lao People's Party (which changed its name to Lao People's Revolutionary Party [LPRP] in 1972) while the quite decentralized Royal Lao Army often challenged central control from headquarters in Vientiane (Stuart-Fox 1997: 145).

For the Kingdom of Laos, military influence in politics and putsches became common between 1959 and 1973. After being promoted to RLA chief of staff, then to commander of Military Region 5, and

Table 6.1: Connections between Lao regional military commanders and regional elites (variously from 1960s until 1975)

Military regions	Military commander	Economic overlord family
Military Region 1 (provinces of Phong Saly, Houa Khong, Sayaboury, Luang Prabang)	Gen. Tiao Sayavong (half-brother of king); the region was also dominated by narcotics bigwig Gen. Ouane Rattikun (Cockburn and St. Clair 1998: 247)	King Savang Vatthana
Military Region 2 (provinces of Houaphan [Sam Neua], Xieng Khouang)	Gen. Vang Pao (Vang Pao's Zieng Khuang Air Transport Company transported heroin (ibid.: 247)	US Central Intelligence Agency, waging a secret war in this Region, provided enormous subsidies. Chao Saykham, Touby Lyfoung
Military Region 3 (provinces of Khammouane and Savannakhet)	General Bounpone Makthepharak (followed by General Nouphet Daoheuang), Deputy Commander Gen. Kane Insixiengmay	Leuam Insixiengmay family (Leuam's wife was sister of Prince Boun Oum Na Champasak); Gen. Bounpon's wife was a na Champasak. The families of Nosavan, Voravong, Chounlamany, and Saycocie also held influence here.
Military Region 4 (provinces of Saravane, Attopeu, Champasak, Sedone, Wapi Khamthong, and Sithandone)	General Phasouk S. Rasaphak (a member of the Na Champasak family), followed by General Soutchay Vongsavanh	Na Champasak family led by Prince Boun Oum na Champasak
Military Region 5 (provinces of Borikhane and Vientiane)	Gen. Phoumi Nosavan followed by Gen. Kouprasith Abhay followed by Gen. Thonglith Chokbengboun	Sananikone family (Gen. Kouprasith's mother was a Sananikone and he was married to a Sananikone)

Source: Soutchay 1981: 23–25.

finally to minister of national defence, Col. Phoumi Nosavan hatched a successful coup in 1959, which was followed by elections. In August 1960, the neutralist Captain Kong Le led a coup d'état against a Phoumi-controlled government, declaring his intention to stop corruption linked to pro-US generals. The putsch temporarily divided the army. Kong Le's regime was eventually overthrown in December 1960 by now-Brigadier General Phoumi, whose return to dominate the country was largely sponsored and subsidized by the US Central Intelligence Agency. Kong Le fled to the countryside and raised his own group, the Patriotic Neutralist Forces, to join the Pathet Lao's war against the state. With Kong Le ousted, Phoumi served as army chief from 1960–65 and, as the CIA's proxy-gone-rogue, personally dominated the country, increasing state repression and corruption to previously unseen levels. According to a later Royal Lao Government Defence Minister, 'The army was his [Phoumi's] ... and he was a gangster ... Casinos, opium and gold is [sic] what the military dealt in.'[3] Yet Phoumi's friction with other army officers eventually forced him into exile in 1965.

Phoumi's demise left a political vacuum in Laos. His protégés included Ouane Rattikone, who succeeded Phoumi as army commander (1965–71); Bounpone Makthepharak, who succeeded Ouane in the same post (1971–75); Kouprasith Abhay, who served as commander of the strategic Region 1 Vientiane (1962–71); Siho Lamphouthacoul, who had grown up in Abhay's household and built up the Lao police force; Bounleuth Saycocie, who in the early 1960s was the army's chief logistics officer; and Thao Ma Manosith, commander of the Royal Air Force (1959–66). Most of these generals seemed to prioritize personal power interests over national security concerns: There were regular coup attempts by one or another of them (except for Ouane) in 1964, 1965, 1966 and 1973, and each seemed most concerned about maintaining regional clan connections and promoting their often illicit business interests (e.g. opium and heroin smuggling) (Webb 2010: 169; Stuart-Fox 2008: 242). In the end, the RLA's disunity, lethargy, corruption and inefficiency – in comparison to the better-organized LPLA – contributed to the demise of the Kingdom of Laos itself in 1975.

---

3. Interview with Defence Minister Sisouk na Champassak, in Kamm 9 August 1971.

The Lao military's political and economic influence since 1975

Following Laos' 1975 Communist revolution, the LPLA was slightly reorganized in 1976 under the tutelage of Vietnam (People's Army of Vietnam [PAVN[4]] advisers had been working with the Pathet Lao since 1953) into four military regions – Luang Prabang, Phonsavan, Xeno and Pakse. Also in 1976, the LPLA was renamed as the Lao People's Army (LPA) (Stuart-Fox, 2008: 184). Despite its own bureaucratic inefficiencies, the LPA became the most functional structure of power left in Laos – and was directly forced to fill a vacuum of bureaucracy and civil management, though the Foreign Ministry retained a large number of its personnel. Four decades later, in 2016, some state civilian structures would remain distinctly weak and inefficient compared to the military. The post-revolutionary Lao military possessed a small defence budget but was dependent upon financial assistance from Vietnam and the Soviet Union (Auclair 1994a: 271–2). The reliance on outside aid was made apparent in the 1980s, during which the LPA, with PAVN assistance, was kept occupied fighting several anti-LPDR insurgencies supported by Thailand, China and the United States, including those of the Hmong and the Chao Fa (ibid.: 280–2). In addition, soldiers of LPDR sporadically engaged in border battles with Thailand's army (1984, 1987–88). Service in the 30-year struggle, the continuing importance of the LPA as an internal security guarantor, and the fact that military leaders (such as Khamtai Siphandon and Sisavat Keobounphanh) had supported the economic reforms of then-Prime Minister (and chair of the LPRP) Kaysone Phomvihane probably enhanced the political sway of LPA officers (Stuart-Fox 1997: 195). As a result, in 1985, the military's influence on the Central Committee of the Lao People's Revolutionary Party increased. Meanwhile, the number of Lao soldiers hovered at approximately 50,000 troops (Stuart-Fox 2008: 181).

Military aid to Laos from Iron Curtain countries started to diminish in the mid-late 1980s amidst growing Soviet Union cut-backs, and it completely dried up with the end of the Cold War in 1991. Moreover, most Vietnamese soldiers and all Russian technical advisors who had been stationed in post-1975 Laos withdrew from the country by 1989 (Ivarsson

---

4. PAVN is referred to elsewhere in this volume as the VPA or Vietnam People's Army.

1995: 21), though some sources have alleged that 'a few Vietnamese military technical specialists ... likely ... remained in Laos' as of 1994' (Auclair 1994a: 271). The loss of financial aid sapped the supplies of the LPA, endangering its ability to provide sufficient internal security. Indeed, encouraged by the United Nations and the International Monetary Fund, the military diminished in size from 55,000 soldiers in 1991 to 37,000 troops in 1994. Armed forces salaries were increasingly delayed and remained low, and many troops resorted to living off the land (as they had often had to do before). The increasingly impoverished Lao military 'embarked on private business ventures to support itself' (ibid.: 272). But 'the military's power [was] also partly a reflection of the weakness of the economy; the military [was] one of the few local organisations with any infrastructure or skills base capable of undertaking large-scale commercial activities.' No other state institution had comparable infrastructural development capacities (Nette 1998).

The Lao military began to reap its fortunes during the 1980s precisely because of the tapering off of foreign aid, Lao state moves toward the privatization of industries, and the military's own monopoly over infrastructure in rural areas. As the Lao military began to take a more active role in the country's economy, its greater clout helped to put a brake on the dwindling number of regular LPA soldiers and concomitant increased reliance on militia forces. With the 1992 death of Kaysone, the LPA also continued to increase its political influence: in 1996, five of the seven positions within the ruling party's Politburo were held by active-duty or retired LPA officers. According to Stuart-Fox (2008), 'the army effectively took over the party' (Stuart-Fox 2008: 187). The military has maintained high levels of influence within the party ever since.

In the 1980s, three military enterprises emerged and came to dominate Lao forestry, later diversifying into other sectors of the economy. Profits from these conglomerates were utilized to buttress the meagre budgets for military operations of military officials based in the Northern, Central and Southern parts of the country. Soldiers were given hiring preferences. To some extent, the military heads of the conglomerates made enormous personal profits. The first conglomerate was the Mountainous Region Development Corporation (*Bolisat Phatthana Khet Phudoi* or BPKP) located in central Lao. The second conglomerate was the Agricultural Forestry and Development Company (AFD) located in the north. The third was the Development, Agriculture Forestry Industry Group (DAFI) located in the South. All three companies were under the purview of the Ministry of National Defence, though they also reported to the Ministry of Agriculture and Forestry. During the mid-1980s, nine state forest enterprises existed, each matched with a foreign donor. By the early 1990s, the three military companies had come to divide the state-granted concessionary operations of the nine State Forest Enterprises among them (see Table 6.2 below).

In 1992 the Lao state abolished logging concessions altogether, handing the monopoly of this industry over to the three military-owned state enterprises. 1994 witnessed passage of a Lao Prime Ministerial Order which facilitated military control over logging quotas within the different regional zones of military companies. Henceforth 'military-owned logging enterprises were granted preferential treatment in the allocation of logging, [wood] processing, export quotas and logging contracts, as well as exemptions from paying royalties' (Asian Development Bank, 2006: 10). Such logistical advantages were further facilitated by link-

Table 6.2: State Forest Enterprises, donors and military enterprises, 1982–92

SFE #	Location	Chief donor state	Military company
SFE1	Borikhamxai	Sweden	BPKP – Gen. Cheng
SFE2	Savannakhet	Vietnam	DAFI – Gen. Bounyang Volachit
SFE3	Vientiane-Borikhamxai	Sweden	BPKP
SFE4	Khammouane	Soviet Union	BPKP
SFE5	Khammouane	Soviet Union	BPKP
SFE6	Xayaboury	HIPA Company (Malaysia)	AFD – Gen. Bouleuth Soulima
SFE7	Savannakhet	Soviet Union	DAFI
SFE8	Champasak	Poland	DAFI – Gen. Khamtai Siphandon
SFE9	Vientiane	Asian Development Bank (Japan)	BPKP

Source: Based upon information in Barney 2011: 158, footnote 88.

ages to Thailand's market, through the assistance of senior Thai military officers such as Gen. Chavalit Yongchaiyudh (Fahn 2008: 133). The operations of these state companies thus became more opaque than ever before, and less accountable to monitoring by those outside of the military itself (Asian Development Bank 2006: 10–11). The ruling party's civilian control became increasingly distant from the economic pursuits of the Lao military (though it had never exercised much control).

The first military company, BPKP, formed in 1984, was headquartered along Highway 8 at Lak Xao (translated as Kilometer 20) city, Borikhamxai province (which was recreated out of Khammouane and Vientiane provinces) on the Lao–Vietnamese border. Its director was ret. Gen. Cheng Sayavong, who servied in the Royal Lao Army until his defection to the Communists in 1963 (Dommen 2010: 835), and then as a Patriotic Neutralist commander, before later starting his profitable stint in the LPA. With infusions of capital from Cheng's BPKP, his state-within-a-state at Lak Xao grew into a large and prosperous border post, complete with airstrip, hospital, poker-room casino, hotels and a zoo. Cheng established this zoo just after the Lao state's 1986 enactment of a law banning trade in wildlife. He stocked it with animals sourced from local villages as well as endangered species, all of which were placed up for sale (Singh 2008: 12). Indeed, Cheng became one of Lao's leading wildlife traders. Moreover, according to US officials, BPKP has been 'also involved in the production, processing and sale of both heroin and marijuana' (International Narcotics Control Strategy Report 1990: 62). Ultimately, BPKP became a 58-company conglomerate and the single largest holder of non-performing loans. By 1995, the enterprise was worth $40 million. In 1998, the government appointed Cheng to the position of vice-minister of commerce and tourism as well as chair of the National Tourism Authority. His BPKP has worked closely with Vietnamese military counterparts, principally in timbering, but later in mining, saw-milling, transportation and the import–export business through central Vietnam (Stuart-Fox 2008: 171, 182). BPKP had extracted profits through logging and helping to facilitate the Nam Theun 2 Dam project. However, following pressure from international institutions for its high debts and corruption, BPKP in 2001 was placed under the Ministry of Finance (ibid.: 171,182–3). Nevertheless, as late as 2010 Gen. Cheng's commercial empire continued to expand as he assumed control over the country's first private television station: Lao Star TV (Smith 2010). Cheng passed away in 2015.

The second military business, AFD, is centred in Laos' north. Founded in the mid-1980s, by the late 1990s it had become arguably the most powerful enterprise in the region. Through its work in Xayaboury, Houay Xay and Oudomxai provinces, AFD has profited first from logging and trucking, then the import–export trade, road construction, cement production and mining (specifically lignite – controlling 25 per cent of the Thai–Lao Hongsa lignite mine) (Walker 1999: 179–80). But perhaps its strategic location as a company centred at the crossroads of China, Thailand and Myanmar has helped AFD the most. Indeed, it handles logging and export–imports with businesspeople in China, Myanmar, Thailand and even northern Vietnam.

The third military enterprise, DAFI, concentrates on business in southern Laos. It was established in the late 1980s as a corporation furthering military interests in logging, mining, construction, fuel distribution and tourism (ibid.: 179). Its power was so great during the 1990s that southern provincial governors could not veto its preferences. In one episode, following DAFI conflicts with the governor of Attapeu province during the mid-1990s, soldiers loyal to DAFI simply arrested and imprisoned him (Barney 2011: 162). DAFI has worked closely with and increasingly subcontracted out its timbering concessions to Vietnamese lumber companies along Highway 9 in Savannakhet province as well as in Attapeu province. Meanwhile, in Stung Treng province, the Royal Cambodian Armed Forces maintains tight economic ties with DAFI: a leading officer in Cambodia's Military Region 1 (Ly Sareth) is the brother-in-law of a senior official in DAFI (Global Witness 1998).

In 2004, BPKP, AFD and DAFI underwent World Bank-monitored restructuring. According to Barney (2011), an economic downturn for the companies in the late 1990s (simultaneous to the Asian Financial Crisis), and the beginning of their restructuring in the early 2000s appeared to demonstrate the 'decline' of the armed forces in the timbering industry while the power of provincial and national state authorities in this sector intensified. (Barney 2011: 164). However, according to Stuart-Fox (2005), Lao military leaders strongly resisted any weakening of their economic power by the state, viewing this as the 'loss of an important source of income for senior officers' (Stuart-Fox 2006: 61).

Though the opaque nature of the Lao state makes it difficult to monitor the exact extent of loss in the military's economic income (both institutionally and among senior brass) since 2004, the consensus is that such direct clout did not in fact diminish. In fact the military increasingly diversified its activities and its economic power became more indirect, 'protected by the political influence it exercises within the Party through … access to senior, ex-military Party officials' (ibid.: 61–2). Regardless of any economic decline in the military's economic strength overall, it apparently still dominates most logging and forestry ventures in both interior and border areas. Though Thais, Singaporeans and South Koreans appear to be willing partners of the Lao military in timbering, the clearest partnerships are those in conjunction with the Vietnamese military (Barney 2011: 165) and the Chinese military (Stuart-Fox 2006: 62). In 2016, these military partnerships persist, though cloaked under greater party and state control.

One area outside of timbering in which Lao military officials have taken part is the wildlife trade, which is a related forest industry. The three aforementioned military conglomerates were heavily involved in the trade of animals, and Lao military officers and soldiers continue to be individually involved in profiting from the wildlife trade. Their network relies on ties to other soldiers, bureaucrats, and businesspeople, both domestic and international. Besides wildlife, these officials have had links to smuggling weapons, narcotics and humans (Butler 2009).

The stature and structure of the Lao People's Army inside Lao society today

Understanding the Lao political economy means comprehending its political and economic institutions, and one of the leading institutions in Laos is its army – among all other Lao Ministry of National Defence-led security forces, including Laos's small air force, navy and militias. Indeed, except for the militia, the largest and best-funded security service is the Lao People's Army. The LPA is tasked with guaranteeing external and internal security, including counter-terrorism and counterinsurgency (United States State Department 2015). Moreover, the LPA manages and oversees Lao village militias (Lao People's Army [website]).

Though the LPA is under the Ministry of Defence in these missions, the Ministry of Public Security (MoPS) shares the function of maintaining state order through its various police services: local police, traffic police, immigration police, security police (including border police) and still other armed police units. Also, there are communications police who are responsible for monitoring telephones, media and internet (United States State Department 2015).

However, the long arm of the Lao state in politics and economics has, more often than not, been the LPA. The LPA has acted as a ubiquitous agent of state interests throughout the country. Nevertheless, though it possesses the monopoly on tools of violence, the economic resources sustaining it have been paltry. The army thus has an institutional interest to increase its economic gains. Individual commanders have also sought to expand their economic clout by increasing military involvement in businesses. As a result, the LPA has become a major player in the Lao economy, wielding enormous economic influence through its corporate subsidiaries or via companies owned by former senior officers, their relatives, or through cooperation with Vietnamese Chinese, Thai and Korean military-dominated businesses.

After some hard downsizing in the armed forces of Laos following the collapse of the Socialist Bloc at the end of the 1990s, the level in forces officially fell to 33,000 troops and then dwindled to approximately 30,000 troops, divided between the much larger army and the tiny Lao People's Liberation Army Air Force (LPLAAF). Regarding the latter, as air force aircraft have increasingly declined in serviceability, many transport tasks have come to be tasked to the state-owned airline Lao Airlines (World Air Forces [website]). The miniscule Navy is only used for riverine patrols. The LPA is deployed in the country's four (or five) aforementioned military regions under a central command centre in the capital of Vientiane. (Vientiane I, Luang Prabang II, Phonsavan III, Xeno IV, Champasak V). (Globalsecurity.org). The LPLAAF follows this same structure. Though Laos is a relatively small country, its large number of military zones have owed to the country's highly mountainous and regionalized nature. Vientiane, though the site of the military headquarters, also serves as the central region of operations for the military.

Though there is a formal separation between the army and police, contacts between the two security services are close. The MoPS-administered police depend upon the advice and support of other security agencies. Indeed, the police are sometimes merely a subterfuge for government and army intentions; in practice, there is no separation of power between the two security agencies, even 65 years after independence from France. Corrupt and abusive qualities of these security forces can be traced back to the formative years of Siamese, French colonial and United States legacies in initially building up a strong military and police. Overall we can calculate that around 1.9 per cent of Lao citizens at an employable age are part of some kind of state security unit though it is unclear which numbers belong to the Interior Ministry and which are under the Defence Ministry. These numbers could be much higher in rural areas.

In 2017, Laos has a population of 6.9 million people, but around 48 per cent of this population is not yet adult and another 9 per cent are too old to engage in labour. This leaves approximately 2.8 million citizens who are available for the national process of generating income (Statistical Yearbook 2013: 21–4). According to the 2014 Report of the International Institute for Strategic Studies, close to 130,000 Lao citizens are said to be formally employed in national defence: military or militia. The same report states that in 2014 the Lao People's Army contained 29,100 active-duty personnel. Nevertheless, these statistics must be viewed as estimates (50,000 active-duty army personnel may be more likely) given that the LPA has generally been wont to reveal exact troop numbers. Moreover, even an estimate on the number of police is simply unavailable (see Table 6.3 below).

Table 6.3: Security forces of the Lao PDR

Active military	29,100 including 3,500-person Lao People's Liberation Army Air Force (LPLAAF)
Navy	600
Police unit	NA
Paramilitary	100,000
Total	129,700
% of population employed in defence	1.9

Sources: for army, IISS 2014: 260–61; for air force, World Air Forces (website), 'Lao People's Liberation Army Air Force', http://www.aeroflight.co.uk/waf/aa-eastasia/laos/laos-af-home.htm; for navy, Stuart-Fox 2008: 178.

Laos' military expenses

Since 1992, Lao military spending has been on a decline. In terms of constant US dollars, share of GDP and percentage of government spending, there has been a gradual decrease in budgetary military allocations since the end of the Cold War. This owes partly to the fact that since the mid-1990s, there has been a drop in military challenges to the LPRP, both internal and external. In addition, given that LPDR is the most impoverished country in Southeast Asia, expenditures for the military have had

Table 6.4: Lao military expenditure

Year	US$ millions	% of GDP	% of gov't spending
1992	251	8.7	–
1993	248	8.1	–
1994	251	7.5	–
1995	210	5.8	–
1996	161	4.2	–
1997	148	3.8	–
1998	101	2.6	–
1999	43.8	1.1	–
2000	34.7	0.8	4.0
2001	33.5	0.7	3.4
2002	30.9	0.6	3.7
2003	27.1	0.6	2.9
2004	25.6	0.5	3.4
2005	25.1	0.4	2.6
2006	25.1	0.4	2.4
2007	25.1	0.4	2.1
2008	23.3	0.3	1.5
2009	19.5	0.3	1.2
2010	19.6	0.2	1.1
2011	21.9	0.2	1.1
2012	22.4	0.2	1.0
2013	23.1	0.21	0.8

Source: Data from SIPRI 2015.

to decrease, especially given the end of subsidies provided by the Soviet Union and Vietnam and the need to shift spending to non-military portions of the national budget. Today the LPDR certainly prides itself on self-reliance. However, the regime spends unbelievably sparse amounts of money for its armed forces. This might be a reason why the army is involved in so many businesses – following Wallenstein's saying that 'der Krieg ernaehrt den Krieg' (the war feeds the war) (Rebitsch, 2010: 24) – perhaps Lao People's Army has to feed itself? In fact, the diminishing budget for the military has forced the latter to rely increasingly upon informal khaki capital (e.g. military enterprises) in order to guarantee the salaries of foot soldiers, ensure sufficient funding for military functions and, in some cases, line the pockets of generals who have become khaki entrepreneurs.

Key political figures in the LPA today

Since the mid-1980s, as the military has become more important within Lao politics, some personalities have emerged who possess clout within the armed forces itself. Such influence enabled them to guarantee the growth of khaki capital in Laos because they all supported policies which facilitated the evolution of the three military conglomerates and a greater role for the LPA in the economy in general. Five of these individuals are examined below.

Lt Gen. Khamtai Siphandon, former president

Born in Champasak Province, Khamtai fought with the Lao Issara against the French from 1947, eventually joining the Pathet Lao. In 2017 Khamtai is one of the final members of the first generation of revolutionary leaders who is still living. He continues to exercise enormous political power. Among his living military contemporaries is Gen. Sisavat Keobounphanh, another original leader of the Pathet Lao. In 1950 he attended its official inauguration ceremony and in 1960 succeeded Gen. Singkapo as commander of the Pathet Lao armed forces. Khamtai was also the first commander of the Lao People's Liberation Army. In 1975 he became Lao PDR's first Minister of Defence. In later years, he also came to oversee the Ministry of Interior and Ministry of Justice. In 1992, with the death of Kaysone, Khamtai rose to become LPRP secretary-general. In the mid-1990s, while President Nouhak Phoumsavan was nearing the end of his term, Khamtai's political influence rapidly expanded. His clout corresponded with a continuing chumminess with the Vietnamese military and, to a lesser extent, the Chinese military, as well as the enhancement of military influence in politics. This latter development was illustrated by Khamtai's elevation to president of Lao PDR in 1998, as well as in greater numbers of senior military officers in high ranking positions of the LPRP. Khamtai served as Lao president from 1998 until 2006, a time during which military officers continued to ascend in great numbers within the party and there was 'growing interpenetration of the armed forces, the Party and the state (Evans, 2002: 220). Upon his retirement, Khamtai saw to it that his trusted military loyalist Lt Gen. Choummaly Sayasone succeeded him (Stuart-Fox 2008: 160–1). As of 2016 Khamtai continues to influence the military and politics through Choummaly and others in his southern Lao political clique.

Lt Gen. Choummaly Sayasone, former president
Choummaly Sayasone was born on 6 March 1936 in Attapeu province (which borders present-day Vietnam and might explain his later close Vietnamese connections – similar to many cadres of the Pathet Lao and the LPLA). It has been said that as early as 1954, when he was just an average teenage soldier, Choummaly became a member of a Pathet Lao-linked armed group in Houaphan Province. In 1955 he joined the Lao People's Party (as a candidate), a forerunner of the LPRP (Lao People's Revolutionary Party). During the 1960s, he became significant as a Pathet Lao tank unit commander on the Plain of Jars. He also became known as a close confidante of Pathet Lao military head (and later President) Khamtai Siphandon. Choummaly was selected as a member of the Central Committee of the ruling LPRP still at its third National Congress in 1982, and became an alternate member of the Politburo of the party's Central Committee and Secretary of the Secretariat of the Central Committee in 1986 (People's Daily, 2011). It was during this period of the mid-1980s that the Lao military began to take a more leading role in the politics of the nation. By 1994, Choummaly had become a very powerful military officer in Lao PDR, given his loyalty to his patron, Khamtai. He served concurrently as minister of national defence and commander-in-chief of the LPA. In addition, at that time, he was the seventh highest ranking member of the ruling LPRP Politburo. As a ranking member of the Politburo, Choummaly was responsible

for formulating both government and military policy. 'As commander in chief, he had absolute power over all internal and external security matters. All state security personnel, commanders of the air and naval forces, and police officials reported to Choummaly (Globalsecurity. org2). Nevertheless, though Choummaly became powerful as a loyalist of President Khamtai Siphandon, he had to share power with other Lao senior brass, especially Gen. Osakanh Thammatheva (who died in 2004). He was elected as Party General Secretary on 21 March 2006, in the aftermath of the Party's 8th Congress by the 1st plenum of the 8th Central Committee, succeeding Khamtai Siphandon, and he subsequently succeeded Siphandon as President on 8 June 2006 (People's Daily 2011). In these offices he served until his retirement in 2016. Though Choummaly has been quite influential in his home province of Attapeu, his economic 'powerbase is linked to big players in Khammouane province associated with his second wife.'[5] Today it is easy to say that Choummaly is a member of the new Lao aristocracy, given his deep roots in the Pathet Lao insurgency and his close contacts with neighbouring countries, especially Vietnam.

Lt Gen. Douangchay Phichit, former defence minister
Like President Choummaly Sayasone, Douangchay Phichit was also a southerner, born in Attapeu in 1944. And, like Choummaly, he was a Pathet Lao soldier who was a loyalist of both Kamthai and Choummaly. Like Choummaly, Douangchay was close to the business interests of DAFI. With Choummaly's support, he rose in the LPA and then in the Ministry of National Defence, serving as Deputy Chief of General Staff, Chief, Vice Minister of National Defence and then Minister (United States Embassy Cable 2006). His wife is also an army officer. Besides DAFI, Douangchay maintained close linkages with Tong Homsombat, an ethnic Chinese businessman with interests in timber and construction (THB 2014). On May 17, 2014, Douangchay, along with 17 other persons (including four Politburo members) died in a plane crash. Other victims included Public Security Minister Thongbane Sengaphone Propaganda and Training Chief Cheung Sombounkanh and Vientiane Gov. Soukan Mahalath (Associated Press 2014). According to one report, the group of four was at the core of a pro-Vietnam clique within

5. Personal interview with anonymous academic expert on Lao politics. 8 July 2016.

the Laos government and China would mostly benefit from the deaths (Anonymous 2014). Nevertheless, Soukan and Cheung were civilians and not military stalwarts, so this story may be mere rumour. When Douangchay died, he ranked seventh in the Politburo and was a potential candidate to be next prime minister. Also, the 70-year-old Douangchay, an old-school military officer chum of Choummaly, had close ties with Vietnam. Had Duangchay lived, 'the old guards' relationship between Laos and Vietnam would be a lot stronger, and more personal;' but with his death, this might be a turning point for the [Lao PDR] communist regime' (Hunt 2014).

It thus seems that, with the death of Douangchay and other victims in the plane crash, an important connection between Laos and Vietnam was destroyed. Their deaths and the 2013 death (apparently from dengue fever) of Major Gen. Sanyahak Phomvihane, son of Kaysone Phomvihane, 'father' of post-1975 communist Lao PDR, could perhaps have produced geopolitical ramifications for Lao foreign policy (such as a tilt away from Hanoi). Like his father, Sanyahak was viewed as being very supportive of Vietnamese interests. With the pro-Vietnamese Douangchay and Sanyahak out of the political picture, Chinese influence with the Politburo could now move forward for the first time since the forced resignation of the allegedly pro-Chinese Prime Minister Bouasone Bouphavanh in 2010 (Anonymous 2014). On the other hand, it must be remembered that all senior-level Lao military officers have studied and travelled in Vietnam and perhaps even the former Soviet Union and China – including Kaysone's children. As such, it is likely that the Lao political leadership would remain close to Hanoi. Perhaps then, any discussion of geopolitics as a result of these deaths is unwarranted.

Instead, one could argue that the deaths of Douangchay and Sanyahak merely produced changing power balances with Lao political factions and in the rivalries among military commanders and powerful relatives. Finally, given that Douangchay and Sanyahak were senior military officers who had helped to improve the political and economic clout of the Lao military, their deaths may have produced a blow to armed forces interests. Their deaths also paved the way for Deputy Defence Minister (Lt General) Sengnouan Xayalat to become Defence Minister in 2014, while (Lt General) Chansamone Chanyalath was appointed his Deputy. Sengnouan was a party technocrat, having previously served as Assistant

Party Secretary of the Ministry of Defence, Party Committee Secretary for the General Political Department.

Ret. Gen. Bounnhang Vorachit, new president, 2016
In January and April, 2016, Ret. Gen. Bounnhang Vorachit succeeded Choummaly Sayasone as secretary-general of the Lao People's
Revolutionary Party and President of the LPDR. Bounnhang and his
whole slate of supporters have been viewed as tilting toward Vietnam,
while the group exiting power is perceived by some to have been more
allied with China. According to one retired Lao soldier close to the
Ministry of National Defence, 'it is clear that after the regime of President
Choummaly Sayasone and Deputy Prime Minister Somsavat Lengsavad
there is no pro-Chinese group' (Radio Free Asia 2016). Born in
Savannakhet, the new President once served under Khamtai Siphandon
in the Lao Liberation Army. 'However, Bounnhang cut his teeth under
other military cadres – most likely Gen. Somsak, Gen. Cham Nien
and Gen. Singkapo Sikhotchounnamali, former Supreme Commander
of the Pathet Lao. Bounnhang is closely linked to Khamtai through
marital ties between the families.'[6] Previously he served as Governor of
Savannakhet Province, Vientiane Mayor and Prime Minister. Amidst
Bounnhang's rise, Sengnouan was elevated to the position of Vice
President of the National Assembly and Chansamone, a Bounnhang
favourite, succeeded him as Defence Minister. Each rose to become
eighth and thirteenth in Politburo rank. In 2016, the Deputy Minister
of National Defence is Maj. Gen. Vilay Lakhamfong and yet another
general, Maj. Gen. Phouvong Vongphom, is also on the rise, heading the
LPA's General Logistics Office. If the LPA increases its political power,
perhaps Chansamone could become a future Lao president though he
would have to compete for that position with Kaysone Phomvihane's
surviving son Xaysomphone Phomvihane, who is a civilian and, since
2016, ranks ninth in the Politburo. Nevertheless, the ascension of these
military men means that army officers will persevere as a prominent
force in Lao politics.

Thongsing Thammavong: from military medical student to prime minister
The career of Thongsing Tammavong offers an example of a political
leader without deep military connections nonetheless serving military

---

6. Personal interview with anonymous academic expert on Lao politics, 8 July 2016.

interests. Born in 1944 in Sam Neua Province, Thongsing served as a Pathet Lao field medic before being discovered and mentored in the mid-1960s. He became head of teacher training in Hua Phan province, the centre of the civil war, and later rose to become, Mayor of Vientiane and Chairman of the LPRP Organization, in which capacity he facilitated promotions of party members and developed a network of close and dependent colleagues. In the 1990s he developed close relations with President (and ret. Gen.) Khamtay Sipandon and cordial ties to Choummaly. In 2010, Thongsing became Prime Minister, succeeding Boussone Boúphavanh, who, despite close military connections with Khamtai, pursued policies that threatened both individual military leaders and the institution as a whole: he sought to enforce laws regarding timber export, land grabbing, wildlife trade and gem mining, and he sought a foreign policy in which China could balance Vietnamese influence in the country (Voice of America 2011).[7] Thongsing's appointment owed to the influence of powerful retired military men. Thongsing was seen as a sufficiently loyal protégé (and alternative to Bouasone) for both Gen. Khamtai and then-President and Gen. Choummaly. Thongsing's appointment thus demonstrated the informal power of military officials to have loyalists placed in top political positions.

Once in office (2010–16), Thongsing oversaw an economic boom in Laos, something with which the military was content. However, increasing friction with Choummaly led to his removal in 2016, following 'allegations of corruption, economic mismanagement and criticism that he was leaning too heavily on China (Hunt 2016).' Before leaving, however, Thongsing managed to place his son, Dethsongkham Thammavong, deep into the management of the country's construction and development business.[8] Because the military heavily influences most transportation

---

7. The official narrative refers to resentments within the LPRP 'that his mistress had used her position to enrich herself and her family (Stuart-Fox 2011). This story, however, is not plausible. Such transgressions were sufficiently common in Lao politics as to not provide a moral foundation for a resignation, particularly by a Prime Minister with powerful patrons. Former president Khamtai Siphandon (see above) was a Bousone supporter and was surely strong enough to help the new Prime Minister weather a moral challenge, but not a direct assault by the military.

8. One project is an $80-million road upgrade linking Laos National University's Dongdok campus to Route 13 North to be managed by Chinese firm The Third Railway Survey and Design Institute Group Corporation (TSDI). See Joshua Lipes,

development projects, the son's success in this project reflects his family's continued close ties to the LPA.

The LPA and khaki capital: master key to Laos?

The Lao military remains a crucial societal actor. Indeed, military structures are surely the strongest and possibly the only bureaucracy capable of delivering development to people in the Lao hinterland. To date, the military has failed at this task, which in fairness it may not have perceived to be a task worth pursuing. Outside of the military-developed infrastructure, civilian-led forms of development have been paltry, partly because of 22 years of civil war (1953–75), and partly because of the endemic poverty of the country. There might be a cadastral land register but it does not cover the entire country. Actually, Lao land is placed under three different jurisdictions, and the military is one of these. Though the state claims general ownership to all land (with private property heavily regulated), specific property ownership has at times remained somewhat unclear. Until today, the police force and public administration remain weak and poorly subsidized. The condition of the LPA is also poor, though it still manages to continue operating. Partly because of a shortage of funds, elements of both the police and LPA have helped some businesses in 'land-grabbing'.

While there are large areas of control by the public administration of Laos, the army knows almost every corner of the country and controls – if not the entire area – the access to those regions that it does not fully control. The army maintains some control over those areas that are central to energy or mining sectors but also for the planning and construction of geographical trade routes such as the Greater Mekong Region's North–South and East–West corridors, both of which pass through Laos. Indeed, throughout Laos, mining, road construction, land concessions and hydropower are the principal areas of military 'development' for the Lao nation. Maximizing this development, which the military needs to pay the salaries of its soldiers, also rationalizes military interference in the domestic economy.

One particular, centralized geographical area is Xaysomboun, in the heavily forested highlands northeast of Vientiane. The region has long

---

'Cost of Lao Road Project Led by PM's Son Vastly Overstated: Expert', 6 April 2015, *Radio Free Asia* http://www.rfa.org/english/news/laos/road-04062015164424.html.

been a centre for the Hmong ethnic minority and Khmu. From 1962 until 1975, most of these Hmong, under RLA Gen. Vang Pao, served as guerrilla warriors for the US Central Intelligence Agency's 'secret war' effort against the Lao communist insurgents. After the 1975 revolution, those Hmong remaining in Xaysomboun suffered from new communist state reprisals after engaging in resistance activities, with some opting to become insurgents against the new regime while others fled abroad. As a result, from 1975 until 1994, Xaysomboun was administered directly by the Lao army and was relatively inaccessible to outsiders. In 1994 it became a 'Special Administrative Zone' but remained under tight military control. In 2006, it was incorporated back into Vientiane province and finally, in 2013, became the country's newest province. Nevertheless, soldiers have remained quite visible here. The military has rationalized its continued sway over Xaysomboun Province mostly because of rumours of Hmong insurgents in this area – a relic of the Second Indochina War. In terms of security, Xaysomboun comes under the purview of central Lao military commanders. LPA authority is enforced in the province through its 584 Brigade, which is positioned there. In late 2015, the LPA began engaging in skirmishes with unidentified Hmong groups in the province, a situation which could be used by the LPA to rationalize an increased military presence in Xaysomboun (Ounkeo 2015). Until the mid-2000s, the late Gen. Cheng's military conglomerate BPKP (which lorded over the central part of the country) had access to the economic potential of Xaysomboun (Robichaud *et al.* 2001: 98) – minerals, forests, hydropower, tourism and opium poppies. Today, with Cheng out of the picture, it is more a question of local people in conflict with the state over development projects that appear to benefit state elites amidst land confiscation and evictions with inadequate compensation. In 2014, the Lao People's Army, other state authorities and the Chinese company Norinco commenced work on building Nam Phay, the largest dam yet in Laos – expected to cover much of the valley in the Hmongs' Long Tieng district in Xaysomboun (Lao Ministry of Energy and Mines [2014]).

The LPA is today increasingly collaborating with foreign interests in plundering Laos of its land, forests and other natural resources, working with companies from China, Vietnam, Thailand, Singapore, South Korea and Malaysia. In northern Laos (Luang Namtha), two Chinese companies (China-Lao Ruifeng Rubber and Yunnan Rubber Company), in joint ventures with the LPA, recently obtained land concessions for 300,000 hectares and 167,000 hectares respectively. Through 'collusion with Lao military higher-ups[,] Chinese companies have forced upland farmers to change their farming practices or abandon their land in the name of development' (Tan 2015: 18).

Meanwhile, Lao active-duty army troops and decommissioned military personnel with patronage links have been working as private security for Vietnamese companies that are increasingly obtaining land concessions from the Lao government, resulting in the displacement of many rural farmers in southern Laos. According to Global Witness, Vietnamese companies HAGL (Hoang Anh Gia Lai Joint Stock Company) and VRG (Vietnam Rubber Group) are expeditiously acquiring land for commercial ventures in mostly southern Lao and have paid Lao soldiers to guard their concessions, a job which often means intimidating, harassing and using violence against Lao residents who have been displaced from their lands by the companies. (Global Witness 2013: 2, 24, 31).

Two other Vietnamese companies, Nicewood and Vinaca Maiphuong, have benefited from murky links with the LPA to transport logs from Laos to Vietnam. The companies have also taken advantage of special legal exceptions and quotas that are given out by high-level Lao government officials (EIA, 2012: 7–8, 12).

Another Vietnamese company working with the LPA is the Company of Economic Cooperation (COECCO), the business arm of Vietnam's own Military Zone 4 Command, a division of the People's Army of Vietnam which is headquartered in Vinh, Vietnam. COECCO has been active since at least 1991 in transporting logs, most owned by the Vietnamese military, from Laos (specifically Lao Military Zone 4) to the Vietnamese ports of Vinh, Danang, and Qui Non for marine transhipment. Many of these logs come from Lao dam clearance sites (EIA 2011b). Lao military officials have guarded COECCO-branded timber from logging site to the Lao-Vietnamese border. As a result, 'COECCO...benefits [s] from a close relationship with the Laos People's Army' (EIA 2012:10).

The principal Thai company involved in logging in Laos is LVT (Lao–Vietnam–Thailand) International. The company's owner, Prakit Sribussaracum, admitted in an interview that in 2007 he paid bribes to Lao 'military officials including a leading general' to obtain logging concessions in eastern Laos. He stressed that he pays 'every step' of the logging process (EIA 2008: 16).

Turning to domestic loggers, the most important Lao company is the Phonesack Group, which is also involved in mining, construction and coal production. Its CEO is Phonesack Vilaysack. Phonesack himself maintains very close relations with former Lao President Choummaly Sayasone and other Politburo members or their relatives (including Sam Lengsavath) (EIA 2011a: 13). He is related by blood to the Pholsenas, a leading Lao political family.[9] This includes Col. Kenekeo Pholsena, the Lao Defence Attaché to the United States, and an increasingly influential officer in the LPA (US Cable 2009). Much of the land which Phonesack Group began to log was previously under the control of BPKP, which had earlier had its licence revoked. Phonesack won the tender on these lands, and its holdings have since continued to grow, thanks to Phonesack's own high-level connections in the Politburo and with the LPA (EIA 2008:16). EIA, an environmental watchdog group, has accused Phonesack of smuggling timber from Laos to Vietnam (EIA 2011a: 12). In 2010, Phonesack also began to carry out gold mining inside of Laos' Nakai Nam Theun National Protected Area, under a contract with and assistance from the LPA (ibid.: 13). To this day, the company's 'links with the military persist overtly' (EIA 2012: 5). Ultimately, the LPA's contemporary plunder of natural resources forms part of a powerful 'iron triangle': military, politicians and businesspeople (foreign or domestic). The other two actors look to the military for assistance because it often holds needed concessions and can use its labour, weapons and infrastructure to guard and assist in the extraction of natural resources, and even help to get it to market.

Nevertheless, the economic activities of the LPA and its subsidiaries are not limited to simple, fundamental businesses such as land concessions, the wildlife trade and logging. Indeed, the LPA is responsible for even more complex tasks such as the issuing of mining licences (cloaked behind the civilian bureaucracy). In fact the LPA has become a crucial Lao player in developing the country's economy (while simultaneously

---

9. The Pholsenas count among them a former vice president of the Asian Development Bank, a Lao Vice Foreign Minister (later charged with hydropower development plans), two cabinet ministers, a member of the National Assembly and a Vice Minister for Industry and Commerce (Boh, 2013; US Cable 2009).

plundering it). This owes partly to the fact that the LPA remains largely unaccountable to civilian bureaucratic authorities and also because it is the most embedded state institution in the country. This political entrenchment has kept the military powerful since the Royal Lao Government was incrementally removed (relative to what happened in Saigon and Phnom Penh in 1975) by the 1975 Socialist takeover of Vientiane, after which the only institution foreign governments could really count on was the army especially since most leading party officials were former and active-duty army officers.

Today the LPLA is active in different sectors of the national economy, operating at various depths. From direct natural resource extraction interests and indirect assistance in hydropower projects to granting concessions in mining and land to security jobs, co-partnerships with foreign companies and some rare management engagements, a multitude of Lao military activities in business can be found – though it is generally not overt. One contemporary example of this is the Dansavanh Casino Resort, constructed in 1996 not far from Vientiane, on the edge of Nam Ngum Lake. 'The casino is managed by a joint venture between Syuen Group, a private Malaysian (Chinese) company and the Lao military, which owns 25 per cent of the share capital' (Tan 2015a). Another current example is UNITEL, Ltd, a telecommunications joint venture, 51 per cent owned by the Laos Ministry of National Defence and 49 per cent owned by Viettel (a state corporation wholly owned by Vietnam's Ministry of Defence) (Vietnam Business Registration 2016). Meanwhile, in terms of energy (an important part of army business in Laos), we can find Lao–Vietnamese cooperation in the close relationship among Petrolimex, a Vietnamese Company, which is the supplier of lubricants for the Lao Army and the Vientiane Oil Company.[10]

Economic activities of the LPA and the environment
Meanwhile, deforestation of the country has transpired at an unbelievably rapid rate. Though the country once boasted a forest cover of 70 per cent, official statistics by 2010 reported a cover of 40 per cent (*Vientiane Times* 2014), thanks partly to the logging of military companies such as

---

10. Petrol Lao Company (PLC) possesses a solid relationship with Petrolimex Laos and Vientiane Oil Company (the Laos Army Oil Company has had close relations with PLC over the past 20 years in the supply of lubricants for the Lao Army). See Long 2014.

BPKP (Smith 2010). Foreign experts say that this number is grossly inflated. Between 2001 until 2014, the total area of tree cover loss in Laos grew from 36,474 hectares to 191,031 hectares (Globalforestwatch. org). At the same time, the army presence in deforested areas has been intense – military-associated timber trucks are still dominating the picture at rural roads. In fact the 'forest belt' between the Mekong Valley and the Plain of Jars has declined from 160 to currently perhaps 60 kilometers wide. This has had a dramatic impact upon the overall environment. Nevertheless, clearly none of these military activities are possible without the approval and sanction of the ruling party, as well as foreign funds and buyers.

In fact, the state has made efforts to curb timbering, representing rudimentary attempts at civilian control over policies that directly challenge military economic interests. In January 1989 the government announced a partial logging ban, though there were numerous exemptions. Taxes were also placed on the export of timber. Nevertheless, by the end of 1989 logging was again permitted and the export of logs increased rapidly. In 1991, the Politburo fired Gen. Sisavat Keobounphanh, the army's chief of staff and the mayor of Vientiane for his involvement in illicit business deals with Thai timber companies. The dismissal was apparently meant to send a signal that dicey deals were not acceptable. Also in 1991 the state announced a second moratorium on logging. But this second ban was never fully implemented and timbering (both legal and illegal) continued to grow (Lang 2001). In 2016, the government announced a new logging ban. However, enforcement looks to be difficult against loggers who are well-connected to (or are colluding with) powerful Lao political and military interests. In addition, even if the moratorium could be enforced, logging could continue under the pretence of clearing land for industrial trees, mining and dam projects (Boliek and Ounkeo 2016). Ultimately, though the Ministry of Agriculture and Forestry exercises de jure responsibility for Lao forests through its Department of Forestry and Office of Forest Inventory, the de facto authority in forest affairs is the Lao army itself (United States Embassy Cable 2006).

The LPA is unlikely to stop its timbering any time soon, given that 'the army ... makes most of the profit from' timber sales, the majority going to Vietnamese buyers (ibid.). Also, there is no formal, if any, civilian monitoring of the military's khaki capital in Laos (ibid.). Meanwhile, with regard to Laos' 20 National Biodiversity Conservation Areas (NBCAs), which were established in 1993 (as the military's economic clout was growing), the Ministry of National Defence directly manages one (Phou Khao Khway, a former RLA military base), which is in parts of Bolikhamxay Province, Xaysomboun Province and Vientiane Province. In addition, in the NBCAs of Nam Pouy (Xayaboury Province) as well as Pou Xieng Tong and Dong Houa Sao (both in Champasak Province), the Lao army has played 'a significant role in controlling access (Robichaud *et al.* 2001: 98).' Moreover, according to a Swedish-produced NBCA Report, the military companies BPKP, AFD and DAFI (as well as successor companies), in their search for timber (but also in their tourism businesses), took advantage of their open access to NBCAs (ibid.: 99) in order to maximize profits. Given that these companies have been non-transparent and unaccountable to the international community, the chance they would exploit the environment within these NBCAs was quite high. Ultimately, despite what might seem to be civilian bureaucratic control in Laos, it is in fact the LPA which holds the keys to the country's environmental treasure box. Nevertheless, the LPA must also give a part of the 'pie' to the Lao police force.

The importance and influence of the Lao security sector by population numbers

Many Lao people work directly or indirectly for Lao security forces. According to the FAO, 80 per cent of the Lao population is active in agricultural subsistence work (FAO 2016) – information that shows how inconsistent statistical data of Laos are – when looking for comparability. This 80 per cent definitely includes children and/or the elderly. However, it does not account for that part of the Lao population which has become migrant labour. Such numbers might show us that a larger proportion of the rural population is at least partially employed as civil servants. Indeed, one can conservatively estimate that nearly 20 per cent of the population at the legal age for work is working for the state. Roughly half of this group – around 10 per cent of the Lao population – is incorporated directly or indirectly with state security forces, with the remainder employed in public service jobs such as road maintenance, community development, social welfare and health sector.[11] This sounds provocative and it is. So let us take a closer look at the connection among army, militia and the agricultural sector.

Interaction between the agricultural sector and the security sector
The army in particular and the security sector in general do not offer attractive career opportunities for the Lao youth despite the wartime call by the legendary leader Kaysone Phomvihane for young people to be patriotic and join in the defence of the nation (Auclair 1994a). Indeed, since the 1991 collapse of the socialist market system, new LPA applicants require qualifications if they aspire to become officers. Many rural people simply do not have these credentials and anyway prefer to continue living in their villages. It is such individuals – mostly working in agriculture – who join village militias. A large number of militia members receive no payment, uniform or armament and are said to be quite poor. With no state provisioning, being a militiaman might only be an honour – but one which requires militiamen to 'live off the land' – even sometimes forcibly collecting their financial upkeep from locals. In fact, most of the time, 'collecting financial upkeep from locals' means little more than going home for dinner. Militiamen and women focus more like scout groups for the village. They do not serve full time and are thus a reserve force. In this capacity, their mission is to act as auxiliary forces to the LPA in maintaining internal and external security, though Laos in fact has no problems with external security.

Why join the Lao militia?
It seems logical that militiamen must also be a part of the normal workforce of the nation. Their volunteer job might bring them some benefits like being issued a gun that can be used for hunting, having a better position in the village social structure and travel to some events and training sessions at the national or provincial capital, but official records report little income to be generated out of any activity for the militia in Laos. Government officials have also often tried to advertise militia positions as a kind of key for better future chances in obtaining political opportunities, sometimes in the exact sense of the word but sometimes also meaning obtaining access to positions in the civil public service or the professional security sector (Auclair 1994b). Even today

---

11. Given the lack of exact information about the number of public servants especially in the security sector (eg. number of police officials), this number is an estimate.

participation in the militias can be especially helpful for young people from the countryside who seek an escape from home. Such a job might be more attractive for young, lower-income Lao than more doubtfully locating a future in trade, industry or finance business. Often people join the militia simply to escape boredom. Militia personnel help guard vehicles at state-sponsored events and receive free drinks and cigarettes. They also get to rub elbows with members of high society while they indulge themselves at parties.

Why join the Lao army?

In general terms, a career in the Lao armed forces is not very attractive for most young people. As in all countries, draftees often try at all costs to avoid the conscription call. Payment is known to be small, equipment for troops is rudimentary and the budget offered for the LPA is a microcosm of the country's paltry national budget, which is further constrained by the choice not to collect taxes that are on the books.[12] One important reason to choose a career at the LPLA is the lack of other opportunities or the hope for a political career. At the same time, family tradition in the military is also important. Children of military officers are often encouraged by their parents to follow in their footsteps. The choice of an army career out of political reasons might include a ticket to the corridors of power – and is in a way logically predetermined for some members of the Lao society. Often 'career officers' are members of army or political families, descendants of families known as having had a place as heroes of the anti-colonial, anti-capitalist war in their genealogical tree. Ultimately, for the enlisted soldier, based in any garrison in the backyard of Laos, an army career might be more a 'cul-de-sac' with poor living conditions, worse payment and embarrassing equipment. Yet for a young scion of a Pathet Lao war hero's family, taking a position as an army officer can be the first step towards ascending into the country's inner circle. Indeed, 40 years after the socialist takeover of Laos and 25 years since the collapse of the Soviet bloc, many in the country's small middle class are finding that a career in the military is still one of the most stable pathways toward a position in the Lao political, administrative and economic structure. Of course, success on this path depends

---

12. Personal Interview with Kirsten Focken, LNTA (Lao National Tourism Administration) Advisor, Vientiane, December 2010.

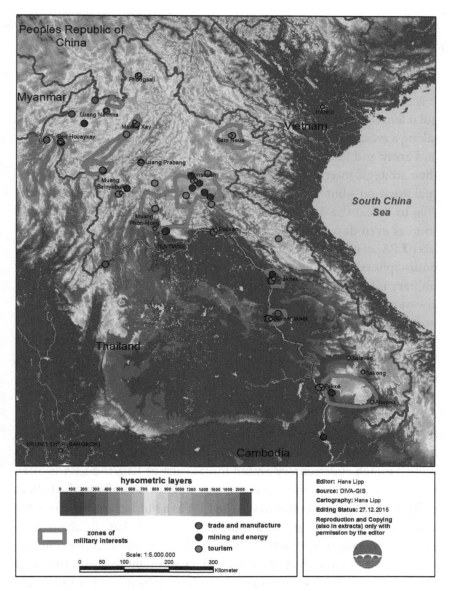

Map 6.1: The economic infrastructure of Laos

Note: This shows that areas of economic activity – like energy, mining and trade – tend to significantly overlap with areas where military interests have been traditionally strong, such as around Thakhek and Savannakhet, but especially in the longtime nearly inaccessible heartland areas in and around Laos' newest province, Xaysomboun – a former military-managed Special Zone.

heavily on which unit(s) one serves in and who one's commanding officers are.

Infrastructure and zones of special army interest

It is difficult to understand Lao military infrastructure through the singular lens of strategic issues. It might become a little more possible when taking a second look at the country's history under French colonial rule and army and later under viewpoints the PAVN had to take to realize their strategic interests. Some might wonder about this seemingly unusual situation – but the LPA does not excel, nor has it ever, though it was able to defeat the Thais in two border battles (1984, 1987–8). Some sources even describe the uniformed cadres of the Pathet Lao and the later LPA as not unlike the Royal Lao Army: relatively poorly trained, undisciplined and sometimes unwilling to fight (Brown, 2001). Lao military infrastructure planning tends purposeful and strategic, but not always with national Lao interests as a top priority. If not serving the economic needs of military officers or soldiers themselves, the LPA partly serves either as a tool of her founders, the Lao People's Revolutionary Party (the vanguard of the nation), or her own neighbours – Vietnam or China.

Travelling through Laos, observers will find many, seemingly abandoned army posts, technical installations like fuel posts, storehouses, fortifications and even airfields, but very few armed persons, and even fewer armed persons who easily can be identified as soldiers or militiamen. Though rudimentary armed forces exist in Lao, the LPA is often hard to see in urban and rural areas. One might even refer to the LPA as a ghost army. Yet it is better to see the LPA as a hidden army or army for profit: a construction group, a transport company that simultaneously acts as a bureaucratic structure – the backbone of the country. Though international sources (e.g. IISS, SIPRI) have sought to count the exact number of Lao troops, such a task is difficult at best and hard to verify. However, regarding the number of Lao air bases, there are quite a few, though many seem to have been abandoned. Taking a closer look it is not difficult to find that on many occasions the 'non-uniformed' militiamen or even some soldiers exchanged their Kalshnikov rifles and army boots for hoes and flip-flops, working regularly in planting vegetables and raise chickens around their army huts while awaiting the next or-

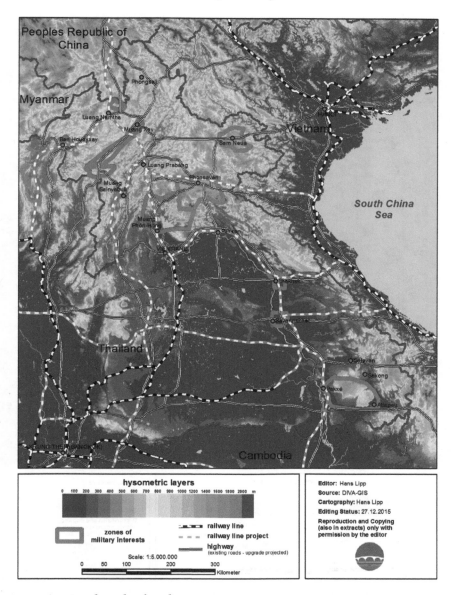

Map 6.2: Roads and railroads in Laos

Note: This shows the positioning of Laos as a strategic key to mainland South-east Asia and its role as 'post colonial' source of raw materials. Most planned lines of infrastructure are designed to pass through the country and remove bulk material to nearby harbours or forward them to processing plants. The Lao military has had a crucial role in helping to erect such transportation projects.

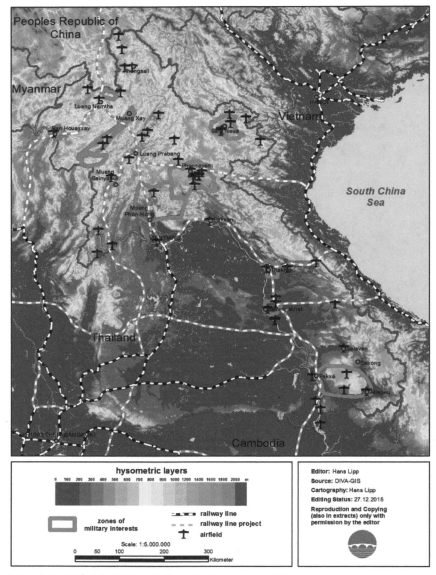

Map 6.3: Airfields and army bases in Laos

Note: Airfields and army bases have to be seen almost always in unison in Laos. Most army outposts come with an airfield sometimes for helicopters or STOL planes, sometimes with paved runways. However most of these airfields are to be found concentrated in traditional military centres around Thakhek, Savannakhet and Bolaven (Paksong). Meanwhile army bases with ground forces bases are marked with stars. Some of these air centres have economic potential for the future of the LPA.

der from any regional operational headquarters. Lacking any external enemy is useful for soldiers with little or no income. Lao army vehicles can be seen transporting household goods, timber, construction materials. Tanks are often parked on dam construction sites. Despite wearing a proper uniform, soldiers often work as a kind of security staff for private companies, many of which are international.[13]

Meanwhile, in terms of national infrastructure today, the military plays a leading role. Most roads and planned future railway lines are connecting Lao to China in the North, Vietnam in the East and Thailand to the West. Route No. 7 from Phou Khoun via Phonsavan was always a strategic road, for the French colonial army, for the Royal Lao Government and later for the PAVN. Accordingly, in the future there will likely be a railway which acts as an extension to the Vietnamese port of Cua Lo.[14] Nevertheless, this project may wait for a long time. Moreover, it can be said with high probability that the Lao Army and its semi-civil substructures are not able to plan the detailed routing of any infrastructure. This job has and will be almost always continue to be done by their often also uniformed foreign interested parties (e.g. Vietnam, China). As with other militaries in Southeast Asia (and as shown on the previous maps) – the LPA holds the legal key to the country's nature treasures. Ultimately, most of the current parts of the Lao Army as well as the subordinated (khaki) 'civil' sector are performing a form of labour which prioritizes economic expediency – different from that which is understood by militaries in 'developed' nations.

Conclusion: Lao military capital toward the future

This study has argued that the Lao People's Army, formally tasked with guarding internal and external security of the country as well as spearheading development in the countryside, has since the 1980s become a major political and economic player in Laos today. As such, it has often prioritized its corporate economic interests while factions of retired and active-duty soldiers under military personalities engage in unmonitored

13. Personal observations of co-author and geographer Hans Lipp, who made extensive visits to Lao PDR (2008–15), using direct observation and interviews with local people in these areas.

14. See International Business Publications, 2010: 173. This is one of the few sources that discuss a planned railway via Xiengkhouang to Vietnam.

economic plunder, often in cooperation with corporations or even militaries from Vietnam and China (and elsewhere). Since pre-colonial times, Laos, hemmed in by neighbours or as a political pawn, has found itself at the crossroads of war. As such, time and again it has suffered from the carnage of invasion as well as civil strife. Laos has almost always been a proxy, buffer state or dependency of one great power or another. The country's endemic poverty and geographic regionalization have made it difficult for the weakly institutionalized central state apparatus to effectively exercise national authority. Lao soldiers since independence have always been paid a paltry salary while their military commanders often use their positions of power to look for licit and illicit sources of income. This pathway through economic history has reproduced itself before and since the 1975 revolution. Since 1975, Laos has possessed an authoritarian-mass party variant of civil–military relations. Formally, civilian control is high given that the Lao People's Revolutionary Party (LPRP) is vested with a monopoly of political power. Yet control by this LPRP-led regime, as in any country, necessitates that it remains protected by security forces – the Lao People's Army. In Lao, the LPA tends to act as the arms and legs of the LPRP. There have been insurgencies against this regime and sometimes there are episodes of chaotic inter-clan competition. The regime thus needs the army to ensure its durability. However, the party possesses only a small amount of financing available for military budgeting. As such, it has allowed the military both formally and informally to locate additional financing through military enterprises. Since 2006, the military faction dominated by retired general and ex-President Khamtai Siphandon has come to exert greater influence over the military. This clique, centred in Laos' southern provinces, has for the most part favoured Vietnam. However, where other countries such as China and Thailand offer lucrative financial opportunities, the Lao leadership has happily cooperated with them as well. The Khamtai faction is likely to continue exerting tremendous influence across the Lao military and in Lao politics under the cloak of the LPRP for the foreseeable future and it, along with the overall Lao military, will likely persist in utilizing unmonitored khaki capital as a vehicle of sustaining the military's political clout. This owes to the fact that such income earns enormous profits for the LPA, ensuring that it remains informally insulated from and unaccountable to civilian bureaucrats as well as the

LPRP. Such lack of effective oversight furthermore owes to the fact that over the last ten years, as prominent politicians (including retired military officers) and well-connected businesspeople (e.g. Phonesack) have come to collude economically with the military as an 'iron triangle', the LPA has become virtually untouchable in its khaki capital ventures. Informal profits from this alliance are earning individual incomes for military officials from the most senior to the lowest ranks, a necessary bonus since the army relies on volunteers and can scarcely budget its commissioned soldiers. Such informal profits are also a vehicle for sustaining the military's political clout.

For the future, it does not appear as if the LPA will ever return to civilians those parts of the Lao economy that the military informally or formally controls – despite the apparent civilian supremacy of the LPRP and civilian bureaucracies over the armed forces. Indeed, it seems likely that the army-influenced sectors of the country will persist as a kind of private domain for different families of the military-connected, post-1975 Lao aristocracy. These sectors correspond to the Lao military zones. Currently the main actors on the Lao economic stage are deeply rooted in the LPRP and the country's security sector and they hold close ties to Laos' neighbours, especially Vietnam and China, but also Thailand, Malaysia and Singapore. Lao military networks provide security and maintenance to keep the Lao economy running. Without adequate security services, regime stability in Laos will become much more difficult. As in the past, the Lao military today continues to earn its keep by maintaining national security while many of its senior brass have profited from capitalist ventures. Meanwhile, it remains the poorest military in Southeast Asia.

List of Acronyms

AFD	Agricultural Forestry and Development Company
ANL	*Armée Nationale Laotiènne* (Lao National Army)
BCL	*1er Bataillon de Chasseurs Laotiens* (First Lao Rifle Battalion)
BPKP	Region Development Corporation (*Bolisat Phatthana Khet Phudoi*)
COECCO	(Vietnamese) Company of Economic Cooperation

DAFI	Development, Agriculture Forestry Industry Group
FAR	*Forces Armées du Royaume* (Royal Lao Armed Forces)
FUA	French Union Army
LPA	Lao People's Army
LPDR	Lao People's Democratic Republic
LPLA	Lao People's Liberation Army
LPLAAF	Lao People's Liberation Army Air Force
LPRP	Lao People's Revolutionary Party
LPRP	Lao People's Revolutionary Party
MoPS	Ministry of Public Security
NBCA	National Biodiversity Conservation Area
PAVN	People's Army of Vietnam
RLA	Royal Lao Army
RLAF	Royal Lao Air Force
RLN	Royal Lao Navy

References

Personal interviews

Anonymous academic expert on Lao politics, 8 July 2016, via Internet.

Focken, Kirsten, LNTA (Lao National Tourism Administration) Advisor, Vientiane, December 2010.

Secondary Sources

Aeroflight. 'World Air Forces: Lao Air Force'. http: //www.aeroflight.co.uk/ waf/aa-eastasia/laos/laos-af-home.htm, accessed 10 March 2017.

Angelfire (2006) 'Laos Airfield and Lima Site Information, Lima Site List', (7 March). http: //www.angelfire.com/home/laoslist/limasitelistweb.html, accessed 10 March 2017.

Anonymous (2014) 'Mystery surrounds death of key Laos officials', *Crikey* (blog) (10 June). http: //www.crikey.com.au/2014/06/10/mystery-sur-rounds-death-of-key-laos-officials/?wpmp_switcher=mobile, accessed 10 March 2017.

Anthony, Victor B., Sexton, Richard R (1993) *The War in Northern Laos.* Washington, D.C.: Center for Air Force History, United States Air Force.

Asian Development Bank (2006) *Lao PDR: Governance Issues in Agriculture and Natural Resources*. Manila: ADB (December).

Associated Press, 'Top Laos lie in state after plane crash', (19 May). https://www.yahoo.com/news/top-lao-officials-lie-state-plane-crash-081152107.html?ref=gs, accessed 10 March 2017.

Auclair, Nicholas (1994a) 'National Security', in Andrea Matles Savada (ed) *Laos: A Country Study*. Washington, D.C.: Library of Congress (July). http: //www.country-data.com/cgi-bin/query/r-7900.html, accessed 10 March 2017.

—————— (1994b) 'Other Military Units.' in Andrea Matles Savada (ed.) *Laos: A Country Study*. Washington, D.C.: Library of Congress (July). http: //www.country-data.com/cgi-bin/query/r-7899.html, accessed 10 March 2017.

Barney, Keith (2011) 'Grounding Global Forest Economies: Resource Governance and Commodity Power in Rural Lao', Ph.D. Thesis, York University.

Boliek, Brooks and Ounkeo Souksavanh (2016)

'Laos Prime Minister Asks Public to Help Cut Down the "Log Mafia"' (9 June). http://www.gt-rider.com/se-asia-motorcycling/threads/new-lao-prime-minister-issues-ban-on-timber-exports.13088/, accessed 10 March 2017.

Brown, Mervyn (2001) *War in Shangri-La: A Memoir of Civil War in Laos*. London: Tauris.

Butler, Rhett (2009) 'Laos Emerges as Key Source in Asia's Wildlife Trade,' *Yale Environment* 360, (26 February). http://e360.yale.edu/features/laos_emerges_as_key_source_in_asias_illicit_wildlife_trade, accessed 10 March 2017.

Cockburn, Alexander and Jeffrey St. Clair (1998) *Whiteout: The CIA, Drugs and the Press*. London: Verso.

Conboy, Kenneth (with James Morrison) (1995) *Shadow War: The CIA's Secret War in Laos*. Boulder, Colorado: Paladin Press.

Dommen, Arthur (2002) *The Indochinese Experience of the French and the Americans: Nationalism and Communism in Cambodia, Laos, and Vietnam*. Bloomington, Indiana: Indiana University Press.

EIA (Environmental Investigation Agency) (2008) 'Borderlines: Vietnam's Booming Furniture Industry and Timber Smuggling in the Mekong Region', (March). https://eia-international.org/wp-content/uploads/reports160-111.pdf, accessed 10 March 2017.

EIA (Environmental Investigation Agency) (2012) 'Checkpoints: How Powerful Interest Groups Continue to Undermine Forest Governance in Laos', (September). https://eia-international.org/wp-content/uploads/EIA-Checkpoints-report.pdf, accessed 10 March 2017.

EIA (Environmental Investigation Agency) (2011a) 'Crossroads: The Illicit Timber Trade Between Laos and Vietnam,' (July). https://eia-international.org/wp-content/uploads/EIA-Crossroads-report-FINAL-low.pdf, accessed 10 March 2017.

EIA (Environmental Investigation Agency) (2011b) 'Vietnamese army named as timber smuggler: Military a key player in illegally transporting raw timber from Laos', (28 July). http: //eia-international.org/vietnamese-army-named-as-timber-smuggler-2, accessed 10 March 2017.

Evans, Grant (2002) *A Short History of Laos: The Land in Between*. Sydney: Allen and Unwin, second edition.

Fahn, James (2008) *A Land on Fire: The Environmental Consequences of the Southeast Asian Boom*. New York: Basic Books.

FAO (Food and Agriculture Organization of the United Nations) (2016) 'Laos at a Glance'. http: //www.fao.org/laos/fao-in-laos/laos-at-a-glance/en/, accessed 10 March 2017.

Globalforestwatch.org (2017). 'Laos.' http://www.globalforestwatch.org/country/LAO, accessed 10 March 2017.

Globalsecurity.org (2012) 'Lao People's Armed Forces', (8 June). http: //www.globalsecurity.org/military/world/laos/lpa.htm, accessed 10 March 2017.

----2 (2012) 'Ministry of National Defence', (8 June). http://www.globalsecurity.org/military/world/laos/mond.htm, accessed 10 March 2017.

Global Witness (1998) '$50 Million Worth of Cambodian Logs Destined for Thailand via Laos in New Illegal Export Deal', 'Press Release', (19 June). https: //www.globalwitness.org/en/archive/50-million-worth-cambodian-logs-destined-thailand-laos-new-illegal-export-deal/, accessed 10 March 2017.

———(2013) 'Rubber Barons: How Vietnamese Companies and International Financiers are Driving a Land Crisis in Laos and Cambodia', (26 May) http: //bit.ly/1ar7lKn.

Hunt, Luke (2014) 'Indochina's Troubled Year', *The Diplomat* (28 May). http: //thediplomat.com/2014/05/indochinas-troubled-year/, accessed 10 March 2017.

——— (2016) 'Leadership Change in Laos: A Shift Away From China?' *The Diplomat* (25 January). thediplomat.com/2016/01/leadership-change-in-laos-a-shift-away-from-china/, accessed 10 March 2017.

IISS (International Institute for Strategic Studies) (3 February 2014). *The Military Balance 2014*. London: Routledge.

International Business Publications (2010) *Laos Mineral & Mining Sector Investment and Business Guide*. Washington: Global Investment & Business Center.

International Narcotics Control Strategy Report Mid-year Update (1990) Bureau of International Narcotics Matters, US Department of State (10

August).https: //www.ncjrs.gov/pdffiles1/Digitization/126991NCJRS. pdf, accessed 10 March 2017.

Ivarsson, Søren, Thommy Svensson, Thommy, Tønnesson, Stein (1995) *The Quest for Balance in a Changing Laos: A Political Analysis*, Copenhagen: Nordic Institute of Asian Studies.

Kamm, Henry (1971) 'Laotian Declares He Has Cut Corruption in Army', *New York Times*, 9 August, http: //www.nytimes.com/1971/08/09/ archives/laotian-declares-he-has-cut-corruption-in-army.html?_r=0, accessed 10 March 2017.

Lang, Chris (2001) 'Deforestation in Vietnam, Laos and Cambodia', in D.K. Vajpeyi. (ed.) (2001) *Deforestation, Environment, and Sustainable Development: A Comparative Analysis*. Praeger: Westport, Connecticut and London. https://chrislang.org/2001/01/03/deforestation-in-vietnam-laos-and-cambodia/, accessed 10 March 2017.

Lao Embassy (2011) 'New Cabinet Members Approved', (16 June). http:// www.laoembassy.com/1.%20NEW%20CABINET%20MEMBERS%20 APPROVED.pdf, accessed 10 March 2017.

Lao Ministry of Energy and Mines (2014) 'Chinese Company to Develop Hydropower in Xaysomboun', (8 April). http: //www.laoenergy.la/page-News.php?id_News=44, accessed 10 March 2017.

Lao People's Army (website), http: //www.kongthap.gov.la/index.php/en/ about-us, accessed 10 March 2017.

Laovoices.com (2013) 'Deal inked for building of Attapeu Airport', (13 May). http: //laovoices.com/deal-inked-for-building-of-attapeu-airport/, accessed 10 March 2017.

Lipes, Joshua (2015) 'Cost of Lao Road Project Led by PM's Son Vastly Overstated: Expert', *Radio Free Asia*, (6 April). http: //www.rfa.org/eng-lish/news/laos/road-04062015164424.html, accessed 10 March 2017.

Long, Nyuyen Duc (2014) 'Petrolimex Laos recorded a high volume in lubri-cant business in 2013.' *Petrolimex* (13 January). http: //www.petrolimex. com.vn/details/specialized-news/petrolimex-laos-recorded-a-high-volume-in-lubricant-business-in-2013/default.aspx, accessed 10 March 2017.

Munzinger Datenbank Preview, http: //www.munzinger.de/, accessed 10 March 2017.

Nette, Andrew (1998) 'Laos: Military Inc Flexes Economic Muscle', *IPS Inter Press Service*, Vientiane (20 December). http://www.ipsnews. net/1998/12/development-bulletin-laos-military-inc-flexes-economic-muscle/, accessed 10 March 2017.

Ounkeo Souksavanh (2015) 'Curfew Imposed in Lao Province After Deadly Violence', *Radio Free Asia* (11 December). http: //www.rfa.org/english/ news/laos/curfew-12112015191818.html, accessed 10 March 2017.

People's Daily Online / Xin Hua (2011) 'Profile: President of Laos Choummaly Sayasone', (16 July). http: //english.peopledaily.com.cn/90001/90777/90851/7411513.html 16.06.2011, accessed 10 March 2017.

Radio Free Asia (2016) 'Selection of New National Leaders in Laos Indicates Tilt to Vietnam', (22 January). http: //www.rfa.org/english/news/laos/Laos-elect-01222016112729.html, accessed 10 March 2017.

Rebitsch, Robert (2010) *Wallenstein. Biografie eines Machtmenschen.* Wien: Böhlau.

Robichaud, William, *et al.* (2001) *Review of the National Area Protected System of Lao PDR.* Vientiane: Lao Swedish Forestry Programme.

Scramble/Dutch Aviation Society (2016) 'Armed Forces Overviews: Laos', http: //www.scramble.nl/orbats/laos/summary, accessed 10 March 2017.

Singh, S. (2008) 'Contesting moralities: the politics of wildlife trade in Laos', *Journal of Political Ecology*, 15(10):1–20.

SIPRI (Stockholm International Peace Research Institute) (2016) 'SIPRI Military Expenditure Database'. http: //www.sipri.org/research/armaments/milex/milex_database (Excel Sheet) , accessed 10 March 2017.

Smith, Beaumont (2010) 'A Tree Falls in Laos', *Asia Times* (5 October). http: //www.atimes.com/atimes/Southeast_Asia/LJ05Ae01.html, accessed 10 March 2017.

Soutchay Vongsavanh, (1981) Gen. *Royal Lao Government Military Operations and Activities in the Laotian Panhandle.* Washington, D.C.: US Army Center of Military History, Department of the Army.

Statistical Yearbook (Ministry of Planning and Investment, Lao Statistics Bureau) 2012: 21–4, Vientiane June 2013

Stuart-Fox, Martin (1997) *A History of Laos.* Cambridge: Cambridge University Press.

——— (1998) *The Lao Kingdom of Lan Xang: Rise and Decline.* Bangkok: White Lotus Press.

——— (2006) 'The Political Culture of Corruption in the Lao PDR', *Asian Studies Review*, March, Voume 30.

——— (2008) *Historical Dictionary of Laos.* Lanham, Maryland: Scarecross Press.

——— (2011) 'Family Problems', *Inside Story* (Blog), 19 January.

Tan, Danielle (2015) '*Chinese Engagement in Laos: Past, Present, and Uncertain Future*', *Trends in Southeast Asia* Special Paper no. 7, Singapore: Institute of Southeast Asian Studies.

——— (2015a) 'The "Casino Strategy" in Laos and Cambodia: a Risky Bet on the Future.' *French Network for Asian Scholars* (July). http: //www.gis-reseau-asie.org/monthly-articles/casino-strategy-laos-cambodia-risky-bet-on-future-danielle-tan, accessed 10 March 2017.

Thanhniem News (2013) 'HAGL starts construction of second international Airport in Laos', (15 March). http: //www.thanhniennews.com/business/vietnams-hagl-begins-construction-of-airport-in-laos-3171.html, accessed 15 March 2013.

THB Group Sole Company Limited, http: //thbgroup.com.la/firstpage1.html, accessed 10 March 2017.

United States Embassy Cable (2006) 'Deforestation in Laos', 06VIENTIANE674_a (19 July). https: //wikileaks.org/plusd/cables/06VIENTIANE674_a.html, accessed 10 March 2017.

United States Embassy Cable (2009) 'Lao Defense Attache to Arrive Washington, D.C.', 09VIENTIANE268_a (6 June). https://wikileaks.org/plusd/cables/09VIENTIANE268_a.html, accessed 10 March 2017.

United States Embassy Cable (2006) 'New Central Committee Line-up', 06VIENTIANE306_a (31 March). https: //www.wikileaks.org/plusd/cables/06VIENTIANE306_a.html, accessed 10 March 2017.

United States State Department (2015) *Human Rights Report: Laos.* Bureau of Democracy, Human Rights, and Labour. http: //www.state.gov/j/drl/rls/hrrpt/humanrightsreport/, accessed 10 March 2017.

Vientiane Times (2014) 'Reaching forest cover target "a challenging task": minister says.' (14 May). http: //www.laolandissues.org/2014/05/14/reaching-forest-cover-target-a-challenging-task-minister-says/, accessed 10 March 2017.

Vietnam Business Registration (2016) 'VietinBank's Laos branch to sign credit contract with Unitel', (6 April). http: //www.vnbusinessreg.com/vietinbanks-laos-branch-sign-credit-contract-unitel/, accessed 10 March 2017.

Voice of America (2011) 'At Party Congress, Lao Communists Maintain Status Quo', (29 March). http: //www.voanews.com/content/at-party-congress-lao-communists-maintain-status-quo-118913784/167268.html, accessed 10 March 2017.

Walker, Andrew (1999) *The Legend of the Golden Boat.* Honolulu: University of Hawaii Press.

Webb, Billy (2010) *Secret War.* Bloomington, Indiana: Xlibris Corporation.

Womack, Sarah (2009) 'Ethnicity and Martial Races: The Guard Indigene of Cambodia in the 1880s and 1890s', in Tobias Rettig and Karl Hack (eds) *Colonial Armies of Southeast Asia.* Oxford: Routledge: 106–25.

World Air Forces, 'Lao People's Liberation Army Air Force', http: //www.aeroflight.co.uk/waf/aa-eastasia/laos/laos-af-home.htm, accessed 10 March 2017.

Appendices

There are a number of areas in Laos connected with or controlled by the LPA. However, the level of connection differs. Indeed, only the length of the list, the number of interests and the amount of military investment shows the real extent of involvement of the military sector in the Lao national economy.

Appendix A: Lao airports/air force and/or army bases

Air bases and airfields have represented potential sites for the realization of khaki capital by military officials in upcountry Laos. The number of existing and usable airfields, airbases and airports is unclear. Information ranges from over 300 venues where planes can be landed and started down to a more realistic 50 usable airfields and airports. All were built for military purposes and thus could be considered a form of military base. Without a doubt any STOL [Short Take-Off and Landing] plane might be able to land also on extended rural roads. There might be a difference between an airfield and what was once called during the US war in Laos a 'LIMA' site. LIMAs were barebones, unpaved airstrips that were used by the CIA air transport company Air America during that war to supply US-backed guerrilla movements on the ground (Conboy 1995). Most of these 'LIMA' sites are defunct. Ultimately, the number of airfield sites is immense. Many of the sites provide the only access to regions where no roads were ever built. Some offer simply easier access to the area, while land transport might take days to reach these locations. The list below offers some details about the number of air bases and airfields which have been used by the Lao People's Liberation Army Air Force and its predecessors. Some of these areas involve mixed civil and military interests. A growing number of these former airfields or air bases today offer real estate or other opportunities for the Lao military to earn income. In some cases they have become centres of income generation (e.g. plantations, special economic zones) for nearby active-duty and/or retired military officials.

Apart from the main military air bases, there are also a number of smaller airports and airfields around the country that are frequently used by the Air Force.

Attopeu Airport (ICAO: VLAP, IATA: AOU)

Type: local airport (light traffic) announced but the area is in the heart of the city and definitely not usable anymore due to being partly overbuilt. Scheduled airline service: none.

The Airport officially served Attopeu, Laos. The area is attractive for business and might sometimes be controlled by the army.

Latitude: 14.814715 | 14 48.882921 N | N14 48 52

Longitude: 106.821699 | 106 49.301949 E | E106 49 18

Field elevation: 344 ft/105 m MSL

26 km from Attopeu (and 170 km south from Saravane) there is a new airport under construction by Vietnamese military-linked investor HAGL. This airport opened in a first phase in early June 2015 with an 1850 x 30 m. runway while a second phase until 2020 contains an extension to 3000 x 45 m. (Laovoices.com 2013). Already built but not suitable for fixed wing aircraft.

Actually there are no regular flights to Attopeu so it can be called a private airport used by HAGL while financing is unclear. However all air activity is licensed and controlled by Lao Air Force authorities.

Ban Houei Sai (ICAO code: VLHS, IATA code: OUI)

Also spelled, Ban Houay Xay and Ban Houeisay, this airfield is located in the north west of the country, close to the Thai–Lao border. Date of construction not known, but it has been used since at least 1982.

Runway data: Paved Rwy ?/?, Length: 4900 ft.

Houeisay (IATA code: HOE)

Houeisay Airport (also spelled Houay Xay) is located in Ban Houeisay. Date of construction not known. It is currently of civilian and LPLAAF use.

Runway data: Rwy ?/?, Length: ? ft, Elev: ? ft, Location: 103 45' 0' E, 20 30' 0' N.

Airport codes: HOE / OIE Type: local airport(light traffic)

Scheduled airline service: yes

Serves: Huay Xai, Bokeo, Laos

Latitude: 20.257299 | 20 15.437965 N | N20 15 26

Longitude: 100.436996 | 100 26.219788 E | E100 26 13

Field elevation: 1,380 ft/421 m MSL

Magnetic variation: 0.491°W

Runways at Ban Huoeisay Airport 4,922 x 75 ft (1,500 x 23 m) – paved – not lighted – threshold 34 displaced 196 ft (60 m)

Khong (IATA code: KOG)

Khong Airport is located in the south of the Khong Island and close to the border of Cambodia. Date of construction not known. It is current not used and not usable. Coordinates are not clear but it seems that the former airfield covers a large area that is still in poor condition. However the area is economically seen as highly attractive.

Runway data: Earth, Length: 3,937 ft, Elev: 250 ft, Location: 14.112068 E, 105.817786 N

Long Tieng

Long Tieng is located in 'Military Region II'. It was used by the US Central Intelligence Agency, the Thai Army and the RLA from 1962 until 1975 for T-28 and Hmong guerilla operations which were led by Gen. Vang Pao. During this time, it was called Lima Site 98 (LS 98) or Lima Site 20A (LS 20A).

Runway data: Date of construction: 1962. No longer used. Runway data: Rwy ?/?, Length: ? ft, Elev: ? ft.

Luang Namtha (ICAO Code: VLLN, IATA code: LXG)

Luang Namtha Airport is located in the north of the country close to the Chinese border at former Casino City Boten. The date of the original construction is not known but there was an extension around 2010. It is currently in civilian use.

Runway data: Paved Runway (Asphalt), Length: 1,600 m., Elev: 1,968 ft, Location: 101 24' 0' E, 20 58' 0' N.

Luang Prabang (ICAO Code: VLLB, IATA code: LPQ)

Luang Prabang Airport is located in the centre of the northern region, close to the Plain of Jars. Date of construction not known, but it has been used since at least 1959. It is in current civilian and LPLAAF use. It houses the regional military HQ.

Runway data: Paved Rwy ?/?, Length: 6,070 ft, Elev: 978 ft, Location: 102 9' 0' E, 19 54' 0' N.

Muang Sing Airfield

Muang Sing Airfield is a former LIMA Site located close to the Chinese border only a few km north from Luang Namtha and actually not in use. The

Airstrip still can be identified on Satellite Photos but there is no equipment or installations left. It is defunct. However next to the abandoned Garrison Buildings in the heart of town another area around the former airfield of 3925 x 125 ft is under control of the LPLA. Location is by coordinates: 21°10'39.0'N 101°08'43.0'E

Muang Vang Viang (ICAO code: ?)

Also known as Vang Vieng, this airfield is located midway between Luang Prabang and Vientiane, in the north of the country. Date of construction not known, but it has been used since at least 1982. It is now defunt and there are ·houses on it. Around the airfield there are restaurants and entertainment for locals – not without allowance of and payments to the LPLAAF authorities. It is current nor in civilian or LPLAAF use – but there's talk about another airfield a little outside the city.

Runway data: Rwy ?/?, Length: ? ft, Elev: ? ft.

Muong Sai (IATA code: UON)

Date of construction not known. It is in current civilian use.

Runway data: Rwy ?/?, Length: 3,380 ft, Elev: 2,067 ft, Location: 102 0' 0' E, 20 49' 0' N.

Oudomxay (ICAO Code: VLOS, IATA code: ODY)

Date of construction not known. It is in current civilian use.

Runway data: Unpaved Rwy ?/?, Length: 3,900 ft, Elev: ? ft, Location: 104 10' 0' E, 20 35' 0' N.

Paksane (IATA code: PKS)

Paksane former Airfield is located around 150 km south from Vientiane by road south east of town with good access (100 m.) to main route Nr. 13. The date of construction is not known. It is currently not in civilian or LPLAAF use but in a transition process to a small business park. A further use as an Airfield is unlikely.

Runway data: Rwy ?/?, Length: ? ft, Elev: ? ft, Location maybe: 103 65' 0' E, 18 36' 0' N.

Pakse (ICAO Code: VLPS, IATA code: PKZ)

Pakse(or Pakxe) Airport is located in the south of the country, south of Savannakhet, south west of Saravane, close to the Thai border. Date of construction not known, but it has been used since at least 1959. It is big enough for large transport aircraft. It is still used by civilian and LPLAAF aircraft. It houses the regional military HQ.

Runway data: Paved Rwy ?/?, Length: 5,330 ft, Elev: 330 ft, Location: 105 47' 0' E, 15 8' 0' N.

Phonsavan

Phonsavan (or Phonsavanh) is located on the Plain of Jars in north-central Laos. It was constructed in the mid 1970s to replace Xieng Khouang. It was used as a MiG-21 fighter base. It houses the regional military HQ. Especially the following Data should not be trusted so the runway must be in my calculation more than 2000 m. in length.

Runway data: Rwy Asphalt, Length: 4,950 ft, Elev: ca 3,600 ft. Location: 19°26'24.54"N 103°10'6.24"E.

There is another former airfield in the heart of Phonsavan known as 'General Vang Pao's old airfield', which has been used in very different ways as an entertainment hub with restaurants, a hotel resort, Karaoke, fairgrounds and sports areas (a golf driving range had to be terminated because of typical regional strong winds. The investor company's Name is 'Golden Mountain', a Company known for its good government contacts.

Sam Neua (ICAO Code: VLSN, IATA code: NEU)

Sam Neua Airport is located in the north east of the country, towards the Vietnam border close to Route Nr. 6. Original date of construction not known but there was talk about an extension is underway. It is currently in civilian use.

Runway data: paved runway (asphalt), Length: 3,400 ft, Elev: ? ft, Location: 104 4' 0' E, 20 25' 0' N. Actually there is a new Airport with a 7,500-ft runway around 36 km north in Nong Khang by Vietnamese Investor HAGL under construction (Thanhniem News, 2013). At the time of writing there was no official aviation information available about when the airport would commence operations.

Saravane (ICAO Code: VLSV, IATA code: VNA)

Saravane is located in the centre of the southern region. Date of construction not known but it might have been in the colonial era. It is currently not in use and not usable but the area is highly attractive for investors as it covers an area 200 m. south of Route Nr. 15 to Vietnam in the heart of the city. In fact, there are houses built over it.

Runway data: Unpaved Runway, Length: 3,477 ft, Elev: 574 ft, Location: 106 24' 0' E, 15 43' 0' N.

Savannakhet (ICAO code: VLSK, IATA code: ZVK)

Savannakhet Airport is located in the south west of the country, more or less in the city around 130 road km south of Thakhek, close to the Thai border and to the invests of Savan Vegas und Seno Savannakhet Special Economic Zone. Date of construction not known, but it has been used since at least 1963. It was home to the RLAF Pilot Training School T-41Ds. It is still used by civilian and LPLAAF aircraft. It houses the regional military HQ.

Runway data: Paved (Concrete) Rwy ?/?, Length: 5,350 ft, Elev: 509 ft, 104 45' 0' E, 16 32' 0' N.

Sayaboury (ICAO Code: VLSB, IATA code: ZBY)

Sayaboury Airport is located where? Date of construction not known. It is currently in civilian use.

Runway data: Unpaved Rwy ?/?, Length: 4,195 ft, Elev: 950 ft, Location: 101 42' 0' E, 19 15' 0' N.

Seno (IATA code: SND)

Seno (or Xeno) is located in the southwest, close to the Thai border, near Savannakhet. Date of construction not known, but it was first used by the AL in 1958. The name Seno was derived from the French names of the four compass directions, Sud, Est, Nord and Ouest. It is in current civilian use. It was big enough for large transport aircraft.

However actually Xeno is on the way to change its business model and become a new special economic zone. Close to the new infrastructure lines along the Greater Mekong Subregion East–West Corridor from Vietnam to Thailand is the Vietnam–Lao joint venture: the Savan Vegas Casino Complex. The former Airbase might become another really successful cash cow for the Lao Security sector. The location is one of the most attractive ones under the control of the Lao People's Army.

Runway data: Paved Rwy ?/?, Length: 3,940 ft, Elev: 607 ft, Location: 105 1' 0' E, 16 40' 0' N.

Thakhek (ICAO code: VLTK, IATA code: THK)

Thakhek is located on the Thai border in the south of the country. The date of construction is not known but it might have been in the thirties when Thakhek was an important Post for the French Colonial Administration. In the second Indochina War Nakhon Phanom on the Thai side of the Mekhong was a much more important base so Thakhek (East) must have been irrelevant even at this time. It is currently defunct and will not be usable as far as the runway might be long enough for STOL Aircraft while other installations don't exist (anymore).

The whole 'Airport' is located in a settlement area around one Kilometer from Route Nr. 13.

Runway data: Unpaved Rwy ?/?, Length: 4,500 ft, Elev: ca. 500 ft. Location (was) 17.3999996 E 104.8000031 N

Thakhek West

Thakhek West seems to be the newer and more usable one of the two Thakhek Airfields. It has an around 2650 feet long unpaved runway and is surrounded by an industrial development area south of the city close to Route Nr. 13. Exact location is 17°22'36.0'N 104°51'44.0'E

Udomxay (Meuang Xay) (IATA code: UDO)

Udomxay is located in the very North of the country close to Chinese and Vietnamese border. The date of construction might be connected with the establishment of the city within the second Indochina war by the Chinese People's Army. It is in currently in civilian use and covers a large area beside the city centre.

Runway data: Paved (Asphalt), Length: 1,200 x 45 m., Elev: 509 ft, Location: 103 49' 0' E, 19 8' 0' N.

Vang Vieng (IATA code: VGG)

Vang Vieng is located in the heart of the country 150 km north from Vientiane and 200 km south from Luang Prabang? The exact date of construction is not known but it must have been in the second Indochina War following the name 'LIMA Site 6'. It is in current not in regular use as an airport even the runway is still paved. Local population uses the area as a market place. Further use is as a bus station. Old hangars and shacks serve as restaurants and storage rooms.

Runway data: Paved (Asphalt), Length: ca. 2,000 m, Elev: ? ft. Location: 18°55'31'N 102°27'1'E

Viengxay (IATA code: VNG)

Viengxay is located at Route Nr. 6 around 20 km from the Vietnamese border and around 30 km from the provincial capital Sam Neua. The airfield was built during the second Indochina war. It is in now only temporarily in semi-civilian use while usage is possible only by STOL Aircraft. The area is further interesting for economical use especially since Sam Neua Airport gets an extension by Vietnamese Investors.

Runway data: Paved (Gravel), Length: 1,500 ft, Elev: ? ft.

Vientiane-Wattay (ICAO code: VLVT, IATA code: VTE)

Also known as Viangchan-Wattay, Wattay International Airport is the only international airport for Laos. It is located 6 km to the west of the Vientiane city centre. It was originally built by the French, and has been used since at least 1958. It is home to much of the LPLAAF, including one MiG-21 interceptor squadron (when it was operational) and the VIP Transport Squadron. It is also home to Lao Airlines - the state domestic airline.

Runway data: Paved Rwy ?/?, Length: 10,499 ft, Elev: 559 ft, Location: 102 34' 0' E, 17 59' 0' N.

Xayabury (IATA code: XAY)

Xayabury is located in Xayabury, the capital of Xayabury province. Date of construction not known. It is in current civilian use.

Runway data: Rwy ?/?, Length: ? ft, Elev: ? ft, Location: 104 43' 0' E, 18 40' 0' N.

Xieng Khouang (ICAO code: VLXK, IATA code: XKH)

Also known as Chieng Khouang, Xieng Khouang is located south east of Luang Prabang, towards the Vietnamese border. Date of construction not known. It was used since at least 1958. It was completely destroyed in the Vietnam War and went out of military by 1977.

Runway data: Runway is paved, Length: 10,500 ft, Elev: 3,500 ft, Location: 103 0' 0' E, 19 30' 0' N.

Xieng Lom (IATA code: XIE)

Xieng Lom is located 200 kilometers southeast of Huay Xai and 100 Kilometers west of Hongsa close to the border to Thailand. The date of construction is not known but it might have been built by Japanese Forces in WW II. If it is in use it is currently only in civilian use. The area is quiet interesting economically because of mineral resources such as lignite around.

Runway data: Paved (laterite), Length: 3,400 ft, Elev: 2,050 ft, Location: 100 49' 30' E, 19 37' 0' N (Aeroflight).

Appendix B: Some current Lao companies connected to the Laos People's Army

UNITEL, Ltd., a telecommunications joint venture, 51 per cent owned by the Laos Ministry of National Defence and 49 per cent owned by Viettel (a state corporation wholly owned by Vietnam's Ministry of Defence).

Dansavanh Casino Resort, a casino jointly managed by the Malaysian Syuen Group and the Lao military, which owns 25 per cent of the share capital. Dansavanh Group (Hotels, Casinos, Restaurants, Tour Operators – Organized with the acceptance of the Army.

Khammouan Army Mining Corporation (Khammouan Military Mineral Mining Co.)

Air Lao: mainly industrial and cargo flights and passenger flights into remote areas and to airfields which are not regularly used by other 'civil' planes. It is said to be indirectly connected to the LPA. Renamed as Lao Skyway

Lao Airlines: Civil Flag Carrier of LPR, restructured with Chinese support of China Yunnan Airlines (today China Eastern). 'The Air Force has close ties with the civil airline Lao Airlines (Lao Aviation until March 2003).' (Scramble).

Lao Holding State Enterprise (Energy – under the official control of the Ministry of Finance)

Lao State Fuel (Lubricants, LPG, Transport, Construction)

Vientiane Oil (Lubricants esp. for Army needs – mainly Army)

Phonesack Group (Mining (Coal & Gold), Construction, Energy)

Phonesack Wood (Logging, Wood Processing)

Lao Star TV channel

Tong Homsombat Business Group (Construction, Timber)

CHAPTER 7

Philippine Military Capital After 1986
Norming, Holdouts and New Frontiers

Rosalie Arcala Hall

Introduction

Since 1986, the Philippines has made inroads in crafting legal mechanisms to subordinate its armed forces to civilian rule, in line with the requirements of democratic civil–military relations. These legal mechanisms have included subjecting the military's budget and promotions to legislative approval, barring the appointment of active duty officers to any government posts, and instituting firmer administrative supervision through a civilian defence agency. Yet persistent elite arrangements in which the Armed Forces of the Philippines (AFP) remains a key player have not fully brought the military back to the barracks. The attempted coups from 1986–89, the military-leveraged ouster of President Estrada in 2001 and the Oakwood mutiny in 2003 all point to the lingering politicization of the armed forces and the concomitant influence the institution wields in policies it considers important: personnel welfare and internal security. The military's political capital, although clipped by legal and institutional arrangements, remains substantial against the backdrop of civilian governance weaknesses.

This chapter describes the trajectory of Philippine civil–military engagements in the formal arena of public fund allocation (government budget) and in informal settings (shadow economies, unauthorized businesses and corrupt activities) after 1986. It examines shifts in military influence in government allocation decisions, including regular appropriation, procurement and pension. It also looks at other sources of military funds (e.g. foreign military assistance and UN peacekeeping funds, which do not come from the government), as well as Trust Receipts and inter-agency transfers for which the institution exercises greater discretion and flexibility when it comes to spending decisions. Oversight and monitoring mechanisms are in place, which suggests a strong 'norming' process in the formal arena. Gaps remain, however, largely owing to deficits in the capacities of legislative committees and civilian oversight bodies.

The chapter proceeds from an insight established in the literature: problematic civilian control in internal security and military organization has largely shaped the growth of as well as normative constraints on the military's influence in budgetary matters. The military's continued preoccupation with internal security and counterinsurgency has been made more pronounced by the war on terror (against the Abu Sayyaf Group since 2001), which provided an impetus for role expansion into civic action and other community development initiatives, and corresponding investments into these non-kinetic military activities. These security strategies accord the military continued influence, even within the established constitutional limits and lags in the civilian appropriations apparatus. As combat and anti-terror operations intensified, more openings (such as renewed US military assistance in the form of training and equipment; re-channelling of AFP modernization funds towards the purchase of equipment for internal security rather than for external defence, as originally intended) have been made to the military for these resources. In terms of its nontraditional tasks, the military has gained access even to funds ostensibly controlled by other national government agencies, having been tasked as the implementer to various infrastructure projects in conjunction with counterinsurgency, most notably through the *Kalayaan sa Barangay* (KBP) and *Bayanihan sa Barangay* (BBP) programmes. With deeper involvement inside conflict zones, the military's economic influence has also increased with weaker national civilian oversight capacity in the periphery. Moreover, corruption cases became harder to detect where monitoring in the conflict areas was already difficult to begin with. Thus while the military's influence in formal economic arenas seems to have been appeared curbed as budget and procurement rules have been normalized in line with other government agencies, there remain elements in the budget process that suggests bulwarks or islands of resistance, such as opaque budget items, conversion practices and red flags on balance sheets that civilian authorities (absent sufficient bureaucratic capacity) are unable or refuse to contest.

Money and the military: Flexing autonomy versus civilian control in democratic settings

Civil–military relations may be defined as a 'strategic interaction carried out in a hierarchical setting' premised on the principle that civilian authorities have to delegate the use of force to the military (Feaver 2003: 54). The military is essential to the state's survival, but civilian authorities must exercise control over the military to avoid possible abuse of force. Civilian control is exerted through a variety of legal mechanisms (e.g. having the elected head of state as commander-in-chief, placing the military under a civilian Defence department, legislative approval of budget and appointments), enabling civilian authorities to monitor or oversee military activities. For Welch (1976), civilian control mechanisms are 'devices through which the ill-disposed towards governmental policies can be bypassed, replaced, co-opted or neutralized.' The military has functional remit and expertise on the deployment of violence (Huntington 1967). Civilian authorities supply the policy objectives while the military presumably enjoys latitude in determining how best to achieve that objective. The military is a professional organization in that it has its own set of rules, norms and standards aligned with its unique skill set, for which autonomy is warranted. Balancing civilian control with military autonomy is a key concern in democratic settings.

Civil–military engagements in the formal arena of policymaking are more nuanced than a straightforward relationship of military subordination to civilian authorities. For Feaver (2003), the optimal form of civilian monitoring involves incentives that lead a self-interested military to do as civilians tell them. For Levy (2012), civilian control depends on exchange: the military agrees to limit its autonomy in exchange for material and symbolic resources given by civilian authorities. The military needs these resources to maintain its organization and obtain public legitimation. State allocations for the military in particular enable the military to recruit, pay its personnel and engage in legitimate action, which in turn affect its corporate status. Poorly equipped and manned armed forces are not just inimical to state interest (poor security outcomes); they are also bad for the military's morale and image.

In societies that transitioned from a political system wherein the military played a key political role, engagements between civilian authorities and the military have come with additional challenges. First, where the new democratic government is beholden to the military (i.e., fearful of military coup threats or dependent upon military support to remain in power), budgetary allocations become 'rent' or a military buyoff (Kimenye and Mbaku 1995: 701). Faced with destabilization threats, the transitional state normally acquiesces and gives the military a larger share of its budget (Tusalem 2014: 483). Second, where the military has 'reserved domains' or policy prerogatives (regarding, for example, the conduct of operations, or military enterprises), an imbalance in civil–military relations ensues. Placing these matters outside the policy spotlight means removing them from civilian scrutiny and contestation (Stepan 1986). Allocation of resources (or accounting of income) in these circumstances is not subject to monitoring and oversight by civilian authorities.

One area in which civil–military dynamics can be examined is military allocations. This is defined as the amount appropriated by the government for the military's upkeep, including expenditures for personnel, maintenance and operation and capital outlay. Levels of military allocations reflect the preferences and insights of policymakers as they grapple with the perennial guns-versus-butter issue of determining how much security they can afford in light of pressing societal and economic needs (Deger and Sen 1990: 6). Government allocations to the military are also a key indicator of the military's corporate well-being; whether sufficient spending is made to take care of the salaries, allowances, hazard pay, pension, equipment and other logistical requirements for the armed forces to carry out their missions. The formal process of deciding how much allocation is given to the military illustrates the exchange described by Levy (2012): negotiations and bargaining between civilian authorities and the military can best be observed during the process of budgetary decision-making. This exchange is seen in various dimensions of the allocation: aggregate, as the percentage of total government allocation and quality of continuing civilian oversight, regarding for example allocation structure (personnel, maintenance and operation or capital outlay) and prioritization of certain missions or tasks. Because government allocation is a formal process, it normally comes with civilian control complements (e.g. procurement and auditing mechanisms) designed to ensure accountability in the way state resources are used. Allocations being an important lifeline to the military and integral to its mission accomplishment, officers are expected to lobby intensely for the biggest plausible share of the pie. Presidents looking to buy off or obtain military support also look at the budget as a useful instrument.

Military access to resources outside of public funds increases the challenges of civilian control. Income sources might include military enterprises, foreign military assistance or payment for participation in international missions such as peacekeeping. While earnings from the sources could be justified as filling the gap between government allocation and legitimate personnel welfare expectations, they could also be sources of corruption (Brommelhorster and Paes 2003: 5). They are not subject to government scrutiny, thus allowing the military to develop their own internal controls, which may be less stringent than those used by other civilian agencies. Moreover, the military's involvement in business is problematic as such runs counter to their core function of war fighting; even during peacetime, running a business should not be a priority (ibid.: 4). Military-run businesses provide an income source, which given their access to crucial material resources like transportation, communication and real estate, could easily be abused. The military could also accrue income from the informal economy, which can take two forms: earnings from the use of military resources for civilian purpose without consent of proper authorities; and involvement in informal economies such as smuggling, sale of weapons and extortion. Either way, these undertakings open opportunities for corruption.

Philippine military influence in shifting political contexts: gains and snares

Civil–military relations in the Philippines evolved in the context of serious deficits in Philippine democracy. While the military generally refrained from intervening in politics prior to 1986, the way the institution related to formal power holders (e.g. the president, Congress and local government officials) reflects the more informal, elitist and clientelistic nature of Philippine politics. Formally, power within government institutions is determined via electoral contest, but with limited participation and contestation between political parties, only a subset of elites actually come into office and these are generally intolerant of opposition (Selochan 2004). The prominence of clientelistic ties is echoed in the relationship between the military officers and civilian leaders, notably the president and key members of Congress whose approval is necessary for one's promotion and for the military's budget. Previous presidents, like Magsaysay and Marcos, utilized these patronage links to the fullest by assigning the military new mission areas beyond defence, embedding the institution further into internal security operations and hand-picking favourites to administrative posts in order to shore up personal loyalties. Marcos adeptly restrained the military's involvement in politics by use of an authoritarian variety of civilian supremacy principles. He provided a strong constitutional justification for the military's expanded role while keeping a tight leash on the institution through crafty appointment decisions based upon personal loyalty to him (Abinales 2005: 29). Under President Marcos, uniformed officers were appointed to lucrative civilian posts, including government-owned and controlled corporations. The military's role expanded to encompass nontraditional tasks such as infrastructure and disaster response, even as its combat role intensified with the dual armed campaign against the communist and Islamic separatist rebels (Hernandez 2008; Hutchcroft and Rocamora 2003: 275). The military also grew in size as it placed the nationalized police force, constabulary and the paramilitary arm, the Civilian Home Defence Forces (CHDF) under its operational control. As it became more centralized, the military as an institution got accustomed to a large degree of autonomy when it came to its budget, its material as well as personnel prerequisites, and the way it conducts its counterinsurgency programme. Along with these, however, came adverse consequences such as loss of professionalism and discipline in the ranks: corruption and outright stealing from communities the military encountered in its anti-insurgency activities were common. Its expanded government budget and mandate, and access to illicit resources, were mediated by the institution's solid support to the dictatorship. Most notably, the military became more politicized as its material fortunes become enmeshed with the dictatorship's survival. Thus, under President Marcos, the distinction between civilian principal and military agent became blurred.

Problematic civil–military relations in the Philippines are historically rooted in the ways that state civilian authorities have organized and deployed violence (Lotta-Hedman 2001; Lotta-Hedman and Sidel 2000). The privatized and localized nature of law enforcement, and the centrality of the AFP's constabulary function (rather than territorial defence), are illustrative of these hybrid formulations. If the military is understood to be an agent of the state (implementing the state's directives, and under Martial Law, by the dictator Marcos), then its abnormality rests in that it was mainly used as a collection of local brokers for the government's anti-insurgency campaign. As a consequence of its prolonged deployment to conflict areas within the Philippines, military units had become de facto power wielders, acting as agents of the state vis-a-vis local warlords. In alternate circumstances, the soldier-agent could also defy the state's order and subsequently redefine such relationships. Former officer-turned-Governor and Congressman Rodolfo Aguinaldo was a key example of a soldier-rebel-politician who played local politics in the same way as civilian-politician rivals (that is, with a private army and financial support from an illegal numbers game or jueteng) (Wong 2008). Continued military deployments for internal security operations to this day embed officers into local politics and the shadow economies of the conflict zone, within which they wield de facto political authority.

Following the democratic transition in 1986, legal and institutional reforms were initiated to reassert civilian control over the Philippine military. These reforms included writing provisions into the 1987 Constitution that barred the appointment of active duty military personnel to government posts (including Government Owned and Controlled Corporations or GOCCs), institutionalization of legislative oversight on military budget and promotions, and the reorganization of a civilian national defence department to supervise to armed forces. The constabulary and police were separated from the military; the paramilitary arm was reconstituted into the Civilian Armed Forces Geographical Unit (CAFGU) with presumably greater checks on human rights accountability and threat-based mobilization and deactivation. The efforts of the Aquino administration to find a peaceful settlement to the armed insurgency, however, were thwarted by military interventions from 1986–89 by factions connected with the Reform the Armed Forces Movement (RAM), leading President Aquino and thereafter President Ramos to roll back on the reforms. While the military's formal capital become more restricted (its budget more or less remained flat from 1986–99), the institution nevertheless maintained its strong influence in the crafting and implementing internal security policies, with Congress and the defence department largely acquiescing (Heiduk 2011: 212). The military did not regain the formal capital lost from US military assistance when it comes to equipment acquisition with the closure of US military installations in 1992. Previously, the military had access to second-hand US equipment and matériel, handled directly by the Defense Department, through the Foreign Military Assistance programme. The AFP Modernization Programme from 1995–99 only delivered a fraction of the 50 billion pesos committed for equipment upgrade under the AFP Modernization Act (Republic Act 7898), but the law effectively brought the military's procurement and acquisition process within the same normative ambit as all government agencies, thus resulting in greater civilian control.

Scholars note that notwithstanding these reforms, deficiencies in civilian control of the Philippine military remained after the 1986 transition. The series of military interventions, including the withdrawal of support to beleaguered President Estrada in 2001 (otherwise known as the EDSA 2 uprising) and the 2003 Oakwood mutiny by the Magdalo group, point to the persistence of contextual factors feeding into interventionist proclivities by segments of the military. The Davide and Feliciano Commissions, which investigated the RAM putsches and Oakwood mutiny respectively, found that three factors abet military intervention: politicization of the military, non-prosecution of previous coup plotters and instigators, and poor material investment in fighting a multi-pronged insurgency war (Croissant 2011; Lee 2008). To those factors, Beeson (2008) adds civilian threats to military corporate interests (defined as access to economic activities, both legal and illicit) as triggers to intervention. Along with this diagnosis, scholars have noted the Philippine military's low level of professionalism (Schulzke 2010), corruption, human rights abuses and engagement in criminal activities (Dressel 2011). Analyzing the extent of civilian control in five areas, Croissant *et al.* (2012) and Chambers (2012: 156) noted substantial military influence in the areas of internal security and military organization. In these matters, they concluded that the military's preference in policy crafting, decision making and implementation bears a strong imprint, largely because of civilian authorities' unwillingness or lack of competence in exercising oversight.

Formal military capital in the Philippines: norming amidst gaps in the budget process

The military's influence in public financial matters is circumscribed by institutional arrangements or rules pertaining to national budget allocation, designating the parameters within which civilian and military leaders negotiate and bargain (Pion-Berlin 1997: 4). The 1987 Constitution established fundamental limitations to military capital, particularly in the area of budgeting. Article VI, Section 24 gives the legislature supremacy on all budgetary appropriations, including that of the military, while Article II, Section 17 prioritizes education among all sectoral expenditures. From these come normative principles that the military must submit to Congressional decisions regarding allocation, including pay and pension increases, equipment and material. Defence is a peripheral sector and its expenditures must not exceed those of education. In addition, the centrality of Department of Budget and Management (DBM, as the government's premier defender of austerity measures imposed by international creditors) in determining spending directions for all government agencies means an extra layer of rules to which the military must subscribe in order to get its budget passed and its allocation released. To these rules are also added the Commission on Audit (COA), the government's accountability body, which monitors whether allocations are used as intended. Where governments are committed to austerity measures and in periods of economic downturn, it is expected that demands for a higher military budget will not find a receptive audience among bureaucrats and decision makers. Conversely, where a surplus is at hand (as was the case from 1992–96), it would still take a lot of political leveraging to convince lawmakers to spend the money on the military establishment, rather than on improved social services. To get the increase, the military must be open to new and additional mandates or task insertions by Congress. Two modernization programmes, funded through national government budget (as provided by Republic Act 7898 in 1995 and Republic Act 10349 in 2012), added more mission areas (e.g. protection of the environment, maritime law enforcement and border controls) for the Philippine military.

Examining budget trends, the military's nominal budget declined then flattened after 1986. Data from SIPRI Yearbook 2016 reveal a downward trend beginning 1997, on account of the Asian financial crisis. From 2.6 billion US dollars in 1996, military expenditure went down to $2.3 billion in 2002, increasing above the 1996 level to $2.6 billion in 2003 and generally keeping to a $2.5 billion threshold for another three years. During the second term of President Gloria Macapagal-Arroyo, military expenditure began its modest upward trend from $2.8 billion in 2007 to $2.9 billion in 2010. Beginning in fiscal year 2013, military expenditures increased phenomenally at US$3.4 billion, further going up in succeeding years to US$ 3.9 billion in line with the five-year AFP Modernization Programme.

The structure of military spending also reflects the government's prioritization of internal security operations amongst the AFP's multiple mission areas, and on personnel welfare. The Capability Upgrade Programme (2006–10) focused on internal security operations (presumably to end the counterinsurgency campaign and to effect the AFP's shift to territorial defence from 2010–18). The Defence System of Management (DSOM), which provided for multi-year planning on resource acquisition and a mission-thrust orientation in the AFP's budget, was also adopted in the same period (Salvador and Santiago-Orate 2013: 17).[1] Internal security operations got 3/4 of the total AFP budget in 2011–12, with the Army receiving the bulk of it (averaging 50 per cent from 2006–10 and 59 per cent in 2011–12) and much of the Army's share going to personnel services (as much as 85 per cent in 2011 and 2012) (Salvador and Santiago-Oreta 2013: 18).

In general, the bulk of the AFP's budget (as much as 70 per cent) went to personnel services. There was slight increase following the staggered salary adjustment for military personnel from 1994–97 (President Ramos was authorized to effect yearly increases, sans Congressional legislation, subject to availability of savings or unspent government al-

---

1. Previously, the AFP's budget followed a functional differentiation, i.e. combat operations, military intelligence, logistics and civil–military operations. Under DSOM, the budget categories were streamlined according to mission areas: internal security operations, support to national development, territorial defence, disaster response, international defence and security engagement, and international humanitarian assistance. The DSOM categories therefore became more explicitly linked the budget with the AFP's performance along these broad mandates.

location from the previous year); the injection of pension payments into the military's regular budget began in 1992. However, the DBM kept a lid on increases in programmed personnel expenditures by imposing a non-negotiable troop ceiling on all major services (maximum number of military and civilian personnel, which in turn was used to calculate the military's allowed personnel services budget). The DBM also imposed an overall budget ceiling using economic criteria such as availability of revenues, borrowing limits and consonance with the national develop-ment plan. An indication of this 'bargaining' process can be gleaned from the decision to create paramilitary, counterinsurgency-oriented civilian volunteers (Civilian Armed Forces Geographical Unit Active Auxiliaries or CAA) whose number was excluded from the troop ceiling and whose size varied year-to-year depending on threat assessments. Unlike regular soldiers, the CAA were cheaper because they were only provided uniforms and a token allowance, creating minimal increases in the military's overall budget. The CAFGU programme remained in place from 2006–10 and, in 2008, a 'special insertion' allowed for CAFGU al-lowances and separation payments to be placed under Internal Security Operations budget category. During 2011–12, the Army's personnel expenditure included the 22 billion peso compensation and separation payment for the CAFGU (ibid.: 20). Meanwhile, parallel initiatives intended to improve soldier morale (such as additional collateral pay for combat duties, expanded housing and payment of pension arrears to veterans), carried out under the Macapagal-Arroyo administration, were funded through a supplemental budget, outside of the regular AFP annual appropriation. Allocation for military and police housing (5.6 billion pesos) was earmarked in 2013 under a lump sum arrangement (Manansan 2013).

Big ticket capital expenditures for the military came as separate legislations. Military modernization (both 1995 and 2012) was funded through their share of the Base Conversion Development Authority (BCDA) proceeds, which in turn are treated as a 'Trust Fund'.[2] The 1995 modernization programme (proposed since 1992) was an example of political leveraging between a Congress that was open to the idea, which came in the wake of renewed threats from the communists and

---

2. About 29.16 billion pesos have been remitted by BCDA into the AFP's Trust Fund from military camp sales proceeds since 1993 (see *Manila Times* 2015).

the Moro Islamic Liberation Front, and of a military establishment that was looking to replace the loss of US military assistance. The Philippine Congress initially refused to approve multi-year funding for armed forces acquisitions in its regular budget. Even when government agreed in principle that it would support modernization, the law mandated additional tasks of disaster response and environmental protection to justify new acquisitions, stretched the programme period from ten to fifteen years, effectively cutting the final appropriation figure to half of what the military had proposed, and suspended the programme altogether in 1998 because of fiscal constraints from the Asian financial crisis.

For de Castro (1999; 2012), the 1995 AFP modernization programme illustrates Congressional assertion and through legalistic and bureaucratic procedures, effective curtailment of military influence on budget outcomes. By contrast, the 2012 AFP modernization got an external boost from the US and Japan, given maritime security concerns in the South China Sea. The modernization is part of a broader Philippines Defence Reform Programme, largely underwritten by the US government, that focuses on improving AFP performance in internal security operations and its transition towards a more long-term external defence role. The cornerstone of this reform package is the Capability Upgrade Programme, which essentially triples the capital outlay budget by investing $114 million every year for five years to acquire equipment to improve the forces' internal security operations performance as well as reduce casualties in the field. Unlike the ill-timed 1995 modernization, the 2012 military modernization programme under the Aquino administration provides for funding of 75 billion pesos over five years, sourced from the domestic budget as well as externally committed assistance mainly from the US. The 2012 modernization programme was riding on the country's improved economic performance since 2010 and a receptive public mood.

The two modernization programmes introduced reforms in the acquisition and procurement processes for military hardware, with the end view of introducing more transparency and accountability. Following the enactment of Republic Act 9184 (Government Procurement Reform Act 2002), the AFP's procurement process was harmonized with the rest of government civilian agencies, making use of mechanisms such as electronic procurement system, annual Procurement

Management Plan, the establishment of Bids and Awards Committee and Pre-qualification, Bids and Awards Committee (Cacanindin and Tingabngab 2003). Rules were also set up for administering the AFP Modernization Trust Fund, seed money for which came from proceeds in the sale or lease of military assets (including land). But as Cacanindin and Tingabngab (2003) note, the reform did not come with the corresponding training and education of AFP and Department of National Defence (DND) personnel on acquisition planning; imposed additional hurdles for multi-year and contracts in excess of 300 million pesos (requiring additional Congressional appropriation); produced long delays or unimplemented contracts due to a long, sequential, time consuming and highly centralized (General Headquarters level) process. For the military establishment, external controls on the acquisition process did not always respond to operational needs on the ground.

Reforms in 2006 carried further changes in the procurement process that took into account possible fiscal limits such as the absence of annual AFP budget for Maintenance and Operating Expenditures (as mentioned previously, most of the AFP budget is eaten up by personnel services). The reform involved four organisational changes: adoption of a multi-year defence planning, programming and budgeting system intended to enforce greater fiscal responsibility that ties in strategies, objectives and needed capabilities and resources within anticipated financial limits; improved logistics capacity; optimizing the defence budget and improving management control; and creating a professional acquisition workforce and a centrally-managed defence acquisition system (Teodoro 2008: 110). As mentioned by Teodoro, this new approach is meant to install more fiscal accountability into the AFP's procurement process. The Defence Reform Programme is also seen as a long-term commitment for which subsequent administrations, with improvements in the economy, will continue investing into the further modernization of the AFP in two phases (2012–17; 2018–23). By and large, the 'modernization' carried out were focused against domestic threat groups and not investment towards external defence (Chalk 2014: 4). The bulk of US assistance went to training and equipping the Light Infantry Company as well as for the Battalion Retraining. The bulk of the hardware purchases are just beginning to come on line, including a modest number of refurbished frigates from US and Japan.

Apart from the Military Modernization Trust Fund, the military also receives shares from other government incomes such as the Malampaya Gas Fund[3] and 'proceeds of sale, lease or joint development, private-public partnership, sale of products from government arsenal, disposal of repairable equipment, donations and interest income.' (DBM, COA and Department of Finance Joint Circular 2013-1, issued 7 November 2014). Shares of government agencies to these incomes are set by prior legislation. The AFP also has Trust Receipts, which are 'accrued income from AFP operations and exercise of regulatory function for which authority was granted to the AFP Chief of Staff' (Executive Order 1002 of 1985). Included in Trust Receipts for instance are payments by other government agencies for use of AFP equipment and facilities in infrastructure projects contracted to the AFP Corps of Engineers (Government Procurement Policy Board Resolution Number 09-2005, issued 28 April 2015). During the Macapagal-Arroyo and Benigno Aquino administrations, the AFP entered into a Memorandum of Agreement with the Department of Public Works and Highways and the Office of the Presidential Adviser on the Peace Process (OPAPP) to undertake infrastructure projects in conflict areas. The AFP Corps of Engineers is the implementing agency, money for the project are to be transferred to the DND-AFP and entered into as an Inter-Agency Transferred Fund. Because this is not part of the AFP's regular appropriation, it is subject to more internal regulation. Following the scandals in 2007 and 2011, guidelines were supposed to have been put in place covering the utilization and monitoring of Trust Receipts, UN funds and Inter-Agency Transferred Funds (Gutierrez 2011).

Unlike other civilian government agencies, the military continues to run its own pension programme, the Retirement Benefits and Separations System (RBSS). The RBSS's impending collapse in 1992, due largely to mishandling by previous generals who were also in charge of making investment decisions, was staved off by a government bailout. The government subsequently assumed military pensions as part of

3. In 2014, the Commission of Audit (COA) flagged the AFP for improper transfer of 61.19 million pesos of the Malampaya Gas Fund to its account after the Supreme Court issued a ruling that the fund could only be used for energy-related projects. The COA ordered the AFP to return the money to the National Treasury. Following the Supreme Court ruling, AFP's access to the fund became more restricted (Forbuena 2014).

the regular allocation, but continued to allow the military to run the pension programme separately from those of other civilian government agencies.[4] Consistent warnings have been made about its underfunding and that its current assets are 'insufficient for future pension commitments' (Rappler News 2013). But the RBSS remains a holdout of military independence in terms of financial management.

In sum, inroads have been made to subject the AFP to the same rules and regulations as all other government agencies, with the end view that congruity in benchmarks for accountability and transparency across civilian departments and the military establishment would make it easier to flag wrongdoings. Yet as Croissant *et al.* (2012) and Chambers (2012: 158) have noted, despite the presence of these legal and normative restrictions, civilians remain lacking in oversight capabilities and compelling incentives to challenge the military's perceived dominance in matters pertaining to security. In terms of regular budget items, the military tends to formulate its own programme, which Congress invariably approves, absent as it is of the expertise that would be required to scrutinize or otherwise question military proposals (Croissant *et al.* 2012: 39).

Public allocations outside of the regular appropriation – such as the Trust Funds, Trust Receipts and Inter-Agency Transferred Funds – enable military access to funds under different and often less strict terms of spending. Corruption has also been alleged involving collusion between the AFP, members of Congress and contractors, particularly involving projects entered under Inter-Agency Transferred Funds. In a scheme named 'return to sender', funds are inserted into the AFP's budget to be turned to cash and collected later by the civilian government official who made the insertion (Mangahas 2011). A Commission on Audit (COA) report on the Philippine Air Force in 2013 pointed to serious gaps in the service's practices, including multiple cash advances and categorizing intelligence expenses as miscellaneous expenses. The COA in its 2007–09 report has also called attention to AFP's ghost pensioners – recipients with no birthdates or addresses – indicating the

---

4. To date, the single largest line budget item category in the AFP's budget is for pensions. In 2012, close to 75 per cent of the AFP's 4.5-billion peso budget (3.1 billion pesos) for the General Headquarters is for military pensions, more than the amounts appropriated for each of the armed services for operations (Manasan 2013: 28).

institution's failure to comply with the need to rationalize its pensioners' list. Practices such as perfected contracts, delayed submissions of supplies contract and unliquidated cash advances for foreign trips by AFP personnel have been cited by COA (Mangahas 2011: 2–3). The military also maintains 'opaque' expenditure categories (e.g. representation, confidential, extraordinary, miscellaneous) that COA finds unacceptable. Emergency purchases of howitzers and mortars (ostensibly for counterinsurgency operations) allow the institution to short-circuit the process of vetting acquisitions. As revealed further in a Senate inquiry led by retired Lt Col. George Rabusa, AFP finance officers played with the books to collect unspent allocations and give 'send-off money' to retiring AFP chiefs of staff (GMA News 2011). Also, in the case of AFP comptroller General Carlos Garcia, fixers have gotten sweetheart deals. (Mangahas 2011a).

Despite the strengthening of legal procedures for acquisition and procurement, problems remain such as overpricing in the procurement-bidding process at the headquarters level and fund conversion, or the practice of turning supplies into cash or other materials (Aguja 2008: 4). Although the COA can reveal malpractices by the military institution, it remains a fact that prosecution of errant officials rests with another agency, the Ombudsman, whose office lacks independent investigation powers (it cannot wiretap, freeze assets or make arrests) and the glacial pace of most corruption cases before the Sandiganbayan court (with jurisdiction on cases involving corrupt practices by public officers and employees) led to a predisposition either to enter into plea bargains or dismiss cases entirely (Bolongaita 2010: 14 and 18). This structural deficiency explains why in the case of former AFP comptroller General Garcia, the state prosecutors agreed to a plea bargain reducing his culpability from plunder to bribery, finally leading to the return of barely half of the assets presumably stolen by him. The mishandling of the Garcia case is indicative of the weak civilian accountability mechanisms in general.[5]

Parliamentary oversight through the House Appropriations Committee and the Senate Finance Committee (with a total of only

---

5. The story of the serendipitous discovery of comptroller General Garcia taking bribes, the filing of charges against him by the Office of the Ombudsman and the eventual plea bargain was covered by the media (Tulfo 2013).

56 personnel as support staff), remains limited. The Congressional Planning and Budget Department is similarly plagued by lack of workforce and resources, as well as a compressed 3-month timeframe to deliberate on the budget of 34 line agencies and 17 special funds (Aguja 2008: 7). Congressional oversight is also hampered by an executive order that requires President's consent before any government personnel can be ordered to appear before Congressional budget hearings (Aguja 2008: 8). Congress- initiated investigations of alleged corruption rarely result in convictions of those implicated, nor have they led to meaningful reforms in military practices. Congress can investigate, but it lacks prosecutorial powers. For instance, the Philippine Senate filed eight resolutions between 1987 and 1998 requesting an inquiry into allegations of anomalies and fund mismanagement within the armed forces. Of these, only one resolution was acted upon by the Committee on National Defence and Security: the investigation on the mishandling of the military pension fund. A case was filed against AFP Chief General Lisandro Abadia of the Ombudsman's office, but this case was eventually dismissed (Arcala 2002: 49–50).

Beyond the budget: military influence in other places

The extent of military influence can also be measured by the degree to which the institution has autonomous or independent access to resources outside of government allocation. These typically are foreign assistance grants that are channelled directly to the military and hence outside routine monitoring or scrutiny by accountability agencies. Until 2012, the AFP independently managed UN peacekeeping assistance for overseas missions involving Filipino troops and was not subject to close scrutiny.[6] Allegations made in 2009, that Philippine–US Joint Military Exercises (called Balikatan) funds remitted by the US government were systematically skimmed off at the command level for side-payments to dealers, internal revenue agents and navy commanders. Commentators

---

6. Testimony from a former state auditor about misuse of the UN peace keeping funds (intended for allowances of Filipino UN peacekeepers) prompted the government to institute more controls over this matter. Previously, the standard practice was for UN peacekeeping funds to be coursed through the AFP, not to the Department of Foreign Affairs. Following the scandal, the AFP was no longer allowed to receive said payments directly.

suggested that corruption of this kind could go undetected as this type of fund was transferred directly to the AFP.[7] As in previous cases, only when these types of irregularities are unearthed by the media do civilian authorities react by instituting more controls over the fund sources.

US military assistance (in the form of grants) also enabled the government to procure additional weapons and defence services from the US without dipping into the national budget. In fact, AFP acquisitions prior to the 1995 AFP Modernization mostly came through Foreign Military Sales (FMS) funds from the US (Cacanindin and Tingabngab, 2003). These are primarily negotiated and decided at the level of the Department of National Defence, without vetting by other civilian agencies. From 1972 to 1981, the Philippine military received over $184 million under the US Military Assistance Program (MAP) and $6.3 million under International Military Education and Training (IMET) The MAP amount declined dramatically after 1981, finally registering modest amounts ($10 million in 1990, $7.2 million in 1991 and $3.8 million in 1992 at the time of the base closures. Allotments for the IMET, by contrast, increased even after the political transition and continued in modest amounts after the removal of the American military bases in 1992.

Following the Philippines' inclusion in the US war on terror, US military assistance has grown steadily, from $10.5 million in 2001 to $42.8 million in 2007 (USAID n.d.).[8] The American rotational troop presence in the Bangsamoro areas of Mindanao have also given their Philippine military counterparts a leg up in their civil–military operations, by providing direct support (in addition to a bigger humanitarian push by USAID) to various development projects (Hall 2010: 37). Accounts of US military-supported development projects in Muslim communities, under the Special Advocacy on Literacy/Livelihood and Advancement for Muslims (SALAAM) programme, for instance, abound (Cpt Gregorio Jose, personal communication 19 April 2013; Yabes 2011: 166–72). Independent funding streams enable local units to carry out non-combat missions and earn vital social capital, but also

---

7. See related stories (*Mindanews*, February 2011; *Philippine Star*, May 2009).

8. The estimated volume of US military assistance varies across authors (see de Castro, 2005; San Juan, 2007). Another news report said US military aid in 2001 was $11 million and increased to $30 million in 2008 (*Philippine Daily Inquirer* 2007).

bring them close to the arena of local politics; they have to engage local chief executives (mayors and village chiefs) to get these projects up and running.[9]

Yet even as inroads have been made in these areas, the military has succeeded in extending its influence on budgetary matters by acquiring mandates to implement programmes by other civilian agencies. Under Presidents Marcos and President Ramos, the military had been tasked to construct school buildings and undertake rehabilitation projects (mostly infrastructure) following disasters, with funding from the Office of the President. The Department of Public Works and Highways also had a school building programme implemented by the military in 2008. Under President Macapagal-Arroyo, the military's civil–military operations activities (previously only funded through their regular appropriations) received an enormous boost with the shift towards a 'holistic approach' in dealing with communist and Islamic insurgency problems (Russell 2013: 154–7). The military's foray into construction (focused on small-scale infrastructure projects and socio-economic activities) outside its regular budget and mandate peaked with the creation of National Development Support Command (NaDeSCom) in 2007.[10] NaDeSCom ran two types of programmes: the *Kalayaan sa Barangay* (KBP) and the *Bayanihan sa Barangay* (BBP). Under the KBP, the military was tasked to implement key development programmes under the Office of the President. The KBP targeted conflict-afflicted communities for infra-structure projects, with the military as implementer.[11] AFP-Department

---

9. Ilagan (2014) provides details of this nuanced engagement between local army commanders/officers and Muslim community leaders in a case study of a fish pond nursery project in three North Cotabato marshland villages. She concluded that the military interventions usurped the right of local leaders to determine the security agenda in their territory and created more divisiveness in the community, ultimately leading to the project's failure.

10. National Development Support Command (NaDeSCom), placed all engineering units under one umbrella. It had operational command authority over five Army Engineer Brigades, one Aviation Engineer Group, one Naval Mobile Construction Battalion and one Civil Relations Group of the Civil Relations Service. NaDeSCom's purported mandate was to undertake infrastructure projects in conflict- and disaster-affected villages, as directed by the national government (GMA News 2007).

11. The Kalayaan sa Barangay Programme is aimed at 'transforming communities previously affected by internal conflict into development areas through infrastructure

of National Defence and Office of the Presidential Adviser on Peace Process (OPAPP) jointly identified the projects (farm-to-market roads, school buildings and classrooms, Level II water system facilities, facilities for electricity, and medical facilities and health centres) and beneficiary villages. By contrast, the BBP involved contracts between the military and other national development agencies, local government units and private sector (foundations, companies and foreign donors) to undertake similar development projects (Arugay 2012: 14). From 2005 to 2009, 905 barangays and over 1200 projects were identified by NaDeSCom under the KBP (Armed Forces of the Philippines Civil Relations Service 2012). Attendant to this role expansion, local military commands were tasked to link the KBP with parallel projects by Department of Social Welfare and Development (DSWD) through Kalahi Convergence at the level of regional planning and development council. Funding for KBP and BBP was subsequently terminated under President Benigno Aquino III in 2010; NaDeSCom was accordingly dissolved and the engineering battalions reverted to the operational control of Brigades. Since KBP's termination, however, the AFP was able to continue inking agreements with the private sector and government agencies for construction projects within their area of operations. For instance, in 2013, OPAPP contracted the AFP to implement two road construction projects in Mindanao under the PAMANA programme.[12] Examining 301st Brigade's school building and low-cost housing projects funded by the ABS-CBN Foundation and Gawad Kalinga, respectively, Hall (2014) found that the projects complemented the brigade's other civil affairs and civic-action activities, enabling it to fulfil its mission of neutralizing rebel influence in target localities where the projects are placed.

The military was also tasked to implement the *Balik-Baril* (cash-for-guns) programme, a component of a comprehensive reintegration package for communist rebel returnees, and acted as conduits for the

---

projects and expeditious delivery of basic services' (Quilop 2007). The programme was terminated in 2010 under President Aquino; NaDeSCom was subsequently dissolved. The current PAMANA (Payapa at Masganang Pamayanan) programme, a development project for conflict-affected communities, is an iteration of the KBP in that it targets former conflict areas, with emphasis on former military camps and communities. PAMANA is housed under OPAPP, not the AFP.

12. The Commission on Audit later questioned the OPAPP about this project as the funds were not liquidated (see Ramos 2015).

government livelihood programmes for this group. An inter-agency body under OPAPP ran this reintegration programme, which as of this writing is plagued with backlogs and accumulated unpaid obligations. Because the military confirms the identities of rebel returnees and often serves as a halfway house for those who face threats from their comrades, individual units (like the 303rd Brigade in Negros Occidental) are able to propose livelihood packages by tapping into local government funds as well a private support for livelihood assistance for these clients. Like its post-conflict reconstruction and infrastructure deals with OPAPP, having this rebel returnee constituency in its fold enables the military to then build networks with other government agencies and the private sector for resources (Hall 2014). As opposed to items under the AFP's regular budget, accountability mechanisms for these projects lie with proponent agencies, which may or may not exercise due diligence in seeing that funds are spent as intended. Because projects are located in conflict zones or deal with subject-beneficiaries vetted by the military themselves, fact-checking can be especially difficult.

No systematic assessment has been done as to the outcomes of construction projects or the *Balik-Baril* programme done by the military, either sourced from their own budget or sourced from outside agencies and institutions. Our tentative survey yields the conclusion that, at best, these projects have allowed the military to maintain a footprint in local communities in a non-combat capacity and, consequently, given them a much-needed image boost among local beneficiaries. The joint projects have also greatly expanded their networks among national government agencies and private sector. Through these projects, local army officers have learned to liaise directly with agencies such as Technical Education and Skills Development Authority or TESDA (for vocational training) and with OPAPP (for livelihood assistance) to access government programmes for the out-of-school youth and rebel returnee constituents in their area of operations (Hall 2016). These initiatives, however, do not necessarily strengthen civilian-local government ownership of the process. Contrary to the role distinction in the AFP's internal security plan, whereby the military 'clears and holds' while civilian agencies 'develop', the military in actuality ends up implementing a lot of the development projects themselves (instead of assisting and supporting civilian agencies) without due diligence in utilizing the local peace and order council framework and conducting community consultations (Arugay 2012: 11). Only in Bohol have civil–military engagements met the normative formula where the local government takes ownership of the projects and military involvement is limited to participation on local peace and development councils (Arugay 2009). Clearly, efforts to bring the military's non-kinetic activities within the ambit of civilian-led frameworks (e.g. Peace and Order Council or Kalahi convergence) have fallen short.

The Philippine military's extended formal capital has been underwritten by civilian authorities looking to the institution as a way to extend government reach in conflict areas. However, rather than funding the military non-kinetic activities through its regular allocation, these are funded instead in contingent, lump sum appropriations under different agencies (Office of the President, Department of Public Works and Highways, etc.) which in and of themselves are more susceptible to abuse. The controversy over the misuse of lumps sum insertions into the budgets of various agencies and special purpose fund of lawmakers (pork barrel) led to inquiries and charges filed against several lawmakers, later prompting the Supreme Court to rule the use of lump sum appropriation as unconstitutional (Porcalla 2015). This new court ruling will likely change the way the military is able to access extra-budgetary formal capital through the government.

By contrast, the military's involvement in disaster preparedness and response, tasks it has historically assumed and from 1995 onwards been legally assigned, is illustrative of the template of civilian control (Hall and Cular 2010). The military carries little formal capital in this mission area. Military budget for disaster response is modest (closer to the 5 per cent calamity fund cap per government agency that the National Risk Reduction and Management (NDRRM) law of 2010 provides); its role confined to search and rescue, logistics and communication during the emergency phase only, and to support of civilian agencies (primarily the DSWD) in relief delivery and to the local police as security augmentation (Quilop 2009: 127). The civilian-led disaster coordination frameworks (disaster risk reduction and management councils) are robust and functional, and co-located military units have pre-designated teams that can 'plug-in' to Operations Centres on the ground. As observed during the response to Typhoon Haiyan, the Philippine military created a separate coordination framework (the Multinational Coordination Council)

from the NDRRM Council to accommodate foreign military and personnel assets sent for humanitarian assistance and disaster response on
bilateral terms by their home-country principals. All of the appointed
regional incident commanders (for Tacloban, Cebu and Panay) were
also military officers. Despite these features, the military kept within
the parameters of their assigned tasks (logistics, and security for foreign
personnel) and generally conceded to the lead of their civilian principals
(DSWD and the Department of Interior and Local Government) with
no contestation (Hall and Espia 2015: 96). The military bore all fuel
costs of their disaster response logistics runs and, as a matter of pro-
cedure, could not bill the cargo owners (DSWD, local government or
NGOs) for the meals of soldiers who it tapped to provide manual heavy
lifting. Disaster response is one mission area in which the military has
no access to external funds nor to other government agencies' coffers for
the tasks it performs. Like construction and civic action activities, the
military is able to build goodwill among the local population through
disaster response and affords local units nominal linkages to NGOs that
may be useful in the future.

Illegal economies: shadow military influence

The Philippine military's deployment in conflict zones where illegal
economies also thrive provides a fertile environment for corrupt activities. In these settings, military officers come into contact with a shady apparatus whose currency of kickbacks and protection money are integral
to their activities. There are many historical antecedents of these cosy
intersections between the military and illegal economies. Hernandez
and Ubarra (1999: 14) note the involvement of the military in illegal
logging, mining, smuggling and numbers games as principals or protec-
tors. Wong (2008) tells the tale of Rodolfo Aguinaldo, mentioned briefly
above (p. 277) whose tactical alliance with illegal business networks
enabled him to run a Robinhood-esque counterinsurgency programme
in his native Cagayan province. In Basilan and Tawi-Tawi, cross-border
traders from Malaysia are levied 'extra fees' (locally called *kotong*) by
the navy, police and other government agencies, so that traders could
avoid having their goods confiscated or so that their boats could dock
and unload, undisturbed, in less conspicuous places (Villanueva 2013:
208). Gutierrez (2013: 132–3) points to Cotabato kidnappings by

Commander Mubarak, the Pentagon Gang and succeeding permutations from 1989–2002 as corporate ventures between politicians, the police and the military, with the standard practice of jacking up ransom payments, with the difference to be pocketed by erstwhile-negotiators. Even contemporary high-profile Abu Sayyaf kidnappings in Mindanao are rife with allegations of payoff to military units, thereby allowing said kidnappers to elude capture (Abinales 2004: 13). The sale of misappropriated military weapons and munitions to insurgents and terrorists by local officers has also been cited in the accounts of kidnapping survivor Gracia Burnham and by the Oakwood mutineers (Rodell 2004: 200).

Reforms have been initiated in the military to address corruption in the ranks, such as the formulation of the AFP Code of Ethics and the creation of an Office of Ethical Standards and Accountability under the General Headquarters directorate (Hernandez and Kraft 2010: 133–4). An Undersecretary for Internal Affairs has also been appointed to oversee the AFP financial and procurement system. Despite these efforts at internal control, the AFP's own personnel admit to continued high risks in their financial management system and practices in the form of collusion of inspector with suppliers, dubious emergency procurement of items, and discretionary power of the unit commander on the use of funds, among other irregularities (Development Academy of the Philippines 2007: 3). I argue that overall weaknesses in the civilian accountability mechanisms at the national level make it difficult to discover errant behaviour, not to mention charging and securing convictions of those involved. Further, serious gaps in local governance in conflict zones mean local military units are able to enter undetected into nefarious practices and arrangements. The incentive structure and pay-offs for involvement in these shadow economies are magnified because the local military officers often function as the proxy 'state' authority in these areas.

Beyond prospects of immediate illegal monetary gain, the military can gain informal influence in the frontline that can translate to lucrative post-retirement/separation employment or business opportunities. Because of the premium for paramilitary support in the conduct of internal security operations, the military finds creative ways to support militias and other civilian armed formations within their area of operations. Except for the Civilian Armed Forces Geographical Unit Active

Auxiliaries (CAA) and the Special CAA (SCAA), which the army controls, all other armed groups have been recently declared illegal.[13] The declaration is particularly targeted toward groups on Mindanao. But before 2011, the military routinely issued Mission Orders (MOs) and Memorandum Receipts (MRs) to civilians, which give the latter legal permit to own guns and to display them outdoors (Quitoriano 2013: 59). In the same period, local government units also executed Memoranda of Agreement (MOA) with local army commands for the deputization of Civilian Volunteer Organisations (CVOs) in their area and with private companies (plantations, mining) for Special CAAs (Quitoriano 2013: 65). While these practices have since been discontinued, local commands continue to craft ad hoc arrangements for managing gun possession and use by civilian armed formations (Hall 2015). The commanders' cosy ties with private companies and local government units or LGUs foreground future employment as 'security consultants' for these firms or experience in putting up their own private security companies. This is the revolving-door equivalent for the military and their clients. The institutionalization of paramilitary formations (both legal and grey) has thus accorded the military undue influence in the local scene, amplifying further its internal security role.

Conclusion

Almost two decades after the democratic transition in 1986 saw the progressive reduction of Philippine military influence, as legal and institutional efforts were pursued to curb military autonomy, particularly

---

13. There had been various attempts by the national government to 'legalize' armed formations as counterinsurgency tool. Under Executive Order 546 (series of 2006), President Gloria Macapagal-Arroyo authorized the deputization of Civilian Volunteer Organisations (CVOs) as force multipliers in the anti-terror campaign, particularly in the Bangsamoro area in Mindanao. These are separate from the Special CAAs, which are armed men hired by private companies to guard vital assets/installations covered by the 1991 National Reservist Law. The SCAA volunteers are trained by the army although their uniform and salary are paid by the company. Following the Maguindanao massacre in 2009 in which over 60 individuals including female relatives of Maguindanao gubernatorial candidate Mangundadato and journalists were summarily executed by security forces (police and CVOs included) loyal to political rival Ampatuan, the CVOs were reclassified as Private Armed Groups (PAGs), rendering them 'illegal' formations.

in regard to its regular budget appropriation, modernization and access to external funds began to bear fruit. Three areas were particularly effective: bringing the military's budget into the ambit of accountability mechanisms such the Commission on Audit, the Ombudsman and Sandiganbayan; the homogenization of rules for procurement and acquisition between civilian and military agencies; and the indexing of modernization initiatives to national economic performance and government fiscal priorities. Instituting tighter internal checks on the use of Trust Funds, Trust Receipts and Inter-Agency Transferred Funds are also welcome additions, even though they do not preclude collusion between officers and civilian agents for private gain, through manipulation of documents. Closer civilian supervision of extra-budgetary access, such as UN Peacekeeping Funds and RP-US Military Exercises (Balikatan) remittances, injects further accountability in the military's international tasks. Despite these gains, military influence remains strong in the area of internal security operations. There remain uncontested islands of military budget practices (e.g. opaque expenditure items and conversion) and grey area transactions such as sweetheart deals with procurers that elude accountability. That these practices come to light only following scandals points to serious gaps in civilian oversight capability. Inherent weaknesses in the government's accountability mechanisms also mean poor legal redress.

The military's presumed prime role in internal security operations has also expanded its capital in conflict areas, especially in Mindanao. Its expanded non-combat role, particularly in construction and civil–military operations gave it access to other pools of money by a diverse array of funding 'principals' – through lump sum appropriations by government agencies, partner private-sector foundations and nongovernment organizations, and US military initiatives to introduce projects in conflict zones. Against the backdrop of weak or nonexistent local governance mechanisms in these zones, local military units function as the de facto state authority, or at least as a reliable bridge for these projects. With few exceptions, these projects proceed outside of the supervisory capabilities local civilian-led frameworks and therefore blur the line of acceptable areas of military remit. With government programmes like the *Balik-Baril* (guns-for-cash scheme for rebel surrenderers) and the Kalayaan sa Barangay (small-scale infrastructure projects in conflict-afflicted communities), the military becomes more fully embedded into local politics and develops a stake in individual or community pathways.

Its immersion into domestic conflict zones also provides officers and the rank-and-file opportunities for corruption, in the forms of taking bribes and protection money. As most AFP budgets are decentralized to the operations level (i.e. various area commands), accountability mechanisms are stretched to their limits. A great deal of malpractice continues undetected because of the sheer difficulty of fact-checking in remote and insecure environments. Local civilian agents are unlikely to contest military authority or even supervise the military implementation of ostensibly civilian-led projects. In such settings, the civilian control mechanisms critical to keep military capital in check are simply absent or non-functional. The military also often resorts to hybrid practices with respect to armed civilian formations (e.g. accommodating them for counterinsurgency support) thus extending their influence further into the local security fabric. These local networks with paramilitary formations and private security groups enable officers to build good relations and open doors for lucrative post-retirement employment and contracts.

The Philippines is at a crossroads as preparations are underway for the military to turn over internal security operations tasks to the police, and concomitantly shift to a territorial defence role, in 2028. With renewed US and Japanese interest in security in the South China Sea, a government enjoying stable economic growth and fiscal cushion, and a public generally receptive to military modernization along the lines of territorial defence, the trajectory of Philippine military capital is evolving. It remains to be seen whether the civilian control complements that come with this military role shift is ready.

List of Acronyms

AFP	Armed Forces of the Philippines
BBP	*Bayanihan sa Barangay*
BCDA	Base Conversion Development Authority
CAA	Civilian Armed Forces Geographical Unit Active Auxiliaries
CAFGU	Civilian Armed Forces Geographical Unit

CHDF	Civilian Home Defence Forces
COA	Commission on Audit
CVO	Civilian Volunteer Organisation
DBM	Department of Budget and Management
DILG	Department of Interior and Local Government
DND	Department of National Defence
DPWH	Department of Public Works and Highways
DSOM	Defence System of Management
DSWD	Department of Social Welfare and Development
EDSA	Epifanio de los Santos Avenue; site of a series of military interventions in 1986 and 2001
FMF	(US) Foreign Military Financing
FMS	Foreign Military Sales
IMET	International Military Education and Training
KBP	*Kalayaan sa Barangay*
MAP	(US) Military Assistance Program
NaDeSCom	National Development Support Command
NDRRM	National Disaster Risk Reduction and Management
OPAPP	Office of the Presidential Adviser on the Peace Process
RAM	Reform the Armed Forces Movement
RBSS	Retirement Benefits and Separations System
SCAA	Special Civilian Armed Forces Geographical Unit Active Auxiliaries
SALAAM	Special Advocacy on Literacy/Livelihood and Advancement for Muslims
TESDA	Technical Education and Skills Development Authority
USAID	United States Agency for International Development

References

Abinales, P. (2004) 'American Military Presence in Southern Philippines: A Comparative Historical Overview', East-West Center Working Paper No. 7.

——— (2005) 'Life after the Coup: The Military and Politics in Post-Authoritarian Philippines', *Philippine Political Science Journal* 26(1): 27–62.

Armed Forces of the Philippines Civil Relations Service (2012) *AFP Kalayaan Barangay Projects*. Quezon City: Kinkapil Press.

Aguja, M.J. (2008) 'Role of Parliament in Defence Budgeting in the Philippines', presentation made during the Expert Workshop on the Role of Parliament in National Security Policy and Defence Budgeting in ASEAN Member States (22 May 2008). ipf-ssg-sea.net/expert_ws.../DefenceBudgetingPhilippines_Mayong.pdf, accessed 20 November 2014.

Arcala, R. (2002) 'Democratization and the Philippine Military A Comparison of the Approaches used by the Aquino and Ramos Administrations in ReImposing Civilian Supremacy', Unpublished dissertation. Northeastern University, Boston, MA.

Arugay, A. (2009) 'Linking SSR and Peace Building: The Case of Boho', in *Developing a Security Sector Reform Index in the Philippines: Towards Conflict Prevention and Peace Building*. Manila: Institute for Strategic and Development Studies (ISDS), United Nations Development Program (UNDP) and the Office of the Presidential Adviser on the Peace Process (OPAPP).

——— (2012) 'The military along the security-development frontier: Implications for nontraditional security in the Philippines and Thailand', NTS-Asia Research Paper No 10. Singapore: RSIS Center for Nontraditional Security Studies for NTS-Asia.

Beeson, M. (2008) 'Civil–military Relations in Indonesia and the Philippines: Will the Thai Coup Prove Contagious?', *Armed Forces and Society* 34(3): 474–90.

Bolongaita, E. (2010) 'An exception to the rule? Why Indonesia's Anti-corruption Commission succeeds while other don't: a comparison with the Philippines Ombudsman', U4 Anti Corruption Resource Centre, No. 4 (August).

Brommelhorster, Jorn and Wolf Christian Paes, eds (2003) *Soldiers in Business*. Bonn: International Centre for Conversion and Palgrave Macmillan.

Cacanindin, D. and A. Tingabngab (2003) 'Establishing the Role, Functions and Importance of Program Managers and Program Management Teams in the AFP Modernization Program Acquision Process: A Comparative Analysis with the US DOD System', Unpublished Master's Thesis. Naval Postgraduate School. Monterey, CA.

Chalk, P. (2014) Rebuilding while performing: Military modernization in the Philippines. Australian Strategic Policy Institute.

Chambers, P. (2012) A Precarious Path: The Evolution of Civil–Military Relations in the Philippines. *Asian Security* 8(2): 138–63.

Croissant, A. (2011) 'Civilian control over the military in East Asia': East Asian Institute Working Paper Series No. 31. East Asian Institute, Seoul, S. Korea.

Croissant. A., D. Kuehn and P. Lorenz. (2012) 'Breaking with the past? Civil–military relations in emerging democracies in East Asia'. East West Centre, Washington, D.C.

Cruz, F. Jr. (2010) 'The Eventual Demise of the Communist Insurgency in the Philippines'. Quezon City, Philippines: Philippine Institute for Peace, Violence and Terrorism Research.

De Castro, R. (1999) 'Adjusting to the Post-US Military Bases Era: The Ordeal of the Philippine Military's Modernization Program', *Armed Forces and Society* 26 (1): 119–38.

——— (2005) 'Philippine defence policy in the 21st Century: autonomous defence or back to the Alliance?' *Pacific Affairs* 78(3): 403–22

Deger, S. and S. Sen (1990) *Military Expenditure: The Political Economy of International Security*. Stockholm International Peace Research Institute and Oxford University Press: New York.

Development Academy of the Philippines. (2007) 'Integrity Development Review of the AFP- Philippine Navy: Executive Summary'.

Dressel, B. (2011) 'The Philippines: how much real democracy?' *International Political Science Review* 32,5: 529–45.

Feaver, P.D. (2003) *Armed Servants: Agency, Oversight and Civil–Military Relations*. Cambridge, MA: Harvard University Press.

Forbuena, Carmela. (2014) 'COA questions AFP transfer of 7.6 billion pesos from Treasury', Rappler News, 23 May 2014. http://www.rappler.com/nation/58573-coa-military-treasury, accessed 14 October 2016.

GMA News (2007) 'AFP to Rebuild War-Torn Areas', GMA News Online, August 24. http://www.gmanetwork.com/news/story/57611/news/nation/afp-to-rebuild-war-torn-areas, accessed 10 October 2014.

——— (2011) 'Corruption mess has Australia worried over aid to AFP', 10 February 2011. http://www.gmanetwork.com/news/story/212709/news/nation/corruption-mess-has-australia-worried-over-aid-to-afp, accessed 02 July 2015.

Gutierrez, Angelo (2011) 'No more malpractices in AFP, says spokesman', ABS CBN News, 10 February. http://news.abs-cbn.com/-depth/02/10/11/no-more-malpractices-afp-says-spokesman, accessed 02 July 2015.

Gutierrez, E. (2013) Bandits, kidnappers and bosses: kidnappers of the southern Philippines. In Lara, Francisco Jr. and Steven Schoofs (eds) *Out of the shadows: Violent conflict and the real economy of Mindanao*. International Alert: Manila. pp. 118–44.

Hall, R.A. (2010) 'Boots on Unstable Ground: Democratic Governance of the Armed Forces under post 9/11 US-Philippine Military Relations', *Asia Pacific Social Science Review* 10(2): 25–42.

——— (2014) 'Life after war in three settings: A comparison of Philippine reintegration programs for CPP-NPA and MNLF ex-combatants', paper presented at the Philippine Political Science Association conference, 2–3 May 2014. UP Visayas, Iloilo City.

——— (2015) 'Neither heroes nor villains: security arrangements between/among collocated armed actors in three Bangsamoro conflict areas', paper presented at the Philippine Political Science Association (PPSA) International Conference, 9 to 13 April 2015. Dipolog, Zamboanga del Norte.

——— (2016) 'Guardians reinvented: the Philippine army's nontraditional engagements in Panay island, Philippines', *Philippine Political Science Journal* 37(2): 1–24.

Hall, R. and A. Cular (2010) 'Civil–military relations in disaster rescue and relief operations: Response to the mudslide in southern Leyte, Philippines', *Scientia Militaria: South African Journal of Military Studies* 38(2): 62–88.

Hall, R. and J. C. Espia (2015) 'The Response to Typhoon Haiyan', in *Frameworks and Partnerships: Improving HA/DR in the Asia Pacific*. Seattle: Peace Winds America.

Heiduk, F. (2011) 'From guardians to democrats? Attempts to explain change and continuity in the civil–military relations of post-authoritarian Indonesia, Thailand and the Philippines', *The Pacific Review* 24(2): 249–71.

Hernandez, C.G. (2008) 'Rebuilding Democratic Institutions: Civil–military Relations in the Philippine Democratic Governance', in Hsin-Huang Michael Hsaio (ed.) *Asian New Democracies: The Philippines, South Korea and Taiwan Compared*. Taipei: Taiwan Foundation for Democracy and Centre for Asia Pacific Area Studies RCHSS Academia Sinica: 39–56.

Hernandez, C.G and M.C. Ubarra (1999) *Restoring and Strengthening Civilian Control: Best Practices in Civil–military Relations in the Philippines*. Quezon City: Institute for Strategic and Development Studies.

Hernandez, K.M. and H. J. Kraft (2010) 'Armed Forces as Veto Power: Civil–military Relations in the Philippines', in Paul Chambers and Aurel Croissant (eds) *Democracy under Stress: Civil–Military Relations in South and Southeast Asia*. ISIS Thailand 2010.

Huntington, S. P. (1967) *The Soldier and the State: The Theory and Politics of Civil–Military Relations*. Cambridge, MA: Belknap.

Hutchcroft, P. and J. Rocamora (2003) 'Strong demands and weak institutions:

The origins and evolution of the democratic deficit in the Philippines', *Journal of East Asian Studies* 3: 259–92.

Ilagan, G.T. (2014) 'Multi-stakeholder Security Strategies that De-escalate Armed Violence in Mindanao', *Open Journal of Social Science Research* 2(3):78–86.

Kimenye, M. and J. M. Mbaku (1995) 'Rents, military elites and political democracy', *European Journal of Political Economy* 11: 699–708.

Lee. T. (2008) 'The Military's Corporate Interests: The Main Reason for Intervention in Indonesia and the Philippines?' *Armed Forces and Society* 34(3): 491–502.

Levy, Y. (2012) 'A Revised Model of Civilian Control of the Military: The Interaction between the Republican Exchange and the Control Exchange', *Armed Forces and Society* 38(4): 529–58.

Lotta-Hedman, E. (2001) 'The Philippines: Not so Military, Not so Civil', in Muthiah Alagappa (ed.) *Coercion and Governance: the Declining Political Role of the Military in Asia*. Stanford, USA: Stanford University Press: 165–86.

Lotta-Hedman, E. and J. Sidel (2000) *Philippine Politics and Society in the 20th Century: Colonial Legacies, Post Colonial Trajectories*. New York and London: Routledge.

Manasan, R. (2013) 'Analysis of the President's Budget for 2012.' Philippine Institute for Development Studies Discussion Paper 2013-31.

Manila Times (2015) 'BCDA generated 29 billion pesos for military modernization,' (27 April). http://www.manilatimes.net/bcda-generates-p29b-for-military-modernization/178952/, accessed 14 October 2016 .

Mangahas, Malou (2011) 'On EDSA's 25th anniversary, corruption devours the Armed Forces', Philippine Center of Investigative Journalism (22 February). http://pcij.org/stories/on-edsas-25th-corruption-devours-the-armed-forces/, accessed 14 October 2016.

————— (2011a) 'Petty, big, routine graft: a lucrative trade at AFP.' Philippine Centre for Investigative Journalism (23 February). http://pcij.org/stories/petty-big-routine-graft-a-lucrative-trade-at-afp/, accessed 20 November 2014.

Mindanews (2011) 'Ex-Navy whistleblower says she has evidence on AFP fund mess' (22 February). http://www.mindanews.com/special-reports/2011/02/22/special-report-ex-navy-whistleblower-says-she-has-evidence-on-afp-fund-mess, accessed 30 August 2015.

Philippine Daily Inquirer (2007) 'US envoy says military aid to RP still work in progress' (6 November).

Philippine Star (2009) 'COA: AFP failed to remit P244-million Balikatan fund' (20 May). http://www.philstar.com:8080/headlines/469094/coa-afp-failed-remit-p244-million-balikatan-fund, accessed 30 August 2015.

Pion-Berlin, D. (1997) *Through Corridors of Power: Institutions and Civil–military Relations in Argentina.* University Park, PA: Pennsylvania State University Press.

Porcalla, D. (2015) 'Palace: Supreme Court declared "pork" illegal', *The Philippine Star* (12 August).

Quilop. R., ed. (2007) *Peace and development: towards ending insurgency.* Quezon City: AFP Office of Strategic and Special Studies.

———— (2009) 'Responding to Disasters: Framework, Challenges and Prospects for the Philippines', in Rosalie Arcala Hall (ed.) *Civil–Military Cooperation in Emergency Relief.* Quezon City: Central Book Supply.

Quitoriano, E. (2013) 'Shadow Guns or Shadow State? The Illicit Gun Trade Conflict-Affected Mindanao', in Francisco Lara, Jr. and Steven Schoofs (eds.) *Out of the shadows: Violent conflict and the real economy of Mindanao.* Manila: International Alert: 49–84.

Ramos, Marlin (2015) 'COA to OPAPP: Where did P 1.14 billion go?', *Philippine Daily Inquirer* (28 April). http://newsinfo.inquirer.net/688049/coa-to-opapp-where-did-p1-14 ... outm_medium=twitter&utm_campaign=social&utm_source=twitterfeed, accessed 29 April 2015.

Rappler News (2013) 'Military pensions in danger as COA reports PhP 47 B fund shortfall' (18 November). http://www.rappler.com/nation/43959-military-pensions-in-danger-afp-rsbs-coa-report, accessed 30 August 2015.

Rodell, P. (2004) 'The Philippines: Playing Out Long Conflicts', *Southeast Asian Affairs*: 187–204. http://bookshop.iseas.edu.sg, accessed 27 July 2006.

Russell, D. R. (2013) 'Civil Military Operations (CMO) in the Philippines: Examining Battle Space Management in the Past and the Present'. PhD Dissertation. Graduate School of Asia-Pacific Studies. Waseda University.

Salvador, A. and J. Santiago-Oreta (2013) 'Defence Budget and Spending: Alignment and Priorities (Philippine Defence Spending 2001–2012)' Quezon City, Philippines: Friedrich Ebert Stiftung and Working Group on Security Sector Reform, Ateneo de Manila University.

San Juan, E. Jr. (2007) *US imperialism and revolution in the Philippines.* New York: Palgrave Macmillan.

Schulzke, M. (2010) 'Democratization and Military Reform in the Philippines', *Journal of Asia Pacific Studies* 1(2):320–37.

Selochan, V. (2004) 'The Military and Fragile Democracy in the Philippines', in RJ May and Vibrato Selochan (eds.) *The Military and Democracy in Asia and the Pacific.* : Canberra, Australia: Australia National University E-Press: 59–69.

Stepan, A. (1986) 'The New Professionalism in Internal Warfare and Military Role Expansion', in Abraham Lowenthal and J. Samuel Fitch (eds) *Armies and Politics in Latin America,* rev. ed. New York: Holmes and Meier: 134–50.

Stockholm International Peace Research Institute (2016). SIPRI Military Expenditure Database: Data of all countries from 1988–2015 in constant USD, https://www.sipri.org/databases/milex, accessed 01 October 2016.

Teodoro, G. (2008) 'Reforming Philippine Defence', *Military Technology* 9: 108–13.

Tulfo, A. (2013) 'General Garcia: how the big fish got away' *Newsbreak* (11 April). http://www.rappler.com/newsbreak/20027-garcia-militay-corruption-deal, accessed 02 July 2015.

Tusalem, R.F. (2014) 'Bringing the military back in: The politicization of the military and its effect on democratic consolidation', *International Political Science Review* 35(4): 482–501.

USAID (n.d.) *US Overseas Loans Grants* (Greenbook). Washington: United States Agency for International Development. http://gbk.eads.usaidall-net.gov, accessed 10 February 2010.

Villanueva, S. (2013) 'Cross-border illicit trade in Sulu and Tawi-tawi: the coexistence of economic agendas and violent conflict', in Lara, Francisco Jr. and Steven Schoofs (eds) *Out of the shadows: Violent conflict and the real economy of Mindanao.* Manila: International Alert: 197–218.

Welch, C., ed. (1976) *Civilian Control of the Military: Theory and Cases from Developing Countries. Albany.* NY: State University of New York Press.

Wong, P.N. (2008) 'Towards a More Comprehensive Analysis of Warlord Politics: Constitutive Agency, PatronClient Networks and Robust Action', *Asian Journal of Political Science* 16(2): 173–95

Yabes, C. (2011) *Peace Warriors: On the Trail with Filipino Soldiers.* Manila: Anvil Press.

CHAPTER 8

The Politics of Securing Khaki Capitalism in Democratizing Indonesia

Jun Honna

Introduction

The military was the backbone of the authoritarian regime led by President Suharto, who ruled Indonesia for more than three decades since the mid-1960s. With the collapse of the Suharto regime in 1998 (following a nationwide democratic movement), public 'back to the barracks' demands pushed the military to conduct reforms aimed to disengage itself from political activism. The military spokesman, Col. Ahmad Yani Basuki, who submitted his PhD dissertation on military reform to the University of Indonesia in 2007, showed that the military completed 31 internal changes between 1998 and 2007 and argued that these reflected a strong institutional commitment to reform (Sinar Harapan 2007). On the other hand, civil society groups denounced repeated military atrocities in conflict areas and generally claimed that military reform had been more show than substance, since military remained unaccountable for its role in several instances of excessive force and resort to violence (Human Rights Watch 2006).

As the country's democratic consolidation went on, especially under the Yudhoyono presidency (2004–14) and the current Joko Widodo government, the public image of the military improved significantly, as seen in opinion polls that identify the military as the most trustworthy institution in the country.[1] Today, Indonesia's military adaptation to

---

1. See, for example, Lembaga Survei Indonesia (2015)..

democratization is also positively evaluated by the international community, which has been disappointed by other democracies in Southeast Asia, particularly in both Thailand and the Philippines, where civil–military relations are apparently vulnerable due mainly to military attempts to challenge civilian political leadership, both overtly and covertly.

Does this mean that the military has successfully reformed itself in line with a civilian effort to establish democratic civilian control over the military, and that military activities are transparent and limited to legitimate ones? I argue that this is not the case. The stabilization of post-authoritarian civil–military relations has been achieved at the cost of allowing the military to maintain its institutional prerogatives, most notably economic interests generated by khaki capitalism. The cost is crucial to an understanding of the stable civil–military power balance in Indonesia's democratic consolidation, and this chapter examines the politics of making a trade-off between stability in civil–military relations and stagnation of reforms intended to make the military genuinely subservient to civilian leadership. To this end, I analyse how military reform aiming to limit the role of the military to 'external defence' has been emasculated by army elites in order to preserve their vested interests, in particular capital accumulation. The study also examines how the principle of civilian supremacy has become a dead letter. These two processes have effectively contributed to the making of a stable partnership between civilian political leaders and military elites, with the cost of consolidating a low-quality civil–military relationship in the age of democracy.

Importantly, the preservation of khaki capitalism in Indonesia today should be understood in this political context. The scale of its capital accumulation shrank dramatically in the post-authoritarian period, due to the pressure to withdraw military activities outside of defence affairs and to streamline unprofitable military enterprises. However, the military still enjoys unaccountable fundraising activities, which enable it to sustain organizational practices that stem from the country's independence. These include unofficial financing of secret military operations that could create favourable politico-security environments for local military commands throughout the archipelago. Until such a space for autonomous self-financing is eliminated, Indonesia's endeavour to establish democratic, civilian control over national governance will be incomplete. Nevertheless, this incompleteness has ironically contributed to the stabilization of post-authoritarian civil–military relations, as it helps to create a pragmatic consensus, or a pact, of mutual non-intervention between military and political elites. The pact is simple: civilian politicians do not problematize the military's core institutional interests, including independent business activities, in return for securing the support of military elites in running civilian governments.

The current mode of Indonesia's khaki capitalism is best understood by contextualizing its function in a broader civil–military political power balance, rather than simply mapping and explaining the details of military business operations. Unlike countries in Southeast Asia where military engagement in business is widespread and legitimized by non-democratic governments, Indonesia's case illustrates how the military attempts to preserve its khaki capitalism in the face of pressures for reform in the age of democracy. Such uniqueness should not be overlooked, and it is against a backdrop of pragmatic compromise on all sides that we will examine the military politics of preserving business activities.

Genesis of khaki capitalism

During the Suharto presidency (1967–98), the military consisted of four services, including the police. The army, responsible for internal security, relied on a territorial command system with ten army divisions based around the archipelago and extending politico-security surveillance down to the village level.[2] The police assumed responsibility for law enforcement and supported the army's often repressive approaches to handling internal security.

---

2. The territorial command system was established in parallel with the government structure. Army headquarters, at the top of the command hierarchy, supervised Military Area Commands (Kodam) at the provincial level. Each Kodam oversaw several Military Regency Commands (Korem) at the regency (*kabupaten*) level. A Korem administered various Military District Commands (Kodim) at the district (*kecamatan*) level. A Kodim was responsible for several Military Sub-district Commands (Koramil), and they supervised commissioned officers, called *babinsa*, in each village throughout the archipelago. In this way, the military network of surveillance and repression was developed to implement the orders of the army chief down to the village level. On the army in the Suharto era, see, for example, Crouch (1988).

Suharto's Indonesia established a military authoritarian polity in which the army played a twin role in national defence and politics. This role was formally known as the 'dual function', or *dwifungsi*.[3] The military and police focused on preserving internal stability and were involved in a range of activities not normally associated with defence responsibilities. Dwifungsi was deployed to legitimize a paramount political role for the armed forces. Moreover, it served as a doctrine to justify the military's involvement in national economic development. Thus, dwifungsi was the core of Indonesia's khaki capitalism, and it was rooted in the history of nation-building since 1945 when the country declared independence after World War II. Indonesia's army was formulated during the independence war (1945–49) against Dutch colonialism, and it was largely a self-financed organization that relied heavily on volunteer fighters recruited around the country. To feed them, and to finance operational costs of their guerrilla warfare, every local command was expected to engage in fundraising activities. These activities typically involved provision of transportation services to local traders and farmers. After independence, however, the peacetime business partnership developed quickly to cover large-scale trade in various goods, typically agricultural products and natural resources.[4] The newly independent country had no capacity to fully finance the military budget, so the government encouraged local commanders to extend their fundraising efforts in order to self-finance military activities.

Khaki capitalism was institutionalized under Suharto's military regime as authoritarian developmentalism. The military established enterprises in various sectors in order to expand economic activities, and they were given contracts for government-managed development projects. During 30 years of Suharto era, the military enjoyed capital accumulation in almost all major business fields, including natural resource extraction, banking, construction, transportation, real estate and tourism.[5] Military enterprises were active in collaborating with state and private companies in strategic sectors. For example, Pertamina, a state-owned oil and natural gas corporation, was a stronghold of capital

---

3. On the discourse on *dwifungsi* ideology and politics, see Honna (2003).

4. Regarding military business in early years of independence, see Sundhaussen (1982).

5. For details, see for example Robison (1987) and Crouch (1988).

accumulation for many high-ranking officers. Mining was also a major business field for the military, as seen for example in Papua, where it operates the world's largest gold mine in a giant joint venture with Freeport-McMoRan. Every service branch, local command and soldier developed business activities to enjoy the fruits of dwifungsi. Apart from military-owned enterprises, men in uniform were active in managing cooperatives and foundations that generated income by owning shares in companies. It was through these business networks that the military established Indonesia's khaki capitalism during three decades of authoritarianism. Suharto's generals typically claimed that military fundraising was needed to compensate for national budget that could not even cover soldiers' most basic welfare needs. This narrative, all the more powerful because it was demonstrably true, provided rhetorical cover for the establishment of military–economic linkages whose profits could be flexibly used for any purposes for the military as an institution, including enriching military elites and, to the extent necessary, covering those basic welfare needs.

During the Suharto period, it was understood that official government defence budget only covered around thirty percent of actual military spending. This meant that the remaining seventy percent was self-financed by the military. Thus, it is clear that the military relied heavily on the khaki capitalism, which generated at least seventy percent of actual military spending, but it is not clear how big the military business was. The khaki funds came from three sources: military enterprises; military's security 'services' to civilian clients; and illegal business activities backed by military personnel (and units). Even with the military, however, the contributions of these business activities to the actual scale of khaki capitalism remain murky. It is also unclear how much of the gains of khaki capitalism were used for 'institutional purposes' and how much went directly into the pockets of individuals.

The fall of Suharto in May 1998 became a watershed for the country's khaki capitalism. In response to a widespread democratic movement triggered by economic crisis, Suharto stepped down from presidency and his resignation created political space for questioning the role of the military and the relevance of dwifungsi. Emboldened civilian leaders in both parliament and civil society criticized atrocities committed by the military and demanded military reform to professionalize the armed services and to institutionalize civilian control over all aspects of military activities. The demand for military reform inevitably extended to calls that the military abandon its involvement in non-military affairs, including political and economic activities. How have military elites responded to these pressures for change?

Reforming the military

The military leadership under General Wiranto was tasked to deal with the end of Suharto's authoritarian government with formulating a vision of military reform. This responsibility was delegated to reform-minded intellectual officers such as Lt General Susilo Bambang Yudhoyono (who in 2004 became the country's sixth president), Lt General Agus Widjojo and Maj. General Agus Wirahadikusumah.[6] One of their first proposals was the separation of the national police from the military.

The idea was formulated in an army seminar convened in September 1998 at which emerged the initial agenda for military reform, dubbed the 'New Paradigm'.[7] In April 1999, the policy proposal for splitting the police and military was implemented and the military returned to the pre-Suharto period organization of three services – army, navy and air force. This functional separation was inevitably accompanied by the redefinition of responsibilities between the police (Polisi Republik Indonesia, or Polri) and the military (Tentara Nasional Indonesia, or TNI).[8] In an attempt to professionalize the security services, the TNI was assigned responsibility for national 'defence' and the police given the role of maintaining domestic 'security' and 'order'.[9] With this arrangement, political elites both in parliament and in civil society expected

6. In May 1998, Yudhoyono served Wiranto as chief of socio-political affairs, Widjojo as commander of Military Staff and Command College, and Wirahadikusumah as assistant for general planning.

7. The official document of the New Paradigm can be found in the seminar report, Sesko ABRI (1998).

8. A list of acronyms is provided at the end of the chapter.

9. The legal basis for the functional separation was prepared in 2000, when parliamentarians passed two decrees in the People's Representative Assembly (MPR) – the country's highest decision-making body. The two MPR decrees are: Ketetapan MPR No.VI/2000 Tentang Pemisahan Tentara Nasional Indonesia dan Kepolisian Negara Republik Indonesia; *and* Ketetapan MPR No.VII/2000 Tentang Peran Tentara Nasional Indonesia dan Peran Kepolisian Negara Republik Indonesia.

that the new role-definition would disengage the TNI from internal security missions and lead it to professionalize its capacities regarding external defence matters.

However, the organization of the army was virtually untouched; the army merely scrapped its departments in charge of political operations without redesigning the military structure. Further, as a result of the reform, there was growing dissatisfaction among TNI officers. Given the reduced number of posts within the TNI and the shifting of domestic security functions to the police (an organization that enjoyed far less prestige and status), TNI officers found gaining promotions much more difficult. These frustrations fanned distrust and resentment of the police and civilian policymakers.

Significantly, the country's political environment over the next few years strengthened such frustrations within the TNI. The major factor was the military's humiliation over Aceh and the independence of East Timor. Wiranto's military was forced to admit mass killing on Aceh that spanned decades, and it was blamed for failing to prevent the independence of East Timor in 1999. In both cases, the army had no effective response to critics who argued that two decades of military-led policies in Aceh and East Timor yielded nothing but dead bodies and international criticism against the military repression. Moreover, in early 1999, ethnic violence broke out in West Kalimantan, and religious wars also erupted in the towns of Ambon (Maluku) and Poso (Central Sulawesi). Soon after, armed conflicts expanded to Central Kalimantan and North Maluku (van Klinken 2007). The escalation of violence in these five conflict areas resulted in ethnic cleansing, mass murder and the destruction of local communities. As violence and disorder spread, post-Suharto Indonesia seemed on the verge of becoming a Balkanized nation (*AAP General News* 2000; *BBC News* 2001).

The inability of the police to contain communal violence and maintain security drew strong criticism from the TNI. Some high-ranking officers argued that the separation of the police from the military had been too hasty because the police force was not prepared to handle security problems.[10] Brushing over the military's own well-documented shortcomings in dealing with communal violence in an ethnically neutral fashion, conservative army officers attempted to reassert a military

10. Interview with Lt Gen. Djoko Santoso (Deputy Army Chief of Staff), 1 June 2004.

role in internal security matters by dwelling on the deficiencies of the police.

Khaki capitalism in crisis

The military propaganda campaign waged against the police in the national media was not only motivated by institutional interests in reclaiming responsibility for internal stability. Importantly, it was also driven by TNI's concern for khaki capitalism. There was also a growing turf war between the police and TNI over the conduct of business activities. Before the separation of the police, it was an open secret that the military profited from offering 'security services' for private companies – including those operating brothels, gambling dens and nightclubs.[11] The transfer of domestic security duties from the military to the police inevitably reduced lucrative opportunities for the military as the newly independent police muscled in on these services. The impact on the TNI was devastating, particularly for local army commands which had relied heavily on revenue from such unofficial business activities to provide for their troops' 'welfare'. As discussed above, military budgets from the central government did not come close to covering operating expenses, and it was expected that the military would engage in entrepreneurial activities to make up for the shortfall. These military enterprises faced serious problems in the 1997–98 Asian economic crisis and many of them were almost to bankrupt due to their bad corporate management.[12] As off-budget income dried up significantly, police encroachment since 1999 was a serious threat for the military. Frustrations with the military sometimes led to outright conflicts.

In 2001, for example, the tension between military and police units in the East Java town of Madiun escalated into a violent clash marked by a pitched gun battle. TNI soldiers ran amok, attacking the Madiun police station, killing two citizens and wounding several policemen. The army chief-of-staff at that time, Gen. Endriartono Sutarto, admitted that the soldiers involved in the clash had been involved with illegal businesses in

---

11. For details of these operations, see Human Rights Watch (2006).

12. The collapse of rupiah in 1997 forced many army enterprises to close down. The most symbolic case included the army newspaper, *Angkatan Bersenjata*. Its bankruptcy led the head of military intelligence to forge currency to pay the militias in East Timor. On this account, see Anderson (2008: 40).

the area, referring to brothels, gambling dens and the drug trade (*Jakarta Post* 2001). In the following year, similar mayhem erupted in cities such as Maumere (Flores) and Binjai (North Sumatra).[13] In response, top leaders of the military and police pledged to tighten discipline of local personnel in the field, but this did not stop the clashes. At least six serious brawls between the military and police occurred in 2007, and even more cases were reported in 2010, for example in South Sumatera, North Maluku, Ambon, Makassar and Papua. The rivalry never ended, as 2014 witnessed seven big clashes in various cities in West Java, Batam (Riau), Papua, Ambon, Yogyakarta and Binjai (Tribunnews.com 2014). In many cases, we saw the clash between army troops stationed at the local military command and the police mobile brigade at the local police command (Baker 2008). This reflected nothing but the fact that local security forces had been engaging in turf wars for illicit business profits throughout the archipelago, and it was a big challenge for the long-established khaki capitalism in Indonesia.

In the eyes of the police, these brawls were basically triggered by 'the jealousy of the military which has no more authority to dictate to society but is still preoccupied with the old thinking.'[14] But it was also evident that local police's illegal racketing angered the public and it frequently developed into communal violence (International Crisis Group 2012). For its part, the TNI has taken every opportunity to undermine the police, encouraged by opinion surveys that repeatedly label the police as the most corrupt institution in the country (Transparency International 2007: 22). Clearly, the rivalry, suspicion, resentment and hostility be-tween the two institutions are now deeply rooted.

In the TNI's way of thinking, the police were an obvious disturbance for the maintenance of khaki capitalism – therefore it should be neu-tralized. In doing so, it was necessary to convince political elites that the police were not trustworthy and were unable to handle domestic security without military assistance. With this, the TNI hoped to offset opinion favouring constraints on its own role in domestic affairs. If the TNI could regain an internal security role, the police would have no choice but to share security-related business turf, including protection rackets, with the military.

---

13. For details, see The Editors (2003).

14. Interviews with police officers in the National Police Headquarters, July 2007.

Furthermore, regaining a role in internal security was crucial for maintaining the size of the military. It was particularly the army that was strongly concerned about pressure to reform its territorial command structure – a holdover from the authoritarian past – which was originally built to deal with internal security problems. By reclaiming a role in internal security, the TNI would be able to maintain its territorial command structure with only cosmetic changes. For most army officers, the elimination of the territorial command structure is unacceptable. They believe that Indonesia – a multi-ethnic nation spread over a large archipelago – may fall apart without the firm grip of the military, and also fear, perhaps even more, that such a reform would inevitably lead to institutional downsizing.

Thus, the need for the army to deal with domestic security has been emphasized against the direction of reform, and – in addition to discrediting the police – the army has staved off this reform pressure by fanning fears about the role of external actors in generating internal instability. All these efforts were expected to strengthen the argument that the TNI's territorial commands were still relevant even though its main institutional duty was external defence. High-ranking military officers were especially interested in preservation of territorial commands, as they could then continue to serve as footholds of khaki capitalism throughout the archipelago.

War on terrorism and military prerogatives

Under such a circumstance, the war on terrorism created an institutional opportunity to regain lost ground and deflect pressures to reform (cf. Institute for Policy Analysis of Conflict 2015). In order to sell the idea that defence and internal security are inseparable, officers have invoked the concept of a 'grey zone'. They assert that Indonesia's geopolitical circumstances require TNI to defend the nation from domestic penetration by external threats, and that domestic security should be an integral part of defence operations. From this standpoint, the army began to criticize the 2002 Defence Law. They problematized Article 7, which states that the role of the military was to respond to military threats but assigned non-military threats to other government institutions. In the eyes of army officers, this law ignores the 'grey zone' and does not reflect the reality of defence–security linkages.

A window of opportunity to become more assertive came following the October 2002 terrorist bombing in Bali. This tragedy revealed Indonesia's vulnerable security conditions. The call for improving Indonesia's security management by the international community, and the need to protect the valuable tourist industry, allowed the TNI to revitalize the activity of *babinsa* – the village level unit in the territorial command – to detect possible terrorist movements. In the aftermath of the Bali bombing, Indonesia's political community was reticent about questioning the military tactic to redeploy territorial command resources for counterterrorism operations.

Subsequently in 2003, when the TNI published its first post-Suharto Defence White Book (Departmen Pertahanan 2003), the army-orchestrated 'grey zone' argument was more explicitly articulated in terms of defence–security syncretism. The TNI claimed that the primary concerns of Indonesia's defence sector had shifted from traditional threats – i.e., conventional military attacks by foreign countries – to non-traditional ones such as terrorism, piracy, illegal migrants, separatist movements and armed rebellions. In order to respond to these new threats, it was argued, the TNI needed to strengthen its capacity and role in operations other than warfare in which the demarcation between defence and security was irrelevant. Since then, the military has intensified internal socialization about the legitimacy of defence–security syncretism by producing guidelines regarding non-traditional military threats and responses (Markas Besar TNI 2003). The Defence White Book was updated in 2008 and in 2015. Both editions strengthen the commitment to developing the seamless role of the TNI in both military and non-military defence (Departmen Pertahanan 2008: 46–51; Kementerian Pertahanan 2015: 45–57).

In 2010, these pro-military arguments began to find their way into government policy. The National Anti-Terrorism Agency (BNTP) was established directly under President Yudhoyono, and the TNI was institutionally included in this domestic security task. This was nothing less than official recognition that TNI is part of the internal security apparatus – a significant retreat from the original reform vision. When the succeeding Joko Widodo government faced a resurgent terrorist threat in Poso (Central Sulawesi) in 2015, the TNI Commander General Moeldoko immediately decided to conduct counterterrorism 'training exercises' in Poso with the purpose of cracking down on militants with suspected links to Syria's Islamic State. This operation was authorized by the President and, with it, TNI learned that it was now possible legitimately to conduct internal security operations under the guise of 'training'.

In this way, TNI has skilfully neutralized pressure to limit its role to external defence by incorporating non-traditional security issues – notably counterterrorism – into the scope of the defence agenda. In redefining defence threats, it has effectively sidestepped laws that attempt to restrict its role to defence affairs. Although TNI's efforts to undo the separation of security and defence partly reflect its long-standing self-image as the sole guardian of the nation, it also reflects institutional resistance to reform targeting the territorial command structure. As discussed above, the territorial commands are vital for the army to promote fundraising, generate economic opportunities and maintain its khaki capitalism at levels sufficient to sustain a force that is the largest – and thus most powerful and prestigious service – within the TNI. It is via this territorial command system that army officers have gained access to the local politico-economic elite and wielded oligarchic power in the provinces (Mietzner 2003; Honna 2006).

As discussed above, Indonesia's khaki capitalism experienced a crisis after Suharto's fall, as many military-owned companies went bankrupt and new competition with the police intensified in the market of the security-provider business. The profits from these military businesses collapsed and many local commands experienced demoralization of soldiers, who started to seek alternative profits in criminal sectors by offering protection rackets for the business of smuggling goods and people. To stop the collapse of the khaki business regime, it was imperative for the TNI to emasculate democratic pressures to reform its territorial command structure, which had been a vital bulkhead for its capital accumulation activities. The military successfully undermined such a pressure by inventing the 'grey zone' theory that attempted to legitimize TNI's domestic security role in the name of defending the country from terrorism.

It is important to note that TNI's business activities have survived thanks to the policy of Yudhoyono, a reputed reformist general and the first popularly elected president in Indonesia. When the parliament passed a new law on the military – which was aimed at defining the role of the military in the post-authoritarian era and supporting the reform for professionalism – in September 2004 (Law No. 23/2004) under the Megawati administration, it was expected that the TNI would be financially accountable in the near future, as the law's Article 76 banned military commercialism and emphasized the government takeover of 'business activities owned and operated by the military' within five years. Following this, in 2009, the Yudhoyono government produced an action plan to take over military business. It was to demonstrate the government's commitment to eliminate the traditional practice of off-budget fundraising of the military. However, as Mietzner and Misol (2013) evaluate, the action plan has left the large field of non-formal fundraising untouched. As shown above, it is now very common to see soldiers involved in illegal fundraising activities, and it has been institutionalized since the post-Suharto crisis of khaki capitalism. This illegal mode of military business was neglected in Yudhoyno's idea of ending military commercialism. Moreover, military-run foundations and cooperatives were technically exempted from the government takeover, and this measure helped local territorial commands to continue their capital accumulation activities throughout the archipelago. Despite the best intentions of reformers both within the military and in the government, the TNI has successfully preserved the long-term economic prerogatives associated with its nationwide territorial command system.

Also under the Yudhoyono presidency, a further setback for limiting the role of the military was administered in 2012 when the law on handling social conflict (UU No. 7/2012 tentang Penanganan Konflik Sosial) was enacted. The law effectively allows the TNI to suppress riots and disturbances without authorization from local government leaders. Now the TNI only needs to notify its suppressive activities to them, a clear setback from the 2004 military law that required presidential permission for the conduct of military operations other than war. Clearly, the TNI has succeeded in lowering the boundary between domestic security and national defence, and it continues to insert itself into roles the police forces believe to be their responsibility.

In retrospect, the separation of the police from the military was the first reform project in post-authoritarian civil–military relations. It was designed with the expectation of promoting military professionalism in external defence matters. However, the TNI is apparently not willing to relinquish domestic security functions to the police, because it adamantly believes that losing this security role would endanger the *raison d'être* of its territorial command system, a key and cherished institutional foundation for the survival of khaki capitalism. Yudhoyono, a retired general who ruled the country for ten years (2004–14), established a stable civil–military relationship based on his personal commitment to protect TNI's institutional prerogatives in the age of democracy.

What, then, is the lesson for civilian political leaders? How can they deal with TNI's lingering perceptions from the Suharto era that resist change and justify, in the minds of officers, sabotage of reform initiatives? The TNI still feels it is the sole arbiter of what is best for the TNI, including the future of khaki capitalism. Under such a circumstance, how it is possible to consolidate a principle of civilian supremacy and establish a democratic civilian control over the armed forces that could enhance institutional accountability of TNI? In examining these questions, we discuss TNI's politics of undermining effective civilian oversight of military activities in the following section.

Emasculating civilian oversight of the military

The principle of civilian supremacy over the military was introduced near the end of the Suharto era in 1998.[15] Under the Habibie administration (1998–99), the principle was not institutionally clarified: General Wiranto served as both TNI commander and defence minister. After the general elections in 1999, the parliament elected as President Abdurrahman Wahid, the leader of Nahdatul Ulama (NU, the largest Islamic organization in the country) and founder of the NU-based political party, Partai Kebangkitan Bangsa). Wahid's administration (1999–2001) was the first to appoint civilian defence ministers, Professor Juwono Sudarsono and Mohammad Mahfud Mahmodin. The next president, Megawati Sukarnoputri (2001–04), also appointed a civilian, Matori Abdul Djalil, as minister of defence, but due to illness he was largely absent from his duties. Since Megawati did not replace him, the Ministry was virtually controlled by secretary-generals who were army lieutenant generals. Under President Susilo Bambang

---

15. Before Suharto's rule, there were civilian defence ministers in 1950s, for example Hamengku Buwono IX and Iwa Kusumasumatri.

Yudhoyono, Professor Junowo Sudarsono was reappointed as defence minister, and then replaced by Purnomo Yusgiantoro in a cabinet shake-up at the beginning of Yudhoyono's second term. Under the Joko Widodo administration (2014–), however, the post of defence minister was given to Ryamizard Ryacudu, a retired army general who served as Army Chief during the Megawati administration. Joko Widodo (popularly called Jokowi) is a member of Megawati's political party, Indonesian Democratic Party of Struggle (Partai Demokrasi Indonesia Perjuangan, or PDI-P), and it is widely understood that the appointment of Ryamizard is her instruction. With this, Jokowi effectively broke the post-Suharto practice of appointing a 'civilian with no military background' as defence minister, and opened the door for a 'civilian with military background in the past' to take over the post in the future.

Clearly, the recruitment of civilians depends largely on the president's political will. There is no legal foundation that institutionalizes civilian leadership in the military structure. Equally important, secretaries-general and all directors-general in the Ministry have been active generals representing the TNI voice and neutralizing civilian initiatives in formulating defence budgets, strategies, deployments and other significant administrative matters related to the military.[16] This arrangement has restricted the influence of civilian defence ministers over the military. Understanding this structural barrier to civilian control, the TNI now has no problem in working with a civilian defence minister whose ceremonial role bolsters the military's reform propaganda of respecting civilian supremacy.

It is also important to examine the relationship between TNI and the legislative branch. Until they were abolished in 2004, military-controlled appointed seats in both national and local parliaments were occupied by active-service officers. These members constituted a lobby group for the military headquarters within the parliaments, enabling the military to exercise political influence in the process of legislative deliberations. In this manner, civilian supremacy was not truly exercised in the parliaments until 2004 when the country held the second general (legislative) elections after the fall of Suharto. It was only after the inauguration of

---

16. Regarding the problem of civilian leadership in the Defence Ministry, see Anggoro (2007).

the Yudhoyono presidency in October 2004 that parliaments were fully occupied by civilian politicians.

Have civilian-dominated parliaments taken the initiative on military reform? Since 1999, the relationship between TNI and the parliaments has been accommodative, rather than competitive. Parliamentarians, especially from the three big political parties – Golkar, the government party in the Suharto era, Megawati's PDI-P, and Yudhoyono's 2009 election-winning Democrat Party – have done little to pressure the TNI to accelerate internal reform. They have been more interested in gaining issue-specific support from the TNI. Most notably, in the half-year process of impeaching President Wahid in 2001, the coalition of major political parties approached military members in parliament to support impeachment. During general elections in 1999 and 2004, both Golkar and PDI-P wooed military leaders in Jakarta and other cities to support their election campaigns in various ways, despite TNI's statement of political neutrality during the elections. During the Yudhoyono presidency (2004–14), the ruling coalition parties in the parliament included Yudhoyono's Democrat Party, which embraced many retired military officers who were not interested in the idea of promoting civilian supremacy over the military.[17] Under the current Jokowi administration, the PDI-P came back as the largest party in the parliament and demonstrated its indifference to the concept of civilian supremacy by placing a very conservative retired army general in the post of defence minister, as discussed above.

It is also widely believed that some elite politicians have been involved in the brokering of arms procurements that has contributed to price hikes for imported military hardware and low transparency in Indonesia's arms trade.[18] Parliaments now have a larger say in the political process, as a result of post-Suharto constitutional reform. However, they have never taken serious initiatives in shaping the roadmap of military reform. The current performance of legislators is largely limited to such activities as enacting military-related bills drafted by the government, conducting 'fit-and-proper tests' for the candidate for military commander appointed by the president and convening ad hoc investigations of alleged military wrongdoing, including human rights

---

17. On Yudhoyono's Democrat Party, see Honna (2012).

18. On the brokerage, see for example *Jakarta Post* (2011).

abuses and other crimes. These activities attract public attention, but there is no sustained commitment to military reform and little participation in defence planning. There is an obvious lack of capability in the parliament to oversee defence affairs (Sebastian and Gindarsah 2013: 298). In the eyes of many politicians, military and defence issues do not attract voters, while a confrontation with generals – who can, *inter alia*, mobilize covert intelligence operations – carries considerable potential risks. Even after 18 years of democratization, parliamentarians remain cautious about pressuring the military.

In reality, the practice of civilian supremacy in post-authoritarian Indonesia is extremely weak despite the appointment of civilians to head the Defence Ministry and formal legislative oversight powers over military policies. Here we see the tension between new institutional arrangements and old practices, which together lead to the 'ceremonialisation' of civilian supremacy. According to the defence law in 2002 and the military law in 2004, the Defence Ministry can exercise control over the military, but in practice, effective military resistance ensures that the law remains little more than an ornament. The military has successfully resisted the placement of its military commander under the authority of the defence minister, just as it has resisted parliamentary oversight. Particularly in parliaments at the provincial, regency and district levels, politicians are seen by the local army officers as patrimonial agents eager to co-opt local military elites into their network of influence. For those local politicians, the practice of civilian supremacy is nothing but an opportunity to develop mutually beneficial relationships with the local military command, such as security protection and business collaboration. Thus, effective and democratic oversight of the military is not happening in local parliaments and civilian supremacy is reduced to a charade. Mietzner (2006) argues that second-generation reforms – which go beyond formalistic civilian control of the military – remain an immense challenge for the country's political leaders. Clearly a breakthrough strategy is required both to close the gap between law and common practice and to promote second-generation reforms in civil–military relations.

There are two issues at the core of the current impasse. First is how to demilitarize a Defence Ministry that has remained under the strong influence of military elites and is now controlled by a retired army general. It is important for the political leadership to ease military suspicion toward the civilian handling of defence policies by convincing generals that the military will gain institutional benefits from the Ministry's 'civilianization'. As seen in many democratized countries, civilianized defence bureaucracies tend to develop professional lobbyist circles that are more sophisticated and effective than military officers in negotiating defence budgets and navigating legal affairs, as well as in promoting peace diplomacy, security dialogue and cooperation in the international arena. With such civilian assistance, the armed forces could deploy their human and institutional resources more efficiently. In post-Suharto Indonesia, there has been little effort towards convincing the military leadership about how it can benefit from such a transformation. Up to now, it sees reform only as a diminution of its power, status and autonomy – including the self-financing of off-budget income.

The second core issue is how to insulate the military from patronage politics in both national and local parliaments. Eliminating the military's parliamentary seats and providing oversight authority to parliaments have been insufficient to consolidate democratic civilian supremacy or to promote transparency and accountability in defence administration. Rather, we have seen the unintended consequence of empowering politicians who seek to use their power to co-opt the military as a means of consolidating political power. As Robison and Hadiz (2003) argue, the transition to democracy was viewed by civilian Suharto-era remnants as an opportunity to develop oligarchic power around the archipelago. In order to do so, they have relied on corruption to incorporate business, bureaucratic, judicial, legislative and military sectors into their oligarchic networks on a 'pay as you go' basis. Decentralization has contributed to a growing trend of 'bossism' in local politics, and democracy has generated opportunities for the fortification of political power under these local strongmen. The military is not isolated from these developments. In fact, local heads and legislators have offered lucrative inducements to mobilize local military institutions and 'personalize' military resources, including security provisioning, intelligence reports and business services, such as the transportation of goods, strike-breakers and the forced removal of citizens for land development.[19] Through such partnerships

---

19. For an excellent report on these military activities, see Kontras (2004). Kontras is a prominent human rights NGO headed by Munir Said Thalib until he was

with local civilian strongmen, the military has deepened its involvement in criminal businesses in the post-Suharto era, notably in illegal logging in Papua, Kalimantan and North Sumatra. Under these circumstances, the idea of empowering politicians, which was introduced in the first decade of democratic reform, has contributed little to promoting military accountability for ending khaki capitalism.

Conclusion

In June 2015, President Jokowi nominated army chief, Gatot Nurmantyo, as TNI Commander. The choice was against the public expectation that the new commander should be a general with an air force background (following the 2004 military law that advocated the rotation of the three services for the post of TNI Commander). The predecessor of Gatot as the TNI Commander had been Gen. Moeldoko, also an army man. Jokowi's choice of Gatot was, to large extent, politically motivated. Jokowi had faced insubordination from top police officers since he became President in October 2014. To counter them, Jokowi was seemingly determined to use the army – a big brother of the police – as his political base. Gatot's nomination clearly indicated how Jokowi – who gained extensive popularity during his governorship of Jakarta and won the country's direct presidential election in July 2014 – sacrificed the goal of military professionalism in order to consolidate his political power. The cost of this was giving the highest position of the military to Gatot who was known as extremely conservative and anti-reformist. Almost a year earlier, when he commanded the Army Strategic Reserves (Kostrad) in 2014, Gatot criticized Indonesia's democratic consolidation as 'too Western' and said electoral democracy was not suitable to Indonesia's cultural values based on the state ideology of Pancasila (*Kompas* 2014). As we have discussed above, this perception reflects the mindset of the mainstream within the army, and it is these army generals who have insisted on the noble role of the army as the guardian of Pancasila and national integration that should not limit its role merely to deal with external military threats. Thus, even after 18 years of democratization, it is still far from civil society's expectation for consolidating democratic civilian control of the military.

---

poisoned to death in September 2004. Many believe that the killing was ordered by military officers in the National Intelligence Agency (BIN).

In retrospect, Indonesia's experiment in military reform has produced some successes and failures. As we have seen, various reform policies were successfully implemented in order to depoliticize the military and demilitarize politics. The TNI institutionally abandoned dwifungsi practices of sending active-duty officers to non-military posts in the bureaucracy and to parliamentary seats. As an institution, TNI no longer formally supports certain political parties and it maintains a policy of political neutrality during elections. It has also abolished internal sections dealing with political affairs. Unlike its counterparts in the Philippines and Thailand, TNI has not tried to influence events by threatening or staging a coup. All of these facts reveal that Indonesia's transition from military-led authoritarianism to democracy is a work in progress.

It should be noted, however, that this progress has not intruded on the military's economic interests. In other words, the progress has been secured because it is limited to the appearance of civilian supremacy and an apolitical military. Any reform project that goes beyond this appearance has been resisted, sabotaged and finally neutralized by the military. A key vested interest of the military involves financial autonomy from state control, which has provided massive economic benefits to high-ranking officers throughout the archipelago. The existing territorial command structure should be maintained, in their eyes, because it is a major source of khaki capitalism. Therefore, reforms targeting this issue have all faced resistance and failed, thanks also to the 'guardian' role played by President Yudhoyono.

This chapter first examined how the army had skilfully reinvented its role in internal security and re-legitimized the territorial command structure in a way that secured the military's economic interests. It then highlighted three ways that the ceremonialised nature of civilian supremacy has extended the endurance of Indonesia's khaki capitalism. First, limited civilian control of the Defence Ministry illustrates TNI's resistance towards civilian intervention in military affairs. Second, severe limitations of parliamentary oversight underline how political incentives to promote and implement military reform agendas have effectively been reduced in the legislative branch. And third, the study saw how local political figures are interested in co-opting the TNI into their patronage networks in order to gain advantages in the escalating 'democratic' competition among civilian elites at all levels of administration, including the presidency. Clearly, a paradigm shift is needed to detach the military from the civilian political game, but the political will to do so can hardly be seen.

This means that the political economy of maintaining a stable (but low quality) civil–military relations remains strong, although the country is now widely praised by world leaders for the 'success' of democratic consolidation with diversity and economic growth. Both US President Obama and British Prime Minister David Cameron, during their visits to Jakarta in October 2010 and April 2012 respectively, applauded Indonesia as a model of democracy in developing countries. Such an international reputation is clearly not helpful to promote further reform but is rather very helpful for anti-reform forces among military and political elites who seek to enjoy the lasting benefits of khaki capitalism, fruits of collusion and deficits of transparency that are effectively camouflaged by the irresponsible international praise for a 'stable democracy'.

List of Acronyms

BTNP	National Anti-Terrorism Agency
NU	Nahdatul Ulama
PDI-P	Partai Demokrasi Indonesia Perjuangan (Indonesian Democratic Party of Struggle)
PKB	Partai Kebangkitan Bangsa
TNI	Tentara Nasional Indonesia (the military)

References

AAP General News (2000) 'Downer warns against Balkanisation of Indonesia', (14 December).

Anderson, Benedict (2008) 'Exit Suharto: obituary for a mediocre tyrant', *New Left Review* 50 (March–April).

Anggoro, Kusnanto (2007) 'The department of defence of the Republic of Indonesia: ineffective civilian control', in Beni Sukadis (ed.) *Almanac Indonesia 2007 security sector reform*. Jakarta: Lespersis and DCAF: 5–18.

Baker, Jacqui (2008) 'A sibling rivalry', *Inside Indonesia* 93, August–October.

BBC News (2001) 'Megawati warns of Balkanisation', (29 October).

Crouch, Harold (1988) *The Army and Politics in Indonesia*. rev. ed., Ithaca: Cornell University Press.

Departmen Pertahanan (2003) *Mempertahankan tanah air memasuki abad 21* [defending the homeland in entering 21st century]. Jakarta: Departmen Pertahanan.

—— (2008) *Buku putih pertahanan Indonesia 2008* [Indonesian defence white paper 2008].

Jakarta: Departmen Pertahanan.

—— (2015) *Buku putih pertahanan Indonesia* [Indonesian defence white book]. Jakarta: Kementerian Pertahanan.

Honna, Jun (2003) *Military politics and democratization in Indonesia*. London/ New York: RoutledgeCruzon.

—— (2006) 'Local civil–military relations in the first phase of democratic transition, 1999–2004: a comparison of West, Central and East Java', *Indonesia* 82 (October): 75–96.

—— (2012) 'Inside the Democrat Party: power, politics and conflict in Indonesia's presidential party', *South East Asia Research* 20(4): 473–89.

Human Rights Watch (2006) 'Too high a price: the human rights cost of the Indonesian military's economic activities', *Human Rights Watch* 18(5).

Institute for Policy Analysis of Conflict (2015) 'The expanding role of the Indonesian military', IPAC Report No.19 (25 May).

International Crisis Group (2012) 'Indonesia: deadly cost of poor policing', *Asia Report* No.218 (16 February).

Jakarta Post (2001) 'Army chief says Madiun victims shot by police', (20 September).

—— (2011) 'Expose arms procurement: lengthy, costly arms deals put TNI firepower at risk', (10 June).

Kompas (2014) 'TNI ragu demokrasi: semua pihak diharapkan bersabar dengan proses' [TNI hesitates democracy: all sides should be patient with the process], (28 October).

Kontras (2004) 'When gun point joins the trade: military business involvement in Bojonegoro, Boven Digoel and Poso', Jakarta: Kontras.

Lembaga Survei Indonesia (LSI) (2015) 'Evaluasi terhadap kinerja 100 hari pemerintahan'.

Jokowi-JK, temuan survei 10–18 Januari 2015' [Evaluation of the performance of Jokowi-JK government after 100 days, a result of survey 10–18 January 2015], (2 February).

Markas Besar TNI (2003) *Naskah sementara buku petunjuk operasi tentang operasi militer selain perang* [Draft of operation guidebook regarding military operations other than war]. Jakarta: Mabes TNI, October.

Mietzner, Marcus (2003) 'Business as usual? Indonesian armed forces and local politics in the post-Suharto era', in Edward Aspinall and Greg Fealy (eds) *Local power and politics in Indonesia: decentralization and democratization*. Singapore: ISEAS, 245–58.

———— (2006) *The Politics of Military Reform in post-Suharto Indonesia: Elite Conflict, Nationalism and Institutional Resistance*. Policy Studies 23, Washington, DC: East–West Center Washington.

Mietzner, Marcus and Misol, Lisa (2013) 'Military business in post-Suharto Indonesia: decline, reform, and persistence', in Jurgen Ruland, Maria-Gabriela Manea, and Hans Born (eds) *The politics of military reform: experiences from Indonesia and Nigeria*. Heidelberg: Springer, 101–20.

Robison, Richard (1987) *Indonesia: the rise of capital*. Sydney: Allen & Unwin.

Robison, Richard and Hadiz, Vedi (2003) *Reorganising power in Indonesia: the politics of oligarchy in an age of markets*. London: Routledge.

Sebastian, Leonard and Gindarsah, Iis (2013) 'Assessing military reform in Indonesia', *Defence and Security Analysis* 29(4): 293–307.

Sesko ABRI (1989) *Peran ABRI abad XXI: redefinisi, reposisi dan reaktualisasi peran ABRI dalam kehidepan bangsa* [The role of ABRI in 21 century: redefinition, reposition and re-actualization of ABRI's role in national life]. Bandung: Sesko ABRI (September).

Sinar Harapan (2007) 'Doktor sosiologi untuk kolonel Yani Basuki: reformasi TNI setelah langkah ke-31' [Doctor of sociology for Col. Yani Basuki: TNI reform after the 31st step], (27 June).

Sundhaussen, Ulf (1982) *The road to power: Indonesian military politics, 1945-1967*. London: Oxford University Press.

The Editors (2003) 'Current data on the Indonesian military elite', *Indonesia* 75 (April).

Transparency International (2007) 'Report on the transparency international global corruption barometer 2007', Berlin: TI.

Tribunnews.com (2014) 'IPW: sepanjang 2014, TNI-Polri sudah bentrok 7 kali' [IPW: TNI and police already clashed seven times during 2014], (14 December).

van Klinken, Gerry (2007) *Communal Violence and Democratization in Indonesia: Small town wars*. London/New York: Routledge.

CHAPTER 9

Khaki Capital: Comparative Conclusions

Napisa Waitoolkiat and Paul Chambers

This volume has focused upon the economic dimensions of the internal power that armed forces have in civil–military relations in selected Southeast Asian countries. Different variations in civil–military relations tend to correlate more or less with levels of military capitalism. The study has identified two forms of such military capitalism – formal and informal "khaki" capital. The former are those khaki-owned economic assets that legally belong to the military. The latter are those military-controlled dividends held either indirectly or about which the law is ambiguous or which are illegally possessed. Examining each type is crucial to comprehending the extent of khaki capital in Southeast Asia.

The study has argued that the greater control of the military over economic resources, the more insulated militaries tend to be from civilian control. Taken together, the cases in this volume generally uphold this contention. Of course, the reverse of this argument also holds: the less the civilian control, the greater the military tends to possess economic resources. The less the parameters of civilian oversight over military attempts to achieve licit and illicit economic booty, the more likely there will be greater military adventurism in a quest for such booty. Where a military controls a large piece of a country's economic pie, such financial sway translates into enormous political influence. Such influence can rationalize military determination to stand firm (in their eyes) against civilian attempts to empower themselves politically *vis-à-vis* the military. A military's economic interests (corporate or individual) in fact often dovetails with more legitimate reasons for militaries to hold on to as much authority as it can – such as the need to ensure internal security or protect the monarchy. Indeed, as it holds the monopoly on violence in the countries of Southeast Asia, the military can easily threaten the survival of the region's nascent or weakly structured democracies. The authoritarian, single-party polities of Vietnam and Laos have a more fused relationship with their militaries.

In this chapter, first we compare each country in terms of history, current state of civil–military relations and khaki capital. Second, we look at what the consequences of khaki capital have been for political and economic stability in the countries examined. Third, we offer recommendations for the future.

In examining our case studies, three variables are significant. First, there is the character of each of the case's regime types. Second is the degree of civilian control over military capital. Third are the similarities and differences in terms of the antecedent variable of historical development. Juxtaposing these together can lead to greater understanding about the reasons for distinctions in the economic holdings of militaries in Southeast Asia today.

In terms of history, it is important to understand that each country case differed in its problems, challenges, method of uniting and success rate in resolving national dilemmas. Relative size and geographical location tended to make the smaller case studies (Cambodia, Laos) more susceptible to foreign intervention or occupation. Direct colonization affected almost every country case herein though Siam (Thailand) experienced indirect pressures from European powers. For Vietnam, Laos and Cambodia, decolonization was violent, giving way to successive civil wars that ended in costly revolutions for all three countries. Continuing foreign occupation of or intervention in Cambodia ensured the persistence of civil war there. Only in 1999 did peace finally arrive, under the personal direction of Hun Sen. Decolonization was much more peaceful for the Philippines and Burma/Myanmar, though the two countries later embarked on widely differing political paths. The Philippines remained a shallow democracy until interrupted by the dictatorship of Ferdinand Marcos, but democracy returned there in 1986. The Philippine military has been influential, especially in terms of checking the spread of insurgent groups. Burma's democracy was suffocated by a military coup in 1962 and the armed forces continued to monopolize society until 2011, when the country again began to democratize. The country today continues to experience multiple insurgencies, though the government has signed ceasefire agreements with several ethnic armies in recent years. Indonesia's military helped to spearhead decolonization but also overthrew the country's elected government in 1965. It remained at the forefront of power, fighting insurgency and working to administer Indonesia, until 1998 when democracy returned. Democracy has since become rooted but a powerful military remains watchful on the sidelines. Finally, Thailand, never colonized, has nonetheless possessed a powerful king who legitimizes the influence of a strong military over a frail democracy. This military has engineered 13 successful putsches since 1932. Today, with Thais politically divided, the Thai military directly rules the country, with the endorsement of the palace. An insurgency in the South is challenging Thailand's rule there.

What Table 9.1 below shows is that, in countries which have experienced the most chaos and which require a strong military, civil–military relations tend to be more lopsided in favour of the military in terms of internal security decision-making. Such autonomy in domestic security has tended to translate into the acquisition by militaries of economic resources in certain sectors of national economies. 'Chaos' means civilian disunity and such disunity has tended to benefit the political and economic empowerment of militaries, as in the case of Thailand where the military rose to power in a 2014 coup. Meanwhile, in the cases of the Philippines and Indonesia, though there has been insurrectionary chaos, most civilians have continued to support elected civilian control. As such, there is some civilian monitoring of the armed forces, though the military does find ways to either avoid civilian scrutiny or try to reinvent its mission to obtain more authority. While both the Philippine and Indonesian militaries receive most of their support from the national budget, each also derives some economic benefits from non-budgetary (licit or illicit) sources. (This is especially true of the Indonesian military.) Ultimately, all seven cases tell us that the greater the history of domestic instability in a given country, the more powerful will be the political role of the military in working towards guaranteeing that country's internal security. This has tended to lead the way towards the military having greater economic clout (see table opposite).

What then are the consequences of khaki capital for political and economic stability plus development in terms of our seven country cases? In

Table 9.1: Comparative patterns: history, civil–military relations and khaki capital

Country case	Type of historical development	Type of civil–mil. linkage	Degree of civilian control	Degree of civilian control over military capital
Cambodia	Highly chaotic; foreign intervention	authoritarian-personal	Highly Personalized civilian control by Hun Sen	Personalized though indirect control over certain aspects of military capital
Vietnam, Laos	Chaotic; foreign intervention; institutionalized revolution	authoritarian-mass	High authoritarian control by communist parties but acquiescing to military autonomy in internal security	Mass party control over certain aspects of military capital and acquiescing to military econ. adventurism
Philippines, Indonesia	Civilian unity in favour of civilian control; occasional insurrectionary chaos	(semi-)democratic-competitive	Formal elected civilian control with enforcement but acquiescing to military autonomy in internal security	Civilian (semi-) monitoring and legally-enforced civilian control over military capital
Thailand (before 2014 military coup)	Powerful king legitimizing strong military; weak democratizing elements; one case of insurrectionary chaos	Parallel state; semi-democracy	Formal elected civilian control alongside a more powerful monarchy above a military which is loyal to the King first	Parallel state semi-control over military capital
Myanmar (since 2011)	Embedded military; nascent democratizing elements; insurrectionary chaos	civil–military coalition	Formal civilian control but legally enshrined veto power for the military; informal military control in multiple venues	Civilian appeasement of and acquiescence to the military's capital holdings, formal and informal
Thailand (since 2014), Myanmar (before 2011)	Powerful ruler legitimizing strong military; two cases of insurrectionary chaos	military oligarchy	Military control but legitimized by monarchy/state council	Direct military control over certain resources

each case, the military remains a powerful institutional actor in society with varying degrees of economic clout depending upon the country. But the military semi-dominion over economic resources is sapping away finances from the national budget that could be put to better use for education, health or assisting the poor. Alternatively, in some cases the military has been involved in land-grabbing, directly evicting poor farmers from their lands. Finally, the persistence of military enterprises hinders free enterprise, denying a balanced playing field to competing entrepreneurs. The issues become even more salient given the fact that Laos, Vietnam, Myanmar and Cambodia are among the poorest countries in the world. Where militaries control sizeable swathes of the economy in these countries, national development in terms of human security is gravely at risk. However, of the four countries mentioned above, only Myanmar may likely witness a diminution of military economic power. This owes to the fact that, in the other three countries, the military serves to safeguard the continuing political monopoly by a ruling party. In Thailand as well, there is unlikely to be a reduction in the large economic share of the budget going to the military or extra-budgetary military sources in the near future. But Thailand has been different. Though it possesses a powerful military, its relatively robust economy has allowed for a relatively high degree of health and education services (relative to other countries in Southeast Asia). In Indonesia and the Philippines, civilians may also increasingly challenge the economic resources controlled by militaries. But in both of those cases, militaries have become increasingly adept at working around civilian governments to maintain their benefits.

Ultimately, all cases lead us to conclude that khaki capital (in terms of both corporate and personal interests) represents a venal objective for the armed forces throughout Southeast Asia and in fact, it has become increasingly embedded as a sort of 'way of life' for the military as an institution as well as for the soldiers that staff it. Khaki capital can and should be diminished to make way for the enhancement of state funding of more pro-people objectives like education and health. A lack of sufficient transparency and accountability also tends to hover around military spending sources and the spending itself. There needs to be much more civilian monitoring of khaki capital in order to reduce its excesses (corruption, for instance). Yet there can be no increased civilian oversight until there is 1) greater freedom for peoples (especially in Vietnam and Laos) to express themselves politically; increased education by and for civilians about civil–military relations and military corruption; and 3) greater civilian unity in favour of making the military much more accountable to civilian control.

For the future, there is enormous need for more studies of this kind. Articles and books about the *political* dimensions of civil–military relations in various countries of the world have been prevalent. This volume considers both the political *and economic* parts of the relationship. But there are few other publications like this. There need to be many more studies about the political economy of security forces in individual country cases in other parts of the world. It would also be interesting to compare Southeast Asia with Latin America or Africa. Finally, looking at the national level is sometimes too large. For example, what might be the political economy of the military in Manila or Jakarta? What about the political economy of the military in war zones? Perhaps the theory and concepts originated in this volume would provide a useful beginning to efforts at understanding this phenomenon in other cases for political scientists, economists and regional specialists alike.

Index

f = figure; n = footnote; t = table;
63[–]66 = intermediate page(s) skipped;
bold = prolonged discussion or term emphasised in the text

economic booms 69, 83, 119, 239, 257–8

economic crises 42, 99, 131, **136–7**, 309, 312. *See also* Asian Financial Crisis; Global Economic Crisis

economic development 44, 104, 114, 118, 134, 136–9, 144, 159, 162, 308

economic growth 133, 218, 297, 325

EDSA 2 uprising (2001) 278

education (and health) 134, 148–9, 246–7, 279, 283, 290–1, 332, 333

Egreteau, R. 109, 125

Ekachai Chanchan Mongkol, Gen. **60**

elites 11, 25, 27, 28

Emergency Provisions Act (Myanmar) 111

Endriartono Sutarto, General 312–13

environment **244–6**, 279, 282

Environmental Impact Assessment (EIA) 82

Environmental Investigation Agency (EIA) **243**, 257–8

ersatz capitalism (Yoshihara) 44, 92

Estrada, J. 271, 278

ethnic groups 15, 98, **111–12**, 148, 148n, 194, 241

ethnic insurgencies **99**, 100, **103–4**, 120, 123, 330

ethnicity 97, 168, 314

Europe 6, **12–13**, 14

exclusive economic enterprises (*doanh nghiệp chuyên làm kinh tế*) 144

Fa Ngum 219

FAO 246, 258

Farmland Investigation Commission **121**

Feaver, P.D. 273, 300

Feliciano Commission 278

feudalism **12–13**

Finer, S. **23–4**, 36

First Lao Rifle Battalion (BCL) 220

Five Provinces Bordering Forest Preservation Foundation (FPBFP, 2006–) 55, **74–8**

Florina, C. 4, 35

Ford, M. **118**, 119, 126

foreign aid 186, 226, **227t**, 271

foreign investment 186, 218

Foreign Military Sales (FMS) funds 288

France 33, 43, **164–7**, 218, **219–20**, 221, 232, 250, 253
Civil Code 185

Franco-Cambodian Modus Vivendi (1946) 165

Freedom House 105

Freeport-McMoRan 309

French Union 221

French Union Army (FUA) 220

FUNCINPEC 172, 173, 173n, 182

Galabru, E. 187

Garcia, C. **286**

Garde Indigène (Laos, 1895–) **220**

Garment Export Company 28 (Vietnam) 143

Gatot Nurmantyo **323**

Gawad Kalinga 290

gems **52**, 118, 119, 125, 186, 239

Geneva Conference (1954) 166, 166n, 221

Global Economic Crisis (2007–8) 131, 133, 149–50, 154–5. *See also* Asian Financial Crisis

Global Witness 113, 119n, 120–1, 126, 242, 258

Government Defence Anti-Corruption Index 20, 21t

Government Owned and Controlled Corporations (GOCCs) 277

Government Procurement Reform Act (Philippines, 2002) 282–3

Greater Mekong Region 18, 240, 267

Gutierrez, E. 293–4, 300–1

Habibie administration 318

Hadiz, V. 322, 327

Hải Phòng export-processing zone 139

Hall, R.A. **xii**, 33, **271–304**